PEACE AS A WOMEN'S ISSUE

Syracuse Studies on Peace and Conflict Resolution

HARRIET HYMAN ALONSO, CHARLES CHATFIELD, AND LOUIS KRIESBERG

Series Editors

PEACE AS A WOMEN'S ISSUE

A History of the U.S. Movement for World Peace and Women's Rights

HARRIET HYMAN ALONSO

SYRACUSE UNIVERSITY PRESS

First Edition 1993
94 95 96 97 98 99 6 5 4 3 2

Portions of chapters 2, 4, and 8 appeared previously, in a much briefer form, in *The Women's Peace Union and the Outlawry of War, 1921–1942,* by Harriet Hyman Alonso. Copyright 1989 by the University of Tennessee Press. Used with permission.

Portions of chapter 4 appeared previously, in a briefer and much different form, in "Suffragists for Peace During the Interwar Years, 1919–1941," *Peace & Change* 14, no. 3 (July 1989): 243–262. Copyright held by the Council on Peace Research in History and Consortium on Peace Research, Education and Development.

The paper used in this publication meets the minimum requirements of American National Standard for Information Sciences—Permanence of Paper for Printed Library Materials, ANSI Z39.48-1984. ∞™

Library of Congress Cataloging-in-Publication Data

Alonso, Harriet Hyman.
Peace as a women's issue : A history of the U.S. movement for world peace and women's rights / Harriet Hyman Alonso. — 1st ed.
p. cm. — (Syracuse studies on peace and conflict resolution)
Includes bibliographical references and index.
ISBN 0-8156-2565-0 (cl). — ISBN 0-8156-0269-3 (pb)
1. Women and peace—History. 2. Peace movements—United States—History. 3. Women's rights—United States—History. I. Title. II. Series.
JX1965.A45 1992
327.1'72'082—dc20 92-9719

Manufactured in the United States of America

For Victor

Harriet Hyman Alonso is Associate Professor of History at Fitchburg State College in Massachusetts. She is a resident of Brooklyn, New York, and author of *The Women's Peace Union and the Outlawry of War, 1921–1942* (1989).

"I have often wondered why it is that a family which would make a great protest if the government took away their automobile or even their dog, says nothing when the government takes away their sons."

—Mildred Scott Olmsted, *Four Lights*

CONTENTS

Illustrations xi

Acknowledgments xiii

Abbreviations xvii

1. Coming to Terms 3
2. Developing a Feminist-Pacifist Consciousness, 1820–1914 20
3. Suffragist-Pacifists versus the Great War, 1914–1919 56
4. Former Suffragists for Peace during the Interwar Years, 1919–1935 85
5. Dilemmas, Quandaries, and Tensions during War, 1935–1945 125
6. The Effects of McCarthyism on Feminist-Pacifists, 1945–1960 157
7. From Civil Rights to the Second Wave of the Feminist Movement, 1960–1975 193
8. Feminist Peace Activism and the United Nations' Decade for Women, 1975–1985 227
9. Conclusion 260

Appendixes:

A. A Chronological Listing of U.S. Women's Rights Peace Organizations and Committees 277

B. A Partial Chronology of the Metropolitan New York Branch of WILPF 279

Notes 285

Selected Bibliography 307

Index 321

ILLUSTRATIONS

1. Segment of "Ladies' Department" column in the *Liberator,* 1832. 27
2. Lucretia Mott, ca. 1870. 30
3. Lydia Maria Child, ca. 1870. 33
4. Elizabeth Cady Stanton, ca. 1870. 39
5. Susan B. Anthony, ca. 1870. 42
6. Julia Ward Howe, 1868. 46
7. Sample of literature from the WCTU's Department of Peace and Arbitration, late 1890s. 50
8. Sunday program literature from the WCTU's Department of Peace and Arbitration. 53
9. U.S. delegation to the International Congress of Women at The Hague, 1915. 67
10. Demonstration in New York City, 1916. 71
11. Members of the New York branch of the Woman's Peace Party preparing for a demonstration, Washington Square, New York, ca. 1917. 79
12. Women at the founding meeting of WILPF, Zurich, 1919. 82
13. Women's Peace Society. 94
14. Pamphlet from National Committee on the Cause and Cure of War, 1936. 107
15. Official delegates from U.S./WILPF at the League of Nations Disarmament Conference, 1932. 119
16. Playful photo of Brooklyn branch of WILPF, 1935. 131

17. Women protesting imminent U.S. involvement in World War II. 145
18. Flier from the Women's Action Committee for (Victory and) Lasting Peace, 1947. 153
19. Emily Greene Balch reading telegram about receiving the Nobel Peace Prize, 1946. 160
20. Emily Greene Balch's Nobel Peace Prize diploma. 161
21. Congress of American Women protesting President Harry Truman's "containment" policy, 1947. 188
22. Flier from WILPF/NY branch demonstration, late 1960s. 200
23. Women Strike for Peace anti-Vietnam War flier, 1960s. 203
24. Women Strike for Peace contingent in anti-Vietnam War demonstration, 1972. 210
25. Women Strike for Peace in 1967 march on the Pentagon. 215
26. Sample of translations of the famous logo for Another Mother for Peace. 217
27. Flier about the 1968 Washington, D.C., demonstration by the Jeannette Rankin Brigade. 221
28. Women from Seneca Women's Peace Encampment preparing for a demonstration at Seneca Army Depot, 1983. 250
29. WILPF members protesting U.S. action in the Persian Gulf, 1991. 266
30. Young antiwar protester demonstrating against the Persian Gulf War, 1991. 273

ACKNOWLEDGMENTS

THERE ARE MANY, MANY PEOPLE to thank for sharing themselves with me during the six years I have been working on this manuscript. Whether good friends or invaluable colleagues (or both), they have each contributed precious time and considerable effort to helping me produce this book. They have helped me to clarify my thoughts, forced me to clean up my writing, challenged me to go further in my investigations and analysis, and provided me with the kind of support that makes researchers and writers keep moving. I want them to know that I cherish their friendship and their enthusiasm for the project—also, that their efforts did not fall upon deaf ears. Rather, I noted every suggestion and carefully considered each one during the various stages of revision. I hope that my friends and colleagues will be pleased with the results but not hold it against me when I chose to ignore some of their suggestions.

I completed most of the research on this project during the time I was the director of the Women's Center at Jersey City State College. The college administration was quite supportive of the project. I would like to thank them, but especially Vice-President Carlos Hernandez, for granting me a partial administrative leave for four months of intensive research. I would also like to thank these colleagues and friends for their support: Rebecca Linn, Annette Sinesio, Adrienne Scerbak, Maria Martinez, Doris Friedensohn, Barbara Rubin, Gail Gordon, and Maria Rost.

I left Jersey City State to accept a much desired faculty position at Fitchburg State College in Fitchburg, Massachusetts. I have had very heartwarming support for my research at Fitchburg. Faculty and staff have asked innumerable questions about "my women." I have especially appreciated the warm show of support from students who have attended lectures, asked questions, and consistently reminded me to let them know when the book comes out. Fitchburg has supplied a warm and friendly environment for me, and I truly cherish and respect the college community's serious commitment to education. In particular, I would like to thank the committee that honored me with two Ruth Butler Achievement Grants. These grants were responsible for the beautiful photographs included in this book. I would also like to thank Shirley Wagner, my department chair, who was extremely thoughtful in scheduling my classes in such a way that I could finish the manuscript in a timely fashion. I would also like to thank Charleen Testagrossa for helping me with photocopying and other chores which far exceeded her job description as departmental secretary, and Keith Glenny, our intern, for helping to compile the bibliography cards.

During the course of writing this book, I gave several conference and class presentations and sent out copies of the rough draft to some of my colleagues for evaluation. I would like to thank each of the people who commented on the work and made various suggestions, which I have indeed taken to heart: Roberta Adams, Anne Marie Pois, Dee Garrison, John Chambers, Linda Schott, Melanie Gustafson, Frances Early, Ruth Roach Pierson, Amy Swerdlow, Blanche Cook, David Patterson, Joanne Meyerowitz, Robbie Lieberman, Ellen Schrecker, Carrie Foster, Ed Thomas, Larry Wittner, and Charles Chatfield.

I am particularly grateful to the WILPF Metropolitan New York Branch History Project for its contribution to the book. I would especially like to thank Brenda Parnes, who created and directed the project, and Yvette Tomlinson, our filmmaker. The three of us shared wonderful (and difficult) times together. I am especially thankful to them for doing most of the interviewing and transcribing, from which I directly benefited. I would also like to thank Anne Florant, Ethel Panken, Ida Friedenberg, Sari Wartell, and Ruth Sillman for participating in the 1990 Berkshire Conference on the History of Women panel on the branch project and Hilda Danzig for answering many questions. All of the women in the New York branch have shown great support for the project, and I hope they will like the results.

I would also like to thank the other people who have shared their experiences as actors in the peace movement, notably Jim Lerner, Nan Wiegersma, Ruth Chalmers, and Norma Spector. Each shared valuable information and gave me great insight into various eras and organizations.

I have also received great help from librarians throughout the years, but I would especially like to note four women: Marie Helen Gold of Radcliffe College; Georgia Barnhill of the American Antiquarian Society in Worcester, Massachusetts; Edith Wynner of the New York Public Library, and Wendy Chmielewski of the Swarthmore College Peace Collection. Wendy, who saw me innumerable times these past few years, was incredibly helpful in hunting down hard-to-remember citations and people and clarifying a few rather confusing points. I enjoyed working with her and the rest of the staff at Swarthmore and hope to have many more projects that take me there.

I have two special acknowledgments to make. The first is to Nancy Tomes, the dissertation advisor who encouraged me to take on this project immediately upon finishing my degree at the State University of New York at Stony Brook. Nancy, a wonderful sounding board, has remained in touch with the project up to its conclusion. She made it possible for me, an "older" change-of-career person, to feel that there was a place for me in my newly-chosen field. She has guided me through the difficult periods, encouraging me to be patient and persistent—and she has been right. Today, I identify myself as a "historian" and love every minute of being one.

The other very special person for me to thank is Cynthia Maude-Gembler, Executive Editor at Syracuse University Press. I met Cynthia when I submitted my manuscript on the Women's Peace Union to the University of Tennessee Press. Since the first day we spoke, we knew that we had each met a soul mate. Cynthia has been responsible for some very wonderful things in my career, including the publication of my two books and my appointment as one of the series editors for the Syracuse Studies on Peace and Conflict Resolution. I appreciate her as a colleague and love her as a friend, and I think the world of peace studies is very lucky to have her and Charles Backus of Syracuse University Press on our side.

Finally, I would like to thank my partner, Victor, for his support, persistence, and love; Pablo, for coming back into my life; my parents for their interest; and Miguel—just for being.

Harriet Hyman Alonso

Brooklyn, New York
April 1992

ABBREVIATIONS

AGS	Anna Garlin Spencer
AMP	Another Mother for Peace
AWP	American Women for Peace
CAW	Congress of American Women
CCC	Carrie Chapman Catt
CIA	Central Intelligence Agency
CIO	Congress of Industrial Organizations
CORE	Congress of Racial Equality
DD	Dorothy Detzer
ERA	Equal Rights Amendment
FBI	Federal Bureau of Investigation
FLL	Frieda Langer Lazarus
FOR	Fellowship of Reconciliation
HB	Hannah Bailey
HCH	Hannah Clothier Hull
HUAC	House Committee on Un-American Activities
ICW	International Council of Women
JAPA	Jane Addams Peace Association
JR	Jeannette Rankin
JWH	Jessie Wallace Hughan
KAOW	Keep America Out of War Committee
LC	Library of Congress, Washington, D.C.

MI	Military Intelligence Division, War Department General Staff, 1917–1941
MNYB	Metropolitan New York Branch—WILPF
MSO	Mildred Scott Olmsted
NA	National Archives, Washington, D.C.
NAACP	National Association for the Advancement of Colored People
NAWSA	National American Woman Suffrage Association
NCCCW	National Committee on the Cause and Cure of War
NGO	Non-Governmental Organization
NOW	National Organization for Women
NYHP	[WILPF Metropolitan] New York [Branch] History Project
NYPL	The New York Public Library, Rare Books and Manuscripts Division, Astor, Lenox, and Tilden Foundations
OP	Orlie Pell
P & D Committee	Peace and Disarmament Committee of the International Council of Women
PanAm Women's Auxiliary	Pan American International Women's Committee of the Women's Auxiliary of the Pan American Scientific Congresses
RU	Rutgers University Libraries, Special Collections and Archives
SANE	National Committee for a Sane Nuclear Policy
Schles	The Arthur and Elizabeth Schlesinger Library on the History of Women in America, Radcliffe College, Cambridge, Massachusetts
SCPC	Swarthmore College Peace Collection, Swarthmore, Pennsylvania
SDS	Students for a Democratic Society
S/L	Rosika Schwimmer/Lola Maverick Lloyd Collection, Rare Books and Manuscripts Divi-

	sion, The New York Public Library, Astor, Lenox, and Tilden Foundations
SNCC	Student Non-Violent Coordinating Committee
SPAR	[Semper Paratus] Women's Reserve of the Coast Guard
UPA	University Publications of America, Inc.
VOW	Voice of Women
WAC	Women's Army Corps
WAMM	Women Against Military Madness
WAND	Women's Action for Nuclear Disarmament
WAVES	Women Accepted for Volunteer Emergency Service [Navy]
WCOC	Women's Committee to Oppose Conscription
WCTU	Woman's Christian Temperance Union
WIDF	Women's International Democratic Federation
WIL	Women's International League
WILPF	Women's International League for Peace and Freedom
WILPF/US	Women's International League for Peace and Freedom, United States Section
WISP	Women's International Strike for Peace
WPA	Women's Pentagon Action
WPP	Woman's Peace Party
WPS	Women's Peace Society
WPU	Women's Peace Union
WREE	Women for Racial and Economic Equality
WRL	War Resisters League
WSP	Women Strike for Peace

PEACE AS A WOMEN'S ISSUE

❮ 1 ❯

Coming to Terms

THIS INTRODUCTION is about process—the process by which I came to realize exactly what this book is about. From the day I began this project six years ago, I have taken many twists and turns concerning the scope, direction, and definition of the work. At times, I have been constricted by sources; at others, by the proposed length. To a large measure, I have also been guided by the ebb and flow of peace activism itself. During some eras, issues consume the organizations involved; during others, organizational concerns and personalities dominate. Like people, political organizations and movements change with time, adjusting their outlook and behavior to the climate around them. In response, my work is framed by these fluctuations. For any given era, I chose to emphasize those characteristics that seemed most dominant. To my own surprise, they were not always clear-cut issues of war and peace.

This whole project came about in June 1986, as I was completing my dissertation on the Women's Peace Union, an interwar-era peace organization that tried to make war illegal through the adoption of a U.S. constitutional amendment. As I faced an uncertain period of partial or no employment and the postpartum depression often accompanying the conclusion of a major piece of writing, I turned to my dissertation advisor, Nancy Tomes, for an encouraging word. "What you need is a new project," she said in her most optimistic tone. Rather impulsively, I agreed.

When I look back at that moment now, I realize that Nancy was right. A new project always helps me to get over the rough times. However, there were moments during the next three years, as I held down a full-time administrative job, revised my dissertation for publication, and tried to have a sane personal life, that I cursed the day I eagerly responded to Nancy's suggestion with "That's a great idea! Now that I've finished with the Peace Union, I'd like to write a book about the history of the women's peace movement—not the definitive study, mind you, but the introductory overview that I've never had available to use when teaching Women and Peace courses." By the time my degree was granted in August 1986, I had mapped out my tentative path and tried it out on Nancy. Our general sense was that it all sounded like a great idea, one that I naïvely thought I could pull together within a couple of years.

Immediately upon plunging into the research, I encountered my first major issue. What exactly did I mean by the "women's peace movement"? If I wrote a book about all women in the peace movement, wouldn't I have to include women's church groups and peace committees of women's clubs? How about women who worked in mixed-gender organizations or on peace issues within political parties? But if I researched *all* these groups, I'd never finish the book. Not only would the volume be massive but it might also run the danger of simply describing each group's work rather than focusing on issues, personalities, tactics, and ideologies.

As I poked around in secondary sources and in archives, and as I reviewed my own past projects, I came to understand *exactly* which women intrigued me. They were, without a doubt, women who made the connection between women's issues and peace. These were women like those in the Peace Union and those active in the 1980s peace encampments. These women were like me. In effect, they were my political foremothers, and as a feminist and a peace activist, I wanted to trace the development of that particular movement to see if a continuum existed through the decades. I cannot describe the thrill of that discovery. Having an overactive imagination, I pictured myself as some kind of gift-giver to my sisters for peace. I would uncover *our* history, and then all the feminists who participated in active demonstrations would know that we have a common history, that we have not been alone in our striving for a peaceful and just world.

So the in-depth research began. Through the Women's Peace Union, I had been able to trace a direct line back to the abolitionist movement of the 1800s and up to the peace encampments of our own times. My job now was to make that link tighter and to investigate how the strands of nonviolence and antimilitarism were reflected in the early women's rights movement, which had evolved from the 1848 women's rights convention held in Seneca Falls, New York. Throughout this process, it became clear that I was once again narrowing my focus. Not only was I going to concentrate on early women's rights activists, but I was also going to limit myself almost entirely to women who came to the peace movement through suffragist organizations. The major link between the suffrage network and the peace movement was the Woman's Peace Party, founded by Jane Addams and a reluctant Carrie Chapman Catt in January 1915. My job was to trace the suffrage line up to the creation of the Woman's Peace Party and then to follow it into the 1920s and beyond. Once the suffragists had died off, I needed to see if their legacy was picked up by modern-day feminists. The line, easy to see from the late 1960s on with the "reemergence" of the feminist movement, is less clear but still evident during the 1940s and 1950s.

I soon came to realize that by zeroing in on the early women's rights activists who then formed suffrage organizations I was not including many women who worked on a myriad of women's issues through 1920 but who did not necessarily address peace. Alice Paul of the National Woman's Party is a case in point. Although a militant suffragist, as well as a Quaker, Paul did not utilize either the National Woman's Party or its predecessor, the Congressional Union, as antiwar vehicles. In an effort to be precise, I decided to use the term *suffragist peace activists* to refer to those women suffragists who organized the peace movement from 1915 through World War II. I alternate that term with two others: *women's rights peace activists* and *feminist peace activists* (or *feminist peace movement*). The way that I use the terms is similar, and in the case of *feminism,* I am using Merriam-Webster's broad definitions: (1) "the theory of the political, economic, and social equality of the sexes," and (2) "organized activity on behalf of women's rights and interests." Even though, as historian Nancy Cott has pointed out, women before the 1910s may not have used the term *feminist* to describe themselves, I have opted for the term to describe their political outlook.[1] I would simply add that the women I am writing about have believed that gender equality will have a trickle-down effect that will eventually result in massive changes in the existing international power structure, and therefore, in how nations are run and, finally, in how men and women are socialized. These women, however, are not necessarily of one political persuasion.

Besides being feminists or women's rights peace activists, in the context of this book, the women concerned are also *pacifists* (again in Merriam-Webster's broad definition), those who are "strongly and actively opposed to conflict and esp. war." Different organizations will define *pacifism* in their own terms, but, in general, they have agreed with the basic definition. The largest divergence came in the 1920s, when organizations like the Women's Peace Society and the Women's Peace Union followed a more Gandhian principle of nonviolent resistance, (or "non-resistance," as activists used the term then), that is, meeting violence head-on with nonviolent protest actions. However, although Gandhi was exceedingly popular during the 1920s, the suffragists' link to nonviolent resistance was through the abolitionist leader William Lloyd Garrison, father of Fanny Garrison Villard, founder of the Women's Peace Society. The two other major suffragist peace organizations during the era, the Women's International League for Peace and Freedom and the National Committee on the Cause and Cure of War, favored a less militant pacifism.

The organizations represented in this book also reflect the women's political agendas and their general belief that only a world without war can provide a climate in which women's equality can flourish. Even during such long periods as that from 1920 to 1968 when the movement appeared to ignore women's issues other than peace, the organizers retained their feminism. What they did was threefold. They stressed the importance of education for women who needed to make wise lobbying and electoral choices. In addition, they not only maintained the female power structure and feminist networking that had been used in suffrage organizations but indeed frequently scorned working with men (who, they claimed, expected women to do all the dirty work while men received the glory). Finally, they utilized the organizing ideology, strategies, and tactics that had been developed and passed on by the suffragists. Even during the 1940s, 1950s, and early 1960s, when most former suffragists had either retired from political activism or had died, their legacy of maintaining organizational control and of claiming peace as a women's issue endured. I believe that the women's working style reflected their feminism as well as their recognition that there are times when antiwar work becomes more urgent to some women than specific women's issues. During these times, women's issues per se may be deemphasized in order to focus entirely on an international or national crisis. However, the feminist sentiment itself is never lost for the organizers.

I have based this study on the peace movement's evolution from one portion of the woman suffrage movement. As I have studied this arm of the peace movement, I have been very aware of its white, middle-class nature, especially in the leadership. Having become very conscious of the organizations' own concern about their homogeneity, I pinpoint how these peace women have tried to diversify their memberships, and then I try to raise questions and analyze their apparent lack of success. My research has uncovered constant self-criticism within this movement over issues of race, class, and age. Self-criticism and guilt have driven these women to continue to seek solutions to inequities, contradictions, and even hypocrisies within their own selves and their organizations. Where solutions have eluded them, I have chosen to focus on the continuing problems rather than divert attention to alternative organizations and movements.

There are moments in this study when I appear to veer slightly away from the continuing theme of suffrage organizations and introduce other clearly feminist peace organizations, especially after World War II, when surviving suffragists were hard to come by. The Congress of American Women and Women for Racial and Economic Equality, rooted in working-class and women-of-color issues and membership, are two such groups, the former organization the foremother of the latter. I gave a great deal of thought to including these and other women's peace groups and decided that their ideologies are so feminist and their presence so important to understanding the modern era, that they must be included. In addition, throughout the years covered in this work, there have been a myriad of organizations through which women have worked for peace. Only one runs almost the entire length of this book. This is the United States Section of the Women's International League for Peace and Freedom (WILPF, pronounced "wĭlpf"), which grew out of the 1915 Woman's Peace Party and in 1990 celebrated its seventy-fifth anniversary.

However, this is not a book about WILPF. It is about the linkage between women's issues and peace, an area in which WILPF has played a major role. Therefore, I chose WILPF to exemplify the major theme of suffragist women's rights, while acknowledging that the same commitment and connections have been made by other groups, each with its own program and interpretation of how to use women's issues to further the cause of peace. I have accordingly chosen to write about several of these independent groups, although I do not claim to have included all of them. In fact, I would venture to add that few people, if any, could keep a count of all of the peace organizations in existence at any given time. There are hundreds of them, many consisting of local people involved in grassroots organizing.

In total, what I have done here is to use my general definition of *feminism* to study women's peace organizations, framing the book within a continuum from 1820 to the 1990s. This line begins with U.S. abolitionists and early women's rights activists of the nineteenth century and ends with the reemerging feminist movement of the 1960s, 1970s, and 1980s. However, it also includes other all-female peace organizations from 1820 to 1990 that have based their ideas on the connection between specific women's issues and peace and that either had overlapping membership with the "suffragist" strain or reflected the same commitment to women's rights and peace.

For me, the main theme that defines this peace movement is the connection made between institutionalized violence and violence against women, whether the institution be slavery, the military, or governmental oppression. This linkage is very complex and becomes more and more sophisticated throughout time but is rooted in the women abolitionists' pleas for compassion toward enslaved African and African-American women in the South. The interesting point for me is that the connection has been consistent from the days of the abolitionist movement to today. Throughout the more than a century and a half of organizing for peace, women's rights peace activists have protested not only the physical abuse of women, but also their psychological, economic, and political oppression. Whether via marriage, sexual exploitation, low wages, or lack of political rights, women's rights peace activists have pinpointed male control in both the private and public spheres as the principal source of the abuse of women.

For these women, the military represents an exaggerated microcosm of all this power and abuse. They continue to stress that the actual, physical, military presence in any country means the rape and economic exploitation of women. It has also meant the worldwide impoverishment of women due to the loss of male breadwinners during wars. In the single-headed households of today, it can also mean the loss of the female parent, resulting in orphaned children. It has meant the governmental creation of a shortage of men, resulting in an abundance of single women who might want male partners but will be deprived of them after a war. It has meant the creation of a population of physically and mentally disabled men and women whom women, not the powers who created the condition, must care for. The presence of the military has often meant that some women will become prostitutes in order to survive economically, that some will bear children they may or may not want but will not be able to afford and for whom they will not receive financial support, and that some will have interracial children in societies that will treat these offspring as outcasts. In addition, the military establishment uses up money that could be earmarked for social programs that would benefit women, including job training, housing, child care, health benefits, and aid to the poor and elderly. In a very physical sense, the presence of the military, whether or not in an actual war situation, has always been bad news for women.

During the 1920s, women's understanding of the connections between the military-industrial complex and violence against women became more sophisticated than in the years before World War I. The interwar feminist peace activists recognized additional types of violence, such as child and animal abuse. Didn't this kind of violence, they asked, come about because people accepted the institutionalized violence of war? After all, in wars like World War I, with its high number of civilian deaths, one learned that life was expendable and killing was easy. Furthermore, the military basis of activities like physical education classes and the Boy Scouts supported the initiation of young boys into this system that would train them to become the kinds of men who would look forward to being soldiers—or, at least, to being capable of accepting or perpetrating violence. In addition, the women of the interwar era often connected capitalistic greed and imperialism with the economic exploitation of all people, but especially of women. These women did not necessarily damn capitalism, and most of them did not spout Marxist ideology. However, they did condemn the overindulgences of the people in government and business who worshiped the mighty dollar, and they did support the idea of an equitable distribution of the world's resources. They valued much of what they felt the U.S. stood for—the many freedoms the people have—but they could not tolerate the inequities that fostered racism, sexism, and poverty.

The most sophisticated connections between militarism and violence against women are evolving at this very moment. From 1968 on, with the growth and development of the second wave of the feminist movement, understanding of the linkages made in earlier generations has reached greater depth. For example, there has been much discussion (and a great deal of writing) about military training and the sexist and homophobic use of language, which encourages soldiers (many of whom are adolescents of eighteen and nineteen) to denigrate women and homosexuals. Young men who do not have the stamina for certain physical exercises are called "fags" or "girls." Chants used in basic training exhort the soldiers to "fuck" this or that enemy. The result, according to modern feminist peace activists, is the creation of an arrogant young man in uniform who feels himself superior to all women and entitled to their bodies, whether his attentions are welcome or not. The popularity of this kind of violent mentality in current films and television movies shows that our society is still pervaded with the belief that women exist for men's pleasure and use. Many contemporary feminist peace activists feel that the result is an easy swing to domestic violence, date rape, and child abuse.

For the most contemporary and all-inclusive analysis of these connections, we must thank the ecofeminist strain of the peace movement. Ecofeminists believe that everything is connected—the toxic waste, the destruction and pollution of the earth and the environment, the nuclear weapons tests, and the nuclear power plant accidents—all represent a rape of the earth, our mother earth. The violence to the planet is the larger manifestation of violence against women. It is all symptomatic of a sick world, one that needs to be remolded using a more female, nurturing approach to life.

Another theme that permeates the organizations discussed in this book is the idea that women, as the childbearers of society, have a particular interest in peace—namely, not wanting to see our offspring murdered either as soldiers or as innocent victims of a war. However, the "motherhood" concern has also given feminist peace activists a special position within a society in which they have never had any real political power, especially in the arena of international affairs. After all, the theory goes, *only* women can experience maternal feelings, and these maternal "instincts" give us an edge over men in understanding emotions, in being compassionate, and in being able to envision peace. In a real sense, throughout U.S. history, our ability to reproduce children has caused men to ascribe to us a moral insight that they claim not to have (or don't want). Understand, it is not necessary even within the context of this theory or of these organizations for all members to *be* mothers; just possessing the proper biology or the emotional capacity to "mother" has been enough to claim the superiority of motherhood. Actually, from time to time, some men have been allowed in as members of these groups even though they have rarely been allowed into the leadership. Moreover, some of the most famous and most revered women, such as Jane Addams, Emily Greene Balch, and Carrie Chapman Catt, never had children.

The motherhood theme, a very real and emotional issue for millions of women, has also added a fundamental uniqueness to almost every one of the organizations here—and it is often used to illustrate just how different the world of men (especially the powerful ones) is from that of women. Although most of the organizations have been careful to define the power problem as "patriarchal dominance in society," it is also clear that almost every group involved has itself portrayed women as more sensitive, more caring, more thoughtful, and more committed to producing a humanistic and compassionate world than men as a whole. This new world would encompass gender equality, and equality that would result in racial, social, economic, and political justice. Women would play a key role in this new world, no longer the abused, exploited, and angry outsiders, but rather the creative, productive, and nurturing insiders.

The motherhood theme has been an essential element in the women's rights (or feminist) peace movement for several reasons. It has provided women a societally acceptable cover for their highly political work. It has also allowed women to be angry and to express that anger within this acceptable context, giving them a certain amount of credibility. In addition, it has given women a unique position that men cannot share and therefore cannot really argue against. It has furthermore allowed women to present a self-image of moral superiority. Above all, it is the most successful organizing tool available to women. (Men in power always seem willing to give "mothers" an audience, even if they don't usually accept their suggestions or meet their demands.) However, motherhood is not just a convenient political tool; it is a very real emotional condition. It has been one of the main forces which has taken me to innumerable antidraft rallies since 1971, the year my son was born, and which made the 1991 war with Iraq even more personally traumatic. For many, many feminist peace activists, to have borne a male child is to have borne all of the male and female children who have been or could be killed or maimed in a war.

A third theme that defines the women in this book is their conviction that women must be responsible citizens, not only locally, but nationally and internationally as well. This concern is very clear, beginning with the abolitionist outspokenness on the injustice of slavery through today's activism against the nuclear arms race and the great powers' bullying of the Third World. The women in the organizations represented here never absolved themselves of their own role in the work of making society more just and equal. Although they consistently lashed out at men for their material greed and lust for power, they also emphasized their own responsibility in cleaning up the mess they accused their partners of creating. Like the social housekeepers of the Progressive Era, including their own dear, peace-loving Jane Addams, women's rights peace activists took it upon themselves to confront what they perceived as men's abuses of society. The very first organized feminist peace organization, the Woman's Peace Party (1915), consisted largely of suffragists who stressed that the elimination of war was not possible unless women not only had the right to vote but also made up half of every nation's governing body. Once the vote was achieved in the United States in 1920, these same women became active in educating their peers on peace issues. Women's rights peace activists during the interwar era became all too aware that men still held the reins of power. Their objective was to activate their newly enfranchised sisters so that each successive generation of voters would be more sophisticated. They also hoped and worked for more female representation in Congress.

As the decades passed, feminist peace activists continued to stress the importance of women's participation in the political process. This concern has been a point of frustration throughout the twentieth century. Organizers have had to rely on the traditionally powerless techniques of lobbying Congress, holding petition drives, marches, and rallies, and trying to convince men in power to support their causes. The unsuccessful efforts to avoid World War II and to exit from Vietnam early in the 1960s were illustrative of this situation. So are the many proposed solutions to end the arms race and the perpetual military aggressiveness of the U.S. government. Being responsible citizens has proven to be the most challenging of all the efforts within feminist peace organizing because of the realization that real political power eludes us.

The final theme pervading this book is the desire of women to attain some semblance of power by working within female-centered organizations. Although I recognize the complex reasons for forming exclusively women's organizations, I have also been struck by the rather simple explanation that throughout the decades women have been sick and tired of being bossed around by men. Throughout my research, I repeatedly ran across references to women who received immense pleasure from making major decisions and, more importantly, getting credit for doing so. One of my favorite examples took place during 1931 and 1932 as the Women's Peace Union planned its lobbying campaign for the League of Nations Conference on Reduction and Limitation of Arms in Geneva, Switzerland. Just when everything was in place, the New York women received a cable from their affiliate, the London War Resisters' International, announcing (not offering politely) their intentions of taking over the final stages of the work. The women were livid. How dare these men attempt to come in and, as usual, reap the credit and satisfaction for their months of hard work and endless fund raising! Needless to say, the Peace Union women forged ahead and completed their own project. Their anger, however, was clear—and in other letters, organizational minutes and in oral histories, I have heard the same complaint and response. Women do the mundane work and, at long last, we shall enjoy the fruits of our labor. In the modern era, this desire for autonomy manifested itself through the radical and ecofeminist communities.

Over the years, feminist peace organizations have been involved in various issues of concern to women, such as the right to vote, the Equal Rights Amendment, reproductive rights, labor laws, child care, and health care. But, throughout, four themes have been the most consistent and best developed: motherhood, the connections between militarism and violence against women, responsible citizenship, and independence from male control. These themes have never vanished, even during the two world wars when out of fear of governmental repercussions or outright support of the war effort, there were hardly any women left to carry on the movement's work. Today, these issues are still the main elements keeping the feminist peace community active and growing.

By this time, I hope that I have presented a clear picture of the direction of this book. At this point, I would like to explain something about the format. The book is shaped not only by my personal interests but also by the resources available to me and my choice of which direction to take with those resources. There is no question that the Women's International League for Peace and Freedom dominates the manuscript. I had not originally planned that to be the case. But because WILPF had its birth within the suffrage movement and because it is the *only* organization that has survived from 1915 to the present, it is only natural for WILPF to take center stage. WILPF also has an inexhaustible number of historical documents on the international, national, and local levels.

My first major decision was to focus on the U.S. women's rights peace movement. If I had decided to investigate the topic of peace on an international level, this would have been a very different book. It is not that the international issue does not intrigue me or that I don't feel that international connections are important. Quite the contrary: I feel that, both historically and currently, global feminism is one of the most important phenomena to face the movement. However, I chose to organize this study around U.S. history in order to understand our own movement better. Working on U.S. women brought writing this book into my own realm of personal experience. In addition, this option allowed me to pursue a subject that really intrigues me: local organizing.

In the past, when I have given papers or talks about women's peace history, I have always been asked about women who have organized on the grassroots level. While it is true that people never tire of reading about the leadership in large organizations, many also want to know what was happening on the local level. I made a very conscious decision to follow this path, because of two specific factors. First, I had already researched the Woman's Peace Party of New York City, founded in November 1914, which became the New York branch of the Woman's Peace Party (later the New York branch of the U.S. section of WILPF). I knew of the tensions between this somewhat bohemian, radical branch and its national board. I decided to follow their story through to today. Secondly, I became the historical consultant to the History Project conducted under the auspices of the Metropolitan New York branch of WILPF. As a well-meaning member (albeit not an active one) of this particular group and as a historian, I became interested in helping to trace the branch's history as part of its seventy-fifth anniversary celebration.

At first, I saw myself involved in two separate research projects. Then one day it struck me that I could interweave the New York branch's history into the broader study and understand more fully the nature of WILPF. So, even though I had decided to look at the relationship between the national leadership and the local organizations, I found myself limiting my study to the example of the New York branch—except for the 1950s. During the McCarthy era, most of the excitement took place between the national board of WILPF and the Denver and Chicago branches. Because of the importance of these two stories in attempting to understand the national organization, I decided to emphasize them.

The texture of this book may not always seem consistent. Some chapters offer a narrow view of one or two organizations within a specific era, while others give a more general picture of several organizations. Some chapters emphasize local branch issues more than others. In addition, some have more details on various national or local personalities. My choice was determined largely by the fluidity within the movement and my personal reaction to the constantly shifting organizational patterns. For example, if I saw that a certain period, such as the 1920s and early 1930s, was intriguing because of ideological stands, I focused on that. In an era such as the 1950s, however, personal challenges seemed much more enlightening than specific international issues, and my emphasis shifted accordingly. What I learned throughout the process was that organizational histories are not so simple. Different external circumstances create various responses within an organization.

A historian, I feel, can benefit by being flexible in her approach to various eras, issues, and personalities. No organization remains static or one-dimensional. They are, rather, complex reflections of their times. Chapter 2, for example, gives a general background on how a feminist-pacifist consciousness evolved out of the abolitionist movement. Even though female abolitionists and early women's rights activists did not take what we could call "antiwar" stands, they did address the issue of violence against women. As a result of the Civil War, several women also began making the connection between militarism and violence, against both women and their children. At this time, the practice of using "motherhood" as a means of protesting male authority entered the movement's rhetoric. Although this early period does not produce a women's rights peace organization, it does lay the groundwork for the creation of the Woman's Peace Party in 1915.

Chapter 3, on the World War I era, emphasizes the development of one organization, the Woman's Peace Party, and places a great deal of emphasis on personalities. In this case, two Progressive Era dynamos, Jane Addams and Carrie Chapman Catt, took center stage. Resolutions to their differing points of view determined the shape the new organization would take. Because Catt gave Addams the sole responsibility for spearheading the peace movement, the Woman's Peace Party took a less conservative stand on suffrage than it might otherwise have. How Jane Addams envisioned the organization and influenced it reflected her background as a reformer more than her own views on suffrage, for Addams was more than willing, at least at first, to provide a place for both the most radical and the most conservative suffragists. I have also emphasized the differences among the national board, the New York, and the Massachusetts branches. Because at the time there was just this one women's rights peace organization, I had the luxury of spending more time and space investigating its internal operations and tensions around protesting the coming of World War I.

Chapter 4, in contrast, covers four unique organizations, with different agendas and leadership styles, from 1919 through 1935. Even though all four groups originated within the context of the suffrage movement, they represented differing stands on pacifism—from accepting any partial move towards peace to absolutely refusing to cooperate with any part of the military system, including buying war bonds or even knitting socks for soldiers at the front. Furthermore, the interwar era was alive with issues that, while not involving major world conflicts, nonetheless provided a background for various options for putting an end to the institution of war. Accordingly, this chapter is by necessity more general than chapters 2 and 3. My interest in following local branches also plays into this chapter with the continuing saga of the New York women of WILPF, the former Woman's Peace Party. During the 1920s, major ethnic changes in the group's membership both determined its future direction and set it apart from its suffrage-based mother organization.

Chapter 5 is concerned with the onslaught of World War II. During this era, WILPF was the only viable women's rights peace organization in existence. The interwar Women's Peace Society and Women's Peace Union were defunct, while Carrie Chapman Catt's National Committee on the Cause and Cure of War had evolved into a group sanctioning force as a means to achieve postwar peace. The absence of other organizations to compete for attention made it possible once again to take a deeper look into the relationship between the WILPF national board and the local New York branch. Because so many of the women involved in the New York group were Jewish, the issues confronting the two parts of the same organization took on quite an emotional tone. During this period, issues of race and ethnicity came to the fore, more uncomfortably prominent than elsewhere in the book.

The tension is also high in parts of chapter 6, which zeros in on the McCarthy era. Even though the New York branch appears quite subdued, the problems that evolve within the Denver and Chicago branches of WILPF and, in turn, these groups' problems with the national organization tell a very damning tale of woman turning against woman. It is also the story of organizational self-perservation. This chapter in WILPF's history is the darkest and, for me, the most difficult to write, yet, at the same time, one of the easiest to tell. It is not always pleasant for those of us who expect women's rights organizations to act more judiciously than other groups to admit that they do not always do so. WILPF, although dominant in this chapter, was not the only organization to have problems during the McCarthy era. However, whereas WILPF's problems were internal, the newly-formed Congress of American Women faced life-threatening harassment from an external source—the U.S. government. By the end of the era, the Congress was defunct.

The 1960s and early 1970s offered an exciting time for women's rights peace organizations because the feminist movement reemerged. The war in Vietnam, which spawned the Vietnam antiwar movement, contributed to the sophistication of feminist peace activism. The war also caused national grief. Chapter 7 examines various women's responses to the war and, once again, because of the proliferation of new groups, from Women Strike for Peace to Another Mother for Peace, the chapter has a broader perspective. Key to this is a description of the reemphasis on feminist ideology within the women's rights peace movement and its effects on the long-lived WILPF. As both this and the next chapter illustrate, not all WILPF members desired to keep up with the changing times. Personal progress did not always keep pace with intellectual evolution. Older and more traditional women found it difficult either to give up the reins of power or to change their leadership style. Feminism, an essential component of WILPF's roots, presented a surprising threat and challenge in its 1968 form.

This challenge, created by the reemergence of the feminist movement, is the focus of chapter 8, which stresses the global feminist connections made possible by the official sanctioning of the United Nations' Decade for Women. Large international meetings and peace encampments were just two of the important developments of the Decade. Both efforts involved large numbers of young women, working women, and women of color. The Decade persisted in challenging the women's rights peace activists to make good on their over sixty-five years of espousing a commitment to peace *and* justice. In addition, the younger U.S. women involved in creating the fervor of peace encampment activities—especially in the home of the women's rights movement, Seneca Falls, New York—challenged the older groups to confront their own class and race prejudices as well as their homophobia. As a result, the Decade influenced organizations like WILPF and Women

Strike for Peace to enter a new era. WILPF would have the strength to take the first step towards a stronger feminist future. At the time of this writing, Women Strike for Peace has faded into the background. During the summer of 1991, the leaders closed their Philadelphia national office. But, who knows? They may be back.

Finally, in Chapter 9, I have tried to sum up a few of the important themes of this movement as well as some of the problems, especially those of class, race, and age. I have attempted to end the book on the same personal note as I have begun it. I have also tried to sort out some of the compelling issues that I find particularly perplexing. Parts of this conclusion may reflect my own sense of frustration with a movement that, I may have to finally admit, most often reflects a minority position within our society. I recently heard that the United States has been involved in over two hundred military actions during its relatively brief history. That is practically one every year. Confrontation, not peace, is our nation's most common international stance. In spite of this fact, women have continued to be optimistic and persistent in their work for peace, equality, and justice. This book speaks to that commitment. It is, in the end, a history written about feminists who have believed in peace, by a feminist who longs for it.

2

Developing a Feminist-Pacifist Consciousness, 1820–1914

Before 1914, no independent feminist peace movement existed in the United States. Individual women spoke out for peace; women's clubs and church members formed peace committees. But there was no organization that linked peace and nonviolence with women's concerns. One reason for this situation was women's lack of political power. On a national scale, they were not recognized as voters until 1920. Locally, married women often did not even have the right to own property, have custody over their children, keep their own wages, or sue in a court of law. It was not until 1848 and 1860 that New York State passed the first really meaningful Married Women's Property Acts, guaranteeing women some rights to their own possessions. However, even though the Territory of Wyoming gave women the vote as of 1869, followed slowly by some other states and territories, women generally felt their influence only on a local level—as members of the school board or town committees.

State or local voting rights simply did not create a sense of influence on the international scene. Indeed, without individual political rights, there seemed to be no rationale for addressing international issues. It was eventually through personal involvement in church activities, club membership, and reform movements that women developed a feminist-pacifist consciousness, which would eventually lead them to address world affairs. This evolution from personal experience to political activism convinced them that the quest for women's equality was directly tied to a world consisting of peaceful international relations, the extinction of militarism, and the practice of nonviolence in both the public and private spheres.

From the early 1800s to 1914, proponents of women's rights became more and more committed to the idea that each human being had the inherent right to develop her or his own potential, regardless of gender, race, ethnic background, or class. Social, economic, and political equality for women were necessary elements of a fair society. In order for women to achieve this personal freedom, however, the wider world needed to free itself of its political, social, and economic injustices. The road to the formation of the feminist peace movement that would attack these issues was long and winding, a convergence of several paths—from the churches, from the temperance and abolitionist movements and, less often, from women's clubs—some with overlapping participants and beliefs.

In these movements, women's specific concerns emerged from the wider picture. As the violence inherent in the slavery system or drunken husbands' attacks on wives and children, for example, came to light more frequently, women abolitionists and temperance workers began to make the connections between gender and the abuse of power. Awareness of the more dramatic forms of violence led to the more personal realization of each woman's lack of her own basic human rights within U.S. society, especially if she was married. Many questions were asked within early reform societies, which offered women an acceptable place to speak out. Unknowingly, these women set the stage for the creation of the women's rights movement and then for the creation of a feminist peace movement that burst onto the scene in 1914, the year World War I broke out in Europe.

A composite picture of an emerging feminist of the nineteenth century who became involved in early reform movements might look something like this: She would most likely have come from a middle-class, white, Anglo-Saxon, Protestant family located somewhere in Massachusetts (usually between Boston and Worcester), upper New York State (along the canal route from Syracuse to Rochester), or in the New York or Philadelphia metropolitan areas. In most cases, although she herself might not have been a regular churchgoer, her parents would have brought her up in a Protestant church. There was a good chance that she would have been a Quaker, a Unitarian, a Universalist, or a member of some other reform-minded Protestant sect. If not, she might have considered aligning herself with one of these churches for her children's sake. In any case, she would have been wary of any overbearing man who leaned towards a literal interpretation of the Bible regarding Adam's rib or other doctrines that inhibited an equal place for women in society. In general, she would have received a good education from a private girls' school. She would also have been well-read and attracted to new trends, ranging from spiritualism to health-food diets to holistic health care, that promised her a healthier, more interesting life. She would most likely have married, although not necessarily at a young age, and had children. In many cases, her husband would have been active in a reform movement, perhaps even earning a living through activist work. Her children would have been reared in a progressive way. Love, understanding, and open reasoning would have replaced corporal punishment and doctrinaire parental attitudes. This budding feminist would have demanded a central role, not only within her family, but also in the reform movements. Her place might have been as a spokesperson for a Quaker meeting, as a speaker on the abolitionist circuit, as an organizer of other women, as a philosopher, or simply as a supporter of others' work. In all probability, the two issues initially attracting her attention would have been abolitionism and temperance. Work in these areas would have eventually led her to the issue of women's rights and then, tentatively, towards peace. Such a woman would most definitely not have been a passive figure but a mover, even a shaker.[1]

Because religion was so dominant in the reformers' lives, it is essential to examine, however briefly, its meaning for them. Among reformers, the Quaker faith was most influential and most widespread, largely due to its social-responsibility component, its philosophy of nonviolence, and its recognition of each individual's equality before God. According to Quaker belief, God existed within every person, giving her or him an "inner light." These Quaker principles were instrumental in pushing women into a more public role. The belief in each individual's self-worth and spiritual equality enabled women to assume an assertive posture both at home and within the religious community. Like other Protestant sects which migrated from Europe beginning in the sixteenth century, Quakers supported marriages that were loving and sharing. They also expected women to speak out at meeting and to take their turn as "ministers," a position that allowed them to speak publicly before audiences of men and women, a custom not generally accepted in the wider society. Because Quaker services consisted of silent meditation until one felt moved to speak, the meetings were more conducive to encouraging women, traditionally intimidated, to feeling more comfortable with open participation than they would in a dramatic atmosphere of lecturing or shouting pastors. Quakers also did not believe in resorting to either personal or institutional violence. Their practice of nonviolence had important effects upon their family life. Because Quaker women generally did not live in any fear of abuse from their husbands, they enjoyed more equitable and open marital relationships than others did. Children gained the same advantage—they were reared not to fear their parents.

In a young nation rife with disputes, the Quakers sometimes represented a positive alternative, though sometimes they also became an obstacle to development. The colony of Pennsylvania, founded as a Quaker experiment in 1681 by William Penn, proved to be a relatively peaceful place to live. Because of the prevailing belief in nonviolence there, the Pennsylvania legislature as well as the residents propagated peaceful coexistence with the Native Americans then also inhabiting the area. The lack of war, however, attracted other non-Quaker settlers who eventually openly confronted the natives. Quakers themselves continued to live side by side with the original population with relatively little trouble. When war did begin, whether with the natives, the French, or the British, other colonists felt they were forced to fight to protect Quaker lives. Resentment was the result, and, even though Quakers did not ask nor want anyone else to be violent on their behalf, they found themselves in a difficult situation. During the U.S. War of Independence, for example, Quakers generally did not take sides. They offered relief to soldiers on both sides but would support neither. As in earlier colonial times, some Quakers were publicly persecuted; some were run out of their homes, and some were treated as traitors and penalized as such. However, most remained true to their beliefs even though doing so often caused them to be seen as outsiders.

For this study, what is most important to keep in mind is that the Quaker practice of nonviolence, which made its believers into an often unpopular minority, also produced strong women who were encouraged and expected to share in family and religious life and to take public stands against other forms of violence. Whether during the War of Independence, over tensions with Native Americans, or regarding slavery throughout the antebellum years, Quaker women represented a very vocal group against war and injustice and in favor of gender equality.

Besides the Quaker faith, early women reformers were also attracted to the Unitarian and Universalist churches, once again because of their emphasis on cooperation between men and women and also because of their concern for human justice. Historian Blanche Hersh has explained that the typical antebellum reformer embraced "the Puritan sense of duty, the evangelical zeal for salvation and the Universalist belief that all men and women are to help each other to salvation as one family under the benign direction of a loving God." Women reformers, while embracing these fundamental beliefs, were at the same time appalled by certain doctrines of some churches, such as the Calvinists' portrayals of Hell and of human depravity. In particular, they hated the concept of infant damnation, for their approach to childrearing emphasized the initial innocence of infants and the importance of having "enlightened" mothers who used love and sound reasoning to raise "superior" children. Their belief in the power of reason was most important to them. According to Hersh, although these women favored the Quaker belief in each person's spiritual conscience (or the "inner light"), they did not care for the sect's emphasis on the importance of spirit over reason. The Unitarian emphasis on "rationality over free will," however, they found quite attractive. They also liked the Universalist belief that Jesus Christ died for the sins of all people, not just for those of a few elect. Furthermore, they were attracted to the Quaker view that Christ was neither male nor female. These early feminists found the image of a "Father-Mother" God quite pleasing.[2]

No matter what religion women reformers embraced, one thing was certain: churches whose male leaders stressed female subservience did not benefit from these women's presence. In addition, activists also often turned away from houses of worship that refused to take a stand against slavery. As a result, women reformers, especially after the initial Women's Rights Convention in Seneca Falls, New York, in July 1848, tended to practice their faith on a private level, directing their evangelical enthusiasm towards secular political issues.

The movement to free the slaves and the issue of temperance were the catalysts for the evolution of these women into women's rights activists and, hence, the awakening of their feminist-pacifist consciousness. Quaker, Unitarian, and Universalist reformers, however, were not the only people to recognize the immorality and institutionalized violence within the slavery system nor to address the issue of alcohol abuse. Many middle-class women from various religions were also attracted by the opportunity to do charity work and to rid their world of social vices. During the late eighteenth century, as commercialism led to a more moneyed urban culture, the ideal of womanly perfection came to be embodied in the woman whose leisure allowed her to become a moral force. As depicted by historian Barbara Welter, this perfect woman was pious, religiously moral, devoted to her husband and pure in body and soul.[3] She stood above men as a kind of moral watchdog. Middle-class men, out into the work world, expected to return home each evening to a haven of comfort and orderliness. This "cult of true womanhood," as Welter termed it, was characterized by a more separate, private women's sphere and a close bonding among women, a "sisterhood" that would lead towards easy cooperation in public action.

Women's entrance into the public sphere was also greatly enhanced by the religious revival movement of the 1820s and 1830s. During this period, numbers of women attended regular church services or revivalist meetings and then raised money and joined in efforts to plan further church-related events. Hence, middle-class women, especially, were able to move out of their homes into the public sphere of volunteer work, either for church activities or as charity workers. The result was the growth of a broad range of women's organizations involved in such issues as reforming prostitutes and attacking the double standard in sexual behavior; raising money to help "worthy" widows get on their feet; and urging such efforts as prison reform, temperance, Bible study groups, urban beautification, sanitation, abolitionism, and peace. By and large, these women were not in the reformers' networks because of their more traditional lifestyles with non-reformer husbands. Their interests and activities, however, dove-tailed with those of the more radical reformer women, especially in terms of temperance and women's rights. In the latter years of the nineteenth century, these women's concerns would begin to merge within the context of antimilitarism with an emphasis on the injustice of society's acceptance and internalization of violence against women.

Understanding the evolution of the feminist-pacifist consciousness can best begin with the abolitionist movement, especially that section of it created and led by William Lloyd Garrison, one of history's firm believers in creating political change and protest through nonviolent resistance and civil disobedience. Garrison encouraged his compatriots, many of them women, to refuse to participate in any institution founded upon the assumption that any form of violence was acceptable. Garrison, for example, refused to serve in the Massachusetts militia or to pay a military tax. In addition, many Garrisonians, as they were called, refused to purchase any items made by slave labor; with this boycott they were following a practice long honored by Quaker women who recognized that even though they had no political authority, they definitely held power as consumers.

Before Garrison's founding of the abolitionist periodical *Liberator* in 1831 and then the New England Anti-Slavery Society, several angry women had spoken out against slavery, although without any organizational structure. One of the earliest advocates of freeing the slaves was Elizabeth Chandler. Born in 1807, Chandler was raised by Quaker relatives after both her parents died. By the age of eighteen, she was contributing poetry and other writings to the *Genius of Universal Emancipation,* a newspaper published by abolitionist Benjamin Lundy. Chandler's writings foreshadowed the nonviolent and nurturing ideologies later utilized by both the early women's rights and the feminist peace movements. In her first column, for example, she immediately called upon women to help end the violence of slavery against other women—like themselves mothers, sisters, and daughters. "Will Christian sisters and wives and mothers stand coldly inert, while those of their own sex are daily exposed, not only to the threats and revilings, but to the very *lash* of a stern unfeeling taskmaster?"[4] Urging more privileged women to try to empathize with slave women by imagining themselves in the same bondage, she gave a graphic account of the slave women's torture in "Mental Metempsychosis": "let the fetter be with its wearing weight upon their wrists, as they are driven off like cattle to the market, and the successive strokes of the keen thong fall upon their shoulders till the flesh rises to long welts beneath it, and the spouting blood follows every blow."[5]

Chandler felt that women had a duty to stand up for other women,

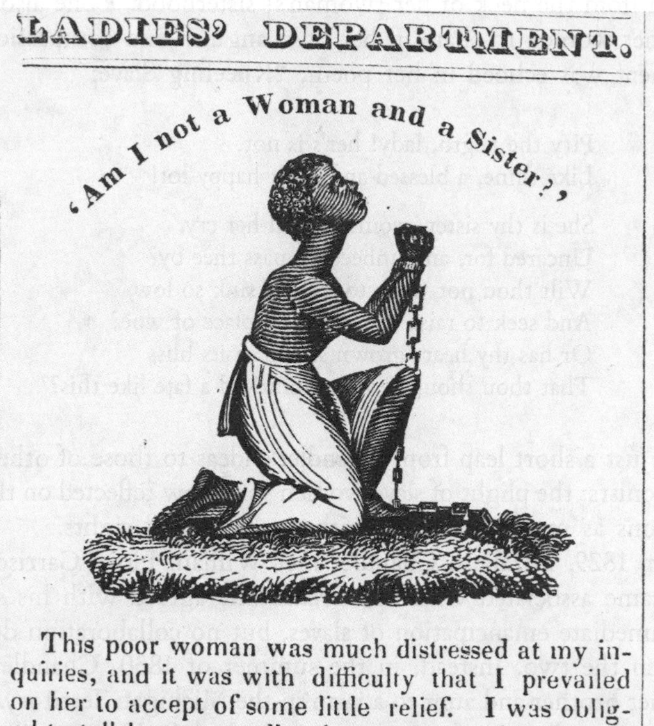

LADIES' DEPARTMENT.

'Am I not a Woman and a Sister?'

This poor woman was much distressed at my inquiries, and it was with difficulty that I prevailed on her to accept of some little relief. I was obliged to tell her repeatedly, but perhaps without convincing her, that all white people were not like those who had treated her with so much barbarity; and that the greater part of them detested such horrid cruelty. '*Why then*,' she inquired with much earnestness, bursting into tears, '*why then do they not prevent it?*'—ABBE GIUDICELLY.

1. Segment of "Ladies' Department" column in the *Liberator,* January 7, 1832. Courtesy of American Antiquarian Society.

and like other activists to follow in her footsteps, she connected violence against women with the fact that political and physical power were firmly in the hands of men. Chandler did not ask for a share of political power—that idea was not even a gleam in anyone's eye. But in her volume, *Poetical Works,* she did desire that man "lift the iron foot of despotism from the neck of her [woman's] sisterhood."[6] She also pleaded for other women to share in her own anguish and compassion. Such sentiment was echoed in her poem, "Kneeling Slave:"

Pity the negro, lady! her's is not,
Like thine, a blessed and most happy lot!

She is thy sister, woman! shall her cry,
Uncared for, and unheeded, pass thee by?
Wilt thou not weep to see her sink so low,
And seek to raise her from her place of woe?
Or has thy heart grown selfish in its bliss
That thou shouldst view unmoved a fate like this?[7]

It was just a short leap from Chandler's ideas to those of other female abolitionists: the plight of slave women somehow reflected on their own situations as married women with no individual rights.

In 1829, Elizabeth Chandler met William Lloyd Garrison when he became associated with the *Genius.* She agreed with his stand on the immediate emancipation of slaves, but no collaboration developed between the two. Instead, in the summer of 1830, Chandler moved with her brother and aunt to a farm in the Michigan Territory. Within four years, at the age of twenty-seven, she had died from an illness, and the abolitionist and future women's rights movements lost a potential leader. In the meantime, Garrison took steps to organize a group of people around the doctrine of nonresistance, that is, actively taking non-violent stands against all forms of institutionalized violence, including slavery and war. In 1829, when he was arrested and fined for consistently refusing to report to his state militia for active duty, Garrison wrote, "I heartily, entirely and practically embrace the doctrine of non-resistance, and am conscientiously opposed to all military exhibitions." Embracing a view then referred to as "Christian Anarchy," Garrison added that he would "never obey any order to bear arms, but rather cheerfully suffer imprisonment and persecution."[8] He felt strongly that abolitionists should not participate in a government that supported slavery. Therefore, they should not vote, hold office, sit on juries, or serve in the military. Some of Garrison's cohorts agreed with him; others did not follow such absolutist practices.

On January 1, 1831, Garrison published the first issue of the *Liberator.* As a forum for his own radical stand on abolitionism, the paper also attracted women who, like Elizabeth Chandler, saw a responsibility to defend their own gender from the violence of slavery. Garrison himself believed in women's equality and therefore was committed to providing a means by which women could develop their independence, even during a time when they were not allowed to participate in or vote at meetings and were ridiculed for speaking in public before male audiences. Against his wishes, his own abolitionist group, the New England Anti-Slavery Society, however, maintained an all-male membership. To give women a forum, in 1833, Maria Weston Chapman and twelve other active abolitionists founded the Boston Female Anti-Slavery Society based on Garrisonian beliefs. Chapman, a Unitarian, had become acquainted with Garrison's work after she had married Henry Grafton Chapman, a strong believer in abolitionism. As the leader of the Boston women's group, she led petition drives for the freeing of slaves in the nation's capital and also worked for better educational opportunities for Boston's free African-Americans. She believed in human rights, claiming that all people had to be emancipated from poverty, religion, and governmental restrictions. In her own words, Chapman claimed to want to free "the whole earth from sin and suffering."[9] This woman became an ardent supporter of Garrison, later becoming known as his "chief lieutenant." In October 1835, she defended his right to speak before an interracial audience in Boston. Facing a potentially violent crowd and an order for women to leave the hall, Chapman replied, "If this is the last bulwark of freedom, we may as well die here as anywhere."[10]

The same year Chapman began organizing women in Boston, forty-year-old Lucretia Mott, a respected Quaker leader, organized the Philadelphia Female Anti-Slavery Society. Mott was born a Coffin, one of the most influential families on Nantucket Island off the coast of Massachusetts. As a Quaker, she attended the Nine-Partners Boarding School near Poughkeepsie, New York, where during her several years there, she got to know James Mott, a senior teacher. They were married in 1811 and settled in Philadelphia, where James Mott became a merchant. As a Hicksite Quaker who supported the Free Produce Movement, Mott would not sell cotton because it was made by slave labor. Like-

2. Lucretia Mott, ca. 1870. Courtesy of American Antiquarian Society.

wise, Lucretia Mott refused to use any article made by slaves or to consider purchasing slaves even in order to set them free.

James and Lucretia Mott had met William Lloyd Garrison in 1830, soon after one of his short stints in prison for having written an inflammatory piece for the *Genius of Universal Emancipation* about a slaveship owner. Becoming good friends with Garrison, Lucretia Mott joined him in working for abolitionism. When he held the first organizing meeting of the New England Anti-Slavery Society, Lucretia Mott made suggestions as to its character even though she was forced to sit in the balcony along with a few other invited women. Her dissatisfaction with the male abolitionists' restrictions on women was the catalyst for the formation of the Philadelphia Female Anti-Slavery Society, one of the few women's organizations of its time to have an interracial membership. In fact, the organization carried on much of its efforts within the African-American community, working with the children and the poor on both civil rights and economic issues.

Women from all the Garrison-inspired abolitionist groups supported the *Liberator,* which emphasized a commitment to women's equality. The newspaper ensured that women's voices would be heard. One column, known as the "Ladies' Department," was headed by a drawing of a kneeling slave woman in chains. The caption read, "Am I Not a Woman and a Sister?" In one editorial, Garrison himself wrote a plea to the women of New England: "If my heart bleeds over the degraded and insufferable condition of a large portion of your sex, how ought you, whose sensibility is more susceptible than the windharp, to weep, and speak, and act in their behalf?"[11]

Spurred on by the influence of their own Quaker, Universalist, and Unitarian upbringings, women of the Female Anti-Slavery Societies concentrated on organizing their own gender around abolitionism. In 1836, for example, Angelina Grimké, a Quaker convert and an exile from her father's South Carolina plantation, wrote a public letter entitled "An Appeal to the Christian Women of the South," in which she asked slave-owning wives how they could live in a society where so many people were kept in chains and suggested that they work to convince their own husbands of the evils of slavery. Grimké's writings so ired church leaders that the Council of Congregational Ministers of Massachusetts issued a pastoral letter condemning her. According to her sister activist, Lydia Maria Child, "One sign that . . . [Grimké's] influence is felt is that the 'sound part of the community' (as they consider themselves) seek to give vent to their vexation by calling her Devil-ina instead of Angelina."[12]

Grimké's effort was followed in May 1837 by the first national convention of U.S. female abolitionists, held in New York City. Over two hundred women from ten states attended, among them several African-Americans from Philadelphia, including Charlotte, Marguerite, and Sarah Forten; Harriet Forten Purvis; and Grace and Sarah Douglass.

The speeches and resolutions that evolved from this and future meetings, although radical in their call for race and gender justice, also reflected the popular Victorian ideology of women's separate sphere and the cult of true womanhood, which placed women as the gentle, nurturing, moral guardians of society. The implication of this ideology was that women's voices represented peace and nonviolence while men's often addressed the opposite. For example, in her resolution presented on May 11, Sarah Grimké, Angelina's sister, proposed that mothers educate their children "in the principles of peace, and special abhorrence of that warfare, which gives aid to the oppressor against the oppressed."[13] Angelina offered another resolution, that it was "the duty of woman, and the province of woman, to plead the cause of the oppressed in our land" through the nonviolent use of "her voice, and her pen, and her purse, and the influence of her example . . ."[14] At the second such convention in 1838, Sarah Smith, reacting against the many men who opposed women's interest and participation in political activities, pointed out the effects a war intended to squelch slave insurrections would have on women: "And when the father, husband, son, and brother shall have left their homes to mingle in the unholy warfare; to become the executioners of their brethren, or to fall themselves by their hands, will the mother, wife, daughter, and sister feel that they have no interest in this subject? Will it be easy to convince them that it is no concern of theirs, that their homes are rendered desolate and their habitations the abodes of wretchedness?"[15]

As the abolition work progressed, other female Garrisonians began to connect the oppression of the slaves with their own, emphasizing the violent nature of the master/slave and male/female relationships. Lydia Maria Child, a Unitarian Church member and a novelist, felt that the comparison between women and slaves was "striking," especially because both had been "kept in subjection by physical force, and considered rather in the light of property, than as individuals."[16] Sarah Grimké also clearly expressed this connection. In her 1838 publication, *Letters on the Equality of the Sexes and the Condition of Women,* Grimké accused most men of entering into "league to crush the immortal mind of woman." She went on to advance Child's argument a step further: "He spares her body; but the war he has waged against her mind, her heart, and her soul, has been no less destructive to her as a moral being." Dra-

3. Lydia Maria Child, ca. 1870. Courtesy of American Antiquarian Society.

matically using imagery very close to that of slavery and echoing the earlier sentiments of Elizabeth Chandler, Grimké added, "All I ask of our brethren is, that they take their feet from off our necks, and permit us to stand upright on that ground which God designed us to occupy."[17]

Angelina Grimké articulated similar feelings in her *Letters to Catherine E. Beecher, in Reply to an Essay on Slavery and Abolitionism, Addressed to Angelina Grimké.* She resented those who felt that women were a gift from God to men. In 1838, she wrote, "She [woman] was created, like him, in the image of God, and crowned with glory and honor. . . . Woman was . . . the first victim of power. In all heathen nations, she has been the slave of man, and Christian nations have never acknowledged her rights." Moreover, she pointed out, "the present arrangements of society . . . are a violation of human rights, a rank usurpation of power, a violent seizure and confiscation of what is sacredly and inalienably" that of woman, namely, her rights "to have a voice in all the laws and regulations by which she is to be governed, whether in Church or State."[18] Both Lydia Maria Child and the Grimké sisters believed that nonresistance was the answer to the violence witnessed through slavery and the oppression of women. "Abolition principles and nonresistance seem to me identical; . . . the former is the mere unit of the latter," wrote Child.[19] For Sarah Grimké, following the "peace principle," as it was called, was the only way to free all people and to avoid war.[20]

Indeed, the female antislavery societies fully utilized the concept of protesting institutionalized violence, such as slavery, with nonviolent action even when confronted by angry observers. In general, they met opposition for two reasons: they spoke publicly before "promiscuous" audiences consisting of both men and women, and their events were frequently interracial, going so far as to having white and black women linking arms while marching down the street. Each inflammatory incident was handled with assertive nonviolence. In 1835, for example, the *Liberator* reported an incident in which a "little band" of women "met and prayed for the slave in the midst of a mob of 5,000 gentlemen of property and standing."[21] Even when, in October 1835, an angry mob disrupted a Boston Female Anti-Slavery meeting, seizing Garrison (who had to be rescued), the opposition was not met by violence. According to historian Margaret Hope Bacon, the most dramatic of the confrontations took place in Philadelphia, where in May 1838 the Anti-Slavery Convention of American Women was scheduled to be held in Pennsylvania Hall, a new structure partially funded by the Philadelphia Female Anti-Slavery Society and intended as a gathering place for reform groups. Because the women abolitionists insisted on having interracial meetings, a hostile crowd, fearful of the results of the "co-mingling" of the races, formed outside the hall. Within days they were throwing bricks and stones and shouting in an attempt to drown out the speakers. When the city's mayor suggested that the interracial nature of the meetings cease, the women ignored him. Finally, one evening after Lucretia Mott led the women hand-in-hand to safety, the mob set fire to the empty hall, burning it to the ground. They then considered torching the Motts' home but settled for several buildings in Philadelphia's African-American community. Rather than disperse, the convention continued the following day in Sarah Pugh's schoolhouse.[22]

The next year, when the women were adamantly refused protection from the Philadelphia police, Lucretia Mott insisted that, if necessary, the women rely on nonresistance to protect themselves. These incidents had long-lasting effects on the women's understanding of the common workings of racism and sexism. Equal rights, justice, and freedom became enmeshed for both women and African-Americans—not only within their own organizations but throughout their society. In addition, both constituencies came to adopt nonresistance as the most effective political tool in seeking social justice. Peace activists would inherit this legacy from their foremothers. As Angelina Grimké so aptly put it, "We Abolition Women are turning the world upside-down."[23]

The women and men of the Garrisonian wing of the abolitionist movement were well aware that another movement, one interested in international and domestic peace, had been established as a response to the Napoleonic Wars. The first U.S. nonsectarian "peace" organizations were founded in 1815, the New York Peace Society by Christian fundamentalist David Low Dodge and the Massachusetts Peace Society by Unitarian minister Noah Worcester. Both organizations used religious terminology in their writings, and both were based on the principle that war was un-Christian and economically wasteful. By 1828, William Ladd, a Maine farmer and former sea captain, decided to organize the several existing local peace societies under one umbrella, the American Peace Society. Over three hundred people joined immediately, including Garrisonian abolitionists. The Society believed in the abolition of all war, whether domestic or international.

Garrisonian abolitionists were attracted to the idea of a peace society because of their strong belief in nonviolence. However, they did not agree with the American Peace Society's easy acceptance of small steps towards peace and nonviolence or with the organization's limitations on women's full participation within the group. William Ladd himself was not adverse to women's help, but he saw their participation in strictly Victorian terms. In a tract written in 1836 and entitled *On the Duty of Females to Promote the Cause of Peace,* Ladd, also writing under the pseudonym "Philanthropos," praised the work of such early Massachusetts female peace societies as the Essex County Olive Branch Circle and the Bowdoin Street Ladies' Peace Society because they concentrated their efforts on educating children towards preferring peace over war. Ladd felt that there were several ways for women to accomplish this and other peace work. They could pray; educate themselves on peace issues through reading the Bible and peace publications; educate their families by singing peace, not war, songs and reading children stories about peace; refuse to attend military balls; write children's peace literature; join female peace societies and distribute literature; and give their ministers life memberships in peace societies. In other words, women were to work for peace within their limited environment and were not to be involved in powerful positions in organizations where male leaders discussed world affairs. For Ladd, women themselves were, quite simply, "the mothers of men" whose natures were not "destructive, but . . . like the mild beams of spring . . . clothe the earth with verdure."[24] The Olive Branch Circles, functioning very much like women's auxiliaries of the men's groups, became quite popular in the United States and England during the first half of the nineteenth century. By 1852 these groups were publishing a newsletter, *Sisterly Voices,* which reflected one of the first all-female international networks.

The Garrisonians reflected a stronger total nonviolent stance than did William Ladd and the American Peace Society. They believed that all violence, especially as exemplified by the slave system in the South and racism in the North, should be ended immediately—no gradual measures. The American Peace Society, in contrast, favored any compromises that would eventually end slavery. Garrisonians also emphasized that women's equality and full participation in all areas of society were part of the entire picture to end violence. At an 1838 meeting of the New England Anti-Slavery Society, Garrison pronounced it "arrogant" for the men to "commend" women "to silence."[25] The American Peace Society members, however, did not wish to accept women as full citizens within their organization. Members within the Society began to polarize around these different perspectives until a confrontation took place in September 1838 at the group's convention in Boston. About two hundred people attended the three-day conference. The more radical members, who leaned towards Garrison's position, wanted to expand the organization's ideology to embrace nonviolence and also to open full membership to women. The more conservative members, who remained the core of the American Peace Society, opposed this idea and after a few hours walked out of the meeting. Those who remained, largely nonresisters, immediately formed a new group, the New England Non-Resistant Society, and then adopted Garrison's "Declaration of Sentiments" as their creed. This document, which influenced both early women's rights and then feminist peace activists, stated:

> Resolved that human life is inviolable and can never be taken by individuals or nations without committing sin against God. . . . We register our testimony, not only against all war, whether offensive or defensive, but all preparations for war; against every naval ship, every arsenal, every fortification; against the militia system and a standing army; against all military chieftans [*sic*] and soldiers; against all monuments commemorative of victory over a foreign foe, all trophies won in battle, all celebration in honor of military or naval exploits; against all appropriations for the defence of a nation by force and arms, on the part of any legislative body; against every edict of government requiring of its subjects military service. Hence, we deem it unlawful to bear arms or to hold military office.[26]

The Garrisonians were not accepted by the more numerous moderates supporting abolitionism and peace. Other abolitionist societies proposed compromise measures, such as gradual emancipation. To them, the nonresistant solution was utopian, unrealistic, and ultraradical. Utopianism and humanitarianism, mixed with ample frustration and anger, however, may very well have been the ingredients needed for the breeding of a separate women's rights movement, for certainly, early on, the Garrisonian female organizers connected their work both ideologically and practically with the end of the oppression of women. Maria Weston Chapman, who devoted a good many years to abolitionist work, caustically commented in one of her poems, "The Lords of Creation," on her male compatriots' efforts to keep women's voices silent and out of men's orbit:

They've taken a notion to speak for themselves,
And are wielding the tongue and the pen;
They've mounted the rostrum; the termagant elves,
And—oh horrid!—are talking to men![27]

All of these early abolitionists set the groundwork for the emergence of the first wave of the women's rights movement in Seneca Falls, New York, in 1848. The central figures in that event were Elizabeth Cady Stanton and Lucretia Mott. Born in 1815 in Johnstown, New York, Elizabeth Cady was exposed at an early age to the legal oppression of women. Her father, a lawyer, allowed her to visit him in his office, where the young girl observed first-hand her father's inability to help married women in property and child-custody cases. As a young adult, she became socially acquainted with reformers in the upstate New York area. There she met abolitionist Henry Stanton, who became her husband.

As a young woman of twenty-five, Elizabeth Cady Stanton had never met either William Lloyd Garrison or Lucretia Mott, though Henry Stanton had earlier had many occasions to speak with them. In 1840, however, she became acquainted with both while on her honeymoon trip, accompanying Henry Stanton to the World's Anti-Slavery Convention in London, England. Both leaders had a profound effect on her. About Garrison she later remarked, "A few bold strokes from the hammer of his truth," and she was "free."[28] In truth, the young woman could not help but be impressed by the abolitionist leader, for when the delegates at the conference refused to allow the women attending to be seated and to participate as equals, Garrison (but not Henry Stanton) sat in the gallery with the women and remained silent throughout the ten days of meetings. Elizabeth Cady Stanton, however, was equally, if not more, impressed by Lucretia Mott, an officially elected U.S. delegate to the meeting. She later recalled in her *History of Woman Suffrage:* "Mrs. Mott was to me an entirely new revelation of womanhood. She came to me at a period in my young days when all life's problems seemed inextricably tangled; . . . I often longed to meet some woman who had sufficient confidence in herself to have and hold an opinion in the face of opposition, a woman who understood the deep significance of life to whom I could talk freely; my longings were answered at last."[29] As the two women strolled around London discussing the sexual discrimi-

4. Elizabeth Cady Stanton, ca. 1870. Courtesy of American Antiquarian Society.

nation they had experienced at the convention, they found themselves dreaming about a women's rights meeting, one which finally came to fruition when they met again eight years later in Seneca Falls.

The beginnings of the separate movement for suffrage and women's rights in the United States in Seneca Falls did not mean the end of the Garrisonian influence. Indeed, several of those in attendance at that first meeting had worked together in the abolitionist cause and had stressed the connection between slavery and the lack of women's rights in U.S. society. Rather, the new movement incorporated the earlier activists' ideologies regarding human rights and direct nonviolent action. Even the document adopted at the Seneca Falls Women's Rights Convention, called the "Declaration of Sentiments," reflected Garrisonianism. Unlike Garrison's own rejection of governmental authority, however, the women's document, combining the form of the U.S. Declaration of Independence with the women abolitionists' expression of the connection between violence and female oppression, emphasized the importance of changing existing laws and working within the accepted legal system to improve women's lot. The document began, "The history of mankind is a history of repeated injuries and usurpations on the part of man toward woman, having in direct object the establishment of an absolute tyranny over her."[30] This preamble was followed by a list of grievances, among them the denial to women of both the vote and participation in government.

The Seneca Falls meeting was followed by a flurry of other women's rights conventions throughout the East and Midwest. At each one, participants decried men's treatment of women and asserted the intention of achieving equal rights. They assailed property rights, child custody, divorce, and wage laws as well as women's invisibility in the political structure. In 1850 in Worcester, Massachusetts, Pauline Wright Davis presided over the first national women's rights convention. Wright had been both a Garrisonian abolitionist and a temperance worker. In her address to the participants, she connected the winning of women's rights with the achievement of a nonviolent, peaceful world:

> The reformation we propose in its utmost scope is radical and universal. . . . an epochal movement—the emancipation of a class, the redemption of half the world, and a conforming reorganization of all social, political and industrial interests and institutions. Moreover, it is a movement without example among the enterprises of associated reformations, for it has no purpose of arming the oppressed against the oppressor. . . . Its intended changes are to be wrought in the intimate texture of all societary organizations, without violence or any form of antagonism. It seeks to replace the worn-out with the living and the beautiful, so as to reconstruct without overturning, and to regenerate without destroying.[31]

Such dreams of peace were cut short by the outbreak of the Civil War in 1861. Even William Lloyd Garrison himself, although horrified by the violence, was forced to admit his pleasure over the emancipation of the slaves. The leaders of the American Peace Society meanwhile declared that the Southern states were in rebellion; hence, President Lincoln had every right to call on the military to intervene. Garrison also supported this idea that the U.S. government (i.e., the North) had the right to defend and preserve itself. Many of the women's rights activists forsook their own political campaigns in order to take on relief work and to help the newly freed people find food, family, and homes. Very few actually spoke out against this specific war. However, their anger at the waste of human life and their commitment to nonviolent resolutions to conflict did not cease. In 1863, in response to the war, Elizabeth Cady Stanton spearheaded the formation of the Woman's National Loyal League. She was joined in this endeavor by Susan B. Anthony, her close friend and suffrage co-organizer. Anthony, a mere five years younger than Stanton, had come to the suffrage cause after working in the New York state temperance movement. Early in her suffrage career, she also lectured on the antislavery issue. A Quaker by birth, Anthony shared humanitarian ideas with other reform-minded women. At first the two women organized the Loyal League around a campaign for a constitutional amendment to end slavery forever. The goal was to obtain three million signatures to present to Congress. The underlying hope was that this work would lead Congress to support a similar amendment resolution for woman suffrage as well as showing support for the North's efforts to free the slaves.

Their work within the League, however, only fueled the women's anger over the violence of this and all war. At one May 1863 meeting, Susan B. Anthony, echoing the spirit of nonviolence she had used in the abolitionist movement, blamed the unlikely pairing of mothers and President Lincoln for the nation's bloodbath. Once again invoking the image of women as politically powerless moral watchdogs of society, Anthony asserted that, if the women of the North had educated themselves and their sons about "the law of justice to the black man," they would not have had to see their sons go off to war. Furthermore, if Abraham Lincoln had freed the slaves and transformed them into "a peaceful army for the Union," the rebellion of the South would have been avoided.[32] Although in a small minority, throughout the war Stanton, Anthony, and others showed their disdain for the events. Lucretia Mott not only advocated nonviolent resistance to the war effort and

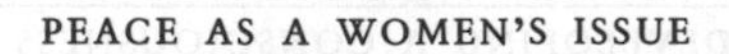

5. Susan B. Anthony, ca. 1870. Courtesy of American Antiquarian Society.

supported the claims of conscientious objectors but also helped found the Woman's Association for the Aid of the Freedmen in Philadelphia.

After the end of the war, the women's outcries against the violence grew louder. Meanwhile, the outrage over the oppression of women did not subside. Rather, the two themes merged, forming a more developed feminist-pacifist consciousness. Both Lucretia Mott and Elizabeth Cady Stanton had shown signs of a developing awareness before the war began. As early as 1849, Mott had publicly stressed the commitment women reformers felt to achieving human justice. "Women as well as men," she said, "are interested in these works of justice and mercy. . . . The blessing to the merciful, to the peacemaker is equal to man and to woman." Mott expressed her disgust with "any view . . . calculated to retard her labors of love."[33]

Eleven years later, only months before the war began, Stanton presented, even more dramatically, her view on why women were natural leaders for reform movements. At the 1860 anniversary celebration of the American Anti-Slavery Society, she emphasized that even though "a privileged class" could never understand what it was like to be enslaved, women were somewhat more able to do so than men. Stanton claimed, "She early learns the misfortune of being an heir to the crown of thorns, to martyrdom, to womanhood. For while the man is born to do whatever he can, for the woman and the negro, there is no such privilege." In Stanton's vision, however, this degradation resulted in a superior human, one who could rise above her situation and create a better future that would leave the oppressors in the muck. "Upward and upward, and still upward, she shall rise. Behold how far above your priestly robes, your bloody altars, your foul incense, your steepled synagogues she shall stand secure on holy mounts, mid clouds of dazzling radiance, to which, in your gross vision, you shall not dare even to lift your eyes."[34]

Mott and Stanton continued proclaiming their feminist-pacifist vision after the war had ended. Mott attended many local peace meetings, speaking out against war toys for children, the advent of military training in schools, and capital punishment. Her favorite theme was the "peace principle" as practiced by the Quakers and espoused by the Garrisonians. At this time Mott also began working within the established peace movement as well as continuing her women's rights activities. The Universal Peace Union, founded by Lucretia and James Mott along with Quaker-Garrisonian Albert Love in 1866, benefited from her membership even though it did not permit women to hold office until 1871. Her local group, the Pennsylvania Peace Society, however, received more of her attention. In 1870 she was elected the group's president, an office she held until her death in 1880.

During this period Mott claimed that the peace issue took precedence over "the woman question, as far as voting goes."[35] Nevertheless, she continued to support the women's rights movement, while also espousing the belief that women were not any more moral than men.

It was just that society liked to portray the two genders as such. Mott's dream was that the two could coexist in harmony, but, of course, equality was a prerequisite. While emphasizing that "arbitration shall supplant the spirit of warfare . . . ," she continued to stress that peace could not be obtained without the equal participation of women in the political sphere.[36] In 1878, Mott, then eighty-five years of age, made a strong statement in support of suffrage even though she restricted her active work solely to peace organizations. At the thirtieth anniversary celebration of the Seneca Falls meeting, she proclaimed, "Place women in equal power, and you will find her capable of not abusing it: give her the elective franchise, and there will be an unseen, yet a deep and universal movement of the people to elect into office only those who are pure in intention and honest in sentiment! Give her the privilege to cooperate in making the laws she submits to, and there will be harmony without severity and justice without oppression."[37]

During the postwar period, Elizabeth Cady Stanton also built upon her understanding that women's rights were inseparable from the attainment of peace. She took a very angry stance, blaming men for the disaster. Her anger was not new. Even in 1848, at the founding of the women's rights movement, Stanton had spoken of men's "moral inferiority," of corruption within government, of "rowdyism" in public places. However, she blamed men's upbringing rather than their "nature" for this condition. Men's "selfishness," she also claimed, resulted in women's "improved . . . moral nature."[38] In 1868, Stanton again lashed out at the "male" values dominating the society. This time, she referred to the male "element" in society as "a destructive force, stern, selfish, aggrandizing, loving war, violence, conquest, acquisition." She accused men of causing "discord, disorder, disease and death" throughout history, "overpowering the feminine element everywhere." She proposed that the new era of postwar expansion should not emphasize the rush for land, gold, or railroads but should embrace "a new evangel of womanhood, to exalt purity, virtue, morality, true religion, to lift man up into higher realms of thought and action."[39]

Once again, in 1872, she stated that peace was a women's issue, but her scope expanded from one nation to all. "As regards international peace," she said, "obviously the woman's mission is to recognize the bond of humanity between all the peoples, the human solidarity deeper and prior to the national."[40] Sixteen years later she was still making the connection: "The true woman is as yet a dream of the future. A just government, a humane religion, a pure social life await her coming. Then, and not till then, will the golden age of peace and prosperity be ours."[41]

The first suffragist actually to attempt to direct this early feminist-pacifist ideology into a separate women's peace movement was Julia Ward Howe. Born in 1819, Howe in her early twenties married a Bostonian nearly twice her age who did not believe that married women should participate in public life. Throughout a large part of her married life, she led a relatively private and inward existence until she gained notoriety for writing the lyrics for the famous Civil War song, "The Battle Hymn of the Republic." Because she was familiar with the antislavery movement in Boston, it was logical that her new public life would lead her to the women involved in this movement. In 1868, Howe founded the New England Women's Club, and a year later became one of the leaders of the newly-founded American Woman Suffrage Association, the result of a split within the post–Civil War women's rights movement.[42]

Ironically, Howe's real interest at the time was in organizing women against war and for peace through suffrage. She stated that women were under "a sort of military subjection to Man—captive of his bow and spirit" and felt that they had to free themselves in order to exercise their "superior moral force" for peace.[43] As a result of her feelings, in 1870 Howe suggested that a Woman's Peace Congress for the World be held in England to coincide with scheduled international conferences among world leaders. She proposed the conference at a peace meeting in New York in December. In order not to alienate the male members of her audience, she emphasized that although the cooperation of men would be helpful, it was up to women to "take each other by the hand" and make "our special impulses and intuitions" felt.[44] Alfred Love, then president of the Universal Peace Union, applauded Howe's idea, supporting woman suffrage and the role of women as the educators of children. The next year Howe tried to organize her Congress in England, but it did not succeed. As she reported, many women wrote to her claiming that they were "helpless" to participate, having neither the time nor independent financial means to travel and meet together.[45]

6. Julia Ward Howe, 1868. Courtesy of Schlesinger Library, Radcliffe College.

Not entirely undaunted, Howe then proposed that a national day be proclaimed to honor mothers, for she felt deeply that mothers, in particular, understood the suffering caused by war. In order to accommodate those women who could not travel, she proceeded to organize "Women's Peace Festivals" to be held in various locations on June 2, 1873. She sent out letters and appeals and organized the Boston meeting herself. Successful informal gatherings were held in Massachusetts, Connecticut, New York, New Jersey, Pennsylvania, Delaware, Illinois, Missouri, and even as far as London, Manchester, Geneva, Rome, and Constantinople. At each meeting women spoke out against war and military training in schools, and in favor of women's participation in decision making regarding war, as mothers, or voters, or both. The Peace Festivals attracted several hundred participants worldwide and continued for years to come, always planned for warm June days when the flowers were in bloom. As late as 1909, thirty-six years after its founding and a year before Howe's death, members of the Pennsylvania Peace Society were still sponsoring the Mother's Day for Peace activities every June 2.

By the 1870s there were several avenues women could take to support peace efforts. Peace work was certainly not in conflict with woman suffrage, and many women joined organizations in both areas. Even women who wanted the vote could join organizations other than suffrage societies in order to concentrate on the peace issue. In 1871, the American Peace Society permitted women, including Julia Ward Howe, to become officers. This was a far cry from the group's 1838 stance, which caused its split. Lucia Ames Mead, a member of the Boston Equal Suffrage Association, also played very prominently in the American Peace Society; in addition, she chaired Peace Committees in both the National Council of Women and the National American Woman Suffrage Association (NAWSA). One-half of the membership of the Universal Peace Union in the 1890s included women; in fact, one-third of its executive committee was female, including Belva Ann Lockwood, the first woman lawyer to argue a case before the Supreme Court and the presidential candidate of the National Equal Rights Party in both 1884 and 1888. Anna Garlin Spencer, a minister from a Unitarian background and an active suffragist, was a prominent member of the New York Peace Society, and Fannie Fern Andrews created the American School Peace League in 1908 to inform and organize educators on peace issues.

Another conduit for peace work was the temperance movement. Even though temperance gained its greatest popularity as a women's issue after the founding of the Woman's Christian Temperance Union (WCTU) in 1873, it had been an important issue for the feminist abolitionists and early women's rights activists as well. Historian Blanche Hersh emphasized in her study of the Garrisonian women that even though many women temperance workers in the antebellum period were not feminists, "every feminist abolitionist felt that temperance was essential to the emancipation of woman and the reform of society."[46] The overriding connection reformist women made between women's rights and temperance was the issue of violence against women. As long as men had a legal right to abuse their wives and children physically, women would remain victims. Their plight was only exacerbated by their husbands' legal right to use both their own and their wives' wages to imbibe alcohol before supplying their families with their basic needs. That the resulting inebriation often made the beatings worse compounded women's unhappy situation. Giving women the vote might be part of a long-term remedy for this intolerable situation. In the short term, however, the right of married women to keep their own wages and property and, even better, to be able to obtain child custody and divorces from violent men would be excellent immediate remedies for these problems. Early women's rights activists emphasized these issues to an even greater extent than suffrage.

In 1849, for example, Amelia Bloomer, the activist who in 1851 introduced Susan B. Anthony to Elizabeth Cady Stanton, founded the *Lily,* a newspaper fostering temperance as a basic component of women's rights. Bloomer's periodical consistently cited "intemperance" as the "great foe to women's peace and happiness," adding in a later issue that no wife should submit to a drunken husband's "blows and curses, and submit to his brutish passions and lusts."[47] Both Stanton and Anthony also worked for temperance. In 1852 the two women founded the New York State Woman's Temperance Society with Stanton as president and Anthony as secretary. At its first convention, Stanton proposed resolutions against married women's remaining with alcoholic husbands. Five years later, Stanton broadened her statements in favor of divorce, likening "the present false marriage relation" to "nothing more nor less than legalized prostitution." For Stanton, "personal freedom" was the "first right" for women as well as men.[48] Women forced to remain with and submit to abusive husbands, women stuck in unhappy relationships, and women caught in the web of slavery were all in the same unjust position. Only public sentiment and legal change could ensure their rescue. In 1860, Stanton and Anthony put their beliefs into practice by helping an abused wife run away from her husband, a Massachusetts legislator. As Anthony had earlier asserted, "Woman will no longer submit to the sufferer, that man may be the *sinner.*"[49]

While temperance remained a concern for the early generation of women's rights activists, its emphasis softened as the movement centered more and more around obtaining the vote. Those women, especially in smaller towns and rural areas, who joined the temperance campaign, did not always see eye-to-eye with women's rights activists. Many chose to join the more conservative WCTU, which at first did not embrace suffrage but which did involve itself with the issues of war and violence against women. Frances Willard, the indomitable leader of the WCTU, wanted to make peace a women's issue because she felt that alcohol abuse and militarism were intrinsically linked. The task of incorporating this slant into the organization's work, however, fell to a Quaker woman, Hannah Bailey, from Winthrop, Maine, who was also a member of the Universal Peace Union, the American Peace Society, the National Council of Women (founded in 1888), and the NAWSA. Bailey organized and headed the WCTU's Department of Peace and Arbitration, founded in 1887. Under her leadership, between 1889 and 1895, the WCTU published two monthly peace periodicals, *Pacific Banner* for adults and *Acorn* for children. In these and in lectures and tracts, the WCTU spoke out against military expenditures and military drills in schools, conscription, war toys, lynching, and even prize-fighting. Even though the WCTU eventually supported the idea of woman suffrage, its main thrusts were temperance and the fostering of the Christian home. Peace played directly into this program. Through leaflets, Bible readings, Peace Sunday programs, and children's peace bands and clubs, the WCTU leaders hoped to rid the world of evil and to promote an ethic of Christian love and humanity.

As in middle-class rhetoric of the time, mothers had taken on the aura of moral superiority. Women organizers either believed in the ideology or else saw its value as an organizing tool. Most likely, they recognized both phenomena. In any case, the role of mothers in saving the world and speaking against injustices became a basic component of their rhetoric. In one WCTU leaflet, for example, the ideal of mother love was presented: "It is the duty of the mother to prevent quarrels, likewise to make peace where contentions exist."[50] In another leaflet, the main job for mothers was stated as "teach[ing] their children that there is a higher form of patriotism than that whose aim is to destroy human life."[51] Because women were not only more peaceable by nature but also the bearers of children, they tended to suffer more from war. Therefore, it was up to them to stand firmly against it.

In 1889, Bailey was appointed superintendent of the World's WCTU Department of Peace and Arbitration. With organizations in North and South America, the Near and Far East, Europe and Africa, the Department's outreach was extensive indeed. Through the World's WCTU, the connections among religion, peace, nonviolence, and suffrage were

WORLD'S AND NATIONAL
W. C. T. U.
DEPARTMENT PEACE AND ARBITRATION.

Blessed are the Peacemakers.

Follow Peace with All Men.

A Dialogue on Peace and Arbitration.

ARRANGED FOR FOUR GIRLS.

MAUD—What do you think, Girls, of the first report of the World's Superintendent of the Department of Peace and Arbitration? I think it very encouraging. There has been a grand work done.

LAURA—Is it any wonder that progress should be rapid when so many eminent lecturers are in the field advocating its claims, and when so many authors of note at home and abroad are deeply interested in this peace and arbitration question?

ANNIE—Have either of you seen that interesting book entitled "Away with War

7. Sample of literature from the WCTU's Department of Peace and Arbitration, late 1890s. Courtesy of Swarthmore College Peace Collection.

all internationalized for temperance workers. One document, widely distributed through this international network, pulled all these issues together. It stated that the group's mission "in the love of God, and of Humanity" was "the protection of the home by outlawing the liquor traffic in alcoholic liquors, opium, tobacco, and impurity; the suppression by law of gambling, and Sunday desecration, the enfranchisement of the women of all nations; and the establishment of courts of national and international arbitration—which shall banish war from the world."[52]

Certainly by the late nineteenth century, U.S. women had a firsthand knowledge of the realities of military intervention, the major tragedy and catalyst for more thought and action being the Civil War. Since this particular conflict, women, especially suffragists, had become more vocal about foreign policy. When the U.S. government found itself in a dispute with Chile in 1891, for example, both the National Council of Women and the WCTU petitioned Congress to avoid getting involved in a war. Four years later, when Venezuela and England had a confrontation over the border of British Guiana, WCTU and NAWSA members again wrote to Congress, this time asking leaders to arbitrate the dispute. Some women reiterated the suffragists' post–Civil War cry that war came as a result of male greed. This anger at male leaders was clearly articulated by Lillie Devereux Blake, a New York public school principal and member of the NAWSA. At the organization's 1895 annual convention, Blake accused men of being willing "to deluge the world in blood for a strip of land in Venezuela or a gold mine in Africa."[53] Blake's daughter, Kathryn, would carry on in her mother's footsteps from World War I through the interwar years, echoing, along with other feminist-pacifists, this frustration with the existing power structure.

The largest outcry at the end of the nineteenth century, however, came over the Spanish-American War in 1898. This war, which established the United States as an imperialist power, presented certain controversies for the activist women because of the variety of issues surrounding the conflict. The first was that of Cuba's independence from Spain. Some women stood against U.S. involvement in another nation's affairs; others supported the government's public stance that helping the Cubans was the right thing to do. The larger issue was that of imperialism. As a result of the war, the United States obtained possession of Puerto Rico, the Philippines, and Guam as well as protectorate status over Cuba. Suffrage leaders had spoken angrily about male greed after the Civil War. They saw clearly the linkage among commercialism, colonialism, and militarism. Some men also made this connection, and in

June 1898, a group of wealthy businessmen from Boston founded the Anti-Imperialist League. Several suffragists—such as Lucia Ames Mead, Anna Garlin Spencer, Jane Addams and May W. Sewall—supported the League, although women were not allowed to serve as vice-presidents until 1904.

Most women's active protest against this war, however, originated within their own organizations. The U.S. occupation of the Philippines particularly angered the activist women, who saw it as a clear-cut case of imposing one nation's will upon another. One petition circulated by the Colorado WCTU protested against the proposed annexation of the islands and the continuing war with the local native guerrilla forces. They characterized the subjection of the Filipinos as the un-Christian "killing and destroying the inhabitants of those islands in order to bring them under subjection."[54] The National Council of Women, the WCTU, and the NAWSA all spoke out against the violence and disease caused by the excessive use of alcohol and the spread of prostitution due to U.S. army bases in the Philippines.

Like the Anti-Imperialist League, the women had a certain fear of how the annexation of the Asian nation might affect immigration and racial purity in the U.S., but the women had additional concerns about moral disintegration and the spread of veneral disease after the soldiers returned home. In 1902 concern over moral decay due to imperialism caused Fannie Gaffney, the president of the National Council of Women, to lament over the "great danger that material things will overshadow things essential to the best interests of humanity." In Gaffney's opinion, it was up to women as the "servator of the human race" to "preserve that general balance between things temporal and spiritual . . . from reverting to gross materialism if not brute ferocity."[55] For all these women, patriotism could not be synonymous with imperialism, war, or greed.

Relief from the scourge of war seemed in sight when a conference on world peace was organized at The Hague for 1899. According to the *Woman's Tribune,* no movement of that generation had so "enlisted the interest of women as this peace conference."[56] Both Lucia Ames Mead and May Wright Sewall organized local educational committees of the NAWSA and the National Council of Women around The Hague conference. Other women's groups, including Utah's Congress of Mothers, the National Woman's Relief Society, the General Federation of

PEACE SUNDAY

PROGRAM

Music

Scripture Reading—Isaiah 2.

Prayer—Ending with Lord's Prayer.

Hymn—America.

Reading—"The Angels of Buena Vista."
J. G. Whittier

Symposium { Peace: Its relation to the { Home / Church / Nation

Singing—"Peace Hymn of Nations."

Recitation—"Is It Worth While?"

Reading—"The Unity of the World."
Written by A. H. Bradford, D. D.

Address—The Peace Congress at the Hague, and what it has accomplished.

Singing—"Sweet Peace, the Gift of God's Love."

Benediction.

Published by H. J. Bailey, Superintendent
World's and National Dept. Peace and Arbitration
Winthrop Center, Maine
Price, one cent each.

8. Sunday program literature from the WCTU's Department of Peace and Arbitration, late 1890s. Courtesy of Swarthmore College Peace Collection.

Women's Clubs, and the Council of Jewish Women, also held meetings and organized events to inform the public about the conference. As the *Woman's Tribune* added, women had meetings of support in more than ninety cities and towns in Utah alone.[57]

During this same year, women also displayed their worldwide solidarity in London at the first gathering of the International Council of Women (ICW). The ICW had been founded in 1888 in Washington, D.C., as an international suffrage organization. May Wright Sewall, however, convinced the founders that the group should feature other issues, such as church and temperance work, in order to attract a broader membership. Julia Ward Howe, while attending this founding meeting, added a plea for the group to adopt a peace stance. In agreement with her was Elizabeth Cady Stanton, who delivered the welcoming address at this first meeting. Stanton, while emphasizing the need for women's political equality, stressed that a woman's voice would add a "more humane" element to the government and court systems. Stanton also emphasized the common bond among women, claiming that the gender shared a "universal sense of injustice."[58] By 1896 the organization had passed a resolution committing its members to a program of peace and arbitration. When the group met in 1899, it certainly resembled the dream meeting Howe had tried to organize almost thirty years before. Representatives came from eleven national councils: the United States, Canada, Germany, Sweden, Great Britain, Ireland, New South Wales, Denmark, Holland, New Zealand, and Tasmania. Together they represented a total membership of over six million women, all aware of the issues of war, peace, woman suffrage, and violence against women.

The ICW, while embracing efforts for both suffrage and peace, became a worldwide voice for women's issues and would play an important role in the feminist peace movement in the years to come. Another important women's organization that grew out of the ICW was the International Woman Suffrage Alliance, founded in 1902 and later known as the International Alliance of Women. This organization worked on only one issue—suffrage—but saw it in an international context. Accordingly, the peace issue became intrinsic to the organization's stance. In the May 1, 1914, issue of the *International Woman's Suffrage News,* for example, the securing of world peace was referred to as "a woman's dream . . . a vision of justice and peaceful evolution." In the same article, the women also recognized their own ability to overcome national differences. "The true spirit of internationalism which pervades the meetings of the Alliance cannot be described; it must be felt."[59]

The first decade of the twentieth century proved fairly quiet for feminist peace activists. The ICW held meetings each year and continued to foster peace, especially through political lobbying and education. Women leaders, such as Anna Howard Shaw of the National Council, continued to question the wisdom of training young boys for military service. Shaw and other suffragists felt that boys should be socialized more like girls had been—that is, to be more caring and less violent. By 1914 feminist peace activists had begun to form a unified voice. They emphasized the necessity of achieving woman suffrage as a means of creating a just society and of ridding the world of violence against women. They questioned the wisdom and the intentions of the male power structure in diplomatic relations as well as the true meaning of patriotism. They pondered over the connections between female biology and peace, espousing the view that women were naturally peaceful because of their ability to procreate and nurture children. Speeches, tracts, meetings, letters, petitions, and peace committee work all raised these issues as well as the all-encompassing concern of women's role in international affairs. This was the dream—a new and beauteously loving world. Unfortunately, the dream was not to be. Instead, the catalyst for bringing these loosely-organized feminist pacifists into a major organizational effort was the outbreak of World War I, then termed the "Great War."

3

Suffragist-Pacifists versus the Great War, 1914–1919

IN AUGUST 1914, amidst age-old border disputes, growing nationalism among ethnic groups, competition in trade and colonial expansion, and a stockpile of newer and more deadly weapons, war broke out in Europe, involving almost all of the major powers. The war created an obstacle for European and U.S. women's rights activists, who depended on their international work for individual support during their campaign for woman suffrage. Women's rights activists in the United States had not formally organized around the Spanish-American War in 1898, but the European conflict of 1914, which threatened to disrupt the worldwide fight for women's rights, inspired a more organized outcry. Having developed friendships and strong working relationships in the International Woman Suffrage Alliance and the International Council of Women, many women in the United States had real concern for the lives of European comrades. Furthermore, by 1914, the sixty-six-year-old campaign for the vote had reached millions of women across the nation. Although not every suffragist was concerned about the European politics that caused the war, enough were to warrant the establishment of an organization to stand for both woman suffrage and world peace. This organization, the Woman's Peace Party, created as a direct response to the European conflict of 1914, became both the suffrage wing of the peace movement and the pacifist wing of the suffrage movement.

The first organized feminist response to the war was a women's antiwar parade held in New York City on August 29, 1914, less than a month after the war began. Dressed in mourning garb, over 1,500 women marched in silence except for the beat of muffled drums. A few of the leaders held a banner showing a dove carrying an olive branch to symbolize peace. Although the people on the sidelines applauded, their hearts perhaps grieving for the suffering in Europe, they demanded neutrality at home.

The Parade Committee that organized this demonstration included some of the most prominent women's rights activists of the day and reflected the broad concerns of the movement. Harriot Stanton Blatch (Elizabeth Cady Stanton's daughter) and Carrie Chapman Catt, for example, represented, respectively, the liberal and conservative sides of the suffrage movement. Lillian Wald and Lavinia Dock reflected social work, and Mary Drier, Leonora O'Reilly, and Rose Schneiderman labor. Mary Beard, Charlotte Perkins Gilman, and Marie Jenny Howe were all involved in feminist history, theory, and activism.

Seventy-year-old Fanny Garrison Villard was chosen as the Committee's leader. The daughter of William Lloyd Garrison, Villard embraced her father's vision of nonresistance. Feeling dissatisfied with such peace organizations as the American Peace Society and the Universal Peace Union, Villard hoped that the Peace Parade Committee would act as the catalyst for a new, all-female peace organization that would be "based upon the principle of the inviolability and sacredness of human life under all circumstances." Expressing her disappointment in the effectiveness of the present male-dominated organizations, Villard hoped that women would take the lead in forging a "new moral movement" that would lead to a nonviolent and warless world.[1]

The parade itself reflected its feminist roots. Along with its expression of horror over the war and its plea for President Woodrow Wilson to act as mediator, the Peace Parade Committee voiced its feeling that women had a unique opposition to war. After all, they were the ones to suffer most, both in the perpetual violence against women during a military occupation and through the deaths of sons, husbands, lovers, brothers, and fathers—a loss both emotional and financial. Like their foremothers, the women expressed their anger at male behavior and determined that they would work separately from men in order to emphasize their special interests and organizational ideas. This new approach to peace work attracted immediate attention. When asked why men were not involved in the Parade Committee, the leaders at first responded innocently that the omission had been just an oversight because the project had evolved so rapidly. Their desire for separatism, however, emerged clearly in a typed memorandum stating, "The idea was originated by women and if it appears the men wish to make a protest they will have to organize a parade of their own."[2]

While Fanny Garrison Villard looked forward to a new women's organization, Carrie Chapman Catt, president of the National American Woman Suffrage Association, did not. Catt believed that women should continue to work through the International Woman Suffrage Alliance and not break off to form a new group. She saw the parade as a one-shot expression of female concern and anger, not as the catalyst for a new organization. Apparently, others agreed with her then, for no new organization evolved out of the Peace Parade Committee.

By November, however, the time was ripe for organizing. The war had been raging for three months with no end in sight, and news filtering in through the international women's suffrage network was filled with reports of brutality and the starvation among women and children throughout Europe. Two European suffragists, one Hungarian and one English, inspired the creation of a new organization. Rosika Schwimmer, a very active and well-known Jewish Hungarian feminist, was in London in August working as the International Press Secretary of the International Woman Suffrage Alliance. Schwimmer, who had been involved with the Alliance since its early years, had gained considerable respect for orchestrating the 1913 International Woman Suffrage Congress in Budapest. By September 1914, Schwimmer, with the assistance of Carrie Chapman Catt, had traveled to the United States to speak with both Secretary of State William Jennings Bryan and President Woodrow Wilson about mediating the war. She carried with her a resolution of support signed by women from thirteen different countries. Schwimmer followed these visits with a speaking tour, urging U.S. women to pressure Wilson into becoming the mediator.

In November, while Schwimmer was on her speaking tour, Emmeline Pethick-Lawrence, a prominent English suffragist, arrived in New York to speak on both suffrage and peace. While there, Pethick-Lawrence met Madeline Zabrisky Doty, a radical lawyer with an interest in aligning the suffrage movement with the newly developed mediation campaign. Doty and her good friend, Crystal Eastman, another radical lawyer and a socialist, arranged for the English woman to speak on the topic at a public forum of the Women's Political Union, the militant suffrage group under the wing of Harriot Stanton Blatch. This event, held on October 31 at Carnegie Hall, resulted in the formation of the Woman's Peace Party of New York, the first formal feminist peace organization in U.S. history.

A local organization, particularly one made up of some of Greenwich Village's "bohemian" residents, was not the most politically astute way to influence the nation's president. Both Rosika Schwimmer and Emmeline Pethick-Lawrence agreed that that job could best be handled by such influential women as Carrie Chapman Catt and Jane Addams, women who moved fairly easily in male political circles and who did not ruffle too many feathers among either men or women. In addition, each woman had influence in a different sphere. At age fifty-five, Catt was most noted for her suffrage activities. In 1914, she was president of both the National American Woman Suffrage Association and the International Woman Suffrage Alliance. Addams, fifty-four years old, was best known for her revolutionary contributions to social work as the founder and director of Hull House, the settlement house in Chicago that she had established in 1889 at the age of twenty-nine. By 1914, Addams, born a Quaker but by then a practicing Presbyterian, was also a respected spokeswoman for peace. As a member of the Anti-Imperialist League, she had previously taken some strong stands during the Spanish-American War. At that time she openly deplored the racist and imperialistic implications of the war, stating that patriotism and duty had to be separated from war-mongering. "Peace is not merely something to hold congresses about and to discuss as an abstract dogma," she said in 1899. "It has come to be a rising tide of moral feeling which is slowly engulfing all pride of conquest and is making war impossible."[3]

By 1902, Addams had begun to formalize her ideas in print. In *Democracy and Social Ethics,* published that year, she stated that the need for war would gradually disappear once the larger society developed the type of collective social morality she had found existed in the crowded immigrant tenement quarters surrounding Hull House. "In this effort toward a higher morality in our social relations, we must demand that the individual shall be willing to lose the sense of personal achievement, and shall be content to realize his activity only in connection with the activity of the many."[4] Five years later Addams produced another tract, *The Newer Ideals of Peace,* in which she introduced the idea that the world needed to substitute "nurture for warfare," and who could do this better than women? The "newer humanitarianism" Addams proposed depended on women's securing the vote and taking "a citizen's place in the modern industrial city" and, hence, the world.[5]

These four women—Rosika Schwimmer, Emmeline Pethick-Lawrence, Carrie Chapman Catt, and Jane Addams—each a seasoned activist in the political world, came together to forge a women's peace organization that still exists today as the Women's International League for Peace and Freedom (WILPF). They could hardly have foreseen the future of their new organization. In late 1914, when each thought about the need for action to stop the particular war in Europe they were experiencing, none perceived that future generations would need such a group. Although Catt and Addams had specific differences and questions they needed to sort through before committing themselves to such a large project, both agreed on four points, each leading to the next: (1) that peace was a special concern for women and (2) that the current peace movement was too male-dominated, but (3) that women should try to work through these existing organizations and (4) that the suffragists should not be the prime movers in the formation of a women's peace organization. Other women, however, perceived the situation in a different light. If, as many agreed, peace was a women's issue and the existing peace organizations were male-dominated, wasn't it necessary for women to form their own movement? Then, if so, what was the role of suffragists in this project going to be and how would the new movement affect the struggle for the vote?

As chapter 2 indicated, women's rights activists had been making the connection between women's oppression and the violence of war at least since the Civil War. Charlotte Perkins Gilman, a philosopher of the feminist movement, put the issue into verse in her book *Women and Economics* (1898):

> The tendency to "sit" is a sex-distinction of the hen:
> the tendency to strut is a sex-distinction of the cock.
> The tendency to fight is a sex-distinction of males in general:
> the tendency to protect and provide for is a sex-distinction of
> females in general.[6]

Later, in *Our Man-Made World* (1911) she ridiculed men's attitudes toward war: "In warfare, PER SE, we find maleness in its absurdest extremes. Here is . . . the whole gamut of basic masculinity, from the initial instinct of combat, through every form of glorious ostentation with the loudest possible accompaniment of noise."[7]

Carrie Chapman Catt, who directly connected the peace issue with the suffrage campaign, in February 1915 vented her anger in a letter to the *New York Times:*

> They tell us men were told *[sic]* off for war, women to care for homes and children, and in time of peace, war, the man's business, gives way to politics, the man's business.
>
> The politics of men have embroiled the world in the most wholesale slaughter of the sons of mothers the world has ever known. That is a case where man's business of war and woman's business of conserving the race have clashed, and women are helpless to defend their own. Hundreds if not thousands of women have been forced to bear children by soldiers of their country's enemy all along the war zone. It becomes the terrible business of the mothers of the race to secure the right of a political protest in every nation. When war murders the husbands and sons of women, destroys their homes, desolates their country and makes them refugees and paupers, it becomes the undeniable business of women.[8]

At about the same time, Jane Addams, in her characteristic way, was gentler, expressing her continuing belief that there were "things upon which women are more sensitive than men, and one of these is the treasuring of human life."[9]

Both Catt and Addams agreed that women had very strong, specific concerns about war that the existing peace societies did not address. In fact, the older peace groups were downright exclusionary in leadership and ideology. Catt wrote to Addams in December 1914, that from what she could tell, the four national peace societies, "all well endowed," were "very masculine in their point of view." She added, "It would seem that they have as little use for women and their points of view, as have the militarists."[10] Addams responded, agreeing that the "masculine management" of those groups was obvious and that she felt there was an eagerness among women for their own action to curb the European conflict.[11] The question arose again and again as to whether the chauvinistic behavior of the men warranted the creation of an exclusively female organization. Addams herself would have preferred to work through the already existing organizations than to create an all-female group. In general, she felt that the very idea of a separate women's peace movement contradicted the idea of sexual equality. However, as she wrote to Lucia Ames Mead, an old hand at dealing with the men in the American Peace Society, "in this case the demand has been so universal and spontaneous over the country that it seemed to me best to take it up."[12]

Although Catt, too, hesitated over the idea of an entirely new, separate movement, she did approve of a female demonstration or a small, informal conference with representatives of the largest and most influential of the women's organizations. Catt would have liked to see these female leaders securing congressional hearings and using their influence on the legislators. Afterwards could follow a mass meeting of both women and men. In any case, Catt did not feel that suffragists should be in the forefront of any peace organization, demonstration, or conference for fear that such a presence might harm the unity of the suffrage campaign. In a letter to Addams, Catt stated her belief that Addams was the right woman to call such a meeting. She herself offered to support the work in New York State but made it clear that she would not head it. Instead, she would "get the right people to do it and . . . give my assistance to it."[13]

At this point, Jane Addams decided to move ahead, and in mid-December she sent out a call, including her own and Catt's names, for a women's peace meeting to be held from January 9 to 11, 1915, in Washington, D.C. On December 29, a distressed Catt wrote to Addams concerning the use of her name. "I wished only to support your effort in an inconspicuous way," she insisted.[14] Catt's hesitancy in being a leading figure in this effort may have had more to do with the presence of the Congressional Union in the Washington event than with anything else. The Congressional Union, a splinter group formed out of the Congressional Committee of the NAWSA in 1913 by more militant suffragists, was a thorn in Catt's side. The union, admiring the aggressive tactics used by English suffragists, wished to duplicate some of these approaches in the United States. Among the tactics they supported were making bonfires out of President Wilson's speeches in front of the White House gates, going to prison for defying the police, and fighting back physically if they felt the need to. The Washington members of the Union were particularly active in organizing the January peace gathering. Catt simply did not want to cooperate with them. Their existence symbolized a split in the otherwise united suffrage movement, and their actions caused embarrassment to the more conservative members of the NAWSA. In addition, Catt's commitment was to winning the vote. As she would later prove, if this meant cooperating in a war effort, she would do so, no matter what her personal feelings were.

The January meeting held at the New Willard Hotel resulted in the formation of the Woman's Peace Party (WPP), with national headquarters to be situated in Chicago so that Jane Addams could easily act as chair. Seventy-seven delegates from such diverse organizations as the Daughters of the American Revolution, the Congressional Union, the Woman's Christian Temperance Union, the American Peace Society, the General Federation of Women's Clubs, the Women's Trade Union League, and the Women's National Committee of the Socialist Party attended, to name but a few. Most of the platform planks passed unanimously. These included the most popular peace ideas of the day: the limitation of arms, mediation of the European conflict, the creation of international laws to prevent war, the substitution of an international police force for national armies and navies, the removal of the economic causes of war, and the appointment by the U.S. government of a commission of men *and* women to promote international peace. The one plank that caused debate was the call for the vote for women. Antisuffragists at the meeting felt that this plank would automatically limit the appeal, size, and effect of the organization—which it eventually did. But Jane Addams and others held strong on the issue, and it passed. As Anna Howard Shaw, past president of the NAWSA said, "A woman who does not want to have anything to say in regard to her nation going to war, has no right to have anything to say in regard to her nation coming out of war. If we cannot have the power to speak before war is declared, we ought not cry out for power to speak after the fighting has begun."[15]

The entire "Preamble and Platform" adopted during this first meeting revealed the unique quality of this new organizational trend in women's history. Here was the first organized effort for world peace on the part of women who still did not have the vote but nonetheless felt that their voices must be heard. At the time, this sense of urgency was so strong that it managed to unite the larger suffrage movement with its radical fringe. Anna Garlin Spencer, a leading suffragist, minister, and pacifist, had reluctantly attended the Washington meeting, fearing that inclusion of the suffrage sentiment would not help a movement for peace. The next week, however, she applauded the "groundswell movement, a great peace crusade within the suffrage ranks."[16] Although she mistrusted the effectiveness of the Congressional Union in dealing with government officials, Spencer did acknowledge "the advantage of the enthusiasm and push of the radical wing." After all, without their hard work, there might not have been an organizational meeting at all. In addition, Spencer hoped that the Woman's Peace Party would have a good effect on the suffrage movement, resulting in a reconciliation of the "straight" and "radical" organizers. The peace organization, she felt, could "give a great practical aim to the women suffragists which will unite and elevate them all."[17]

The element of the new organization that appealed to both factions of the suffrage movement was chiefly its position that women, as "the mother half of humanity," had a unique role to play in the world. The "Preamble" made this perfectly clear. Women, the document proclaimed, had "a peculiar moral passion of revolt against both the cruelty and waste of war." As their foremothers had stated in the nineteenth century, women were fed up with the "reckless destruction" wrought by the patriarchal power structure. If women were the ones "charged with the future of childhood and with the care of the helpless and the unfortunate," then they would no longer "endure without protest that added burden of maimed and invalid men and poverty stricken widows and orphans" that war created. Women, in other words, were sick and tired of being exploited as a result of poor governmental judgment, greed, and violence. They wanted "a share in deciding between war and peace," and that share included equality in the home as well as in all aspects of public life.[18]

The general appeal to women's rights activists worked well. Within a year the Woman's Peace Party had grown from eighty-five charter members to a membership of 512, and there were thirty-three local branches by the next year. By February 1916, membership reached a peak of 40,000, and even though numbers of women would drop out after the United States joined in the war effort on April 6, 1917, that December the organization still included two hundred local branches and affiliated groups. Branches existed from California to New York, the largest number of members living in Connecticut, New Jersey, Pennsylvania, Massachusetts, Washington State, and Illinois.[19] Conflicts between the Congressional Union and NAWSA supporters, however, were never totally resolved. The leaders in Chicago and an active branch in Massachusetts reflected a more staid and cautious aspect of the group's philosophy, an aspect that emphasized peace and not suffrage. Women like Jane Addams in Chicago and Lucia Ames Mead in Massachusetts concentrated their efforts on trying to achieve the cooperation of U.S. officials to head off involvement in the war and to remain neutral. The greatest number of the "radicals" were in the New York branch. These women were interested not only in appealing to national leaders but also in seeking societal changes that would end the causes of war, especially where those causes had become ingrained within the economic and legal structures of the United States.

The dominant force behind the Woman's Peace Party organization formed in New York City in 1914 was Crystal Eastman, one of the two women who originally rallied behind Emmeline Pethick-Lawrence's call to help her European sisters. Eastman, a self-proclaimed socialist-feminist, was educated at Vassar, held a master of arts in sociology from Columbia and a law degree from New York University. Long involved with political issues, Eastman was appointed New York's first woman commissioner of the Employer's Liability Commission in 1909, and while with that group she wrote New York State's first workers' compensation law. In organizing the New York City branch of the Woman's Peace Party, Eastman was joined by other women who took a militant stand not only on suffrage but on reproductive rights, labor organizing, and other issues as well. Margaret Lane, Anne Herendeen, Freda Kirchwey, Katherine Anthony, and Madeline Doty were all close friends with common interests. Several were members of the Congressional Union or of Heterodoxy, an informal network of New York feminists often meeting for Saturday lunches, complete with political, literary, and personal disucssions. As historian Barbara Steinson has pointed out, the

New York branch of the WPP was a youthful group, with an average age of thirty-five; the national average was fifty-nine.[20]

Throughout the World War I era, tension existed between the New York branch and the national board, rooted primarily in the basic difference between the two philosophies of organizing within the suffrage movement, one aligned militantly with the Congressional Union, the other more conservatively with the NAWSA. Age and political leanings added to the problem. Yet, until the United States entered the war in April 1917, the two factions managed to cooperate with each other. There was no conflict more severe than some verbal complaints, either from Chicago or Massachusetts that the New Yorkers were being too bold or from the New Yorkers that the others were being too meek. The tie that bound them together, and seemed to override the suffrage division, was their belief in their special position as mothers "or potential mothers," as Crystal Eastman put it, "who offer more meaning and passion . . . to end war than . . . an organization of men and women with the same end."[21] In fact, the New York City group was so active that by November of the first year, 1915, the national board awarded it representation equal to that of state branches.

During these first two years, the Woman's Peace Party in general was very productive in reaching out to the suffrage network in Europe. Official contact came in April 1915, when forty-seven U.S. women, many of them members of the organization, sailed aboard the *Noordam* for The Hague in the Netherlands. The passengers, including Jane Addams and Alice Post as the official WPP delegates and Madeline Doty of the New York branch, were heading for the first international meeting of women to discuss the ongoing war. Organized chiefly by Aletta Jacobs, a physician and president of the Dutch suffrage organization, and Chrystal Macmillan, a Scottish lawyer and secretary of the International Woman Suffrage Alliance, the meeting was the suffragists' response to the cancellation of their annual international meeting planned for Berlin. Because of the war, women from countries now belligerent could not travel to each other's lands. Accordingly, the meeting was moved to the neutral Netherlands, and "peace" was substituted as its central rallying point.

The meeting brought together women from both the warring and neutral nations in the spirit of "solidarity" and "mutual friendship."[22]

9. U.S. delegation to the International Congress of Women at The Hague, 1915. Jane Addams *(front row, second from left)*. Courtesy of Swarthmore College Peace Collection.

In all, 1,136 delegates from twelve nations attended, despite efforts by a few governments to prevent them. For example, British authorities held up the *Noordam* for three days, causing the U.S. women to arrive just in the nick of time. One hundred eighty British women were refused passports, and the closing of the North Sea prevented even those with passports from reaching their destination. The only British women who attended were Emmeline Pethick-Lawrence, who was on the *Noordam,* and Chrystal Macmillan and Kathleen Courtney, who were already in the Netherlands. Because of the war, no Russian or French women attended. The French were especially adamant in their feelings that to attend would be disloyal to their motherland. Women from Sweden

(12), Norway (12), Italy (1), Hungary (9), Germany (28), Denmark (6), Canada (2), Belgium (5), Austria (6), Great Britain (3), the United States (47), and the Netherlands (1,000) made up the Congress, an interesting combination of largely neutral and "enemy" nationals.[23]

The real purpose behind the meeting was made clear in the proceedings left behind. Not only did the women want peace, but they also wanted equality with men. The concluding document contained the following statement: "The International Congress of Women is convinced that one of the strongest forces for the prevention of war will be the combined influence of the women of all countries. . . . But as women can only make their influence effective if they have equal political rights with men, this Congress declares that it is the duty of the women of all countries to work with all their force for their political enfranchisement."[24] Only through the equal participation of "the mother half of humanity" in all governments everywhere could war and its consequences be ended, especially the victimization of women and children.

Among the resolutions developed as a result of the meeting, suffrage took a major position. Equally important was a recommendation for neutral mediation, based on a plan entitled "Continuous Mediation without Armistice" by Julia Grace Wales, a Canadian who taught English at the University of Wisconsin. The plan called for U.S. involvement in the creation of a body of neutral nations that would continuously suggest peace plans for the belligerents to discuss until peace was reestablished. Further proof of the women's determination to be included in the political sphere came in two actions: the resolve of the group to plan a meeting to be held at the same time and place as the end-of-war treaty meeting so the women could pressure the major powers to include women's equality in the peace plank and the creation of two delegations to visit national leaders in an effort to promote mediation.[25]

This latter action was suggested by Rosika Schwimmer, who, in an impassioned speech, had urged the women to visit the leaders. Schwimmer appealed to the women's sense of motherly duty: "If brains have brought us to what we are in now, I think it is time to allow our hearts to speak. When our sons are killed by the millions, let us, mothers, only try to do good by going to the kings and emperors, without any other danger than a refusal."[26] As a result of the speech, two delegations were formed immediately after the Congress adjourned. Jane Addams, Aletta Jacobs, and Rosa Genoni of Italy met with the leaders of England, Germany, Hungary, Italy, France, Belgium, the Netherlands, and Switzerland. Emily Greene Balch, Chrystal Macmillan, Rosika Schwimmer and Cor Ramondt-Hirsch of the Netherlands visited Denmark, Norway, Sweden, Russia, and the Netherlands. From May to August the two groups paid a total of thirty-five visits to leaders in both neutral and belligerent nations, asking each directly if he would like to see the war mediated, ended, or both. Addams planned to return to the United States to present the responses to President Wilson, with the continuing hope that he would serve as the neutral mediator needed to resolve the conflict.

Jane Addams came home as the first president of the newly formed International Committee of Women for Permanent Peace, of which the Woman's Peace Party was the United States Section. With her usual modesty, Addams stated that she was elected because the organization wanted a leader from a neutral country as far away from the fighting as possible.[27] Upon her arrival, she addressed a mass meeting in Carnegie Hall, revealing her dismay that stimulants such as alcohol were being used on the battlefields to enable men to kill each other, especially when bayonets were called for. In a later report written about the conference, Addams stated that many young men she had spoken with did not want war and "considered the older men responsible for it." Addams held to her belief that men were against war as much as women, even though the mothers of the world probably had "a peculiar revulsion" to seeing their children destroyed.[28]

The press lambasted Addams for her views, and in the years to come, both the press and the U.S. government portrayed her as an unpatriotic subversive out to demasculinize the nation's sons. Bad press, however, did not prevent Addams from trying to achieve an end to the war through neutral mediation. From July to December 1915, she paid six visits to President Wilson. Emily Greene Balch saw him in August and Aletta Jacobs in September. None of the three women left feeling confident in the possibility of Wilson's seeking mediation. Part of the problem was that after the Germans sank the British passenger ship, the *Lusitania,* on May 7, Wilson had begun to shift away from mediation towards preparedness. After all, the ship, in which 128 U.S. citizens met their deaths, had also been carrying arms shipments from U.S. munitions makers to England.

In November 1915, Wilson officially announced that he supported a full preparedness program. The Woman's Peace Party leaders, who had placed so much trust in the president's leanings towards peace, were taken aback by his strong turn towards militarization. For many of them, it meant their own necessary shift in rhetoric and action from a movement for peaceful mediation to a movement against preparedness. By January 1916 peace activists in general began to speak out against the large budgetary increases needed for the nation to be "prepared." That month Jane Addams testified before a House committee against proposed increases in military expenditures. Much Woman's Peace Party activity was aimed at the prevention of using public school physical education classes as a means of imposing military training on young boys. The women acknowledged the benefits of compulsory physical education classes, but declared the classes were not the proper place for military training.

The New York City branch emphasized this issue on a local level. In January the members organized a mass meeting at Cooper Union in New York City "to protest against the invasion of our public school system by military authorities and enthusiasts."[29] That spring the branch participated in a public demonstration about the same issue. Fifteen young women dressed in white and displaying antiwar signs and banners handed out literature to the watching crowds. Two trucks preceded them. The first, decorated with German and French flags and carrying young boys wielding baseball bats, bore the message "Boys are boys in Germany and France." The second truck, which carried boys with rifles, was labeled "Boys are now soldiers in New York State."[30]

The New York women continued to protest the state law outlined in the Slater Bill, which allowed for the educational system to institute military training. The bill also mandated that all boys in New York State between the ages of sixteen and nineteen attend three hours of military drill per week; only those already employed were exempt. In addition, all boys had to spend from two to four weeks during the summer at a special military training camp. Although causing much protest, the law remained in effect well into the interwar era. The national board of the Woman's Peace Party protested similar legislation

10. Demonstration in New York City, 1916. Courtesy of Swarthmore College Peace Collection.

on the national level. In this effort, the women cooperated with the American Union Against Militarism, a mixed-gender organization led by a combination of WPP leaders such as Jane Addams and Crystal Eastman and other such prominent leaders of social reform as Lillian Wald and Roger Baldwin. By lobbying Congress, participating in hearings, and organizing demonstrations and letter-writing campaigns, the antipreparedness forces were able to prevent the passage of a bill mandating the nationwide use of physical education classes for military training.

During the spring of 1916, the New York women also initiated a successful "War Against War" art exhibit in Brooklyn that averaged 6,000 to 8,000 spectators within its first few days. It later traveled to Manhattan and then on to Massachusetts and Chicago. The main feature of the exhibit was a huge, armored dinosaur designed by Crystal Eastman's artist husband, Walter Fuller. The dinosaur, meant to symbolize the military establishment, was large and well protected but had a brain about the size of a pea. Along with the creature was a display of political drawings and paintings.[31]

Throughout its first year the Woman's Peace Party continued the anti-imperialist stance it had inherited from the responses of peace leaders, including their very own Jane Addams, to the Spanish-American War of 1898. In July 1915 the organization protested the presence of U.S. military troops in Haiti. It also criticized the pressure the U.S. government was exerting on Haiti to sign a treaty allowing the U.S. to administer Haiti's customs and finances for the next twenty years. The group also protested the expenditure of $3 million for U.S. military bases in Nicaragua, for U.S. troops in the Dominican Republic, for the existence of colonial rather than independent governments in the Philippines and Puerto Rico, and for the U.S. purchase of the Virgin Islands from Denmark without a vote of consent from the Virgin Islanders.

When, therefore, U.S. and Mexican soldiers clashed at Carrazil in June, some Woman's Peace Party members exploded. At the time, there was already great tension between the United States and Mexico, especially over two issues: the desire of the Mexicans to nationalize oil interests then held by U.S. companies and the periodic flights of Mexican revolutionaries across the U.S. border to avoid capture or to secure provisions. During this particular incident, U.S. soldiers actually crossed the border into Mexico in pursuit of Pancho Villa after his raid on a border town. There was immediate consternation on the part of the U.S. antimilitarists about this border conflict. The Massachusetts branch of the WPP sent telegrams of protest to President Wilson, while the New York women held public demonstrations, collected petitions, and sent a telegram to the women of Mexico via the editor of *La Mujer Mexicana,* the leading women's magazine in that nation. Their message emphasized the need for international female solidarity and the achievement of international laws, rather than military actions, to ensure world peace.[32]

This incident illustrated the direction the Woman's Peace Party had moved in during its first year of operation. Even though there was a national board of strong women, the actual work depended on local organizers. The Massachusetts and New York branches were the largest and most active. Unfortunately, the two groups were so different in character that there were few actions they could cooperate on. Sponsoring the "War Against War" art exhibit was one; protesting the Carrazil incident was another. The national board moved more and more into the background at this time, basing almost all of its actions on the feelings of Jane Addams. During the Mexican affair, for example, the national board did nothing because Jane Addams was in Bar Harbor, Maine, on vacation and could not be reached quickly enough. As Eleanor Karsten wrote to her on June 24, "It is remarkable how lost we feel in an emergency when we realize that we cannot call you up over the phone and put the question to you."[33] This inability to respond quickly did not bode well for events that would take place the next year.

Despite opposition to Wilson's stand against woman suffrage and anger at his refusal to foster mediation in Europe, most of the women peace activists supported his reelection in November 1916. Charles Evans Hughes, Wilson's opponent, promised women he would support suffrage, but he would not promise to keep the nation out of war. Wilson, on the other hand, ran for reelection with the slogan "He kept us out of war." Making the avoidance of war their primary concern, many women worked for Wilson's reelection, even if they did not reside in the few states where they could vote. Soon after his November 7 assurance of another four years in the White House, Wilson delivered his now famous "Peace Without Victory" speech, in which he urged all nations to take care of their own concerns and not to interfere in the politics, trade or self-determination of others. This speech lifted the spirits of many peace activists, but the hope was short-lived, for on January 31, 1917, Germany announced plans to resume unrestricted submarine warfare on all ships—armed or not, neutral or belligerent—that sailed through designated areas. Three days later, on February 3, the U.S. severed diplomatic relations with Germany.

As war approached, Congress began passing certain acts that proved to be disastrous for dissenters. The first appeared before the actual April declaration of war. On February 14 the passage of the Threats Against the President Act made it treasonous to criticize Wilson in any way. Woman's Peace Party meetings that took strong stands against militarism came under scrutiny from their local membership. Several members quit, calling the meetings "an act of disloyalty to the President and all but an act of treason."[34] Other members actively opposed the legislation by continuing to hold meetings and lobbying Congress. In either case, the new legislation and steps towards war caused severe divisions within the organization. After Wilson had severed diplomatic ties with

Germany, for example, the WPP executive board, concerned that U.S. involvement in the conflict was imminent, took a stand supporting the idea of a popular referendum on participation in the war, a position that did not garner favor with much of the membership. The Massachusetts branch supported Wilson's stand and opposed the referendum idea. Several of the other branches, including Los Angeles, Pasadena, and St. Louis, had recently ceased peace work or were dependent on a few remaining members to carry on. The New York branch angrily continued its clear antiwar protestations, using its controversial newsletter, *Four Lights,* as its main communication vehicle. The national executive board then made several proposals intended to help prevent direct war. The women publicly suggested that U.S. citizens stay away from war zones so that any provocation could be avoided. They also stressed the need for the United States and Germany to arbitrate their differences and for the United States to continue to remain neutral so that it could act as a mediator for the warring nations. The idea of sending any U.S. troops overseas made the women's blood run cold.

At this point a serious split occurred once again within the broader community of suffragists. Soon after President Wilson had severed diplomatic relations with Germany, the New York State Woman Suffrage Association, under the leadership of Vera Whitehouse, offered Governor Charles Seymour Whitman prospective war service on the part of all New York's suffragists. A month later the executive committee of the National American Woman Suffrage Association, headed by Carrie Chapman Catt, extended the offer to Woodrow Wilson on a national scale. As a result, the New York branch of the Woman's Peace Party removed Catt from its membership rolls and from her position as honorary vice-chair.[35] Anna Garlin Spencer, then an active member of the New York branch, was outraged that the two women had taken it upon themselves to speak for all of the suffragists, especially for those so committed to the WPP. She immediately confronted Catt about her actions. A rapid-fire exchange of letters resulted.

In a letter on February 17, Spencer warned Catt that any attempt to "commandeer" the members of the NAWSA for war service "would split the body from stem to stern." Furthermore, reminding Catt that "woman suffrage is founded upon democracy," she stressed that as a proponent of democracy she resented the authoritarian action.[36] Writing Catt again on March 1, Spencer emphasized that the suffragists covered "every shade of opinion respecting war and peace from the non-resistant to the go to war enthusiast." A suffrage organization, she added, should stick to suffrage and not other issues. "The vital point of the position taken . . . is that every single member of the woman suffrage party has an inalienable right to determine for herself what form of patriotic service she shall offer to her government or to society in general at this troubled time."[37]

Spencer reported she had learned that while Whitehouse's comments to the governor had been "rather a clear jingo incitement to 'war psychology'," Catt's had emphasized her own "belief in peace and abhorrence of war." Still, the fact remained that Catt had inappropriately pledged *all* suffragists to war. Spencer stressed that if Catt could not understand the "operation of minds which can object to the action taken," then it was "a new Carrie Chapman Catt" she would now have to get to know. "The one I thought I knew," she added, "and have so much admired for so many years has stood with the greatest clearness and strength of leadership."[38] Catt's initial response was one of hurt that she had been publicly attacked. She claimed that the NAWSA executive council had sent a note to the President "announcing its hope and faith that there would be no war. . . . It added that if the worse came to worst, it would like to use its organized strength, so far as it had authority to do so, to save the country from the sufferings [into] which a sudden change in economic conditions plunged all the European countries. It declared its loyalty to its own Government in peace or war and beyond this, it said nothing."[39]

A few days later Catt added that the NAWSA had not offered help to the War Department but, rather, to the government. She also claimed that they had not offered the assistance of any members who did not want to cooperate. She stated that the NAWSA had done nothing contrary to its constitution or principles. "We are working so hard to get the vote that we have no time to consider peace or war. The difference apparently lies in the degree of faith in peace. Those who have a different degree from mine feel that some great principle has been violated. I do not see it that way, nor do any of the working members, so far as I know, of our Association."[40]

As a result of her ouster from the New York branch, Catt resigned from the national Woman's Peace Party as well. What seems like sour grapes, however, was probably an astute political move as a part of Catt's efforts to win Wilson over to suffrage. But in the meantime it meant that Catt, a long-time pacifist, would have to turn her back on the peace movement. In addition, although she and Spencer both lamented the radical nature of the New Yorkers, they differed over the advantages of having a broad political spectrum within the feminist peace movement. Spencer wrote to Jane Addams that she felt the radicals were "of priceless value" and that the attitude of Catt, Whitehouse, and other suffrage leaders added up to "the most serious set-back the peace cause has had in that it will make the path of the W.P.P. more rocky and the solidarity of the suffrage movement less a strength to democracy."[41] In the long run both sides won. Women achieved the vote in 1920, and the Woman's Peace Party survived the war and grew into the longest-lasting women's peace organization in U.S. history.

Wilson's actual request for a declaration of war on April 2, 1917, severely crippled the remaining members of the Woman's Peace Party. A last protest came from the formidable suffragist Jeannette Rankin, newly elected to the House of Representatives (and the only woman), who voted against it. Although the national board itself did not immediately respond to the war declaration, some individual branches took a stand. The women in Massachusetts supported Wilson and promptly turned from peace activism to relief work. The New York women, in contrast, questioned the move, demanding that the president explain to the public exactly what U.S. soldiers were supposed to be fighting for and on what terms the nation would accept peace.[42] Further militancy, however, was greatly curbed by the passage of the Selective Service Bill in May and the Espionage Bill in June, the latter calling for up to $10,000 in fines and twenty years in prison for disloyalty, refusal to serve in the armed forces, interfering with the recruitment, or enlisting of soldiers and "aiding the enemy" in any way. The Espionage Bill also allowed for the banning of any antiwar or so-called antigovernment materials from the mails. No longer was it easy to carry on draft resistance or to publish peace materials.

The Woman's Peace Party's national board took no official stand on conscientious objection during the Great War. This issue was left to such mixed-gender groups as the Bureau of Legal Advice and the

Civil Liberties Committee of the American Union Against Militarism. The national board also did not agree on the role of relief work within the organization. Jane Addams herself supported the idea of relief work and in early 1918 became very much involved in Herbert Hoover's Department of Food Administration. The Administration campaigned for women to help conserve food while also supporting the increased production of food products. Addams felt that feeding the hungry would help to unleash a positive force in the world that could lead to peaceful coexistence among nations.[43] Other national Woman's Peace Party leaders, however, felt that participating in relief work meant the loss of the true meaning of the organization. On the local level, sentiment was also divided. The Massachusetts branch took up relief work for the remainder of the war. Needless to say, New York did not.

In an effort to hold the national organization together, Anna Garlin Spencer wrote a statement on behalf of the executive board to make the Woman's Peace Party's stand clear. "Our business is to help mitigate all horrors of war by consistently refusing to make any sacrifice of human fellowship and good will. We throw back no verbal brick bats; on the contrary, we set ourselves to sympathetic understanding of those from whom we differ, and to grateful recognition of their contributions to that common fund of ethical idealism and of wise mastery of political problems upon which the reconstruction of the world depends."[44] In addition, the organization issued "A Program During Wartime" brochure, in which it reaffirmed its patriotism and internationalism, committing itself to work against racism and ill will towards pacifists; to strive to decrease human suffering, poverty, and crime; to support legal solutions to war, and to protect civil liberties. The document ended with a statement of hope: "The constitution of the United States offers a sacred guarantee of the rights of minority opinion. It often happens that the minority of today is the majority of tomorrow. Let us who are outvoted be neither abashed nor discouraged. Let us hold fast the truth as God gives us to see the truth. Let us never allow ourselves for one moment to feel discredited in working to promote the reign of Peace on Earth among Men of Good Will."[45]

Organizationally, the Woman's Peace Party remained intact throughout the war. The office in Chicago was kept open. No records were removed, and membership lists were kept in a conspicuous location.

Jane Addams related how unpleasant it was to enter the place. "If a bit of mail protruded from the door it was frequently spat upon, and although we rented our quarters in a first class office building on Michigan Boulevard facing the lake, the door was often befouled in hideous ways."[46] Knowledge that the Department of Justice was keeping various leaders, especially Jane Addams, under surveillance did not help promote activity. As a result of these external pressures and the tensions among the remaining branches, especially as continuously exemplified by Massachusetts and New York, the national board decided to restructure the organization. It took over the international affairs; local branches were to handle their own activities and issues. But as the war progressed, even the international work slowed down. The board went so far as to refuse to send the customary annual greetings to the International Committee on the grounds that because the United States was at war, the women could not be in friendly communication with all of its members. When Wilson announced his Fourteen Points on January 8, 1918, the national board expressed its support and maintained it throughout the war.

Local branches did not fare so well. Many disbanded or took up relief work during the war years. The two strongest, Massachusetts and New York, did continue to function. The Massachusetts women kept on with relief work, moving more and more away from a pacifist stance. By November 1917, their executive committee came out in support of a peace only after the defeat of Germany and the implementation of a new international structure as proposed by President Wilson in his Fourteen Points. A few months later the Massachusetts branch officially changed its name to the League for Permanent Peace, thereby breaking off official relations with the Woman's Peace Party.

The New York branch remained active throughout the war but in December 1917 also decided to change its name to the Women's International League (WIL), following a pattern begun by European women peace activists. According to one member, the only reason for the change of name was to make it easier to rent a lecture hall: "Woman's Peace Party is difficult . . . because it sounds too radical." On the other hand, the WPP's name was also no longer useful because the Massachusetts members, who had not yet changed their organization's name, were knitting for the Red Cross, making the name sound "too conservative."[47] Other matters were more important to local New York members. For

11. Members of the New York branch of the Woman's Peace Party preparing for a demonstration, Washington Square, New York. Anne Herendeen *(far left)*, Crystal Eastman *(fourth from left)*, Inez Milholland Boissevain *(fourth from right)*, ca. 1917. Courtesy of Swarthmore College Peace Collection.

one thing, Governor Whitman had responded to the declaration of war by ordering a "Census and Inventory of the Military Resources of the State." According to this decree, every woman in the state between the ages of sixteen and fifty was required to submit to the government her educational background, training, and availability for war service. In a letter to the members, the New York Executive Board protested that the census neglected to ask "whether she is *willing* to lend her energies to the prosecution of the war." The board suggested that each woman, to avoid possible arrest and imprisonment, give the information but insert a phrase like "But I object to aiding war" or "As a conscientious objector to this war, I claim exemption from either direct or indirect war service."[48]

Perhaps the most militant venture, the most collective effort but also the most irritating project of the New York branch of the Woman's Peace Party was the publication of its magazine, *Four Lights.* Begun in February 1917, just before the U.S. severed diplomatic relations with Germany, *Four Lights* had a relatively short and rocky existence. The editorship of the periodical was rotated among a group of about thirty members, all college-educated, militant suffragists; branch members submitted articles and letters and volunteered help. Journalistically, *Four Lights* was direct and confrontational. For example, immediately after war was declared, the editors decided to publish an article on Jeannette Rankin's antiwar vote in Congress along with a cartoon of her drawn by Lou Rogers, a popular feminist cartoonist of her day. Off to the right was a tiny sketch of a battle scene complete with dying men. To the other side, standing behind Rankin with her hands "affectionately laid" upon her shoulders was to be Susan B. Anthony saying, "Well done my daughter!"[49] The cartoon and article received ridicule for its unclear drawing and its unpatriotic fervor, but it certainly reflected both the pacifist and suffragist spirit of the organization.

The most notorious issue of *Four Lights,* however, appeared on July 14, 1917, with an article entitled "The 'Sister Susie' Peril." Written by Katherine Anthony, an active feminist-pacifist who wrote biographies of such famous foremothers as Margaret Fuller and Susan B. Anthony, the article was a direct attack upon the women on the Woman's Peace Party's national board and those in other branches, especially Massachusetts, who had taken up relief work—specifically, the knitting of woolen stockings for soldiers. Anthony accused these "Sister Susies" of taking work away from self-supporting working women in the knitting mills and garment factories. Relief work, she said, was "a peculiarly infantile form of patriotism . . . ," a dumping of "unskill and inexperience on a disturbed labor market." The government, she urged, should "legally restrain" the women who "did not have to roll bandages and grow potatoes to be patriotic."[50] The article angered a number of women, especially those on the national board and in local branches who were deeply involved in relief work, and made the already tense situation even worse.

In addition, *Four Lights* faced harassment under the Espionage Bill, coming under the clause allowing the Post Office Department to withhold any periodical it judged to be treasonous. Two issues of the magazine fell into this category. Despite appeals, the only response the New York branch received was a visit from a representative of the U.S. Department of Justice who wanted to know how many of the editors of *Four Lights* were German citizens. Carefully surveying its collective of editors, the New York WPP organization issued a press release stating that fourteen of the twenty-nine editors were eligible for membership in the Daughters of the American Revolution; six had English heritage, one French, one Irish, one Scots, one Scandinavian; one had a mixture of ethnic groups, three had ancestors from the Central Powers, and one had a grandfather who had come from Germany.[51]

In spite of the necessary acceleration in antiwar work, the New York WPP members also continued to campaign for suffrage. In fact, after New York State approved suffrage for women in late 1917, the members amended their own constitution to include the use of voting power in its work. Throughout the war the New York branch organized programs in which candidates could express their views before the newly enfranchised state voters. With the new voting power, the City group expanded its influence to become the New York State branch of the Woman's Peace Party. Although the dominant force, the branch now involved women from as far as Buffalo.

The war officially ended on November 11, 1918, with the signing of the armistice. As they had planned, the women who had been at The Hague in 1915 began organizing their congress. Unfortunately, they could not meet in Versailles, where the Peace Treaty negotiations were being held, because German women could not travel there. So, instead, they met May 12–17, 1919, in Zurich. The participants included twenty-three delegates from the U.S., twenty-three from Great Britain, three from France, twenty-seven from Germany, nine from other Central Power nations, and 126 from neutral nations. As a group, the International Congress of Women agreed that the blockade of Germany should be lifted so that food and other products could relieve some of the human suffering. They then protested the terms of the Versailles Treaty, which placed blame for the war on Germany. How could disarming only one nation create world peace? Wouldn't the result simply be resentment, leading eventually to another war? In principle, the women approved of the League of Nations provided for in the treaty, but they felt that membership should be open to all nations (especially

12. Women at the founding meeting of WILPF, Zurich, 1919. Jane Addams *(third from right)*. Courtesy of Swarthmore College Peace Collection.

Germany) and the operating principles should be more democratic. Self-determination for all nations, a reduction in arms, free trade, and the abolition of child labor, racism, and labor exploitation were all issues the women felt needed to be handled in both the treaty and the League of Nations.[52]

The women also urged that a "Women's Charter" be incorporated into the treaty, stressing equal rights and opportunity for all women, including suffrage; protection against slavery, especially from the white-slave trade; property and civil rights after marriage; the same child custody rights as the father; the right to retain their own citizenship instead of automatically losing it upon marriage to another country's national; open education; open job opportunities; equal pay for equal work; the end of the prostitution trade; legitimizing the rights of a child born out of wedlock and the responsibilities of the father to that child; food for children; and "economic provision for the service of motherhood."[53]

Finally, and most importantly, the women decided to continue their international sisterhood as the Women's International League for Peace and Freedom (WILPF). Their new constitution pledged the organization's support for "movements to further peace, internationalism, and the freedom of women" as well as supporting resolutions made at various international conferences.[54] Membership was open to women from any nation, with representation of any nationalities that thought of themselves as separate from the group in power. This opened the way to the many ethnic groups displaced by the Versailles Treaty. Headquarters were to be wherever the League of Nations had its headquarters. This ended up to be Geneva. Jane Addams was elected president and Emily Greene Balch the first secretary-treasurer, setting a trend of strong U.S. leadership. In November 1919, the U.S. Woman's Peace Party voted to become the U.S. Section of WILPF. Anna Garlin Spencer took on the chair as Jane Addams devoted her time to being the international leader.

Reorganizing the U.S. Woman's Peace Party into the U.S. Section of the Women's International League for Peace and Freedom was no easy task. Government harassment of peace activists and suffragists, among others, proved to be a problem. Jane Addams was one of the first to be publicly ridiculed. Although Addams was personally inured to it, the adverse attention paid to her and others was detrimental to attracting new members. In January 1919, for example, Archibald Stevenson, a New York lawyer employed by the Military Intelligence Division of the War Department, testified before the Overman Senate Sub-Committee, producing a list of sixty-two names of people whom he labeled "dangerous, destructive and anarchistic."[55] Jane Addams and Emily Greene Balch were both on the list that the newspapers dubbed the "Who's Who of Pacifists and Radicals." The year before, Emily Greene Balch had lost her position on the faculty of Wellesley College because of her peace work, finding herself at the age of fifty-two unemployed after twenty-one years of service. Addams was again victimized in 1920 by the Lusk Commission of New York State, which printed a report on "Revolutionary Radicalism" accusing Addams of using both the national and international women's peace movements to foster her socialistic views.[56]

The "Red Scare," as these actions came to be called, persisted into the 1920s and may have been one of the causes for the eventual divisions among the New York WPP branch members who lived in New York City. The branch had been the strongest, most vibrant, and most independent of all those existing during the World War I era. Other considerations, however, must be taken into account. For example, the actual ratification of the Nineteenth Amendment to the Constitution in 1920, giving the vote to all U.S. women, changed the feminist-pacifists' emphasis from suffrage to peace. In addition, the end of the war, combined with the winning of the vote, meant a reevaluation of all the goals of the organization as a whole. Where did the issue of women's rights fit in? Or did it? Perhaps the entire role of women within U.S. society needed to be rethought. Were women simply the mothers of humanity, or were they more than that?

Anna Garlin Spencer, the woman most open to the various political stands of Woman's Peace Party members, started her term as national chair on an optimistic note which indicated that exciting changes for the new era were welcome and encouraged. Under her leadership the board of officers at the annual meeting in November 1919, when the organization officially changed its name to the Women's International League for Peace and Freedom, issued a statement of hope and encouragement:

> This group of women came together to protest in the name of Womanhood against the cruelty and waste of war, and to give united help toward translating the mother-instinct of life-saving into social terms of the common good. . . . The inner bond of a common devotion to securing permanent peace, and to make good women's share in that devotion has held firm all the while; and now the end of war allows us to become wholly reunited, not only in ultimate convictions, but in every-day service.[57]

The interwar years would prove to be a greater challenge to feminist-pacifists than any of the women could have imagined. Struggling for women's rights, defining non-violence, debating international law, and opposing the rise of fascism would be just a few of the compelling issues they would have to face.

4

Former Suffragists for Peace during the Interwar Years, 1919–1935

At first, the interwar years seemed most auspicious. Once the vote was won in 1920, former suffragists gave their full attention to working for world peace. They saw this campaign as an extension of their successful work in government reform. They had achieved suffrage—why not peace? Many former suffragists, outraged by the tragic deaths, injuries, and illnesses caused by "the Great War," banded together to pressure those in power into taking immediate steps to end violent responses to economic and political problems. In their eyes, the Treaty of Versailles, which ended the war by blaming Germany and punishing it economically, was not a peace treaty, but rather one of revenge. Critics of the treaty believed that the terms would only increase the desperate poverty and starvation already rampant in Germany and result in resentment, new aggression, and another war.

Women throughout the nation, whether former suffragists or not, were revolted by the violence and waste of the war. Trench warfare and modern weapons—tanks, automatic machine guns, airplanes, and poison gases—resulted in high civilian as well as military casualties. Young veterans with missing limbs, destroyed lungs, and emotional problems ("shell shock") appeared in every area of the country. More than one hundred thousand soldiers never returned home at all. Although the number of U.S. casualties was small compared to those of the European nations, the public response was great.[1] People wanted to know exactly why these lives had been cut short or ruined. Many critics of World War I who began researching and debating the real causes of that war and all others concluded from their investigations that big business was to blame for the tragedy. Feminist peace activists almost unanimously concurred: greed, not democratic ideals, had once again produced a war. As in 1915, the women pointed an accusing finger at the men in power, claiming that their warmongering leadership was incompetent, selfish, and inhumane.

In 1921, Carrie Chapman Catt, soon to reestablish herself as a pacifist by founding her own antiwar organization, commented on men's love of violence, pointing out that "war is in the blood of men; they can't help it. They have been fighting ever since the days of the cavemen. There is a sort of honor about it."[2] Another woman went further: "It has evidently got to be the women who must stop war—men are too steeped in tradition to brave such a break."[3] Still others echoed their foremothers by linking war with violence against women. One 1919 statement released by the New York branch of the Woman's Peace Party (WPP), now renamed the New York branch of the U.S. section of the Women's International League for Peace and Freedom (WILPF), claimed that "by aiding men to release themselves from their bondage to violence and bloodshed, we shall also free ourselves, for women can never know true liberty in a society dominated by force."[4]

Jessie Wallace Hughan, one of the original members of the New York branch of the WPP, was still more specific: men, even the most politically radical, were more interested in their own achievements than in caring for human life. Emphasizing motherhood, as the Woman's Peace Party had done, Hughan explained this "preoccupation" as being "doubtless biological." Women, she said, might feel "discouraged" when they saw men who two years before had "braved jail in protest against killing now immersed in problems of industrial control and effective economic organization." Women, unlike men, understood that whereas economics was the basis of a free and equal society, "that the foundation is not all."[5]

The motherhood argument remained strong throughout the 1920s, but the era also produced a somewhat more sophisticated approach to the peace issue. Many newly enfranchised women, especially former suffragists and social reformers, saw it as their duty to effect legislation and cause changes in government policy to better the social conditions of women, children, and economically and socially oppressed men. As long as money was being poured into the war machine, they felt, there could be no reforms in the standard of living, medical advances, education, or working conditions. Sincerely believing that women had a "duty" as responsible citizens to use their newly gained political power, lobbyists flooded Washington. Peace was but one issue they worked for; child labor reform, the equal rights amendment, working women's concerns, and birth control legislation were all addressed.

Victory in suffrage work and experience in the Woman's Peace Party proved to many feminist peace activists that it was no longer advantageous to work with or be guided by men. Women had to build upon and maintain their own power. As Madeline Doty remarked in 1924, "We will never build up a strong group of women, capable of doing effective things, if we let men lecture to us and then adopt what they say."[6] Dorothy Detzer, then Executive Secretary of WILPF, added, "The more I think of it, the more important it seems to have it [a discussion of economic imperialism] really in the hands of our women rather than leaving the final word to technical gentlemen!!"[7] Anna Garlin Spencer, the immediate postwar national chair of WILPF, noted both the importance and the vulnerability of the new class of voters to the continuing development of a feminist peace movement:

> We have millions of new voters among the women of this land. We have great bodies of organized womanhood already pledged to philanthropic effort, to educational advance, to better labor conditions, to full legal rights of women and the saving of child life, and to a finer political method and spirit of action. All that these women are pledged to accomplish may be nullified in a moment when men are set to kill one another by wholesale, as the most sacred of duties.
>
> Unless the women now invested with full power and responsibility of citizenship can rise to the supreme need of the hour, the need for clear thinking and fearless speaking concerning these ordered ways of legal and political, of commercial and industrial, of educational and social organization of world interests to the end of just and permanent peace, they are building upon the sand.[8]

The subtle shift in feminist peace rhetoric from the emphasis on possibilities *if* women had political power to a belief in women's actual influence also reflected two other contemporary political moods. First, during the 1920s, there was much interest in legal solutions to war.

The League of Nations, established through the Treaty of Versailles, was part of this solution. The League was to be a meeting place for the world's representatives to discuss and settle problems—trade agreements, labor unrest, white slavery and drug traffic, economic and social development for example. Like its successor, the United Nations, the League was to enforce peace by means of collective armed intervention. For several reasons, including partisan opposition to Woodrow Wilson (a Democrat) and an "isolationist" trend to avoid European conflicts, the U.S. Senate refused to ratify the Treaty or the League. Instead, in 1921, President Warren Harding (a Republican) finally signed a separate peace treaty with Germany, formally ending the U.S. war with that nation.

A second possible solution to national squabbles was the use of an international court of justice such as the one mentioned in the early 1840s by William Ladd, president of the American Peace Society. As part of the League of Nations, the World Court, situated in The Hague, was expected to settle international disputes voluntarily brought before its multinational panel of judges. Because this procedure meant the U.S. could no longer invoke the Monroe Doctrine of 1823 to determine the fate of Latin American countries unilaterally, the U.S. Senate refused to sanction participation in the Court.

A third legal approach, first mentioned in the 1800s and known as the "outlawry of war," called for laws making war an international crime. Of course, this idea was not readily adopted by nations intent on expansion and colonization. After World War I, however, the concept held more appeal. As a consequence, in 1921, Salmon O. Levinson, a Chicago lawyer, founded the American Committee for the Outlawry of War. The committee, composed of prestigious business and religious leaders, convinced Senator William Borah, a Republican isolationist from Idaho, to support their position. In 1923 he proposed a resolution to Congress recommending that nations sign a treaty agreeing to peaceful discussions before declaring all-out war. Starting in 1928, through the continued efforts of many, including French foreign minister Aristide Briand and U.S. secreatary of state Frank Kellogg, sixty-two countries stepped forward to sign the Kellogg-Briand Peace Pact. The document passed the U.S. Senate with a vote of 85 to 1. The signatories agreed to Borah's original suggestion but in their own interpretations exempted military action in self-defense. Many critics held that this point rendered the Peace Pact useless.

Besides legislative alternatives to war, pacifism, combining both religious and ethical commitment, became the other strong political mood of the twenties. Most members of religious sects such as the Quakers, the Mennonites, the Moravians, and the Amish had always refused to participate in war, and by World War I they had been joined by other Christians as well as Jews, Ethical Culture humanists, and socialists. In the 1920s, furthermore, Mohandas Gandhi, the leader of the Indian independence movement, became very popular in pacifist circles, and with him emerged a renewed public interest in a nonresistant approach to violence. Gandhi, who acknowledged having studied the works of William Lloyd Garrison, preached that violence resulted only in more violence. The only effective way to oppose it was to face hostile forces nonviolently. This did not mean being passive, however. In fact, the approach called for quite aggressive behavior—blocking entrances to work places, holding general strikes, standing quietly before armed soldiers, and refusing to be led into any violent behavior even if the result was bodily harm or even death. Gandhi believed that the violent power structure, eventually realizing that it was senseless to annihilate its own population, would either change its ways or crumble in defeat.

The women who had participated in the Woman's Peace Party—from Carrie Chapman Catt to Jane Addams, from the conservative Massachusetts branch to the radical New Yorkers—were already attracted to both the legal and the pacifist alternatives to war. However, because the strategies they chose to follow in the 1920s and the degree of pacifism each sought differed, it became impossible for the one organization to represent the entire movement as it had tried to do from 1915 to 1919. The differences that had been played out primarily in Chicago, New York, and Massachusetts became too big to handle. As a result, the suffrage wing of the peace movement separated into four major national organizations. Although ideologically somewhat different, they still managed to agree on one goal: a world at peace, where women enjoyed full equality with men.

While many former suffragists chose to continue their work in an exclusively female setting, others opted to work with one or more of the hundreds of mixed-gender groups, also created in the 1920s, that depended upon their female members for active support. The general prosperity of the decade made it easy for numerous groups dependent on monetary donations to coexist. The four major feminist peace organizations reflected the sentiments of the hundreds of smaller women's organizations that arose all over the United States to ensure that another world war would not rob women of their husbands, sons, brothers, lovers, and friends. These four groups were the Women's International League for Peace and Freedom (WILPF), the Women's Peace Society (WPS), the Women's Peace Union (WPU), and the National Committee on the Cause and Cure of War (NCCCW).

The mother organization of three of the groups was, of course, WILPF, the 1919 international reformation of the U.S. Woman's Peace Party and the International Committee of Women for Permanent Peace. However, the details of the reconstruction of the organization between 1919 and late 1920 are a bit hazy. When Jane Addams gave up leadership on the national level in order to be freer to support international work, the role of national chair fell to Anna Garlin Spencer, then residing in New York City. Spencer viewed her leadership role as temporary, but necessary. She knew that she needed to be flexible in dealing not only with the two former suffrage factions, but with the various stands on pacifism as well. Because she had always supported diversity within the League—the New Yorkers' radicalism as well as the Massachusetts women's conservatism—Spencer decided that she was the right person to forge "a link" between the older members and potential new members.[9] Under her leadership, the organization began to revive. Membership grew from just about one hundred in 1919, to five hundred in 1920, and to over two thousand in 1922.

A new constitution, adopted at the WILPF annual meeting in Chicago in April 1920, spelled out the group's intention to continue its work for peace. Specifically, the women wanted to ensure basic human rights, such as food, freedom of speech, the vote, and an end to racism. In addition, they supported all peace-related issues, such as the return of all prisoners of war, a revision of the Versailles Treaty, and the existence of the League of Nations in order to promote real coexistence with Germany, and, most importantly, the evolution of universal disarmament. In order to be able to lobby consistently, the organization established a Washington, D.C., office. Initial lobbying efforts on Capitol Hill were focused on protesting the food blockades against Germany and Russia and speaking out against the enforced deportation of political dissenters and immigrants from the United States.[10]

The issues taken up immediately after World War I occupied the group through the 1920s. Who was to do the work, however, was another question. The national board was not very cohesive at this time. Jane Addams and Emily Greene Balch concentrated on events in Geneva. Moreover, Addams was neither young nor healthy. Suffering from continuing bouts of tuberculosis of the spine, she divided her decreasing energy between Hull House and the international WILPF organization. Lucia Ames Mead, also aging, continued her work in Massachusetts, as did Eleanor Karsten, Mabel Hyde Kittredge, and Lucy Biddle Lewis in Chicago. Because Anna Garlin Spencer lived in New York City, it was logical for her to want to guide the organization's business from there. Accordingly, in 1920 the national office of WILPF moved from Chicago (where Jane Addams had established it) to East 37th Street, right in the heart of Manhattan.

At this point, the national history of WILPF becomes a bit murky. For a while, it was no longer clear who made up the New York branch and who composed the national board. What most likely occurred during this transitional period was that the remainder of the New York City members of the New York branch merged with the national board, thereby creating a two-pronged directorate and causing considerable identity confusion for those women still operating out of Chicago. Before trying to sort out what transformation the national organization of WILPF went through during the first few years of the 1920s, however, it is necessary to backtrack a bit to see what happened within the New York branch itself.

After World War I, the unified New York State branch of WILPF broke up into struggling local branches within the broader state branch.[11] Throughout the period, the New York City women had consistently stood against war and for a world without economic, political, and social oppression. The conclusion of the war proved to many of the City branch leaders "a failure." The boycott of food shipments to Germany, the continuing violence against Bolshevik Russia, and the general interest on the part of the "peacemakers" from the major world powers to end the fighting without addressing the basic concerns of the average person all added up to creating some bitterness in the New York City women, especially as several of the leaders considered themselves socialist-feminist-pacifists. As a result, at the end of the war, the New York City branch issued a scathing statement against the patriarchy, which they felt dominated and oppressed all women: "War to end war has proved a failure. The war is won, yet nowhere is there peace, security or happiness. Hate, fear and greed still rule the world. . . . We failed, not because we were wrong, but because we had no power. The control of the world is still in the hands of men who have no respect for human life, or for the counsel and needs of women."[12]

In order to foster women's rights, in March 1919 the New York branch organized a "Woman's Freedom Conference," attended by over six hundred women.[13] The main objective of the conference was to demand that women play an equal role in the reconstruction of the postwar world. To prepare for this work, sessions were held in the areas of education, work, the family, and government. Workshops included such topics as "Modern Education for Girls," "Professional Opportunities for Women," "Labor Legislation for Women," "Women and Trade Unions," "Divorce," "Day Care," "Community Kitchens," "Women and Children in Soviet Russia," "Women and National Politics," "Women and International Government," and "Women and Political Action." All through 1919 the New York branch propagandized for the equal political participation and representation of women in the world's governments. They stressed the need for laws to protect a woman's citizenship rights no matter what her husband's country of origin was. They also emphasized equal rights and responsibilities for husbands and wives and abolition of "the common law conception of a wife as a chattel, owing personal service, i.e. consortium and household labor in exchange for her necessaries."[14]

Yet a certain discontent had surfaced during the work on the Woman's Freedom Conference. The conference expenses threw the branch into virtual bankruptcy. By the time the meeting was over, the group had a deficit of approximately $800. By May, it was over $2,000.[15] Far worse than a monetary problem, however, was the fact that several of the members felt that the group had moved away from its antiwar position towards one of "violent revolutionary attitude." They claimed that the March conference had not stressed pacifism at all. This unhappiness was echoed by several of the leading members, including the branch chair, Elinor Byrns; the honorary chair, Fanny Garrison Villard; and several of the members of the executive board. Crystal Eastman, who had been criticized for her radical stands since 1915, bore the brunt of the antagonism. Lillian Wald, Jane Addams, Lucia Ames Mead, and Anna Garlin Spencer had all, at one time or another, expressed disdain for Eastman's leadership. At this point, Spencer had even decided to break with the New York branch if Eastman continued to be its primary force.[16] The problem of leadership was solved by May, when Crystal Eastman left to pursue her journalistic work in New York while carrying on a commuter relationship with her husband, then residing in England. Eastman eventually spent more time in Europe than in New York.

For the next four months, the branch struggled along, but on September 12 it suffered a severe rupture when those women who desired a more strictly pacifist organization—based on William Lloyd Garrison's nonresistant philosophy—resigned from the New York City branch to form the Women's Peace Society (WPS). These included Elinor Byrns, Fanny Garrison Villard, Caroline Lexow Babcock, Katherine Devereux Blake, and Mary Ware Dennett, all former suffragists and women's rights activists. The object of the new organization was not merely to protest a specific war but to resist actively all war in the spirit of the nonviolent, nonresistant philosophies of Gandhi and Garrison.

The Women's Peace Society was chaired by the highly respected Fanny Garrison Villard, then seventy-five years old. Villard was a wealthy woman, and her financial generosity kept the Society afloat for a number of years.[17] Her power over the purse strings, however, also gave her unprecedented control over organizational matters, a factor resented by other Society members, especially Elinor Byrns, the creator of most of the ideological statements and organizing pamphlets for the group. Byrns, born in 1876 in Indiana, was a much younger woman than Villard. She was, unlike Villard who had married into wealth, a single, working woman—the sole support of a chronically ill brother who required a housekeeper to tend to him. A graduate of the New York University School of Law, Byrns maintained a full-time law practice in mid-town Manhattan while also participating in local politics (including running for local office on the Socialist party ticket), campaigning for peace, and lunching frequently with the women of Heterodoxy.

As a nonresister pacifist, Byrns agreed with Villard that the Women's Peace Society should be built on "moral principle and not just anti-war activity," a clear differentiation from the New York City branch

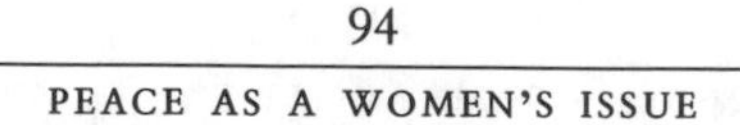

13. Women's Peace Society. Fanny Garrison Villard *(far right).* Courtesy of Swarthmore College Peace Collection.

of the Woman's Peace Party.[18] In the spirit of William Lloyd Garrison, they also agreed that WPS members should neither aid nor sanction any war, whether offensive, defensive, international, or civil; neither make nor handle munitions; neither subscribe to war loans nor use their labor to free others for war work; and neither raise money nor perform tasks for relief organizations. The aim of the group was to work for nothing less than complete and universal disarmament. To join, a woman had to sign a pledge that she believed it wrong to destroy human life under any circumstances and send it, along with twenty-five cents, to the Women's Peace Society.

The Women's Peace Society devoted most of its energy to educational campaigns in support of lobbying efforts in both Washington, D.C., and Albany, New York, that emphasized disarmament conferences and legislation against military appropriations and compulsory military training as part of physical education in the state's public schools. Never exceeding about 1,600 members, most of whom lived in the New York City area, the WPS was the smallest and least active of the interwar women's rights peace organizations. A major reason for its small size was internal strife between the supporters of Villard and those of Byrns. In 1921, Byrns wrote Villard that she intended to propose that the WPS pledge be altered in order to discourage anyone but true nonresisters from joining. "Where you think it desirable to have members in larger numbers, regardless of what they would do in a war . . . ," she wrote Villard, "I would gladly reduce our membership to fifty, if only fifty are ready to be practical as well as theoretical nonresistants."[19] Villard felt it wrong to change the pledge after over 1,400 women had signed it. This seemingly minor conflict actually reflected other problems within the organization. Byrns and others felt not only that Villard was too idea-oriented and not sufficiently action-oriented but also that she held too tight a control over the WPS, often referring to it as "my organization."[20]

By mid-1921 the problems within the Women's Peace Society led to a split within the organization, a change that, true to pacifist ways, was very civilized and not in the least traumatic. Quite coincidentally, in 1921, Christine Ross Barker, a member of the Canadian section of WILPF, wrote to the Women's Peace Society praising its philosophy and suggesting that a conference be held to bring Canadian, U.S., and Latin American women peace activists together. The WPS leaders took an enthusiastic lead in planning the conference, held August 19–21 on the Canadian side of Niagara. Although no women from Latin America were able to attend, plans were made to include them, along with the U.S. and Canadian women, in a single new organization; based on the same nonresister philosophy as the Women's Peace Society, the Women's Peace Union of the Western Hemisphere was to use its pressure to obtain complete disarmament.

Very soon, however, the founding members from the WPS saw the difficulties facing a small, unendowed group of women beginning an international organization. They quickly narrowed their vision, reorganizing a U.S. section to be known simply as the Women's Peace Union (WPU). The active members were those who had been unhappy with both the New York City branch of the Woman's Peace Party and with the Women's Peace Society—namely, Elinor Byrns, Caroline Lexow Babcock, Elizabeth Ellsworth Cook, and WPS member Gertrude Franchot Tone. All were former leaders of the New York State suffrage campaign. Immediately, the women instituted a pledge that Women's Peace Union members would not aid in or sanction any war, use their labor to free others for war work, or even participate in relief work. Run by a collective working committee of no more than fourteen members at any one time, the Union kept a mailing list of thousands. Although the Women's Peace Society had lost its major organizers, and Fanny Garrison Villard remained confused about the split, the two groups remained on friendly terms, supporting each other's work throughout the interwar years.

What did eventually differentiate the Women's Peace Union from the Women's Peace Society was its single-issue program and its uncompromising stand on the need for immediate, total disarmament with no interim stages. The way to reach this utopian goal was simple: to make war illegal. The Women's Peace Union was most likely influenced by the ideal of Salmon O. Levinson's American Committee for the Outlawry of War, but the women took the idea further and developed a program to put it into action. In 1923, Elinor Byrns and Caroline Lexow Babcock drafted a resolution for an amendment to the U.S. Constitution that would have made all war, defensive as well as offensive, illegal within the United States and its territories. To turn this dream into a reality, Union members lobbied every senator in Washington, D.C., to find a sponsor. This work took close to three years. Finally, in 1926, Senator Lynn Joseph Frazier, a North Dakota Republican known for his populist and antiwar stands, agreed to sponsor the resolution. Together with Byrns and Babcock, Frazier and his aides reworked the resolution into the form it took as he introduced it into every congressional session from 1926 to 1939. The main section read: "War for any purpose shall be illegal, and neither the United States nor any state, territory, association or person subject to its jurisdiction shall prepare for, declare, engage in or carry on war or other armed conflict, expedition, invasion, or undertaking within or without the United States, nor shall any funds be raised, appropriated, or expended for such purpose."[21] In support of their amendment resolution, the Women's Peace Union also organized three Sub-Judiciary Committee hearings held in 1927, 1930, and 1934 and led a campaign to have the Kellogg-Briand Pact amended to require that similar outlawry legislation be introduced into the governments of all the signer nations.

Unlike WILPF, however, the Union would not support U.S. participation in the World Court or the League of Nations because both institutions proposed the use of force to keep peace, a tactic that made no sense to the absolute pacifists of the WPU. The women believed that because they, as suffragists, had brought about nonviolent revolutionary change by winning the vote, they could do the same with peace. They also believed that, as with suffrage, the best approach was to limit themselves to one issue. They felt that by focusing all their energy and resources on their amendment campaign, they would ultimately meet with success.

Despite their split from the original New York Woman's Peace Party (via the Women's Peace Society), the women in the Peace Union maintained their feminist stand, consistently drawing on the belief that militarism and societal inequalities resulted in violence against women and children. Their attacks on institutionalized violence led them on a campaign against the Boy Scouts, whom they referred to as "a kindergarten for war" and on attacks against child and animal abuse.[22] They also continued to emphasize the effects that military presence had on women, including rape, unwanted pregnancies, and starvation as well as the loss of loved ones. Only through a constitutional amendment could this type of violence be stopped. As newly enfranchised women, it was their duty to create, campaign for, and ensure the passage of the law to end all wars.

By late 1921 the suffragist wing of the peace movement had subdivided itself into three major organizations: WILPF, based in Chicago, New York, and Washington, D.C.; and the Women's Peace Society and the Women's Peace Union, both in New York City. Ironically, that meant that the bulk of the suffragist peace movement was headquartered in proximity to the former Woman's Peace Party's most radical branch, and, in fact, these women were essential in rebuilding feminist-pacifist activism within WILPF, the Women's Peace Society, and the Women's Peace Union. At this time, the least stable of the three organizations was WILPF. The fracturing within the local New York branch and the shift in leadership within the national board had greatly weakened the organization. The national board was barely operating out of its three separate locations, and for the year that the main office was in New York City under the leadership of Anna Garlin Spencer, the national WILPF organization did not have a clear division between itself and the remaining members of the New York branch.

Spencer had hoped to utilize the New Yorkers in rebuilding the national board of WILPF, but her initial efforts merely confused the situation and diluted the organization's original character. In frustration, Spencer resigned as national chair in September 1920. However, she remained in charge of a virtually nonexistent New York branch until 1924. Although the local organization participated in antiwar marches, mass meetings, and small teas throughout 1921 and 1922, building a reliable New York office structure proved to be almost impossible. In 1923, Spencer hired Christina Miller to act as secretary and to raise money. The two women successfully raised $500 but were so discouraged by the uncooperative local women that they decided to send the money to the D.C. office. Spencer wrote to Amy Woods in the Washington office that the "forces" in New York were "too much divided" to count upon. She seemed stymied by the various transformations going on in New York, referring to the conditions as "peculiar."[23] Within months the office had been physically moved five times. Spencer had virtually given up, and Miller had handed in her resignation.[24] Only through the most concentrated effort of a few loyal women was the New York office maintained.

In the meantime, most of the national organization's emphasis was shifted to Washington. The national board, headed in 1923 by Mabel Hyde Kittredge, agreed with Spencer that, for the time being, it was best that the remaining New Yorkers simply concentrate their efforts on raising money for the upcoming WILPF international convention. When the board, once again operating out of Chicago, requested the Washington office to choose a field secretary to work in New York, assuming all responsibility for her salary and expenses, the women working in the D.C. office refused to oversee the New York work, leaving the branch to sort out its chaos by itself.[25]

Until mid-1924, a few of the remaining New York WILPF members cooperated with Anna Garlin Spencer in reviving local activism as well as in stabilizing the national board.[26] Madeline Doty, Katherine Devereux Blake, Agnes Leach, and Freda Kirchwey all maintained contact with both groups. Their concentration on national board business, however, left the New York branch without goals and an individual identity. By 1924, Doty and Blake had become part of the national executive board while it operated out of both New York and Chicago. They were joined by Ellen and Mary Winsor, two sisters from Pennsylvania who also had roots in the militant suffrage movement. Emily Greene Balch resigned as international secretary in 1922 and returned to the United States to act as vice-chair of the national board. Her peace work during World War I had included close ties with socialists such as Crystal Eastman. In 1924, even though Hannah Clothier Hull, a Pennsylvania Quaker, had taken over as national chair and tried to move WILPF in a more moderate line in order to avoid Red Scare attacks, the national board still reflected a strong New York influence. This mellowed as work became more and more concentrated in Washington, D.C., under the leadership of the new executive secretary, Dorothy Detzer, hired in 1924 by the national executive board.

Detzer, only thirty-one years old at the time, was not a WILPF leader of the traditional mold. The young woman from Fort Wayne, Indiana, did not come from a wealthy family, and she had only a high-school diploma, not a degree from an elite women's college. Nor had she been trained as a suffragist, even though both of her parents had supported woman suffrage and her mother had belonged to a suffrage society. Rather, she came to WILPF as a pacifist who had developed her beliefs through first-hand experience. Her much-loved twin brother had died as a result of prolonged lung damage from poison gases used during combat in World War I. In 1920, after working for some time at Hull House, she signed up with the American Friends Service Committee to perform relief work in war-torn Europe. Upon witnessing the ravages of war, she became a committed pacifist.

Detzer's youth and background caused some elderly WILPFers

to doubt her abilities, but her performance soon allayed their fears. During the 1920s she was a frequent visitor to the Capitol, pressuring senators to vote for any and all legislation that might lead to disarmament and peace as well as supporting antilynching laws, voting rights, child labor and wage laws, and rights for women. In addition, she traveled extensively, giving speeches that were apparently so dynamic that they consistently attracted new members. Detzer's most visible WILPF success of the twenties was her lobbying effort for the ratification of the Kellogg-Briand Pact, an effort that Senator William Borah claimed clinched the Pact's becoming law.

While Detzer was reinvigorating WILPF's work, the New York branch revived its independence, and in January 1925 it once again became an official state branch. Dorothy Detzer tried to convince Anna Garlin Spencer to renew her work with the local group, hoping that her presence might "balance" out the continuing radical nature of the branch.[27] But Spencer, apparently tired of the difficulties in New York, abandoned her leadership role. Like so many former suffragists, she was aging and burning out. Katherine Devereux Blake, however, also an elderly former suffragist, continued to work for the New York branch throughout the period. Blake was the principal of Public School 6, named after her mother, Lillie Devereux Blake, a former suffragist and peace activist; her peace sentiment was well known to the New York City Board of Education. In 1914 her own pacifist version of the nation's then unofficial anthem, "The Star-Spangled Banner," was adopted by the president of the Board of Education for use in the public schools. Until the United States entered World War I, one of the stanzas New York City children sang, thanks to Blake, went:

O say can you see, you who glory in war,
All the wounded and dead of the red battle's reaping?
Can you listen unmoved to their agonized groans,
Hear the children who starve, and the pale widows weeping?
Henceforth let us swear
Bombs shall not burst in air,
Nor war's desolation wreck all that is fair,
But the star spangled banner by workers unfurled
Shall give hope to the nations and peace to the world.[28]

Katherine Devereux Blake revitalized the New York branch of WILPF by recruiting hundreds of public school teachers as members, changing the branch's entire personality. In 1925, out of 144 new members, 118 were teachers and principals; in 1928 she signed up 233 more teachers, bringing the state membership up to 1,284. In 1930 the New York membership list included 766 teachers. The recruitment had a profound effect on the organization. It was clear by this time that the feminist arm of the peace movement—at least, in New York—could no longer be carried on by the militant suffragists. Most of those still active were working through the Women's Peace Society and the Women's Peace Union. Others were aging—retired or semiretired from political activism—or were dying off. New blood was needed. On the national level, new leaders, such as Mildred Scott Olmsted and Hannah Clothier Hull, were emerging from the pacifist population in Philadelphia. New York City, however, offered a unique opportunity for traditional suffragists to recruit ethnically diverse and socialist-minded women, many of them from the middle-working class, to reshape the branch.

Jewish women, in particular, were at the forefront of this change. Usually second-generation citizens, they knew of the injustices their families had suffered in pre–World War I Europe and were concerned about European Jews as fascism grew in popularity. Furthermore, because many of the new WILPFers had roots in the working-class socialist and labor movements, they were attracted by an organization touting as its causes peace, freedom, and justice. By 1927 an active WILPF branch was operating in Brooklyn, one of New York City's five boroughs. The chair and founder of that group, Rose K. Edelman, became a mainstay of WILPF in New York City, organizing throughout the interwar era. She was particularly active in keeping the largely Jewish Brooklyn branch productive and growing. In the same year a Jewish philanthropic organization, the United Order of True Sisters, with over 12,000 members, voted to affiliate with WILPF. Half of its thirty-four lodges were located in New York State.

Recruiting women of color was another way to diversify membership. In general, past efforts of feminist peace activists had not successfully crossed racial lines. One reason why the organizations did not attract women of color lay in their suffrage roots. Suffragists had all too frequently accepted Southern racism in an effort to woo white Southern women to their cause. As a result of this policy and the suffragists' own unconscious racism, African-American women in particular had turned to their own organizations to work for abolitionism, race and gender equality, and social reforms. All too aware of the racial homogeneity of their movement, the national leaders had made a few attempts to incorporate African-American women into the Woman's Peace Party. Throughout the early years Jane Addams had sought out African-American women's club leaders who would adopt the peace cause. Among them were Mary Church Terrell, Mary B. Talbert, Charlotte Atwood, Mary F. Waring, and Addie Hunton.[29]

In 1915, Mary Church Terrell, one of the founders of the National Association of Colored Women, became a member of the Woman's Peace Party's executive committee and in 1919 was elected to represent the organization in Zurich at the founding of international WILPF. There she noticed that not only was she the only African-American woman representing the western nations but indeed she was the only woman of color from any country at all. Terrell wrote in her autobiography, "it is . . . truthful to say that women from all over the white world were present. . . . It was my privilege to represent not only the colored women of the United States, but the whole continent of Africa as well. . . . In fact, since I was the only delegate who gave any color to the occasion at all, it finally dawned on me that I was representing the women of all the non-white countries in the world."[30]

In 1921, Terrell experienced the racism that even the most liberal of feminist organizations seemed unable to avoid. The WILPF executive committee, responding to a report claiming that French colonial African troops in occupied Germany were sexually exploiting local women, asked Terrell to sign a petition seeking their removal. She refused, charging that WILPF's motives were racist: according to an investigation ordered by Carrie Chapman Catt, the Africans were victims of unfounded propaganda to make them appear bestial when, in fact, their behavior was quite proper. Although Terrell felt moved to resign over the issue, Addams asked her not to. She remained a member, but in name only, devoting her efforts to civil rights and African-American women's organizations. Incidents such as this were not unusual throughout WILPF's history, but neither were efforts to improve race relations within the organization and to learn from past mistakes.[31]

The New York branch of WILPF made consistent efforts to recruit African-American members. While the organization was still the New York Woman's Peace Party, the leaders had lamented their lack of racial diversity. The editors of *Four Lights,* in particular, had criticized the homogeneity of their own publication, berating themselves for drawing contributors only from their own membership ranks and for not seeking out women from other nationalities or races to work with. In the 1920s, Katherine Devereux Blake and Margaret Loring Thomas, another WPP alumna, made a concerted effort to bring in women of color to the branch. In February 1929, for example, the New York women sponsored their first interracial meeting, attracting over thirty African-American women to hear a talk about India.[32] Then again, in 1930, they were successful in having Helen Curtis, one of their first African-American members, make a citywide speaking tour on behalf of WILPF. Eager to include many different types of women in their transforming branch, other members spoke at various interracial meetings.[33]

Yet even this branch, the most radical and most ethnically mixed, did not fare well on issues of importance to the African-American community. In 1934, for example, the New York City branch members squabbled over whether to pass a resolution, suggested by African-American member Addie Hunton, supporting the Anti-Lynching Bill, which was being proposed in the Senate for the umpteenth time. The resolution passed the branch but not without a battle. Sadie A. Cohen, a Jewish member of the branch, was outraged by the members' behavior. She wrote to Dorothy Detzer that the branch chair, Grace Hoffman White, suffered from a "Mayflower complex" and would fare better in the DAR than in WILPF. "Among other things," wrote Cohen, "the name 'Sirovich' came up and White said, 'Why don't those people get some real American names?'" Cohen went on to relate the tale of the Anti-Lynching Bill: "But what a tragic illustration that each group must fight for their own lives! . . . Surely there is no greater blot on American life than our southern justice." Going on, Cohen included her Jewish self in this anger against the White Anglo-Saxon Protestant tradition in WILPF. "Must we Jewish women speak for ourselves when our souls are so burdened? Can we not expect those by whose side we have labored in the cause of World Peace to speak for us in our direst need? . . . I'm afraid that many of those who profess to be internationalists really have very little feeling for minority groups. They do only lip service to Peace and that doesn't quite satisfy us."[34]

Addie Hunton, who had brought the antilynching issue before the branch, had had much experience in political organizing, both in the African-American community and in WILPF.[35] Along with Mary Church Terrell, she was a leader in the National Association of Colored Women as well as the International Council of Women of the Darker Races, of which she served as first vice-president in the 1920s. As an activist, Hunton had stood for racial dignity. In 1914, for example, she organized a protest around the placement of the proposed "Mammy Statue" in Washington, D.C. Had she not succeeded, tourists to the nation's capital might have observed the statue of an African-American nursemaid holding a white baby while her own child was crying at her side. Because Addie Hunton believed that more and better education was the path to racial pride, understanding, and, eventually, world peace, she was attracted to WILPF and served not only the New York branch but the national board as well.

By 1928, Hunton was chairing the national organization's Intra-Racial Committee, designed to recruit African-American women for the organization. Under the guidance of Mildred Scott Olmsted, the small committee organized speaking engagements at clubs, schools, universities, and churches in the hopes of attracting new members. By the early 1930s, WILPF had made some progress in including a small number of African-Americans on its national, state, and local boards and in producing literature and welcoming speakers who addressed racial discrimination.

During her years in WILPF, Addie Hunton worked tirelessly to improve race relations, but in 1934, because of her daughter's "serious and continuous illness," she decided to curtail all her activities except for the antilynching campaign.[36] However, she also decided that the organization simply could not overcome its racial bias. Even though the national organization of WILPF had made antilynching legislation one of its main concerns and had exerted much pressure in Washington, D.C., Hunton noted that its efforts to educate and integrate its own ranks had not been very successful. Her experience with the New York branch had obviously left a bad taste in her mouth. In a letter to Dorothy Detzer in 1935, Hunton expressed both her respect for Detzer and her discouragement with the larger organization: "Please know that now and forever that I know no person of your race for whom I have greater esteem, whose sincerity I believe in more than you. In fact, I feel rather too much in love with you at times when you are so courageous. It is true however that for a year or so I have felt less and less sure of the fact that the organization was really ready for an inter-racial program. I don't know, but it does not seem so."[37] Addie Hunton's message to WILPF was both taken to heart and ignored. On the one hand, the organization consistently made racial discrimination one of its chief issues; on the other, it did not confront its members' own personal problems with race.

Throughout the 1920s, at both national and local levels, the torch to continue WILPF's work was passed on. Although some older suffragists like Mildred Scott Olmsted, Katherine Devereux Blake, Emily Greene Balch, and Madeline Doty continued their work, the newer voices started to grow stronger. In Philadelphia, the Quaker influence grew; in New York, the Jewish; in Chicago, the working class on the South Side; in Denver, the activists from the mining towns; and in California, women's rights activists and socialists. At times, the entire organization seemed to adopt a new form, one that appeared to emphasize women's issues less and less. Nonetheless, throughout this period WILPF never lost its basic premise that women had a special reason to organize for peace. For some, the cause was motherhood; for others, the responsibility assumed with the gaining of suffrage; and for yet others, the fact that women needed to work together so that men could not usurp the credit for their work. Whether the transition from a basically suffragist organization to a women's peace organization was intentional or not, it saved WILPF from wasting away, as later happened to the Women's Peace Union and the Women's Peace Society. In 1979, Dorothy Detzer, reflecting on the period, attested to the fact that the majority of WILPF members "followed the leadership of Miss Addams and Miss Balch. They actively supported the policies formulated at the Annual meetings of the League and the programs to implement those policies thru political undertakings."[38] Only a minority of members wished to make the Equal Rights Amendment their primary goal, carrying on the organization's women's rights heritage. An even smaller number wished to be absolute nonresisters but not to leave WILPF for more uncompromising groups, such as the Women's Peace Society or the Women's Peace Union.

The multiple divisions within the New York feminist peace network in the late 1910s and early 1920s may have caused consternation for such leaders as Anna Garlin Spencer and Fanny Garrison Villard, but for Emily Greene Balch, then international secretary, the splits did not present a threat at all. She wrote to Fanny Garrison Villard in 1920: "I should like to see a city like New York have half a dozen really active peace groups of different types following their own lines freely, not worried by one another's acts or policies, but cooperating fully on all their common aims and tactics."[39]

It was fortunate that Balch and other feminist peace leaders respected the formation of new groups, for in 1923, at the same time that WILPF was finally getting its feet back on the ground, Carrie Chapman Catt launched another major women's peace effort. Having fallen from grace with many WILPF members because of her behavior during World War I, and still suffering some resentment over being ousted and blasphemed by the New York branch, Catt decided to follow her own instincts in working for peace rather than on trying to return to WILPF. Moreover, like other suffragists, Carrie Chapman Catt missed the days of organizing around suffrage. In 1924, she echoed the sentiments of Caroline Lexow Babcock, Elinor Byrns, and others when she wrote that she "longed for the good old days—the struggle, the comradeship, the thrill of working for freedom for women of all ages."[40]

Catt's zest for political work and her desire to concentrate on peace finally led her to plan a new strategy appropriate for her conception of the postwar era—an approach involving the unification of the major women's social, professional, charity, and reform organizations under one large umbrella. Catt envisioned "a really active, progressive and yet moderate organization of women for world peace" that would sponsor educational programs concerning the League of Nations, the World Court, and U.S. government–supported disarmament conferences.[41] In 1924, Catt formally organized the National Committee on the Cause and Cure of War (NCCCW). The organization was a consortium of eleven large and influential women's clubs: the American Association of University Women, the Council of Women for Home Missions, the Committee on Women's Work—the Foreign Missions Conference of North America, the General Federation of Women's Clubs,

THE PRESS PROJECT
National Committee on the Cause and Cure of War

Carrie Chapman Catt

WHY NOT WRITE

TO CREATE PUBLIC OPINION

TO STRENGTHEN PEACE MACHINERY

TO REDUCE WAR MACHINERY

TO SECURE EVERY NATION AGAINST WAR

14. Pamphlet from National Committee on the Cause and Cure of War, 1936. Photo of Carrie Chapman Catt. Courtesy of Swarthmore College Peace Collection.

the National Board of the Young Women's Christian Associations, the National Council of Jewish Women, the National Federation of Business and Professional Women's Clubs, the National League of Women Voters, the National Woman's Christian Temperance Union, the National Conference of American Ethical Union, and the National Women's Trade Union League.

The Cause and Cure of War affiliates each had a Peace Committee that organized activities on a local level and expressed their own points of view. On the national level, Catt became their spokesperson. Study groups, round-table discussions, and regional, state and yearly national conferences were all part of the program for promoting what Catt called "sane liberalism."[42] Men, as well as women, were encouraged to participate in affairs sponsored by the Cause and Cure of War, although the leadership remained exclusively female. By 1935 there were approximately eighteen state and local Cause and Cure of War branches, but the eleven cooperating organizations represented a combined membership of over five million women throughout the country, about one-fifth of the adult population of the U.S. at the time. As a large, umbrella organization, the Cause and Cure of War had a policy of not trying to reach a consensus, which would clearly have been impossible, but rather to keep educational discussions going constantly. Catt and many of the members, however, supported only legislative means of ending war, including U.S. participation in the League of Nations, the World Court, the Kellogg-Briand Pact, and all treaties leading to disarmament. Like WILPF, the Cause and Cure of War supported any and all measures that might result in lasting world peace, but unlike WILPF, Catt's group did not address controversial issues that might alienate politically cautious members.

The Cause and Cure of War gave new hope to others besides the clubwomen for whom Catt designed it. Anna Garlin Spencer, recovered from her 1917 confrontation with Catt, praised both the organization and its founder for "getting ready . . . to do [women's] old work of mothering the race on the largest possible scale." Whether it led efforts for ending war, abolishing poverty, or eliminating racism, Spencer saw the Cause and Cure of War as being in the forefront of dealing with social problems "that touch the family at its vital heart."[43] Although she had been severely harassed for her suffrage work, Catt was correct in believing that she could avoid most of the attacks of the Red Scare if she stayed clear of WILPF. To reach that end, under the pretense that the general public, and not pacifists themselves, needed to be educated, she also insisted that peace organizations not be eligible for membership under the Cause and Cure of War umbrella. Members of WILPF, the Women's Peace Union or the Women's Peace Society who wanted to attend the annual Cause and Cure of War conferences in Washington had to do so as individuals, not as representatives of their organizations.

At about the time that Catt spurned the three suffragist-created peace organizations to form the Cause and Cure of War, WILPF was also shunned by the National Council of Women, of which it had been a member since 1915. Three of the Council's member organizations had passed very strong resolutions condemning the outspoken pacifism of both the U.S. and the International Sections of WILPF. As a result, WILPF was asked to resign from the Council. After much debate, the national board decided to comply, but noted that they did so because their program was "perhaps too advanced" for some of the Council's members. Their statement of resignation repeated their antiwar program and ended thus: "We are willing to endure the unjust criticism that comes to pioneers in any movement, but we do not wish to force others into a position which is uncomfortable for them."[44] In 1928, after the Kellogg-Briand Pact had been ratified and peace was at its apex of popularity, WILPF was invited to return to the Council and accepted.

Meanwhile, all of the feminist peace activists had to deal with the Red Scare on some level. During this period the membership pledges for the Women's Peace Society and the Women's Peace Union became derisively termed the "Slacker's Oath." The *Woman Patriot,* a monthly newspaper whose masthead proclaimed a dedication to opposing feminism and socialism, strongly attacked the pledge. Drawing its articles from various other periodicals, the *Woman Patriot* quoted the *New York Tribune,* for example, as advocating that any woman who signed the pledge should lose her U.S. citizenship.[45] The Women's Peace Union, furthermore, was characterized by the director of women's relations of the U.S. Army as being "the most radical and violent of the 'peace' societies. It is unscrupulous in its falsehoods and particularly violent in its attacks on the War Department," largely because the women campaigned against military appropriations.[46] The Union leaders paid little attention to these slurs on their character, even when Rear Admiral Fiske accused them of "imperilling national security" by organizing women to oppose those wars "carried on to protect them."[47] Instead, they went about their business, writing letters or press releases to protest the harassment.

WILPF came under particularly ruthless surveillance. The Washington office, located directly across the street from the War Department, was raided from time to time by the military, who would break in over the weekends, stealing files, disrupting the filing system, throwing ink on documents, and generally causing confusion. The organization was also criticized in articles and pamphlets. One such piece, entitled "Peace at any Old Price," reported on the 1923 WILPF annual national conference. According to the author, R. M. Whitney, the conference was "probably the most subversive, certainly the most insidiously and clevery camouflaged, thoroughly anti-American and un-American" public meeting since World War I. The women "branded" the U.S. government as "corrupt," Whitney asserted, and "boasted" of "slacking" during the war by refusing to buy war bonds, roll bandages, or participate in relief work. Furthermore, like "the Moscow Communists," the women were set on abolishing the Gas and Chemical Warfare Division of the Army, the branch of the military "most effective in suppressing riots and the Communists."[48]

The Military Intelligence Division of the War Department also kept a detailed file on WILPF throughout most of the 1920s, with copies of leaflets, speeches, and conference programs. Government agents attended such conferences as the WILPF Congress of 1924 and wrote up reports on the proceedings. According to one report, WILPF was "of Communist conception," standing for the "abolition of all sentiments of national loyalty and patriotism." The reporting agent came to this conclusion after reading "Disarm the Nursery," a WILPF circular opposing the purchasing of war toys and the playing of war games. The agent concluded that "any individual organization that deliberately seeks to destroy a national spirit and the sentiment of patriotism is deliberately working to destroy civilization and Christianity."[49] Amidst these allegations, organizing was fraught with difficulty. In May 1924, for example, U.S.-WILPF sponsored an International Congress in Washington, D.C., to be followed by an International Summer School in Chicago. To expedite travel between the two events, the organization chartered a train, calling it the "Pax Special," to carry the twenty-five visiting European delegates and their U.S. hosts to Chicago.[50] The plan was to make stops in a number of cities so the delegates could meet local WILPF members and be entertained by them. Implementation, however, was not easy, for local conservatives and members of the American Legion and Daughters of the American Revolution verbally attacked the contingent in the press, accusing the WILPFers not only of being un-American but also of serving as Bolshevik spies. For many of the European visitors, this first glimpse of U.S. life was not a particularly favorable one.

The general maligning of the feminist peace organizations was accompanied by a more personal attack on several of its leaders, especially those, like Jane Addams, Madeline Doty, and Mabel Vernon, who had been instrumental in both the national and international suffrage, peace, and social reform campaigns. The most notorious attack occurred in 1923 in a document known as the "Spider Web Chart." Signed by Lucia R. Maxwell, a librarian of the Chemical Warfare Services of the War Department, and approved by Brigadier General Amos A. Fries, the chart was headed with a quotation from the Lusk Report of New York State, the multivolume Red Scare study of peace, suffrage, and labor leaders of the World War I era. The quotation read: "The Socialist-Pacifist Movement in America is an Absolutely Fundamental and Integral Part of International Socialism." The chart was crisscrossed with lines linking individual women to organizations tinted from red to violet. The names of Madeline Doty, Emma Wold, Mary Gertrude Fendall, Inez Haynes Irwin, Belle LaFollette, Florence Kelley, Freda Kirchway, and Mary Winsor were all underscored in red on the original chart, the color also used to signify WILPF.[51] Later versions also highlighted Jane Addams and Emily Greene Balch.

Balch had already been a Red Scare victim. Unable to gain reappointment at Wellesley College in 1918 because of her peace efforts, she was consistently labeled a Communist dupe. In a response to the Spider Web Chart for the WILPF organ, *PAX,* she characterized the assaults as attacks on women's rights and reform organizations in general. "It is evidently related to the fact that women have succeeded in carrying through certain reforms, that they are believed to stand behind prohibition, and that they seem likely to effect other social advances, such as a lessening of the national reproach of child labor." Balch also pointed out that because WILPF opposed all violence, militarism, and any form of dictatorship, it was "moonshine" for anyone to believe the organization was connected to Soviet Russia, a nation steeped in military rhetoric and openly sanctioning violent revolution.[52] In the same vein, Jane Addams could provide a blanket denial of being connected to the Communist party because such people believed in violent class warfare. Addams was particularly disliked by the conservatives; her work with WILPF had her labeled a "radical pacifist," a slacker, and a traitor. In 1926, when she was sixty-six, her consent for the use of Hull House as a meeting place for strikers led one federal agent to call her "one of the most active radicals in this country." He added, "Bear in mind, that this was a Communist inspired meeting and Miss Addams knew it, for no one has ever claimed that she was senile and did not have a good set of brains to think with."[53]

Carrie Chapman Catt was not perceived as being as dangerous as Jane Addams. In 1922, for example, government agent J. V. McConville acknowledged Catt's past connection with "many pink organizations" but dismissed her as basically unimportant because "her pet hobby," suffrage, was no longer an issue.[54] Unlike many of those under surveillance, however, Catt did not ignore any assault on herself or Jane Addams. Throughout the 1920s she wrote letters to the *Woman Patriot,* the Daughters of the American Revolution, and other sources of attacks, pointing out their lies and revealing their roots in the extinct antisuffrage movement. Catt claimed that with the end of the suffrage era, the opposition merely followed its game into the peace movement. Although Catt herself saw WILPF as "the radical wing of the peace movement," she respected its members' right of free expression.[55] In 1927, she wrote that it was "truly shocking to note how untrue, how misleading, how contemptible are the charges made against this body. Call it radical if you wish, but cease charging it with conduct little short of treason."[56]

Attacks on Jane Addams particularly irked Catt, who saw her peer as "one of the greatest women this Republic of ours has produced. She has given her life to serve others. She knows no selfish thought. You slap her on the right cheek; she only turns the left. Sticks, stones, slanders, you cast upon this highest product of American womanhood and not a protest passes her lips. She is the kind of Christian who might have been thrown to the lions and would have gone cheerfully."[57] Catt was not alone in her admiration of Addams. In 1931, four years before her death at the age of seventy-five, Jane Addams was awarded the Nobel Peace

Prize, sharing it with Nicholas Murray Butler of Columbia University.

The Red Scare harassment of the 1920s did not affect the enthusiasm the feminist peace activists had for their work. On the contrary, the attempts to unnerve these women only made their resolve stronger. In fact, during this period, when Red Scare and antiwar sentiments vied for domination of the private and public sectors, the various feminist peace organizations were at their busiest, combining forces on several projects. Generally, three of the major organizations (WILPF, the National Committee on the Cause and Cure of War and the Women's Peace Union) desired links with other women in the Western Hemisphere, not only to build hemispheric female solidarity but also to support a noninterventionist U.S. foreign policy. Carrie Chapman Catt picked up the spirit of her pacifist foremothers and peers as early as 1924, when she declared that the Monroe Doctrine of 1823 was "outworn," a mere "defense of commerce and of big business . . . false in theory and pernicious in practice."[58]

In 1922, Catt had supported the formation of the Pan American Association for the Advancement of Women under the auspices of the National League of Women Voters. As honorary president, she was to work with an executive committee consisting of Dr. Paulina Luisi, Elena Torres of Mexico, Ester Niera de Calvo of Panama, Narrva Surrez de Coronado of Colombia, and Capurro de Varela of Uruguay, the last two residing in Washington. The organization's aims were to better educational opportunities for women in Latin America and to help them gain their property, parental, and suffrage rights. A successful Pan American Congress was held in April 1922, in Baltimore, but by 1924, Catt had become discouraged by the distance and expense connected with such international work. Rather than pursuing these efforts, she turned her attention to the formation of the National Committee on the Cause and Cure of War. Although she continued to include Latin American concerns in the organization's work, she realized that a women's rights movement, "desperately needed in South and Central America," had to develop indigenously before an effective international network could be established.[59]

From its inception, the Women's Peace Union also tried to establish connections with the women of Latin America.[60] However, the Union was hampered by its desire to form a coalition of nonresistant pacifists that would support its program of legislative amendments to end war. The leaders saw this as a way of ending U.S. intervention in Latin America as well as a way of uniting women. In 1923, Anna Graves, a Union supporter who had lived in Mexico for some time, helped the organization to establish communications with the Consejo Nacional de Mujeres Mexicanas (National Council of Mexican Women). For three years, the Consejo wrote supportive letters to the sponsor of the Peace Union amendment, Senator Lynn Frazier, but this was the extent of its efforts. As Anna Graves informed the WPU leaders, Mexicans were generally suspicious of the nonresister stance, which they surmised was just one more U.S. ploy to gain control of Mexican property and, perhaps, the government itself. Because the Peace Union did not address other concerns of women, its efforts in Latin America did not produce very positive results.

WILPF, also attempting to establish connections with Latin American women, was especially concerned with ending the U.S. military presence in their nations. In 1925, for example, a task force of five women and one man spent three weeks in Haiti examining the effect of the U.S. military on the living conditions of the native residents. (Two of the women, including Addie Hunton, were African-American, lending credibility to WILPF's attempts to combat its own racial imbalance.) From that trip came a book, *Occupied Haiti,* written by the team and edited in 1927 by its leader, Emily Greene Balch, which maintained that the immediate removal of U.S. troops, which had been stationed on the island since 1915, was necessary in order for Haitians to achieve economic and social progress. After President Herbert Hoover's own later investigation confirmed that opinion, the troops were finally withdrawn in 1934.[61]

The U.S. section of WILPF also continued the policies of the World War I era Woman's Peace Party by criticizing the U.S. military's presence in the Dominican Republic, Puerto Rico, and Nicaragua. By the 1930s the organization had a branch in Mexico as well as contacts and emerging groups in Argentina, Nicaragua, Cuba, Puerto Rico, Costa Rica, Peru, Paraguay, Venezuela, Guatemala, and Bolivia. Most of its efforts were devoted to supporting peace treaties that would prohibit U.S. intervention. However, WILPF organizers also hoped that through building local branches in Latin America, they could address other human rights issues.

In dealing with Latin America, the former suffragist peace leaders generally did not cross class lines but instead cooperated with women of comparable economic and educational backgrounds. Their Latin American counterparts were generally wealthy, well-educated, European-oriented women. No organization exemplified this tendency as much as the Pan American International Women's Committee formed out of the Women's Auxiliary of the Pan American Scientific Congresses (PanAm Women's Auxiliary). Founded in 1915 by the wives and daughters of the male members of the Pan American Scientific Congress, the PanAm Women's Auxiliary brought together influential women to discuss both their national differences and ways to improve the plight of Latin American women.

As an organization, the PanAm Women's Auxiliary was the closest this nation has ever come to having a government-sanctioned peace organization, and although not of suffragist roots, the organizers reflected the attitudes of more conservative women's rights activists such as Carrie Chapman Catt. The first of the Auxiliary presidents was Eleanor Lansing, the wife of Robert Lansing, then secretary of state. When he retired in 1920, so did she. Although the organization insisted on her staying, she soon deferred to Antoinette Carter Hughes, the wife of the new secretary of state, Charles Evans Hughes, a woman "of culture, refinement and ability," as one member described her.[62] The other members of the International Committee were recruited solely through their respective ambassadors. By 1922, Argentina, Bolivia, Brazil, Chile, Colombia, Cuba, El Salvador, Ecuador, Guatemala, Haiti, Honduras, Mexico, Nicaragua, Panama, Paraguay, Peru, Uruguay, and Venezuela were all represented.

Inspired by the "real personal touch—the hand clasp of woman with woman" that had occurred during the first Pan American Scientific Congress, the PanAm Women's Auxiliary concentrated on two types of activities to tighten friendships: distributing bilingual literature and planning for the next major congress.[63] Much of the literature tried to analyze the legal and social positions of females in the various nations so that U.S. and Latin American women could understand each other better. There was also much concern with child welfare, education, and domesticity (the last a particularly middle-class interest). One way to help poorer women, the PanAm Women's Auxiliary felt, was to educate them in home economics and child care. Such a Victorian attitude reflected their own desire for women to effect changes in their immediate home and family environment without revolutionizing the patriarchal and capitalistic systems.

The greatest success for the PanAm Women's Auxiliary was its Columbus Day events, held on October 12, 1923. Simultaneous conferences of Latin American and U.S. women were held in all the member nations (the largest in the United States), in order to show "the spiritual element underlying the relationship which ought to exist between the members of the American Family of Nations."[64] A master plan was distributed suggesting that three sessions be held, one each on women of the past, the present, and the future. This plan was adjusted for each country. Generally, emphasis was placed on legal advancements for women in such areas as child welfare and women's rights. The PanAm Women's Auxiliary held its second and final major conference in 1924 alongside the third and final Pan American Scientific Congress.

These small efforts at hemispheric unity during the interwar era were important expressions of the internationalism felt by U.S. feminist peace activists. Money and distance, as well as class and race differences, however, greatly hampered these efforts. Furthermore, as the 1920s faded into the 1930s, U.S. eyes became riveted on Europe, where fascist and expansionist actions led by Benito Mussolini and Adolf Hitler were resulting in a growing war fever, and on Asia, where Japanese imperialism threatened world stability. As before World War I, all four suffragist peace organizations worked tirelessly for some solution to the European problems. Some women supported such existing structures as the League of Nations, the World Court, and arms limitations talks, while others worked for new alternatives, such as the outlawry of war. All opposed any increase in military appropriations, advocating instead the instituting of social reforms. To obtain peace, they said, the world must be rid of all economic, racial, and gender injustices. WILPF and the Cause and Cure of War supported such League of Nations efforts as the International Labor Organization and the committees to oppose white slavery and drug traffic in the hope that these campaigns might alleviate war pressure. The Women's Peace Society and the Women's Peace Union, however, believed that war had to be outlawed before such reforms could be instituted. The Union was especially adamant about the weaknesses of the League, calling it a "compromising body" that was "powerless to do anything" in its present form, especially because it had no provisions for universal disarmament in its charter and supported collective security through force.[65]

Disarmament was the key element in each group's program. WILPF, the Women's Peace Society and the Women's Peace Union all cooperated on any proposition supporting universal disarmament. They also attended demonstrations in support of any arms limitations treaties. Accordingly, they all eagerly participated in the parade to support President Warren Harding's Washington Naval Conference of 1921 and in the international No More War parades of 1922 and 1923. The best example of combined pacifist efforts in spite of tactical or philosophic differences, however, was work in support of legislation for the outlawry of war. The Women's Peace Union, the one organization to support the outlawry idea unconditionally, devoted its entire program to working for its constitutional amendment resolution. The Women's Peace Society, although also supporting the idea, did not have the resources for a large campaign, especially after the death of Fanny Garrison Villard in 1928. Instead, its leadership threw its support behind the WPU, sending representatives to each of its senatorial hearings and producing literature in support of the idea.

WILPF and the Cause and Cure of War came into the outlawry movement when, starting in 1928, sixty-two nations signed the Kellogg-Briand Pact. In addition, at the 1930 congressional hearing, WILPF's Dorothy Detzer and Katherine Devereux Blake spoke on behalf of the Union's amendment, supporting it as a logical extension of the Kellogg-Briand Pact. Even Carrie Chapman Catt's moderate Cause and Cure of War joined the effort. As early as 1924, Catt acknowledged her feelings that the outlawry of war could possibly generate "the spiritual Strength of the World," even though she seriously doubted its practicality.[66] By 1929, the Cause and Cure of War had made support of the Kellogg-Briand Pact part of its program.

The one problem with the Pact was that it had no provisions for peace talks in the case of a nation's defending itself from invasion. Many members of the Women's Peace Union felt that this deficiency made the treaty almost useless unless each nation's legislature passed an outlawry resolution similar to the Union's own constitutional amendment resolution. From 1928 to 1932 the Union added this proposal to its own amendment resolution program, making itself into a two-issue organization. The Union continued to insist that if war were really outlawed, there would be no such thing as a "defensive" war. Although Carrie Chapman Catt agreed with the Union in principle, she wrote that the "old system of defense" could not and should not be eliminated until "a safe and sane substitute" could be found.[67] Catt, along with WILPF leaders, supported the general idea of gradual disarmament until a legal system, based on the Kellogg-Briand Pact, a World Court, and the League of Nations, could be established. The Women's Peace Union supported only complete and universal disarmament based on outlawry legislation.

Spurred on by the spirit behind the Kellogg-Briand Pact and the work of the Preparatory Disarmament Committee of the League of Nations, women all over the world prepared for the 1932 League of Nations Conference on Reduction and Limitation of Arms, to be held in Geneva. The Cause and Cure of War and the U.S. section of WILPF joined an international women's peace petition campaign launched in August 1930 to pressure representatives at the League of Nations Disarmament Conference to create and put into effect definite disarmament plans. Although petitions had been a mainstay of the suffrage movement, the presentation of such a petition to an international peace conference had taken place only once before. In January 1930 two Japanese women had presented a petition, signed by 180,000 of their countrywomen, asking the London Naval Reduction Conference to produce concrete plans for worldwide naval cutbacks. Carrie Chapman Catt, noting that U.S. women were also present at the conference, predicted that women would "attend each disarmament conference and . . . carry upon each occasion a larger petition than went to the preceding conference."[68] True to her words, the next campaign, coordinated by the International Council of Women (ICW), consisted of the circulation of a "Polyglot Petition for Disarmament," calling for a general reduction of arms to be followed by the eventual elimination of weapons and war as begun through the Kellogg-Briand Pact.

In order to facilitate the collection and presentation of the petitions as well as to carry on educational projects, the International Council formed a separate Peace and Disarmament Committee (P & D Com-

15. Official delegates from U.S./WILPF at the 1932 League of Nations Disarmament Conference. Meta Berger *(left),* Hannah Clothier Hull *(center),* and Katherine Devereux Blake *(right).* Flowers sent by Eleanor Roosevelt. Courtesy of Swarthmore College Peace Collection.

mittee) in 1931, basing it in Geneva. Fourteen women's international organizations, altogether representing millions of women around the world, worked under the umbrella of the P & D Committee: the International Council of Women itself, the World's YWCA, the International Alliance of Women for Suffrage and Equal Citizenship, WILPF, the World Union of Women for International Concord, the World Organization of Jewish Women, the European Federation of Soroptimist Clubs, the World's Woman's Christian Temperance Union, the International Cooperative Women's Guild, the International Federation of University Women, the League of Jewish Women, the League of Iberian and Latin-American Women, the League of Mothers and Educators for Peace, and the International Federation of Business and Professional Women. The officers of the P & D Committee were all established leaders of various wings of the international women's movement. President Mary A. Dingman, for example, was a U.S. citizen educated at Columbia University who had done relief work during World War I and had traveled and worked in China for the YWCA. Vice-President Kathleen Courtney, of Great Britain, was a founder of WILPF, and another vice-president, Rosa Manus from the Netherlands, was a leader in the Dutch suffrage movement.

During 1930 and 1931 four different petitions were circulated under the International Council's sponsorship. The WILPF petition, which originated during the organization's International Congress at Prague in August 1929, was the impetus for the campaign and the model for all the other petitions. Also circulated were a British WILPF version of the WILPF petition, the International Alliance version, and the Cause and Cure of War version. In content, all four petitions were basically the same. In tone, the most moderate was the Cause and Cure of War version, which called for the "bold reduction of every variety of armament" in order to avoid "fresh war talk."[69] The WILPF petition was more aggressive. Connecting "competition in armaments" with an insecure world and future wars of "extermination," it asked for no less than "total and universal disarmament."[70] The goal of these petitions was to pressure all governments to instruct their Geneva representatives "to examine all proposals for disarmament that have been or may be made, and to take the necessary steps to achieve real disarmament." The ultimate end, as seen by the P & D Committee, was a weapon-free world with "equal rights and security for all peoples," as stated in Article VIII of the League of Nations' Charter.[71] The Women's Peace Union, as a noncompromising organization, refused to participate in the International Council's petition campaign. To the Union's leaders, the P & D Committee's position appeared weak and compromising. The Union's own petition called for immediate, complete, and universal disarmament through amendments to every country's governing documents and to the Kellogg-Briand Pact as well.

The U.S. section of WILPF (guided by Mabel Vernon, director

of the Disarmament Campaign, who was a former suffragist, a member of the National Woman's Party, and an active women's rights activist) spent the greater part of 1931 on work related to the Geneva meeting. Along with the Cause and Cure of War, the National Woman's Party, and the Women's Peace Union, WILPF lobbied President Herbert Hoover for the appointment of a female delegate to the conference. At first, Judge Florence Allen, a staunch, outspoken feminist and pacifist, was selected for this honor. But because Hoover, a Republican, did not wish to have a Democrat appointed to this extremely visible position, he rejected her. The groups then proposed a Republican, Mary Woolley, president of Mount Holyoke College. Hoover approved, and Woolley became one of the very few female delegates to the conference.[72]

Woolley's performance, however, disappointed some women peace activists. According to Dorothy Detzer, Woolley was too "timid" for the job, afraid of antagonizing the other delegates and of making her feminist position felt.[73] Representatives of the Women's Peace Union agreed with Detzer's assessment of Woolley's performance. All of the groups regretted that Judge Allen had not been chosen to attend the conference. Woolley herself lamented that there were only five female delegates—one each from the United Kingdom, Poland, Uruguay, Canada, and the United States. In an article in the *New York Times Magazine,* she stressed that this conference was just the "beginning" of future joint efforts between men and women.[74] Perhaps she had simply felt overpowered by the dominant male presence in an international arena so unlike her own female world at Mount Holyoke.

More success came from the petition drive. After thorough preparation, the U.S. section of WILPF held nationwide meetings in observance of National Goodwill Day on May 18, 1931. At each of these meetings, resolutions were passed urging President Hoover to instruct the U.S. delegation to work for "real" disarmament. The meetings were followed by a transcontinental peace caravan that began in Hollywood, California, on June 21 and ended 9,000 miles later on October 10 in Washington, D.C. WILPF's founder and honorary president, Jane Addams, accompanied by more than seven hundred supporters, presented President Hoover with more than half a million signatures collected in twenty-five states and 125 cities and towns across the United States. By January 1932, when the official U.S. delegation was ready to leave for Geneva, WILPF had organized public farewell meetings. The gathering in Washington attracted 2,000 people; in New York over 5,000 attended, including 1,200 high school students and the Salvation Army band. The farewell ceremony on the ship received nationwide radio coverage.[75]

Activities reached their peak in February. A national observance of World Disarmament Day was held on February 2, again to pressure Hoover for positive results in Geneva. On February 6 representatives from several organizations presented resolutions to Hoover in Washington, while at the same time in Geneva the Peace and Disarmament Committee of the International Council of Women presented petitions containing more than nine million signatures from all over the world to the president of the Disarmament Conference. Great Britain alone accounted for one and one-half million of these signatures. Switzerland had the greatest number of signatures in proportion to its population: 311,000 names out of a population of four million. These petitions were then placed on exhibit in the Disarmament Building attached to the Secretariat of the League of Nations and remained there for the duration of the conference. Efforts of the P & D Committee did not end with the presentation of the petitions; they also sponsored innumerable workshops, luncheons, and study groups on disarmament.[76]

On February 5 the Women's Peace Union chose to present to the conference its own, very small petition calling for outlawry amendments in every country. The Union had two representatives in Geneva: Frieda Langer Lazarus from Brooklyn, New York, and Isabel Ashby, a War Resisters' International affiliate from England who had corresponded with the Union leaders for more than ten years. Lazarus, the daughter of immigrants and an active member of the Ethical Culture Society, was another of the few Jewish leaders in the U.S. feminist peace movement. She and Ashby made their presence in Geneva felt in three ways. First, they had literature printed in English, French, German, and Italian and distributed it from a shop where they had rented space. Next, the two women personally interviewed as many delegates as they could, stressing the Peace Union's stand on legally abolishing war. Finally, Lazarus rented the only electric sign in Geneva, arranging for the words "Total Disarmament Now" to be flashed thirty-five times every evening.

Frieda Lazarus felt strongly that the Women's Peace Union's work was the only serious attempt at disarmament made at the 1932 conference. Angry at leaders of the U.S. section of WILPF for joining the International Council's petition campaign, she claimed that once the nine million signatures had been delivered, the P & D Committee deteriorated into a social club. Lazarus' feelings illustrated an unfortunate division between the Peace Union and the rest of the remaining former suffragist peace activists. WILPF had not necessarily compromised its pacifist position or its support of the Union's campaign to outlaw war; rather, its leaders, in an effort to respond to the shifting mood of the thirties towards militarism and fascism, had attempted to influence the conference at least to begin actual disarmament. In addition, the U.S. section of WILPF was part of an international organization that had to follow those guidelines established by its mother group headquartered in Geneva. Nor did the P & D Committee become sedentary, as Lazarus claimed. While the Women's Peace Union representatives left Geneva in February, and lack of funds and effective leadership prevented the group from following up on its work, the P & D Committee remained in Geneva throughout the early 1930s, holding study conferences and public meetings, writing and dispersing literature, and lobbying various representatives at the continually weakening international meetings. The women "failed" at Geneva, as Frieda Lazarus put it, not because they did not support the Peace Union's uncompromising approach to campaigning but because the militarists and munitions makers in power were deliberately drawing the world closer to war.[77]

Dorothy Detzer of WILPF was probably the woman chiefly responsible for exposing this manipulation to the general public. In April 1932, while the Geneva Disarmament Conference was still in session, the annual meeting of the U.S. section of WILPF voted on a resolution to work for a congressional investigation of the munitions industry and its connection to the U.S. decision to enter World War I. Lobbying the Senate for a sponsor, Detzer found one in Gerald Nye, a Republican from North Dakota who agreed with the pacifist beliefs of Lynn Frazier, sponsor of the Women's Peace Union's amendment. On February 8, 1934, Nye introduced a bill calling for an investigation. The Senate accepted the proposal, allocating $15,000 for the committee's expenses.

On Dorothy Detzer's recommendation, Senator Nye proposed that Steve Raushenbush, an economics instructor at Dartmouth College, be appointed chief investigator.[78] Raushenbush was aided by a staff of three: Josephine Burns (whom he later married), Alger Hiss, and Robert Wolforth. The Women's Peace Union joined this effort, using the theme of this Senate Special Committee Investigating the Munition Industry's Work for its final senate hearing in 1934, a hearing dominated largely by testimony from other peace organizations, including WILPF. In its final report, the Nye Committee maintained that the munitions industry had clearly tried to influence the congressional vote for war in 1917. The connections between war and industry, which most people had a hint of, became public knowledge. The phenomenon would later be termed the "military-industrial complex."

The work of the Nye Committee marked the end of the period in which the suffragist-inspired peace organizations were most productive and most successful. What had begun in the abolitionist movement of the nineteenth century evolved into a full-fledged feminist peace movement. Women's rights and world peace had become so intertwined that organizational leaders maintained a feminist consciousness even when the times dictated that they address only issues of war and peace. The 1920s was one peak in the movement's growth. During that decade many people sincerely wanted peace, and world leaders made some overtures towards it. During the first half of the 1930s, however, organizing became increasingly less successful. The groups were plagued by low membership caused, on the one hand, by the economic hardships of the Depression and on the other hand, by the growing war fever resulting from the growth of European fascism and Japanese imperialism. The general climate was not conducive to the development of political dissent, peace movements, or women's equality. As elderly suffragists died, new feminists were needed to carry on the work. Recruiting new members was not an easy task. Yet organizing, as difficult as it was, did not cease but persisted despite internal organizational strife and external pressure. In particular, the coming of World War II, surrounded by so many complex issues, sparked intense debate within the entire feminist peace movement. Although the war itself brought on much emotional heartbreak, in the long run it also elicited a renewed commitment to peace.

5

Dilemmas, Quandaries, and Tensions during War, 1935–1945

Up until 1935, feminist peace activists maintained a positive, although somewhat cynical, view of international events. They persisted in their efforts to purge the world of war while at the same time keeping a careful eye on the male power structure. As the 1930s faded, it became painfully clear that neither the vote nor all their lobbying efforts had resulted in a permanent peace. The ten years from 1935 through 1945 proved to be so difficult for the movement that by the end of it, only one of the four original suffrage peace organizations, WILPF, would still be intact. The Women's Peace Society and the Women's Peace Union would be gone. The Peace Society, in fact, disbanded as early as 1933; after Fanny Garrison Villard's death in 1928, the group lost its inspiration and initiative. The National Committee on the Cause and Cure of War would be transformed into the Women's Action Committee for Victory and Lasting Peace, an organization whose emphasis was so different that there was no longer even a resemblance.

Issues such as Japanese aggression in Asia (especially in China) and the growth of fascism in Europe—and along with it, the persecution of the Jews, leftists, pacifists, feminists, ethnic minorities, and the handicapped—presented dilemmas for activists in the United States. The Spanish Civil War, Roosevelt's Neutrality Acts, the rise of Hitler and Mussolini, and the war itself all produced tensions and, in some instances, splits within previously harmonious organizations. Foreign policy issues began to dominate, whereas in previous years they shared the limelight with women's issues. Groups like WILPF and the Cause and Cure of War lost most of their emphasis on women's rights. Although they remained as peace organizations run by women and rooted in the suffrage tradition, they addressed the issues of peace and human rights without emphasizing women's particular concerns.

With its small base for members and leadership, the Women's Peace Union, crippled by both its one-issue constitutional amendment program and its inability to raise funds, ceased really active work after its 1934 Senate hearing. Several elderly supporters had donated money to the Union (though more from friendship and former suffrage ties with Caroline Lexow Babcock than from commitment to the amendment resolution), and when these women died, the organization lost much of its financial support. Moreover, the Union was in the unique position among the four original organizations in having leaders who also held jobs, especially after 1929. Depression economics also came into play. Working women with families had little or no time to volunteer for their favorite causes. Meanwhile, because neither the Union nor the Women's Peace Society attempted to recruit younger members, they withered away from natural attrition. By 1933 the Women's Peace Union, never broadening its program, was barely surviving. Once Senator Lynn Frazier, the sole sponsor of the amendment resolution, lost his bid for reelection in the 1940 primaries, the organization had no reason to exist. From 1934 to 1942 its voice was small while its remaining leaders, Elinor Byrns and Tracy Mygatt, argued over whether to temper the organization's program to include neutral mediation. By 1942 the Union's office space was turned over to the War Resisters League (WRL), and although the group never officially disbanded, it was never active again.

WILPF, which did survive the period, is an excellent example of how an organization can be transformed. As we have seen, the national leadership of WILPF had been going through changes throughout the twenties and the first half of the thirties. Immediately after World War I, Jane Addams had given up her role as national chair to assume leadership of the entire international WILPF organization. A series of former suffragists led the U.S. section through its period of rebirth in the early twenties. Much of the active work became centered in Washington, D.C., under the guidance of Dorothy Detzer, who supported suffrage but had come to WILPF after working in a settlement house and serving in the post–World War I European relief effort. In addition to Detzer, the Washington office drew organizational strength from Emily Greene Balch, who had returned from Geneva to devote time to the U.S. section of WILPF, Mildred Scott Olmsted, and Hannah Clothier Hull, active leaders of the Pennsylvania branch.

Like many WILPF members, Hull was a former suffragist. She was also a devout Quaker who was married to William Isaac Hull, president of Swarthmore College, a school founded on Quaker thought. Hull served as the national chair from 1924 to 1928; chair of the national board from 1929 to 1933, and president of the U.S. section from 1933 to 1939.

The dominant force in WILPF affairs from 1922 through the 1980s was Mildred Scott Olmsted, a well-educated, upper-middle-class woman from the Philadelphia area. Olmsted soon became a paid staff member and remained so for most of her life. In 1934 she was named executive secretary of her branch. Like Detzer, Olmsted, born in 1890, had worked in postwar Europe with the Quakers and the YMCA. Unlike Detzer, she represented the more traditional WILPF leader. Like other activists, she had campaigned for the suffrage cause while a student at Smith College. Even though her professional interests were focused on social work, she devoted immense time and energy to WILPF for most of her adult life. From 1934 through 1946 she was the national organization's secretary, from 1946 to 1964 the administrative secretary, and from 1964 to 1966 the executive director. From 1935 to 1959, Olmsted added participation on the international executive committee to her already formidable WILPF responsibilities.

With Hull's and Olmsted's leadership replacing the weaker one offered in New York, the emphasis of the entire WILPF national organization shifted. No longer depending solely on suffrage personalities and networks to set its goals and plan its activities, the national organization drifted away from its women's rights orientation towards a more pacifist one. This is not to say that it became a utopian or spiritually directed organization, for it did not. Instead, the concern for women's equality, which had already been tempered when suffrage was achieved, became secondary. Although "equal rights" remained among the organization's stated objectives, the issue, submerged in the flood of panic to avoid another war, did not resurface as a vital part of WILPF's activities until the 1970s and 1980s. The organization retained its tradition of being women-led, even though by the 1930s men were being admitted as full members, and in January 1940 the executive board even entertained the idea of dropping "women" from its name. Like the Progressive-era social reformers and suffragists who led it before, the national board decided to maintain WILPF's cautiously pacifistic stance as a liberal organization open to women of all political views who were determined "to study, make known and abolish the political, social, economic and psychological causes of war, and to work for a constructive peace."[1]

The New York branch in Manhattan, on the other hand, continued its radical ways even though it, too, had lost its suffrage base. Older suffragists like Katherine Devereux Blake and Madeline Doty had moved on to work with the national board. (Doty also acted as international secretary in Geneva from 1925 to 1927.) A number of the newer New York City members, especially in the burgeoning Brooklyn and Bronx branches, were working-class women with experience in labor unions, social welfare groups, the Socialist party, and student activism. In Denver as well, several WILPF leaders emerged from the mine workers unions. The South Side branch in Chicago, like the Brooklyn and Bronx branches in New York, reflected a working-class base; the main Chicago branch still attracted middle- and upper-class women. Accordingly, by the mid-1930s many of the local WILPF branches had lost their previous sense of homogeneity, based on the suffrage movement, and instead became a diverse network of groups, each reflecting the ethnic and political nature of its constituency. Up to the advent of World War II, this diversity helped WILPF to grow. In 1935, the year of Jane Addams' death, for example, the organization claimed 61 U.S. branches with a total of 9,115 members. By 1939 this number had increased to 118 branches with a total of 13,600 members.[2]

Nonetheless, WILPF retained from its suffrage days a decision-making process centered in discussions to reach consensus. "We all try to discuss in such a way as not to gain votes, but to find the general will, as Rousseau used to say," explained Emily Balch. "We try both to create agreement and to bring clear expression to all the agreement there is latent among us. We must all the time be trying as much to agree with others as trying to get others to agree with us. This is as new in debate as peaceful settlement of disputes is new in international politics."[3] Besides seeking peaceful, collective answers for making decisions, the WILPF leaders also maintained the original founders' belief in a uniquely nonviolent female character, from time to time adding a new twist. As Mildred Scott Olmsted remarked years later, "The use of non-violent methods comes more easily to women than to men if only because women cannot compete on the physical level and therefore have long been forced to use their wits rather than their fists. I don't mean to say that women don't fight; they can and do; but usually by tongue or by egging on men by indirect methods of personal pressure."[4]

Encouraged by Dorothy Detzer, WILPF, during 1933 and 1934, attempted to broaden its pacifist base by cooperating with coalitions that opposed the growth of fascism in Europe and feared another imminent war. At the time, new organizations were forming throughout the country to deal with international issues as well as the economic depression at home. In 1933, after President Roosevelt officially opened diplomatic relations with the USSR, more and more activists openly expressed support of the young communist nation and more fervently opposed the Nazi regime that threatened its survival. As a result, numerous groups—especially on college campuses, in cities, and on the grassroots level—were organized more to protest fascism than simply to support peace. While advocating support of anti-fascist efforts, however, they felt that the United States should avoid getting involved in any wars.

Dorothy Detzer understood the need for WILPF to remain abreast of the times and at least to cooperate with the new groups springing up around it. Otherwise, the organization faced certain isolation from the broader antiwar movement—and possible extinction. Her interest in gaining support for WILPF projects, such as the Nye Senate Special Committee Investigating the Munition Industry's Work, as well as her concern for unity among the antiwar activists may have been the catalysts for her decision to link WILPF with a coalition of liberal and left-wing organizations calling itself the American League Against War and Fascism. Founded in 1933, the League had a small pacifist, Communist Party, and working-class leadership core, but it had an outreach to millions of people. Detzer felt that aligning with it gave the national WILPF organization the opportunity to reach out to a new constituency and to "identify" itself more closely "with the struggles and aspirations of the working class."[5]

Detzer's recommendation and outright support of the League,

however, did not go uncriticized by more politically cautious WILPF members. Throughout the 1920s the group had been unfairly red-baited. The WILPF national organization, always encompassing the liberal views characteristic of the Progressive-era reformers, supported the political, economic, and social betterment of society, a goal they believed could be achieved only by the elimination of war. More radical views expressed by such local branches as New York (and later by Denver and the South Side of Chicago) had always been countered and dismissed or qualified by national leaders. Therefore, Detzer's immediate support of the American League Against War and Fascism, demonstrated when she signed their first organizing letter, led to several complaints within WILPF. These comments, reflecting a wary attitude towards Communists, foreshadowed some of WILPF's later actions during the McCarthy Red Scare of the 1950s.

Ironically, the first opposition to WILPF's relationship with the American League came from the New York branch, which took an uncharacteristically conservative stance on collaboration with the group. Part of their cautiousness may actually have stemmed from their experiences with personal harassment during the Red Scare of the 1920s. Another part may have derived from uncertainty about the various factions within the Communist movement—Stalinists versus Trotskyites, for example. The women may have wanted to avoid becoming involved in partisan politics which would have clouded over their primary issue, peace. Whatever the cause, it can only be a point of conjecture, for the branch's documents themselves do not reveal the debates over the women's reactions to the American League.

In any case, on March 30, 1934, a Mrs. A. Rosenberg of the New York branch in Manhattan asked Detzer to clarify the national organization's stance on the League. Apparently, Rosenberg wanted to know exactly where WILPF stood vis-à-vis "Communists." Detzer explained that she and other pacifist supporters had been "very careful to see that the League should not be Communist-controlled." To achieve this goal, the non-Communist groups had "insisted" that the National Executive Committee of the American League reflect "a five to one balance . . . against the Communists." Detzer herself lacked confidence in an organization that resorted to such techniques to control one element. In her reply to Rosenberg, she tried to put a positive slant on her bal-

16. Playful photo of the Brooklyn branch of WILPF taken at August 4, 1935, march sponsored by the American League Against War and Fascism to mark the anniversary of the outbreak of World War I. Over 50,000 people participated. Courtesy of James Lerner, National Youth Secretary, ALAWF.

ancing act: "The Communists are so active and vital, so full of zeal and so sure of their goal, and have such a very definite technique of work, that they tend to dominate committees and it is only by vigorous and concerted effort to hold them down that the control remains in the hands of other groups."[6]

Evidently, the New York members were not totally satisfied with Detzer's response. In October another New York member asked her to clarify her opinions and those of WILPF on cooperating with Communists. Detzer responded that at its last annual meeting, a majority of the WILPF national board had agreed to cooperate with any group that "seriously" opposed war. Detzer added, "The Communist Party opposes International war, but does not oppose Class war. I believe that we should cooperate with the Communist Party, in so far as we could do so, openly declaring our opposition not only to international war, but to all war." Detzer, feeling that up to this time she had been very successful in differentiating WILPF's position from the Communists, stated that WILPF should cooperate and press its point of view with the political right as well as with the left.[7] What she did not mention was that her affiliation with the American League did not win overwhelming support with the national board either. The women on that body, although not as adamant as the New Yorkers, also doubted the wisdom of Detzer's actions.

A conflict continued to rage among the New York women, and soon the entire branch located in Manhattan began to express dissent with national board policy. In 1935 the board of directors of the Manhattan group requested that Caroline Singer, one of the few remaining World War I activists and former suffragists, draft a memorandum to the national board opposing its blanket support of the American League Against War and Fascism. Singer began her letter with a disclaimer, stating that what she was about to write was not an attack upon Communists or Communism per se but, rather, a heartfelt and objective examination of the policy of the American League in relation to that of WILPF. Singer maintained that although the American League was not identical to the official Communist party, it was not secret that the organization was led, inspired, and dominated by Communist leaders.

Because WILPF did not support armed conflict and communists did—at least in respect to class warfare—and because, as Singer asserted, the American League opposed only those wars waged by capitalist countries and those dictatorships termed "fascist," its stand was not reconcilable with WILPF's own. Singer concluded by requesting that the national board "cancel its wholesale endorsement" of the League, leaving it up to the "autonomous branches" to determine when and how to cooperate with that organization.[8]

The uneasy relationship among national and local WILPF boards and the American League Against War and Fascism that continued throughout the 1930s can be seen in the correspondence and actions of the New York women. The Brooklyn branch (240 strong by May 1935) raised a particular issue with Detzer in February 1936. Unlike the Manhattan women, the Brooklyn branch wanted to cooperate with the League in protesting the showing at the Loew's theaters of a film entitled *Riff-Raff,* which they felt had a "vicious anti-labor stance." Because the Manhattan chapter opposed any cooperation with the American League, Eleanor D. Brannan, the executive secretary of the Brooklyn division and a member of the League, wrote to Detzer directly to see whether the Brooklyn women could go ahead with their action.[9]

The issue continued to plague WILPF's internal mechanism. Yet the national board, seemingly unwilling to break off from the League, continued to support it, at least in name, until 1937. However, it also supported other coalition groups, such as the Keep America Out of War Committee (KAOW), of whose national committee Detzer was an active member. The KAOW, which leaned more heavily on pacifist, labor, and socialist support than on Communist party members, tried to counteract the influence of the American League in neighborhoods where it was particularly strong.

Nonetheless, by December 1939 the Manhattan, Bronx, and Brooklyn branches had experienced prolonged, adverse effects from WILPF's previous attachment to the American League. Throughout 1939, members witnessed attacks on friends and relatives who supported the nonaggression pact between the Soviets and Germany. Soviet-supporters —who believed that the Soviets were buying time to build their military before an anticipated Nazi attack—nonetheless became equivalent to Nazi-lovers. Because the German threat had become a reality in Europe, pro-Soviet groups were regarded as traitors even if the United States was not yet involved in a war. The branches' members had also witnessed persecution of those who had joined the international brigades in 1937 in order to fight on the antifascist side during the Spanish Civil War (1936–1939). Reflecting on their organization's relationships with other groups, they feared government-instigated repercussions. Moreover, the New Yorkers in general felt that they had lost members and money, not only because WILPF had supported the American League Against War and Fascism, but also because the League changed its name in 1937 to the American League for Peace and Democracy and was therefore easily confused with the Women's International League for Peace and Freedom. The New York women further asserted to the state branch that the Brooklyn and Bronx branches had been particularly affected by their affiliation with the American League as the League had tried to undermine the branches' autonomy. Women had practically fled the organization because of their fear of officially being labeled "Communist." As a result, Brooklyn, with over seven hundred members, was "reorganizing" its branch and the Bronx was "without leadership."[10]

The problem continued into 1940 when Eleanor Eaton, the executive secretary of the New York State branch of WILPF, which included the city branches, reported to Dorothy Detzer that "Communists" and "ex–American Leaguers" had made large inroads into the branches. She told Detzer she felt strongly that WILPF branches should be "warned of the plans of the C.P. to take over W.I.L. and other such organizations."[11] Within a month the New York State board, "under the interpretive privileges granted branches of the U.S. Section of the W.I.L.P.F.," had instituted a mechanism to protect itself from what it perceived as infiltration of its local organizations. At that time it resolved "that all applications for membership should be accompanied by a signed blank indicating that the member has read and agrees with the principles of the W.I.L. including opposition to all forms of totalitarianism, whether Nazi, Communist, Fascist, or Militarist."[12]

From 1935 to 1945, WILPF also developed a new strategy. In order to appear more appealing to the general population, which might favor peace but was cautious about affiliations, it intentionally developed a pattern of spawning new, timely subcommittees that proceeded to become independent organizations. Unlike the post–World War I splits that had resulted in the Women's Peace Society and then the Women's

Peace Union, the People's Mandate Committee (1935) and the National Committee to Oppose the Conscription of Women (1943) were developed deliberately by the WILPF national board to reach out to new constituencies for immediate, short-term actions.

The People's Mandate, a WILPF international project, was launched in 1935 on Jane Addams' birthday, September 6. The U.S. Committee came under the leadership of Mabel Vernon, a former suffrage leader, an active participant in the National Woman's Party, and the chief organizer of the 1931–1932 Peace Caravan petition drive. The purpose of the People's Mandate was to collect petitions entitled "The People's Mandate to Governments to End War," to submit to the world's leaders. Moneys raised through the campaign would fund a peace delegation's goodwill visit to South America. For the most part, the mandate campaign echoed the purpose and strategies of the 1932 Geneva Disarmament Conference petition drive. By having local branches organize activities for the traveling campaign members, WILPF could activate women and men all over the country and get its message across to millions of people.[13]

By January 1936 the Mandate Committee had taken on a life of its own, even though it was in actuality a branch of WILPF. Across the nation, local WILPF branches sponsored luncheons, speeches, lectures, and fairs to raise money and collect signatures for the Mandate Committee's work. As expected, the project received criticism from the usual conservative elements. In 1939 a report issued by the National Affairs Conference Board accused the Mandate Committee of raising money to send a group of "Communists, parlor pinks, fellow travelers and innocents" on a "good-will junket" to South America. These pilgrimages, "planned . . . and manned entirely by women," were led by one Mabel Vernon, "reputed to be one of the smartest lobbyists in Washington, D.C."[14]

The need that the WILPF leaders felt for diversification, through either building coalitions or spawning new organizations, was motivated largely by a growing sense of panic that fascism in Europe would continue to spread and result in another world war. In 1933, Hitler had already been appointed chancellor and been granted dictatorial powers through the Enabling Law. Within twelve months he had instituted the boycott of Jewish businesses and had authorized the construction of Germany's first concentration camp to house his political, social, and religious "enemies." On the other side of the world, Japan, with its expansionist eyes on China, the Philippines, and Southeast Asia, withdrew from the League of Nations and renounced its 1922 and 1930 treaties, opening the way for naval and military growth. In 1934, while Nazism was spreading throughout Europe, Hitler and Mussolini met and began their alliance. By 1935 the Germans had repudiated the Treaty of Versailles and instituted compulsory military training. The world was no longer in the peace-seeking mode cherished by suffragist peace activists in the 1920s. During the 1930s the entire peace movement had to move to the defensive side of politics, trying in any way possible to fend off the diplomatic blows to the peace gains of the 1920s and the early 1930s.

The central issue confronting each of the feminist peace organizations was how to react to President Roosevelt's series of neutrality acts designed to keep the United States out of a European war. The Women's Peace Union, WILPF, and the National Committee on the Cause and Cure of War all supported the concept of neutrality and the legislation created to support it. However, within the organizations there were divisions over the morality of remaining neutral when so many people were living under fascist systems. President Roosevelt and Congress produced three laws that sparked some debate within the organizations, especially WILPF. The Neutrality Act of 1935 specified that U.S.-made arms were not to be sold to any nations that the president had officially recognized as being in a state of war. In 1936 the act was expanded to forbid loans to any warring nations. In 1937 an amendment allowed belligerents to trade with the United States on a cash-and-carry basis only. Nations wishing products had to bring their own ships to pick up the material and had to pay cash upon delivery of the goods. In addition, U.S. citizens were forbidden to travel on belligerent ships. Because the Neutrality Acts treated nations equally, there was no recognition of aggression or of the spread of fascism. The feminist peace activists perceived a narrowness in the Neutrality Acts that stymied them. Although eager for a warless world, they were at the same time sensitive internationalists. The legislation caused them great consternation.

In 1935, when well-armed fascist Italy invaded underdeveloped Abyssinia (then renaming it Ethiopia), there was little discussion of neutrality among the feminists. Each organization apparently felt that, while the act of aggression was hideous, the U.S. government was correct in refusing to sell arms to either side. The Spanish Civil War of 1936–1939, however, presented more of a controversy, for the efforts of another fascist, Francisco Franco, included the overthrow of the legitimately elected republican government in Madrid. Franco's war, signaling a further, very dangerous, expansion of fascism within Europe, came close on the heels of the Italian move into Africa. In addition, because Franco received weapons and troops from both Germany and Italy, he had a military advantage. Although both the Women's Peace Union and the Cause and Cure of War accepted neutrality towards Spain without question, WILPF was not in agreement on either the national or the local level.

The additional expansion of Nazi Germany, which resulted in many tales of horror, also caused heated discussion. German military buildup through 1935 led to the occupation of the Rhineland (the demilitarized zone bordering Belgium and France) in 1936; of Austria and part of Czechoslovakia in 1938, and then the rest of the latter nation and Poland in 1939, bringing Great Britain and France to declare war on Hitler. At the same time, the USSR's move into the other half of Poland and into Lithuania, Latvia, and Estonia raised many questions about support of the Soviet Union. Whether to accept their actions as a ploy to hold off the Germans and protect their own borders or to condemn them as aggressors made neutrality less simple.

The national directorship in WILPF tended to divide into two camps over the issue of neutrality. Dorothy Detzer and Hannah Clothier Hull maintained that mandatory neutrality was the only sane choice for the United States. Detzer, in particular, felt that the nation should not take sides "in the old imperialistic struggle for the control of Europe—by trade agreements with other nations, and by helping in every constructive way possible to deal with the basic factors making the world chaos." Unless the United States could establish a world government to mediate all of the age-old conflicts, it should remain absolutely neutral.[15] Emily Greene Balch and Mildred Scott Olmsted, however, disagreed. Both believed that the United States should resist the expansion of fascism and aggression but use nonviolent methods derived from cooperative international effort. Moreover, they feared that the Neutrality

Acts put too much power into the hands of the president, giving him the authority to cut off even the shipment of humanitarian aid.[16]

The main point of contention among the WILPF leaders was whether economic sanctions could be used as a substitute for war or whether, in fact, they helped foster war. At one annual meeting during this trying time, Olmsted and Balch prepared statements supporting economic sanctions, while Detzer and Hull did the same for complete neutrality.[17] In 1939, Emily Greene Balch also stressed that neutrality was "impractical, amoral" and selfish in that it encouraged people to turn their backs on other nations' problems as long as they themselves were not harmed.[18] Reiterating this concern in 1941 in a personal letter to Dr. Alice Hamilton, she pointed out that "it is *not* enough to sweep before your own door, nor to cultivate your own garden, nor to put out the fire when your own house is burning and 'disinterest yourself,' as the diplomats say, when the frame house next door is in flames and the children calling from its nursery windows to be taken out."[19] Although the discussion became quite intense, the WILPF leaders felt that gaining consensus was important to holding the organization together. Even though they feared the growth of fascism, their desire for group coherence and for the avoidance of war led to their acceptance of neutrality, but with a hope that Roosevelt would seek an opportunity to act as a mediator. They in no way supported U.S. military presence to stem the spread of fascism whether in Spain, Italy, or Germany.

The national board's stance did not altogether please the New York branches, whose Jewish and working-class members were more intimately affected by events in Europe. In the case of Spain, the New York City branches supported the concept of Roosevelt's acting as a mediator but opposed the mandatory embargo of war materials unless the same embargo was placed on all belligerents. The embargo should include, for example, the banning of oil sales to Italy, which relied on the product to carry on its wars in Ethiopia and later in Albania. Furthermore, the New York members felt that unless the United States pulled all of its military personnel and ships out of Asia and Latin America, neutrality was a hypocritical policy anyway.[20] In 1938, the same year that Dorothy Detzer changed her mind and decided that in the case of Spain, where Italian and German military support had ensured Franco's victory, the Neutrality Acts had been unjust, the Bronx branch decided to withdraw from WILPF after seven years of active organizing. The group pinpointed the issue of neutrality as the reason for its action. In a letter to Hannah Clothier Hull, three of the Bronx women stated, "Specifically we find ourselves at variance with the Women's International League for Peace and Freedom policy on neutrality, since we believe that taking neither side in a conflict is analogous to helping the stronger side, namely the aggressor." In the case of Germany, the Bronx branch was firm in its belief that there could be "no peace unless this greatest threat to peace were eliminated or at least checked." Although military action was not the preferred approach, "the mere effort to keep America out of war [was] not enough."[21]

By the next year the leaders of the Brooklyn branch had also resigned in protest of the national board's neutrality stance. At this point, the New York City branches decided to consolidate in order to regroup their strength. On March 1, 1939, they formed the Greater New York branch, including smaller branches in Manhattan and Brooklyn. In 1972, Mildred Scott Olmsted, reflecting on the controversy within the organization, particularly lamented the loss of members WILPF suffered because of the neutrality issue: "at the time of the Spanish Civil War many of the liberals pulled out . . . because we wouldn't support the shipment of arms to the Spaniards. We said we were against the shipment of arms at any time to anybody. During the Second World War we lost many of our Jewish members. . . . During the Italian conquest of Ethiopia, we lost black members who felt that we should go into active support of Ethiopia . . . [but] we steadily opposed war."[22] The price of neutrality was high, for as war drew closer and womanpower more necessary, membership declined.

The other two organizations also suffered as war drew closer. By 1940 the Women's Peace Union was virtually nonexistent. Most of the active members had moved on to other organizations, leaving only a handful of women still interested in an outlawry of war program. For most of the organization's past supporters, the Union's program was simply unrealistic. Tracy Mygatt, the woman most responsible for Union activities at the time, felt that the group should actively support a program of neutral mediation, similar to the Woman's Peace Party's stance in 1915. Elinor Byrns, however, felt that a new approach would dilute the essence of the organization. She recommended that the Union become a study group on the theories of nonresistance, especially as taught by Gandhi. Then, when times were more peaceful, the Union would be prepared to begin campaigning once again for a constitutional amendment to end war. Mygatt, insisting that by 1940 mediation was "the only big tool" left for peace workers, tried to inject the plan into Union work.[23] She did not succeed. Instead, Byrns and Mygatt entangled themselves in a personal battle that eventually led to the demise of the already decimated group.

The National Committee on the Cause and Cure of War also needed to cope with the question of neutrality. At first the organization's leaders favored all of the neutrality legislation, although Carrie Chapman Catt herself seemed to agree with the sentiment expressed by the Bronx branch of WILPF. In 1939 she wrote that developments in Europe might just "create a situation which, if we do not go in, will place us in a dishonorable position."[24] As war drew closer, many of the more conservative groups under the umbrella of the Cause and Cure of War, aligned themselves more closely with the militarists, and, therefore, membership dropped. To accurately represent its constituency, the organization had adopted a far from neutral stance by 1940. At its annual meeting its leaders voiced support for President Roosevelt's public declaration of his intent to keep the United States out of war and requested financial and humanitarian support for refugees and victims of war. However, while supporting neutral mediation, not only in Europe but also in Asia between the warring nations of China and Japan, the women also seconded Roosevelt's policy of withdrawing economic aid from the Japanese aggressors and giving aid to China.[25]

Part of the dilemma over neutrality involved the Nazis' political repression of European suffragists, pacifists, and socialists as well as their religious repression of the Jews. During the 1930s feminist peace activists, committed to U.S. neutrality, reacted somewhat ambivalently to early indications of persecution. By the end of the decade, when reports of imprisonments and executions became daily news, the women took a more aggressive stance. In an interesting way, each organization reacted to fascism and the question of neutrality in a way consistent with its own pacifist or feminist ideology. For example, the Women's Peace Union, with fewer than fifty truly active members but a following of close to two thousand, had difficulties explaining its belief in nonviolence to a population frightened by Hitler's words and deeds. At Union headquarters Tracy Mygatt, attempting to express consistent concern for the European Jewish population, in 1936 amended the organization's membership pledge to include taking a stand "against every form of racial violence in thought, speech, or deed."[26]

However, neither Mygatt nor the other Union leaders wished to blame Hitler, the man, for his actions. In true nonresistant style, the Union chose to condemn the concept of Nazism, *not* the person behind it. In this way, the women could maintain their belief in the basic good within every human heart and deny the possibility that any one person could become the scapegoat for the crimes of a political system. To support this notion, in 1938, Mygatt wrote that there was a need for a "strong Jewish statement, pro-Jewish and *not* anti-Hitler."[27] The official Union policy stated that because Hitler was a product of World War I and the unfair terms of the Versailles Treaty, "In place of the hate-breeding slogan, 'Stop Hitler!', there should be one saying, 'Stop War!'"[28] The decrease in Union membership during this time might very well have reflected many members' inability to accept such a concept.

WILPF, with over 9,000 members and 61 branches in 1935, also stayed aloof from the Jewish issue, generally turning the existence of Nazism into fuel for intellectual discussion rather than concrete action. Dorothy Detzer, in a way, echoed Tracy Mygatt's sentiment when she generalized Hitler, saying that his rise to power was not a particularly German phenomenon, but, indeed, could happen in any nation where governments failed to cure economic and political ills. Blaming Nazism and fascism on the general economic and political upheaval caused by World War I and the Versailles Treaty, Detzer argued that the 1920s had seen "six new nations, six new currencies, six new armies and seven thousand miles of new tariff walls."[29] She maintained this view throughout the thirties, although the organization did show a humanitarian concern for its European sisters. In 1934, for example, Mildred Scott Olmsted joined an international WILPF delegation that traveled into Germany to inquire about its members, especially those being held or questioned by the Nazis. In the late 1930s the group consistently pressured a reluctant U.S. government to admit Jewish refugees fleeing from Europe. By 1940, Detzer was sick at heart—and enraged—over the horrors of Nazism but nonetheless remained committed to neutrality, continuing to assert that the problem belonged to Europe and not the United States.[30]

Once again, the New York City branches of WILPF did not take kindly to the stance of the national board, especially because so many of its members were Jewish, including approximately seven hundred of its Brooklyn branch participants. As early as 1934, Dorothy Detzer had identified some of the tensions between the national organization and the New York branches of WILPF as stemming from problems of "race," by which she could have been referring to either the Jews or the African-Americans, who had encountered difficulties in getting the more conservative New York WILPFers to support the Anti-Lynching Resolution. Although a substantial number in New York, Jewish women were a minority within the national organization. In fact, New York represented the only WILPF local area not dominated by a white, Anglo-Saxon, Protestant majority.

Dorothy Detzer wrote in 1934 that she thought it was "tragic that one should feel, in the W.I.L., at least, that each group must fight for itself," indicating that this was especially true with the New York branches, which simply could not go along with all of the national board's stands.[31] The New York women continued to feel a need to fight their own battles, some of which were based on ethnicity. In 1936, for example, the Brooklyn members supported a boycott sponsored by the American Jewish Congress against the buying of German goods or the use of German services. However, because such an action was frowned upon by the national board, the women were prevented from officially endorsing the boycott; if they wished to participate, they were forced to do so as individuals.

It is interesting to note that Carrie Chapman Catt, the head of the most far-reaching, yet most conservative, of the feminist peace organizations, the National Committee on the Cause and Cure of War, actually took the most visible stand on Jewish rights. The Cause and Cure of War, consisting in 1935 of 739 branches in 42 states, had a constituency of close to five million women through the organization's member groups.[32] As early as 1933, Catt began her petition and lecture work on the Jewish issue, the next year receiving the American Hebrew award for her efforts. Catt did not respond to news of discrimination by abstract attacks on Nazism as a concept. Rather, she chose to use concrete terms. In 1933 she wrote that the Cause and Cure of War leaders were "well informed" about conditions in Germany and felt that it was "worse than anything that has been told."[33]

Catt was also concerned about anti-Semitism within the United States. To one correspondent she wrote, "We ought to face this question frankly and if the Jews are worthy of equality in our midst, we ought to make bold inquiries as to why there is discrimination."[34] Because of her well-known position against discrimination, Catt sometimes received requests for help from individuals who felt they had experienced anti-Semitism within this nation. In a few cases she followed through on their complaints, worrying that the U.S. might be "getting Hitlerized."[35] But when push came to shove, Catt did not always act as boldly as she asked others to. After investigating the case of one young man who had not been admitted to the University of Pennsylvania Medical School, Catt concluded that the fault lay with the student and not the school. Basing her opinion on letters from a school official, Catt came to believe that in the case of Jews in the United States, extreme sensitivity may have resulted in "imagine[d] discriminations that are not really intended."[36]

The Cause and Cure of War spoke out consistently on this issue, especially because Catt, like the WILPF leaders, was personally concerned about the safety of her many Jewish comrades in the International Alliance of Women for Suffrage and Equal Citizenship. In 1933, at the start of her petitioning and lecturing efforts, Catt expressed her worry for the leaders of the German branches of WILPF and the International Alliance, both of which had received orders to dismiss their Jewish members. Both organizations chose to dissolve rather than to do so, and Catt, out of fear for the women's lives, broke off communications with them. She lamented her decision, hoping that someday things would be "different" and that "the German men and women, with a better sense" would "rise again and struggle to recover their rights."[37]

Throughout World War II, Catt tried to keep track of her European feminist colleagues through an active correspondence with Margery Corbett-Ashby of England. Although elderly and ill, she agreed to act as honorary president of the Suffrage Alliance throughout the war, arranging with Corbett-Ashby that, if it were necessary, she would house the organization's papers in the United States for safekeeping. Catt's correspondence during the war was filled with fear for the safety of those leaders whose fates she only later learned—one hanged by the Gestapo in Czechoslovakia, and at least four others, including Rosa Manus, liquidated in concentration camps. In 1939, realizing that the United States would soon enter the war, Catt resigned herself to the onslaught and turned her eyes towards the future. "The main thing to talk about at this time is not how to keep out of war or if we should go into it. It is to make ready for the peace treaty which will end this present war some day. If there are not brains enough in the world to think out a plan that will smash war to smithereens so that it can never come to life again, we are a poor lot."[38]

The Japanese bombing of Pearl Harbor on December 7, 1941, precipitated the U.S. entrance into the war. Japan and the United States had long vied for imperialist dominance in Asia. This war would finally decide the issue. Because of the Tripartite Agreement, the U.S. declaration of war on Japan brought a reciprocal German and Italian declaration of war against the United States. Neutrality was thus invalidated, and the nation entered the worldwide chaos. The National Committee on the Cause and Cure of War seemed to devote little discussion to the declaration of war. For WILPF, however, the situation presented a very real dilemma, one settled in much the same way as that faced by the Woman's Peace Party on April 6, 1917. Rather than protest the war declaration and face governmental repercussions, the organization decided to acknowledge the fact of war, to work for the protection of civil liberties, and to plan for the peace to follow. At an emergency meeting held on December 10, 1941, in Washington, D.C., WILPF leaders announced their acceptance of "the decision of the elected representatives of the people," adding that because it was their basic policy "not to obstruct the carrying out of the will of the majority," they would try to serve the United States by cooperating with the British section of WILPF in preparing to meet the problems to be faced in the postwar world.[39] The statement, prepared by Emily Greene Balch and Amy Woods, both original members of the Woman's Peace Party, exhorted all WILPF members to work for basic human understanding throughout the war: "Let us therefore do all we can individually and together to foster good will, tolerance, and understanding. Expressions of hate or to have those opposed to us suffer are unworthy of humanity."[40]

17. Women protesting imminent U.S. involvement in World War II, May 15, 1941, Washington, D.C. Courtesy of Swarthmore College Peace Collection.

At the same time, however, the women could not keep from expressing their anger at a government that had sold weapons and "helped to maintain in power the military power in Japan" rather than trying to create a less militaristic world. "It is one of the world's great tragedies," they complained, "that once again, efforts were made too late and that the awful suffering of war falls on the innocent peoples of Japan and the United States alike." Yet, in spite of their disappointment with even their own country, the leaders of WILPF maintained their stand that people must continue to work for peace. Their statement concluded with a reaffirmation of their beliefs: "Finally, we would point out that the entire breakdown of political efforts into active warfare convinces us anew that neither the United States nor the rest of the world can ever be truly free until the conditions of peace have been established for all nations and all peoples. Mankind must some day be released from the violence and suffering and waste of this recurring tragedy. For us, war remains the final infamy."[41] WILPF pledged to continue its search into the causes of war so that when peace was finally reestablished, the organization would be prepared to be active and vital once again.

Not all WILPF members were pleased with the organization's response to the war. Anna Graves, an active interwar feminist pacifist, expressed her frustration to Emily Greene Balch in April 1942. "Can't you see that Peace Societies can never have any effect when Governments *see* that when war comes they always crumble?—that their leaders are sure not to keep their faith when trial comes? What incentive is there for joining . . . when one sees that one cannot count on the loyalty even of the leaders of their own cause?"[42]

During the war years WILPF membership dwindled drastically. By 1943 sixty branches had disbanded. By the next year membership had dropped from a prewar high of 14,000 to only 4,708. At the war's end, only 3,789 members remained. But activity did not cease. Although the annual meetings for 1942 and 1943 had to be canceled for lack of a quorum, WILPF members continued to have study groups, to help refugees, to fight racial and ethnic discrimination, to support conscientious objection, and to plan for a peaceful postwar world. Consistently protesting the discriminatory policy of relocating U.S. citizens of Japanese extraction to internment camps, WILPF women often worked with the Japanese community both in and out of the camps. In addition, much of the WILPF international work was shifted to the United States (to New York City and Princeton, New Jersey), especially after the Nazi occupation of Paris in 1940. Gertrud Baer, one of the international chairs, was in the United States working to maintain the international group. When Gertrude Bussey, unsure that she could maintain the pacifist stand she felt that leadership of WILPF required, resigned her national presidency in 1941, Dorothy Robinson took over.

In early 1942, after looking around at all the peace organizations that had collapsed as a result of the U.S. entrance into the war, Mildred

Scott Olmsted marveled that WILPF had survived the first month and a half. She credited the organization's survival to its "roots," the fact that it was one of the "older, better established" organizations that might be able to survive the war. Olmsted also showed great excitement over the plans to establish the United Nations, a project that President Roosevelt had been working on with both Winston Churchill of Great Britain and Joseph Stalin of the Soviet Union. She told the national board:

> Few of you, I believe, will accuse me of being too enthusiastic about President Roosevelt! Nevertheless, I think we must recognize that in spite of the trouble he has got this country into, he is also giving us a kind of opportunity that we have never had before. The war is already shaking people out of their comfortable lethargy and making them accept completely revolutionary ideas about their own responsibility to society and about America's responsibility for the rest of the world that might have taken years and years of ordinary educational work to accomplish. . . . It is the opportunity and the duty of the W.I.L., which has long emphasized the connection between peace and freedom, to try to channel this new thinking into places where it can be most effective in creating a truly warless world.[43]

Olmsted emphasized the need for local work to continue through the branches. In 1943, Dorothy Detzer aided in this effort by traveling throughout the country to encourage the branches to keep operating. She reported that Michigan and California were active and that there was hope for a branch revival in New Orleans.

Even though membership decreased rapidly during 1942 and 1943, the Greater New York branch maintained an active program throughout the war, emphasizing refugee work, reaching out to women of color and educating themselves on the politics and philosophy of both war and peace. The reorganizing of the remaining Brooklyn, Bronx, and Manhattan members helped to strengthen and rebuild the politically strained Bronx and Brooklyn branches, which had lost most of their leadership because of WILPF's stand on neutrality and its relationship with the American League Against War and Fascism. Aging suffragists such as Katherine Devereux Blake, Frances Witherspoon, Tracy Mygatt, and Caroline Singer all continued to work out of the Manhattan branch. Throughout the war years, *Stepping Stones,* a brief branch newsletter, was distributed to the New York membership and to the national board. (It is ironic that *Four Lights,* the name of the much-criticized New York newsletter of the World War I era, became the name of the U.S. national newsletter in June 1941 and remained so through January 1970.)

For many of the members, the most important aspect of their work was the struggle against racism. Accordingly, they made an effort to build a truly interracial organization. Throughout the 1930s and the war years, all the New York City members held meetings specifically designed to recruit African-American women. Members like Addie Hunton of Manhattan were asked to be on the local boards, and branch leaders expressed a commitment to have women of color in all branches and on all committees. The one stand which the New York branches, in particular, took was that special "Intra-American" committees recommended by the national board were not appropriate. According to Caroline Singer, the New York state board member in charge of such local matters, it was discriminatory to have special committees for recruitment. The less racist path was to include women of color on the regular membership committees as the New York City women were doing. Singer lambasted those women whose perception was that "work with Negroes will involve close association with a culturally backward group; that W.I.L. members will go forth, like missionaries, nobly bearing elementary enlightenment to the heathen."[44] Rather, WILPF should emphasize that self-education and constant cooperation would be the keys to ending racism.

As a result of this concern with racism, the projects of the New York branches during the war years tended to cross color and national lines. During 1942, when most of the branches had dissolved into study groups, the Brooklyn members collected knitted items to send to workers in the coal fields of West Virginia, to seven segregated schools in the South, to migrant worker camps and sharecroppers, to refugees from Europe, and to an ambulance unit in China. In 1943, when news of the death camps surfaced, Mercedes Randall, then president of the Manhattan branch, emphasized the need to work for the release of Jews from Germany. The New York women were also concerned about the conscription of African-American men, who neither at home nor in the military received equitable treatment, and the exclusion of the Chinese from refuge in the United States because of racist immigration laws.

The draft, in particular, became a focal point in the national WILPF organization, and the result, once again, was an offshoot group with a life of its own. This effort, organized in December 1942 by such peace movement notables as A. J. Muste, Mildred Scott Olmsted, and Frederick Libby, led to the creation on January 7, 1943, of the National Committee to Oppose the Conscription of Women. Olmsted was hired to be its director, and the organizing committee assumed that women would do the work and make the policies and decisions. The Committee was originally created to protest the proposed Austin-Wadsworth National War Service Act of 1943, which, if passed, would make all women between the ages of eighteen and fifty subject to conscription. Speculation had it that the younger women would face induction into the military as WACs, WAVES, and SPARS, while the older ones would be sent to work in the war industries. Only those who were pregnant, who had children under eighteen, or who were caring for sick or elderly dependents would be exempt.[45]

WILPF leaders felt that, in a time of jingoistic excitement, it was wise to form another independent organization that could reach out to people who would not be attracted to a so-called peace organization during a time of war. The Committee's board of directors nonetheless reflected a strong WILPF presence, including such old-timers as Emily Greene Balch, Katherine Devereux Blake, Dorothy Detzer, and Hannah Clothier Hull. At its height, the Committee had 150 members on its governing board (although few did more than offer their names) and had over three thousand names on its mailing list.

In trying to appeal to as broad a constituency as possible, the Committee's propaganda utilized an interesting combination of both feminist and traditional arguments about the role of women. Although claiming to deny their opposition to the bill "on the basis of special privilege of sex," the Committee actually exploited the accepted sexual stereotypes and role divisions within the society. In general, the group took an antimilitarization approach to the issue, stating that the conscription of women would complete the process of regimenting society. Because this action would disrupt the very "root" of society, the family, the results would include "juvenile delinquency, the loss of family morale, and the dislocation of the foundations of the home." Furthermore, "the value of voluntary sacrifice to the community" would be "destroyed." Rather than forcing women into the military, the government should encourage their traditional roles as mothers, teachers, and social workers in order to maintain stability of the society while so many men were away from home.[46]

Just over a year after the Committee's initial meeting, Mildred Scott Olmsted made a radio broadcast opposing the idea of drafting women. She pointed out that because the military had enjoyed such little success in recruiting women, it was now attempting to exert force to accomplish its goal. In her argumentation, Olmsted once more emphasized the detrimental effects of regimentation, but she added an element of traditionalism that would have caught the ear of many listeners. "All" social workers, she claimed, acknowledged that women did not "take as easily to regimentation as men" and, therefore, were not attracted to "all the pretty posters and the flattering speeches" the armed services had produced. In fact, because women were so reluctant to enlist, they would obviously be inefficient workers if forced to serve. "A woman kept in any job for which there is no inner compulsion and against her will," she added, "is likely to act like a cat on a leash. Don't forget that a man may have the strongest will, but a woman has the strongest won't."[47]

In order to strengthen her argument that women were independent but emotionally oriented people as well as to appeal to the general U.S. public, Olmsted drew on the most traditional of gender stereotyping. Women, she said, were "naturally and rightly the home makers, producers and conservers of life." Both men and women found it "shocking" to envision women taking an active part in war, an intention "to destroy life." It was more natural, desirable, and acceptable for women to "keep the home fires burning until the boys come home." Men did not want women to fight, nor did they want them to share their public sphere. Rather, "sweethearts, husbands and brothers" in the armed forces wanted their women "to *stay out.*" They wanted them at home, maintaining what normalcy they could, raising children and "trying to hold communities together."[48]

On the other hand, Olmsted could not seem to rid herself entirely of her feminist roots in the suffrage movement and WILPF. She referred to the gains that the war had allowed women to make in both industry and the professions—gains that, she asserted, were beneficial to both husbands and wives. Women had finally been given an opportunity to earn enough money to be economically independent. Because army pay was so little, women had to be able to support their families—and they were. Moreover, women had fought for years "to be free from the domination of men." They had finally obtained the right to vote, to be educated, to work, and to remain unmarried, if they so desired. All of these gains would be destroyed in the military, where women would be given only minor jobs. There they would have "no real influence" and would fall once again under male domination, treated as inferiors, and lose their long-fought-for freedoms.[49]

Olmsted ended her speech with rhetoric echoing past generations of feminist peace activists who had portrayed women as the moral watchdogs of society. Ignoring the fact that millions of men did not go into the military, Olmsted concluded:

> In the insecurity that comes to everyone in a war period, the maximum possible stability in the home and community *must* be maintained if our American way of life is to survive, and only American women are left to save it. Compared to this essential service, the question as to whether women are equal to doing clerical work for the army becomes relatively insignificant. We cannot afford to draft women lest, as the Bible warns, 'we gain the whole world and lose our own soul.' America must keep its women free to preserve America.[50]

The Committee was correct in estimating that popular opinion would kill the Austin-Wadsworth Bill. Indeed, by the fall of 1943, the legislation had been put on hold because of the tremendous outpouring of public sentiment against it. By 1944 it seemed clear that the immediate threat of drafting women had passed. As a result, the Committee turned its efforts towards opposing conscription in general, changing its name to the National Women's Committee to Oppose Conscription. At this point, many of its more conservative supporters, who had simply wanted to preserve the traditional roles for women and to protect the family, dropped out, leaving mostly WILPF women to carry on. This they did, emphasizing the issues of racism in both the military and the society at large and opposing the lowering of the draft age to eighteen, which would "undercut the education of the next generation."[51] The Committee continued until 1950, with many state groups reporting that the work rested primarily on the shoulders of members of WILPF, the Fellowship of Reconciliation, and local churches.

It is remarkable that with the war and popular sentiment raging against them, WILPF and the National Committee on the Cause and Cure of War managed to survive. In 1943, although no longer active, Carrie Chapman Catt supported the transformation of the National Committee on the Cause and Cure of War into the Women's Action Committee for Victory and Lasting Peace. (After the war, the words *Victory and* were dropped.) The official transformation took place on April 8, 1943. The Committee, still in the hands of such former suffragists as Vera Whitehouse, Mary Dingman, and Laura Puffer Morgan, supported the idea of a United Nations. It also spoke in favor of a postwar International Police Force as part of the UN "to police the enemy countries of the Axis to avoid rioting and even civil war" and accepted the fact that some U.S. "boys" would have "to be prepared to fight to uphold the rule of law . . . before war spreads all over the world."[52] Catt, herself, hoped that the Women's Action Committee would continue the work of the Cause and Cure of War and that Catt's other creation, the National League of Women Voters, which had evolved from the National American Woman Suffrage Association, would also get involved in organizing a conference to propose new ways to restructure the postwar world. She felt that, after eighteen years, the members had come to accept that "the love of power and prestige is at bottom the real cause of war," and hoped that the new group would work to discover the cure.[53]

Indeed, in August 1945, at the end of the war, in a letter to Margery Corbett-Ashby, Catt supported proposing a "World Charter for Women," similar to the one composed in 1919, as a way of reuniting what was left of the International Alliance. "Women have done enough and suffered enough to deserve justice," she maintained, "and they should now demand it." Catt felt that because most nations were in a sympathetic mood and very desirous of building "a better world," there would be great interest in addressing several women's rights issues, in-

"THERE ALWAYS HAVE BEEN WARS—
THERE ALWAYS WILL BE WARS."

SKEPTICS SAID REGARDING:

The first steamboat
"It won't work."

The early automobile
"Get a horse."

The wireless
"It isn't practical."

Yellow fever
"It can't be stopped."

Human slavery
"There always have been slaves."

The airplane
"Man was not made to fly."

"IT WON'T WORK."
Courtesy Educational Policies Commission

There have always been skeptics. If the world had heeded them, it would have stood still.

Progress comes slowly, but the world does move.

Men used to settle personal disputes by duels. Today duels sound ridiculous.

For centuries war has been the accepted way of settling disputes among nations, but the time is coming when war will be as old fashioned as duels.

HOW SOON THAT WILL BE DEPENDS ON YOU AND ME.

We have the United Nations—a going concern. It needs your understanding and faith to keep it a vital force. Will you give it your support?

Or do you prefer the alternative? Death and destruction! In World War III no place on earth would be safe from the Atomic Bomb.

SHALL WE LIVE, or SHALL WE PERISH?

Women's Action Committee for Lasting Peace
1 East 57th Street New York 22, N. Y.

I wish to join the Women's Action Committee. I enclose ☐ $10 dues as a sponsor; or ☐ $1.00 dues as a general member.

Name........................ Address........................

181 Leaflet No. 180

Revised, January 1947

18. Flier from the Women's Action Committee for (Victory and) Lasting Peace, January 1947. Courtesy of Swarthmore College Peace Collection.

cluding suffrage for many of the world's women who did not have it, women's labor issues, and family concerns.[54] Catt died in 1947, and the Women's Action Committee disbanded two years later. By supporting Roosevelt's general policies, the Women's Action Committee had held on. However, with the death of Catt and the loss of the organization's basic emphasis on peace through disarmament, the group had little appeal to its original constituency.

WILPF, on the other hand, had maintained its antiwar stance, even though it too had muted its dissent, transferring much of it to the Committee to Oppose the Conscription of Women. Although the organization was down to a few thousand members, international, national, and local leaders prepared to rebuild it. In 1946 their efforts were bolstered by the presentation of the Nobel Peace Prize to Emily Greene Balch for her WILPF work. Of immediate concern for those still active in the organization was the establishment of the United Nations. Many WILPF leaders, while applauding the reborn League of Nations, questioned its charter, designed by the World War II allies who seemed to want another vengeful peace like that after World War I. Determined to have a say in the postwar world, WILPF women were present at the San Francisco founding of the United Nations. In recognition of its many years of international work, WILPF was granted Consultative Status with the UN Economic and Social Council in 1948.

Although the organization would eventually have to sort out its philosophical position, membership was an immediate, practical concern. Dorothy Detzer felt that the organization had a good chance of surviving if it acted quickly and reorganized. If not, she feared—unrealistically, as events proved—that the Women's Action Committee would "take over the field which should and can be ours."[55] But the job would not be hers. Detzer resigned in 1946, and Mildred Scott Olmsted was appointed to her position. At the same time, the national headquarters was moved to Philadelphia.

One of the main goals of WILPF in the postwar years needed to be the recruitment, not only of women of color, but also of younger women. Detzer, who was known for her stylishness, had identified this need in the early 1930s when she expressed a desire for young blood in the national office. She felt that utilizing older former suffragists would only make the organization more of an "old woman's" group "made up of tired people who belong to a feminist age which is past—conflict with men, and looking as unattractive as possible." WILPF could either recruit younger women or "lose ground."[56]

Detzer's reading of the situation was correct. WILPF did not attract large numbers of women under the age of thirty-five. In their quest to find out why, Roberta Kramer, chair of the Committee on "Youth and the W.I.L.," carried out a letter survey in 1944 of young WILPF members. One of the main responses, as Kramer reported, touched upon the organization's roots: "Our devotion to tradition leads naturally into our organization's identification with suffrage [but] . . . suffrage means practically nothing to almost all of my generation." Kramer continued, "To many in the W.I.L., the understanding has not yet come that the struggle for women's rights means little to us now. In fact, a mild counter-action has set in and to be very frank, militant demands for women's rights, in the vague theoretical sense, strikes us as somewhat ridiculous." Kramer went on to report that many young members felt that WILPF leaders gave "lip service" to economic change but really did not want it. Moreover, interest in race, civil liberties, and labor was "all too passive. . . . As one letter stated—the W.I.L. dresses too well. I might also add—they sit too much."[57]

Kramer recommended that both the national organization and local branches change leaders more often so as to appeal to the younger women's sense of "adventure." She also commented that young women could not usually attend "luncheons and teas"; that the organization did not offer them any "definite" jobs or "positions of influence"; that, in fact, the old guard often treated younger women in a condescending way. The organization needed to find a way to cut across class and age lines and, finally, to be more precise on its "basic minimum essentials of peace . . . as youth detests vagueness."[58]

Indeed, WILPF had its work cut out for it. Not only did the organization have to recoup its wartime membership losses, but it also had to redefine its relationship to issues specifically women's. A shift to younger leaders depended upon the recruitment of such women. In the meantime, it was obviously going to be the die-hard old-timers who would revive the organization. WILPF had confronted hard issues from 1935 to 1945. Neutrality, fascism, racism at home, war fever, and loss of members and donations were but a few of them. The Women's Peace Union and the National Committee on the Cause and Cure of War had faced similar challenges but had failed to survive.

On August 6 and 9, 1945, the United States dropped the atomic bombs on Hiroshima and Nagasaki. It was now the only nation in the world to hold such a devastating weapon, and the peace activists in WILPF were faced with a whole new international trauma. Because little was known about the bomb at the time, the group could not immediately grasp its significance. Within months, however, atomic weapons development became WILPF's central concern. In a chain-reaction response, the newly spawned nuclear arms race led to the domestic horror of the McCarthy era, when the "Communist threat" became a national pastime, and being a peace activist turned into a personal liability. This era would prove to be one of the most difficult for WILPF's integrity and survival.

6

The Effects of McCarthyism on Feminist-Pacifists, 1945–1960

THE POST–WORLD WAR II ERA included the worst Red Scare in the history of the United States. In the same breath that peace was declared, the Cold War with the Soviet Union was resumed. Allies during the war became enemies immediately after, and, as in the 1920s, those people within the United States who had opposed war and supported societal reform became targets of a raging government campaign to uncover "Communist traitors."

Of the issues igniting the Red Scare, the one of greatest importance was the existence of the atomic bomb—and thus the beginning of the nuclear arms race.[1] Several scientists working on the Manhattan Project to develop the atomic bomb during World War II had warned U.S. government leaders that it would be only a matter of four or five years after the United States had successfully built a bomb before the Soviet Union could have one of its own. This was not mere conjecture. Before World War II, and predominantly during the interwar years, research in atomic energy had been shared openly among members of the international scientific community. Until hostilities began, the atomic research community—particularly in England, France, Denmark, Germany, Italy, Japan, and the United States—had been homogeneous, as the scientists not only published internationally but moved freely among one another's laboratories and shared a network of personal relationships. Except in the United States war activity had slowed down the research, but the end of the conflict signaled the reinstatement of atomic research projects, especially after the August 1945 bombings of Hiroshima and Nagasaki.

With increased U.S.-Soviet tensions, the USSR was all the more interested in accelerating its own research, and in August 1949 indeed tested its first atomic bomb. The prediction of U.S. scientists had proved correct. Nonetheless, the U.S. government claimed that the communist nation could not possibly have accomplished such a feat without the use of spies. In 1950, Klaus Fuchs, a scientist from the Los Alamos research center, where the atomic bomb had been assembled, was arrested in England for confessing to turning over secrets to Soviet agents. The arrest of Fuchs was followed by those of Morton Sobel and Ethel and Julius Rosenberg, also for allegedly recruiting and supervising a spy at Los Alamos. The Rosenbergs were later convicted of espionage and in 1953 executed in the electric chair at Sing Sing prison.

Charges of disloyalty, treason, and un-Americanism did not result entirely from the development of the bomb. Government harassment of dissenters had been continuous in the United States even before the Bolshevik Revolution of 1917. During the Depression, when recognition of the Soviet state had resulted in new trade, the chilly atmosphere had warmed a bit, but events surrounding World War II had brought a resumption of distrust. Antiwar and antifascist organizations were watched carefully. In 1938, for example, when the Special Committee on Un-American Activities of the U.S. House of Representatives held public hearings, WILPF was criticized for its alliances with the American League Against War and Fascism and the American Committee for Protection of the Foreign Born, both suspected of being connected with the Communist party. Such harassment contributed to the internal conflicts experienced within organizations such as WILPF in the 1930s.

Even though the USSR itself was not perceived as a threat during World War II, the general public believed that Marxist-Leninist ideology was dangerous. As a result, Congress in 1940 enacted the Alien Registration Act, commonly called the Smith Act. Under this law, it was not only unlawful to advocate the overthrow of the U.S. government by force or violence, but it was also forbidden to belong to any organization supporting this concept. The Communist party and so-called Communist-front organizations were seen as falling into this category because Marxists talked about class warfare and the potential for a workers' violent overthrow of capitalist systems of government.

The growing paranoia about Communists taking over the U.S. government, starting from the local level and working up, was fed by

Canadian claims that a Soviet spy ring was operating from within its borders. As a result, in 1947, President Harry Truman ordered investigations into the loyalty of well over three million U.S. government employees. Three years later, anyone labeled a "security risk" was fired. There were no avenues of recourse, and many young careers were ruined. Soon, others were being discharged simply because of guilt through association. If a friend, relative, or acquaintance was suspected of disloyalty, so were you. No one was safe. Repercussions from accusations eventually reached the ranks of labor unions, college campuses, and the media. By 1949, with the Soviet A-bomb test, the rise of a communist China, and the continuing development of communist governments in Eastern Europe, anti-Communist sentiment in the United States reached an all-time high and was still growing. In 1950, when Senator Joseph McCarthy claimed to have a list of over two hundred names of State Department employees who were Communists, the hysteria entered a new stage.

Now labeled "McCarthyism," the Red Scare evolved into a series of nonstop hearings before the House Committee on Un-American Activities (HUAC). Individuals, organizations, labor unions, members of the motion picture community, and many others were ordered to appear before the committee. Organizations, in particular, suffered from the 1950 Internal Security (or McCarran) Act, which required members of government-labeled "Communist-front" organizations to register with the Subversive Activities Control Board and prohibited them from holding defense jobs or from traveling abroad.

The McCarthy era proved extremely trying for WILPF and other more recently developed women's peace organizations. Even though in 1946, Emily Greene Balch had won the prestigious Nobel Peace Prize for her work with the organization, the members still felt they were under suspicion for their antiwar activities. As the only feminist peace organization to survive World War II, WILPF strongly felt the arm of McCarthyism from its national board down to its local branches. During these years membership did not easily expand, and meeting places were sometimes hard to come by. But worse, WILPF members became suspicious of each other. The paranoia rampant in the broader society played itself out within specific branches of WILPF, ripping the organization apart from within. Weak national board policy only added to

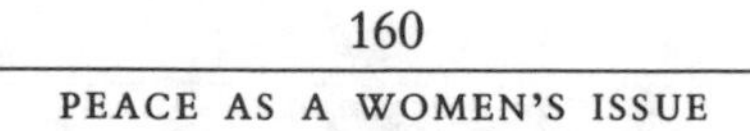

19. Emily Greene Balch in hospital reading telegram about receiving the Nobel Peace Prize, 1946. Courtesy of Swarthmore College Peace Collection.

the problem, and the WILPF legacy for the 1950s was marred by paralyzing distrust. In addition, socialist and working-class feminists who tried to form such new organizations as the Congress of American Women and American Women for Peace were also hampered by the

20. Emily Greene Balch's Nobel Peace Prize diploma, 1946. Courtesy of Swarthmore College Peace Collection.

laws and attitudes of the McCarthy era. Indeed, the period from 1945 to 1960 was extremely discouraging for those who wished to keep the feminist peace movement alive.

WILPF's story is one of the most dramatic. Just before Dorothy Detzer resigned as executive Secretary in 1946, she tried to expand the board's vision about what the new nuclear age meant to WILPF's own development. Even though the leaders of WILPF had reacted to the new threat soon after the atomic bomb was dropped on Japan, Detzer was one of the first to develop a clear antinuclear policy in terms of the organization's structure. "The atomic bomb fell not only on Hiroshima and Nagasaki but, in a psychological sense, on all of us," she said. Accordingly, the new era would require a reorientation of WILPF towards its work. Detzer asked whether being a "women's" organization would now be a disadvantage. Perhaps it was time to work more closely with men. Criticizing WILPF for having too many "Special Committees" that divided the work base, she sought a more centralized assignment of tasks. Moreover, she fretted over the lack of funds. "The world is not static," and, she added, "neither are organizations. We must evolve to meet the requirements of a new age or we shall disintegrate like all organisms which have served their purpose and must give place to the dynamic surge of new energy and new life."[2]

Detzer was replaced as executive secretary by Mildred Scott Olmsted, who worked with a series of national presidents—including Annalee Stewart, Elsie Picon, Ruth Freeman, Meta Riseman, and Orlie Pell—during the McCarthy years. Leadership thus remained in the hands of veteran activists, some of whom had experienced two world wars, the suffrage movement, and the active quest for peace in the 1920s. Olmsted, like Detzer, recognized the importance of rebuilding the organization to fit into the postwar world. Accordingly, WILPF needed to pay special attention to the work of the United Nations as well as to speak out against nuclear weapons development. In 1948, therefore, Olmsted pushed for the establishment of a WILPF office to be located near the United Nations in New York City. This arrangement would enable the group to be more effective in utilizing its Consultative Status with the UN Economic and Social Council. In addition, Olmsted favored the creation of the Jane Addams Peace Association (JAPA). Established in 1948 as a tax-exempt arm of WILPF dedicated to developing educational programs, JAPA was, in reality, another in a long line of WILPF-inspired offshoots created to attract a broader constituency than the mother organization could.

Throughout the latter half of the 1940s, WILPF leaders emphasized the great importance of its support of the United Nations. In a pamphlet on the subject, the organizers emphasized that the UN, like the League of Nations, was a necessary force in achieving diplomatic cooperation and "the abandonment of violence in international relations." As one of seventy-one international nongovernmental organizations (NGOs) to have Consultative Status, WILPF supported all UN efforts towards "the peaceful settlement of international disputes; the complete disarmament of nations; universality of membership in the UN; respect for the worth and dignity of the individual as expressed in the Universal Declaration of Human Rights; self-determination of peoples, and the increased use of the Specialized Agencies to promote world reconstruction by peaceful means as an alternative to world destruction by war."[3]

The WILPF leadership also recognized the connection between U.S. foreign and domestic policy. Because foreign affairs greatly affected the U.S. economy, WILPF felt that the best way to ensure progress and peace at home was for the government to actively support the United Nations. In evaluating U.S. behavior towards UN work, however, the national board found the nation lacking. In 1948 they pointed out various ways the United States could improve its behavior with other countries: (1) better U.S. relations with Latin America; (2) U.S. opposition to apartheid in South Africa; (3) civil, not military, control of Germany; (4) the end of the military occupation of Japan; (5) more women representatives in government; and (6) the general demilitarization of our own society.[4] As one national board of WILPF document said:

> The increase in military influence in civilian life is one of the most alarming trends in contemporary life. The appointment of military men to important government positions and the infiltration of military influence in many different channels constitute a threat of military domination never equalled in our history. . . . we are convinced that military domination not only increases the danger of war, but likewise endangers our freedom in times of peace, since the military system goes counter to the practice of free democracy.[5]

The national board urged, therefore, a "prompt reversal" from military to "effective civilian control."[6] Only in this way could the world begin to revert to peace and to nonviolent methods of settling disputes.

Closely tied to this desire to see the United States working through the United Nations to achieve a demilitarized world was a specific concern about the continuing development of the atomic bomb. WILPF had quickly reacted to the bomb's existence, as early as 1945, publishing a leaflet entitled "The Atomic Bomb and Its Message to You," which warned that the world needed to "Make Peace or Perish."[7] From this point on, work against nuclear weapons development became the focus of its program. In 1945 and 1946, while the United States and the Soviet Union unsuccessfully wrangled over how to control further nuclear developments through mutual inspection systems, within the United States itself, a struggle was waged over who should control nuclear energy at home—the military or a civilian-led Atomic Energy Commission. WILPF leaders favored civilian control, which was achieved in 1946. Three years later, immediately after the USSR exploded its first atomic bomb, Emily Greene Balch and others wrote a letter to the *New York Times* recommending that until a solution to the international control of the weapons could be reached, all nations "agree to stop simultaneously and at one time" the production of atomic bombs and the stockpiling of atomic fuel.[8] Although Balch and other members of the national board abhorred the new weaponry, they did concede that atomic energy, used for peaceful purposes and controlled through the United Nations, might be of some benefit to humankind. Atomic weapons, however—as well as conventional arms and chemical warfare—should be eliminated.

While dealing with the primary issues of international peace and stability during the postwar era, WILPF still had to confront its need to recruit a new constituency. Even though Dorothy Detzer questioned the wisdom of keeping WILPF a single-gender organization, the rest of the leadership favored the organization's traditional approach of finding a unique women's perspective on each situation. Suffrage had long since disappeared as an issue, but WILPF still emphasized the importance of women's self-education and political action. Throughout the 1950s the national board designed short radio spots encouraging women to speak out about the nuclear arms race. Specifically addressing traditional housewives and mothers, the spots were a reflection of the times, which emphasized the ideals of home and family. In one appeal the writers played on the name of the organization, bringing the concept of "peace and freedom" from the international sphere directly into the home:

> What we want to talk about is simple. So simple that it can be summed up in two words—PEACE and FREEDOM; we don't believe that the two can be separated. World peace and freedom! World peace so that you and I—and all the mothers all over the world—can go to sleep without thinking about the terrors of the Atomic Bomb or the H-Bomb . . . or any new, nightmare way of killing people. . . . Women do not want to send their husbands and their children to another war. None of us do. As a matter of fact, we know by this time that another war would reach us all. Our cities, and our homes would be battle fields; everyday people as well as soldiers would be the victims. You know . . . a bomb doesn't care in the least whether you are wearing a soldier's uniform or a housewife's apron.[9]

Another spot, once again concentrating on wives and mothers, emphasized the intelligence and patriotism of women. Unlike much of the media hype of the period, however, the WILPF radio messages emphasized that women who bought into the postwar suburban dream still had integrity, independence, and guts:

> We recognize that it takes more intelligence and harder work to achieve PEACE than to engage in War. . . . As women, as wives and mothers, and as good citizens of the United States, we believe it is important that we learn to understand peoples of various cultural and political backgrounds. That is one thing we CAN do—open our minds to new, and we hope to better, ways of living together. . . . No one has the right to withdraw from the world of action at a time when civilization faces its supreme test. The Emergency Committee of Atomic Scientists has offered this challenge, which is particularly significant to women . . . for in nearly every country, women today constitute a majority of the adult population and of the voting population. Therefore, if women were to use their influence unitedly on any issue—and especially on the issues of Peace and Freedom—they could change the direction of their own nations' policies and the world's thinking.[10]

As always, WILPF's work depended on grassroots organizing, and once again, the New York City women proved to be essential to its continuing efforts. Because of their geographical location, they had a natural potential for leadership in the UN work, which encompassed many issues of the nuclear age. Therefore, it became imperative to revive the depleted Greater New York branch once again. The problem was that many members had left the branch, some out of anger over the neutrality stance, others because of the lack of action to save Hitler's victims, and still others from fear of Communist party infiltration through the organization's relationship with the American League Against War and Fascism. By 1948 the few members who had remained through the war years decided to revive their branch. In June, Sarah Lifton notified Mildred Scott Olmsted that the group had been resuscitated as the Metropolitan New York branch, covering all the five boroughs of New York City and the "surrounding area."[11] Only the Far Rockaway branch in Queens decided to remain independent.

A year later, however, the branch was still suffering from a lack of active participants. The problem was not unique to New York City. During the war, several upstate New York branches which had, along with the City, made up the New York State branch, had either disbanded or, as in the case of Buffalo, moved over to the Women's Action Committee for Victory and Lasting Peace. When the Action Committee disbanded in 1947, the former WILPFers did not necessarily choose to rejoin the organization. Reestablishing a state branch seemed to make no sense at the time because New York was so large and membership so low; accordingly, each group fended for itself. At last, in October 1950, shortly after the newly reconstructed Metropolitan New York branch had decided to give up, Mildred Scott Olmsted convinced Orlie Pell to act as "leader" and try, once again, to revive the group.[12] Pell was a wealthy New Jersey resident who was then a publications and research associate with the American Labor Educational Service in New York. Olmsted and Pell had become acquainted at a national peace conference that Pell was attending as a member of the War Resisters League. Olmsted told Pell that she was determined that the New York City women be organized, not just for UN work but also to help the many national and international WILPF leaders who would be visiting the UN. New York, once an enigma to the national WILPF organization, had become an appealing focal point for its operation.

Pell set to work amid resignations, many precipitated by the growing threat of McCarthyism. At this time, the branch not only had trouble finding members, but it also could not easily find a meeting place. No one was willing to rent a room to the group until the Carnegie Endowment for International Peace offered them office space in their new building located opposite the United Nations. By 1953 the branch had once again become an active component of WILPF; from this time on, the national and local groups functioned more like allies than adversaries, with several New York City women sitting on national committees and participating actively in UN work.

Nonetheless, in true New York style, the women acted independently when they felt they needed to. On one occasion, for example, these WILPF members were involved in a protest against New York City's Civil Defense drills. The city government ordered the public to pretend that an H-bomb was about to fall on their heads, killing about 5,700,000 people. When the air raid sirens went off on June 15, 1955, the residents of one of the world's largest cities were to stop everything and take cover. Peace activists were particularly appalled by this hypothetical attack, and especially by its potential to frighten children. As a protest, twenty-seven people sat on benches in City Hall Park, refusing to obey police orders to report to bomb shelters. All twenty-seven were arrested, placed in police wagons, kept in jail for twelve hours (the women were denied food), and arraigned in New York City's Night Court. Among them was Orlie Pell, who, along with the rest of the group, was charged with a misdemeanor, that is, violating a section of the New York State Defense Emergency Act. Normally, such a charge would have resulted in a small fine and immediate release of anyone arrested. However, the presiding magistrate, one Louis Kaplan, set bail at $1,500 each and scheduled a trial date for June 23.

At the time, Orlie Pell was the treasurer of the War Resisters League as well as president of the Metropolitan New York branch of WILPF. Because the national board of WILPF had not as yet taken a stand on Civil Defense Drills, Pell could not officially represent them at the demonstration. Instead, she declared herself to be there under the auspices of the WRL. But once she was arrested and bail set, it was members of the Metropolitan New York branch of WILPF who went into action. They raised $1,000 of her bail by nightfall, not enough to set her free. As a result, Pell spent the night in New York's infamous Women's House of Detention in Greenwich Village. By morning, though, the branch had completed its fund-raising drive, and Pell was released.[13] According to Bess Cameron, an active member and future president of the branch, the publicity received over the event resulted in a spurt of new members.[14]

Even though the national organization was extremely active, WILPF, on the whole, suffered great setbacks from the rampant anti-Communist spirit of the late 1940s and early 1950s. While letters from HUAC dated 1952 and 1955 verified that the organization had not been cited as "Communist-front" or "subversive," the leaders still felt it was absolutely necessary to defend themselves and the organization against media slurs and personal attacks.[15] Unlike many other peace organizations during this era, WILPF took strong stands: it protested the nuclear arms race and U.S. military activity in Korea and worked to achieve civil rights for African-American citizens. Such stands as these put the organization in the center of controversy. So did the group's stand on free speech.

The leaders of the national organization spoke out strongly and consistently about both the red-baiting and governmental legislation intent on punishing political progressives. At its annual meeting in 1949, the organizers issued this statement: "We vigorously oppose all forms of discrimination against individuals on the basis of political opinions." Yet the women also seemed to feel it was necessary to add some type of disclaimer: "Fully recognizing the danger of fascist and communist totalitarianism, the League believes that such forces can be best opposed by open discussion and by the strengthening of our own democratic procedures, rather than by attempts at direct control."[16] The superiority of democracy to totalitarianism became a central argument in the national board's defense of WILPF. Because the Communist party embraced the concepts of class warfare, a one-party system, atheism, and revolution, Communists could not possibly fit into WILPF, an organization that, according to Emily Greene Balch, was "diametrically opposed to class war," favored a broad-based political system while endorsing no one party, abhorred revolution while favoring evolution, and welcomed people of all religious and political faiths. Balch, reflecting upon the rigid political system implemented by Stalin, asserted, "I feel that no honest person can be at once a member of the WIL and a supporter of Communism in the current sense."[17]

In 1938, WILPF had been described in testimony before the Special Committee on Un-American Activities as a "left bourgeois organization," which saw as its duty "to facilitate and hasten by nonviolent methods the social transformation which would permit the inauguration of a new system, founded on the needs of a community and not on profit." Dorothy Detzer, though described as a non-Communist in the testimony, had been labeled as "one of our original united-front workers" due to her efforts to cooperate with the American League Against War and Fascism.[18] Because of all this early negative publicity and the harassment WILPF had experienced during the post–World War I Red Scare and the knowledge that many Communist party members supported war, the organizers in the 1950s tried to walk a very thin line between defending free speech and denouncing the ideology of "communism." According to the national leaders, one of the "difficulties" WILPF faced was that of "working for goals which the Communists and other groups *seem* to be working for also" (emphasis mine). Just because the goals might appear similar did not mean the groups had anything in common. "We must insist that because we are espousing a cause which the Communists are also working on, does not mean that we are communists, fellow-travelers, communist-infiltrated, etc. OUR WORK MUST BE JUDGED BY WHAT WE STAND FOR, AND THE REASONS FOR THIS STAND. *NOT* BY WHO ELSE IS ALSO WORKING FOR A SIMILAR PURPOSE."[19]

WILPF's stand on world disarmament, accordingly, was not to be perceived as a means of weakening the United States, but only as a way of abolishing war—an organizational policy dating back to 1915. Similarly, the organization opposed the execution of the Rosenbergs because it had historically opposed the death sentence; it voiced no opinion on the couple's guilt or innocence. In regard to the Soviet Union, international WILPF policy was that each national section's main responsibility was to evaluate its own government's policy, not that of others (even though, as a group, WILPF did speak out against injustices such as apartheid, anti-Semitism, and slave labor). Therefore, the U.S. section could voice no opinion on the behavior of the Soviet government because its members did not live there. As in the past, national (or local) branches of WILPF, while not being required to support the international (or national) board's policies, were not allowed to work against them. In this way, the organization maintained both autonomy and cohesion.

This sense of togetherness was extolled by Mildred Scott Olmsted. In 1953, writing to the national board, she pointed out that as in the 1920s, WILPF, especially the branches, most likely had attracted some Communist or "near-Communist" members, who needed to seek out new anvenues for their work because they could not "dare" to organize openly. Even though WILPF, with its open membership, could not "disavow" them, it could control them because of its policy of not going against the national board's decisions. Olmsted emphasized that "the important thing, the essential thing, then as now is that our leadership always remained clearly in the hands of the genuine pacifists. Those who thought to 'infiltrate' us had either to content themselves with working within our framework and putting their energy into promoting our program or they go out. Eternal vigilance and hard work ourselves, not ejection and timidity, is the price of peace within our organization."[20]

Straddling the fence on the issue of Communism, however, became complicated. While the national board tried to present the organization as non-Communist, it was still strongly "anti-anti-Communist." As such, WILPF was one of the few groups that continuously supported the right of Communist party members to free speech even though its leaders disagreed with the Communist party's politics. Among WILPF's priorities for the 1950s was the opposition to all national, state, and local acts that attempted to restrict freedom of speech. There was thus strong antagonism to the Smith Act of 1940, the McCarran Act of 1950, and the Communist Control Act of 1954—the last particularly threatening because it set up a new classification of "Communist-infiltrated organizations" and provided for the imposition of sanctions against them. WILPF also opposed the use of loyalty oaths as an "infringement of the right of freedom of thought," the congressional investigating committees, and the "vigilance groups of 'super patriots.'" All of these tactics, the leaders of the national organization believed, resulted in a move towards a society based on "unthinking conformity, enforced silence, and . . . the penalizing of courageous dissent," that, in effect, "undermine the foundation of the American government."[21] Quoting from a pamphlet entitled *Militant Liberty,* published by the U.S. Defense Department in 1955, the national board used the government's own description of a free society to drive its point home: "the right of individual conscience being the fundamental difference between a democratic America and a totalitarian communist society."[22] In a democracy, the women stressed, dissent was a necessity.

National WILPF leaders developed their own interpretation of McCarthyism, one designed to further their quest for world peace. "The fear of subversion and treason," they wrote, "further encourages the extension of militarism and the police state in ever-increasing areas of national life."[23] Because of the Red Scare, they asserted, racism ran rampant, especially in the South. Moreover, the news media were censored, as in the case of a radio commentator in Oklahoma who lost his job for quoting a poll, published in the Communist newspaper *The Daily Worker,* that showed 71:1 popular support for withdrawing U.S. troops from Korea.[24] In addition, freedom of movement was curtailed when people were being denied passports on the basis of their political beliefs.

On an international level, the national board of WILPF attacked the Truman doctrine of "containing" the USSR through military, as well as other, means. Olmsted wrote, "We feel that our political leaders have used the great power and prestige of America not to heal the terrible aftermath of two frightful world wars but to deepen the schisms, to continue the destruction, and to fasten militarism upon our own and other reluctant countries, which, having suffered more than we, are wiser. We, like ignorant and foolish adolescents turned loose with plenty of money, plenty of egotism (self-confidence) and boundless energy are spreading insecurity everywhere." Warning the public that the United States, with its militarism, lack of respect for other nations' self-determination, and own domestic repression, was heading down "the path toward totalitarianism," Olmsted continued, "We who were so cruelly critical of the Germans for not resisting the demands of the Nazi government should look now at the smoke in our own eyes. The path toward totalitarianism in the U.S. is plainly visible to those who watch certain developments more than words and is shocking to those whose confidence in the deep rooted quality of American tradition has never wavered before."[25]

WILPF leaders, dismayed that all of this unguarded political control resulted in a frightened, repressed population, consistently expressed their opposition to an "alarming doctrine that accusation implies guilt, and that destruction of one's reputation and livelihood can be justified by denunciation by a political demagogue, an unknown accuser or a professional informer." The only possible solution the organization saw for "the return to basic civil liberties" was an alleviation of international Cold War tensions and "the reliance on negotiation rather than reliance on war or threat of war."[26]

In spite of—or because of—its strong stances against political repression yet its ambiguity on the issue of Communism, WILPF suffered during the 1950s. National membership hovered around only 4,336 in January 1955. Episodes in three local WILPF branches shed some light on the effects of the political climate on the organization as a whole. In such local branches as Metropolitan New York, Denver, and Chicago, the fear of being sucked into the national maelstrom of McCarthyism produced internal organizational disruption. Least is known about the Metropolitan New York branch, but from the information available, it appears that sufficient tension existed to cause disruption. The women still in the branch today do not like to discuss the 1950s, claiming that internal rifts have been mended and should be forgotten.

It must be remembered that the Metropolitan New York branch had always included a number of socialist-minded women. When in the 1920s the constituency of the group changed from Greenwich Village "bohemian" radicals to more working-class and Jewish women, the prevailing political bent did not alter very much. However, because the number of women had increased and the demographics had shifted from one neighborhood in Manhattan to the five boroughs of New York City, there was a broader political spectrum represented within the membership. Furthermore, although a number of the women favored socialism, it appears that only a minority were actual members of the Communist party. The effect of this diversification was evident during the late 1930s when the Bronx branch withdrew from WILPF and the Brooklyn branch leaders resigned because of WILPF's relationship with the American League Against War and Fascism. WILPF members who were frightened by the concept of communism and the possibility of Communist party infiltration of their organization began to look suspiciously at even their closest friends within their own branch.

In 1953, Mildred Scott Olmsted reported to the national board that WILPF was "remarkably free from outside attack," unlike its situation in the 1920s. Instead, the organization was now being disrupted "from within, by our own members who have become frightened by the current hysteria and want us to start labelling members and changing our traditional tolerant attitude." Olmsted feared the repercussions of these internal suspicions. "Attacks solidify as is well known to political leaders, but *internal* suspicions and lack of confidence, secret whisperings and the growth of cliques and factionalism can break down an organization faster, can be more fatal to its spiritual life, to its health and to its usefulness than any number of outside attacks."[27]

That same year Olmsted's fears became a reality. The Metropolitan New York leaders, in their fervor to keep die-hard Communists out of the branch, inspected prospective members before incorporating them into the group, a practice very distant from the usual WILPF openness. As one member reported, when most members of the Chelsea Women's Committee for Peace wanted to link up with the Metropolitan New York branch of WILPF in 1953, the women were informally visited in their homes by representatives of the branch.[28] Whether the Metropolitan New York branch was more wary of "ex-American Leaguers" or card-carrying members of the Communist party, however, is not clear. References to the American League Against War and Fascism abound in the New York branch records, whereas references to the Communist party itself are fairly scant.

The hints and innuendos evident in the Metropolitan New York branch records seem minor in comparison to the problems faced by the Denver, Colorado, branch in early 1954. At the root of the Denver problems was a 1952 incident in which the loyalty of an active Denver WILPF member, Eunice Dolan, was called into question. In the 1940s, Dolan's husband, Graham "Cozey" Dolan, had been the publisher of the Communist newspaper *Challenge* and an official of the International Union of Mine, Mill and Smelter Workers, which was headquartered in Denver. Eunice Dolan's participation in her husband's political work and her guilt by association became a branch issue. At the time, several members of the branch resigned, claiming that Dolan's presence represented an attempt by Communists to take over the organization. As they later reported, they felt that WILPF should "be on the alert" lest they get into their ranks persons whose methods were "counter" to their own. Being vigilant was the only way to prevent the organization from "being corrupted from within." Other members protested the accusations, reiterating many times that WILPF's "avowed policy" was "not to inquire into the politics or past activities of any prospective members" as long as they worked "WITHIN THE FRAMEWORK OF THE WIL"—and Eunice Dolan did.[29]

The local branch apparently continued to be active despite its loss of members until February 1954, when the issue was raised again. The instigator was one William B. Fogarty, a man claiming to be a member of the War Resisters League, the Fellowship of Reconciliation, and the Episcopal Pacifist League who had served time in prison during World War II as a conscientious objector. In 1952, Fogarty had moved to Denver, where he worked as a freelance publisher. On February 2, 1954, he joined the Denver branch of WILPF and reopened a Pandora's box that had been closed with some success two years before, thus causing several branch members to wonder whether his forthcoming actions had been preplanned. Fogarty conveniently had a publication, *Memo,* a newsletter reporting on the events and activities of the various Denver peace groups.

At approximately the same time he joined the branch, Fogarty distributed three hundred copies of *Memo,* which included statements about Eunice Dolan that had appeared in the January 15 issue of the *Denver Post,* alleging that she was both an active member of WILPF and had "Communist sympathies."[30] Fogarty's own article also named Virginia Jencks as another branch member with a questionable past. Apparently, Jencks' husband, an official of the same union as Dolan's, had been convicted the previous month in El Paso, Texas, of lying "when he swore he was not a Communist" and sentenced to five years in prison. Fogarty called for a "clarification of the issue," indicating he planned to emphasize it before the organization's April elections.[31]

The local board, which met on February 10, generally felt that Fogarty had "acted in bad faith" by reprinting the *Post*'s accusations of Eunice Dolan. Other individual members responded in various ways, including some resignations. The local board's minutes reported that one "octogenarian with all the fire and superior mental equipment of her useful life still intact" was shocked by the seriousness of the incident. She was "all for having the FBI notified of this real threat!" Another woman, a Ph.D. who had had a long career in the public schools, was "distressed" by the whole affair and resigned, taking another member with her who claimed, "I can't afford to stay in. . . . I have my job to consider—and my place in the community life." One woman (a "devout" Christian Scientist), however, said she was "much more worried about Catholic dangers to the U.S." and could not find time to worry about Communist threats.[32]

By early March, the Denver branch of WILPF had appealed to the national organization for help. Bertha McNeill, chair of the Committee on the Special Problems of Branches, began to sort through the details of the affair in an effort to save the branch from complete disintegration. McNeill, a resident of Washington, D.C., was one of the very few African-American leaders of the organization during the 1950s. An active community leader and member of several organizations besides WILPF, McNeill was asked to be in charge of handling one of the most sensitive problems ever to face either the national organization or its local branches. Letters between various Denver women and Bertha McNeill and Mildred Scott Olmsted illustrate the complexities of dealing with the internal purges occurring within the local branches.

One of the first issues to be addressed was William Fogarty himself. Who was he? What were his intentions? Officers of the branch, while suspicious of Fogarty, tried to handle the issue as diplomatically as possible. They told McNeill in early March that they believed Fogarty was "an egoist and a publicity seeker" because, even though he might sincerely desire to rid the branch of Communists, he handled the issue without regard for the reputation of the individuals involved or for the organization. Furthermore, the officers feared that Fogarty, in his quest for notoriety, might turn his attacks on the national organization "and do greater harm" than he already had done. The "basis" for their concern was, they said, his "peculiar actions, threat, and apparent unsympathetic disregard of the results."[33] When they had requested that Fogarty retract his statements, for example, he adamantly refused.

Fogarty's credibility was questioned again five days later when the branch officers further described him to Bertha McNeill. Even though the local women saw him as "pleasant," "young" and "nice appearing," with good pacifist credentials, they questioned his motives because he had managed to obtain the branch's mailing list without any of the officers knowing how.[34] Furthermore, Fogarty's article about the branch very deliberately and aggressively brought up a sensitive, but previously resolved, issue. His attack on Eunice Dolan was particularly pointed. "Some time ago," he wrote, "the question of Communist infiltration into the local WILPF, in which Mrs. Dolan figured prominently, came up . . . and a number of members withdrew in protest, while among those who stayed there have been expressions of a determination to press for clarification of this matter, and of a determination to protect their organization from perversion from within."[35]

In another letter, this one to Mildred Scott Olmsted, the branch's publicity chair, perhaps out of disbelief that a women's organization was being torn asunder by a male member possibly working as an agent for the FBI, inquired about the national organization's policy on male members. She also mentioned that Fogarty had just popped up one day—no one really knew anything about him. She questioned his judgment because in a city with military training bases and therefore well-known FBI inspections of the mail, Fogarty had been so incautious as to send her a postcard announcing that he had once been in prison.[36] Olmsted, obviously alarmed by the entire chain of events, asked the Metropolitan New York branch to check Fogarty out through their War Resisters League connections. The WRL responded that Fogarty had been a good member in the past and had done some organizing for them on the West Coast. Other than that, there was not much known about him. A follow-up letter from WRL organizer Arlo Tatum went so far as to say that if Fogarty had found a problem with the Denver branch, then there obviously had to be one.[37]

Meanwhile, at least two members of the local board had reason to believe that Fogarty was in cahoots with the FBI. One woman was approached by FBI agents three times before notifying the WILPF national board of the situation. Another woman—the only board member who had stood against Eunice Dolan after Fogarty's article had been printed—actually cooperated with the agency. At the same time that some officers of the Denver branch were furtively writing to WILPF headquarters for advice, this member sent a letter of quite a different tenor. She reported that in 1952, Dolan and her friends had taken over the leadership of the branch and that she had remained to try to "wrest it back into legitimate hands." She then introduced her "hush-hush" reason for writing the letter and to illustrate just how far the branch had "fallen." It seemed that she had been called upon by members of the FBI, who had sworn her to secrecy, a pledge she stood by until she decided to write to WILPF headquarters. She felt sure that Bill Fogarty had referred the agents to her, as she and Fogarty and his "charming German born wife" had become good friends. The FBI men told her that they had no intentions of "labelling" anyone but that they had "orders from headquarters" to "get the goods" on certain persons, notably Eunice Dolan. The agents asked this woman for her cooperation in pointing to "real subversive action" within the group.[38]

Believing that her actions were truly beneficial to the branch, the woman complied. In her letter to WILPF headquarters, she remarked that her behavior did not represent any "hysteria" on her part, for she had already "lived" with the situation for two years. However, "the weight of public opinion," already so against the continuation of the group that many of the "fine things" done in the name of "WIL" came to "naught," made her believe that she had to help purge "the disease in the body politic." Hence, she began naming names and, literally, spying on her peers. She had watched the activities of one new member, recently arrived from Chicago, who she was informed had been instructed by the Communist party to contact "the wife of Gosey *[sic]* Dolan." She also mentioned another member (recently resigned), whom, she alleged, the FBI called "practically in so many words" a Communist. One of the agents, she said, even attended a branch gathering "in company with a lady" and told her that he recognized "several Communist workers" in the audience. The woman also claimed to have heard from Fogarty that one active member of the branch, an African-American, was "somewhat suspect of being subversive," but she felt that this woman and her husband were driven to work with the "extreme leftist crowd" because of their frustrations over racism. As she concluded, "All the REAL workers for peace from the churches, FOR, WRL, and other groups" stayed "well away" from WILPF, "letting this undesirable crowd take control."[39]

Whether out of her McCarthy-era paranoia, her disdain for Stalinist policies, or her own concern over her place in the Denver community, this woman, like so many other normally responsible and concerned citizens, cooperated with the FBI. The Denver agents were able to feed her their ideas and manipulate her into giving them back the information they wanted to hear. Although William Fogarty was able to produce disruption in the Denver branch of WILPF, this woman was the force who could actually sow discontent and spread the suspicion and ill-will capable of crippling the group. Unable to deal with all that was happening, she resigned from the branch at the end of March.

As the national headquarters of WILPF became more aware of the complexities of the Denver situation, they had to decide to take action. The traditional WILPF policy, however, was to allow branches complete autonomy. In this way, although some guidelines were mandated on specific issues, the local membership could be as diverse and independent as possible. Throughout the 1950s the national board tried to retain its hands-off policy, but it was not always possible or helpful. In the case of Denver, in mid-March 1954 the Committee on the Special Problems of Branches called an emergency meeting. Overall, the national leaders of WILPF still wanted the Denver women to solve their own problems. However, the committee did take three decisive steps. First, Bertha McNeill offered recommendations regarding the upcoming branch elections. She urged the branch, on behalf of the committee, not to run any member for office who was "under suspicion" of being a Communist or any person who had joined the branch within the last year. The first suggestion followed the WILPF national board's private policy of being wary of a Communist takeover; the second suggestion would prevent William Fogarty from running for office. As McNeill stated, the branch's situation demanded that there be a new slate of officers who would be "above question" in the community.[40]

Second, the committee sent one of its most valued members, Kitty Arnett, to Denver to offer practical advice and on-the-spot help. Third, McNeill wrote a letter to Fogarty, deploring his actions as "non-pacifist and unrepresentative of the methods of the Women's International League for Peace and Freedom." She lambasted Fogarty for not first drawing the problems to the attention of the national board so that much of the bad publicity could be avoided. She also commented that his "method" was "such a striking example" of what WILPF was *"not"* that the committee could not help but feel that the branch's complaints about him were warranted.[41]

Kitty Arnett's visit to Denver helped by showing a parent body's support for its offspring. However, her short visit did not produce the concrete results the national board desired. To the credit of the remaining branch members, two other leaders with "questionable" politics were retained as officers. Mildred Scott Olmsted thought, on the one hand, that perhaps Kitty Arnett could have gotten other names on the ballot if she had had more time, but on the other, she acknowledged the branch's intention not to make "any more changes" than was necessary. This was especially true of one African-American member's position; the branch informed Olmsted that they wanted to keep her because of "her color and her liberal attitudes." Kitty Arnett disagreed with Olmsted's desire to elect new branch officers in order to solve the branch's problems. She felt that the Denver women were up against very serious red-baiting and that getting people who were above suspicion to serve as officers was exceedingly difficult. Once Eunice Dolan had resigned, much of the publicity surrounding her membership had subsided. Nonetheless, the leftist influence in the branch was still very visible. As Olmsted wrote to Bertha McNeill, those remaining Denver board members who were traditional WILPFers would be "very much subject to management by the strong-minded very leftist members of the committee, and perhaps that is the best which we can do under the circumstances."[42]

In spite of personal persecution, especially of the husbands of branch members, the Denver group continued to function. (One man was fired from his position as a senior chemist at a major corporation because his wife was a member of the Denver branch, and despite letters from Olmsted and others, his requests for the reinstatement of his security clearance were repeatedly denied.) Several members lamented the loss of both Eunice Dolan and Virginia Jencks, one local board member expressing her regret in a letter to Bertha McNeill, with a personal note added to Kitty Arnett. The letter reflected a deep-seated belief that labels are not what a woman is. She is, rather, her actions and her ideas.

> With regard to infiltration of the Denver Branch, you know that none of us ever suspected either before or after the Bill Fogarty affair that Eunice and Virginia Jencks were Communists. We do not know it now, and certainly neither of them said or did anything that would make us believe or suspect it. The policy of the

> WIL as we interpreted it was to judge a member by whether or not she was working in the organization according to the principles and policies. Neither of the girls held an office, except that Eunice was chairman of finance, as you know, and a very hard and efficient worker for the Branch. It is difficult to replace her. Both appeared to be sincere in their loyalty to our democratic form of government, though deploring what is being done to curtail our civil liberties at this time, as don't we all? We are all "sick" about the husbands of two of our most devoted members having been demoted and fired, respectively. I do hope no suspicion will be cast by some "faceless informer" on my own dear husband because I am in the WIL. But I intend to work for the branch as hard as I can, though inconspicuously, if possible.[43]

While the Denver women were wrangling with their problems, WILPF members in Chicago were facing similar frustrations. Women in Chicago, the original home of the Woman's Peace Party, had felt the sting of red-baiting back in the 1910s when Jane Addams was in charge. At that time, the office had been ransacked and defiled several times. In the 1950s the Chicago branch of WILPF, like the Denver one, suffered from internal membership purges. During this period, the Chicago branch had its traditional white, upper-middle-class membership as well as women from the city's South Side, a multiethnic, working-class neighborhood. Many of the South Side women, if not workers and union members themselves, were the wives of men who were. In Chicago, as in Denver, the problem centered around exactly how to handle the issue of perceived Communist infiltration into the group.

The women in Chicago demanded leadership from the national board, who would not provide it. Years later, Mildred Scott Olmsted recalled how the "struggle" in Chicago "came to a head" when the local branch president appeared before the national board, threatening that if "a very clear anti-communist statement excluding communists per se from WIL membership" did not come forth, then she and the entire Chicago branch would withdraw from the national organization. "I am happy to say," reported Olmsted, "that our Board kept its head and we refused absolutely to make any such statement." As a result, several members of the Chicago branch did resign, and the South Side section discontinued its own separate meetings. Others, however, remained with the organization while continuing to struggle with the issue. According to Olmsted, some of the "old-time" Chicago members who had resigned continued to plague the organization for years after. "Every time anybody came and wanted to join or a new person moved there," she added, "one or the other would quietly take them aside and tell them that we were a communist front organization."[44]

By April 1954, the Chicago branch of WILPF, like the Denver one, was crippled by the effects of McCarthyism. Membership was down, donations were dwindling, and husbands who were afraid of losing their jobs pressured their wives into quitting the organization. Some of the remaining older members continued to be suspicious of women they believed were infiltrating the branch in order to pursue Communist goals. These experienced WILPFers worried that the new local board, "who have not read enough or had experience enough to realize the danger we are in of the pro-Communists taking over," would not be able to prevail.[45]

Unlike the Denver branch, the Chicago women split into two groups, the more conservative attacking the more liberal. One member wrote to Kitty Arnett that the situation had caused *"great nervous strain"* on the "accused" women. She commented that the victims were mostly "mature women, several with children," whose husbands were situated in high positions in such places as the CIO and the University of Chicago; a few of the women were employed as social workers and teachers. According to the letter, at least four of them maintained that they had joined WILPF "joyfully, on discovering a Peace Group such as they had been looking for for years, and insist, in spite of the treatment they have received that they want to continue." This woman hoped that because seven of the older members had resigned, the new local board would "take a new attitude" and issue a "moral reinstatement" of these members so that they could once again function as full members of the local branch.[46]

The problems in Chicago lasted into the fall. Members continued to resign, several because, as one member put it, they had "lost confidence" in the national office for "its failure to long ago recognize the communist threat to peace and freedom, and its techniques for infiltrating and taking over organizations, and also the failure to give guidance to branches in meeting the communist threat." As this woman perceived it, WILPF had been infiltrated, and, even after two years, the national board seemed oblivious: "Sooner or later the communist group will take over."[47]

During the midst of this raging madness in Denver and Chicago, the national board, under pressure especially from Chicago, formed a committee that issued a "Packet on Infiltration and Attack."[48] The eight-page, single-spaced, typed memo was designed to aid each branch in its struggles with the effects of McCarthyism. The national committee indicated that it did not wish to create alarm if none existed or to cause branches to look for problems where there were none. Nonetheless, the national board was aware that "some" branches felt very strongly that WILPF faced "two dangers: (1) attempts by 'leftists' to use WIL for their own ends and (2) attempts by 'rightists' to accuse WIL of communism and thus discredit us and render our work ineffective." As a result, the committee felt a need to remind its members that the organization was devoted to the concepts of "PEACE AND FREEDOM," not only on the international level, but right down to the grassroots level of the community. But, the national board, in its efforts to advise its members, once again took an anti-Communist stand while declaring WILPF to be open and broad-minded. The opening statement concluded with rather a positive, yet cautious, tone: "Therefore, in our effort to keep our organization free from subversion and to defend it from overt attacks, we must neither abandon our basic principles and program nor stoop to the totalitarian methods we abhor. The challenge before us is, not to ignore the realities of our situation, but to deal with them by sane and worthy means" (p. 1).

The first section of the packet, which emphasized the importance of members "maintaining confidence" in WILPF's basic principles and nonviolent methods of operation, pointed out the number of times the organization had been misunderstood by the government, the media, and the public. During World War I, the women were accused of being "German sympathizers" because they opposed the war. During World War II, they were "charged with ignoring the moral issues involved" because they did not "join in the chorus of hate" against the Germans and the Japanese. Then, in 1954, the organization was "sometimes" accused of being "sympathetic" with communism. This latter accusation was more difficult to avoid because Communists often spoke in terms of "peace and freedom" and often supported goals similar to WILPF's, such as "peace, the rights of subject peoples, the meeting of men's basic economic needs" (pp. 1–2).

The danger to WILPF, as the national leaders perceived it, was from both Communists and anti-Communists. "The danger from the Communists is the more obvious, both because of their power and of their confessed totalitarian philosophy. But in many places, their opponents with different political creeds are using similar methods in an attempt to control men's minds" (p. 2). WILPF's job was to fight Communism "and other forms of totalitarianism" by using "democratic" means. "We do not have to choose between communist infiltration and methods of witch-hunting, character assassination and demagoguery. Both are evil; both are threats to freedom and democracy. We repudiate both" (p. 2). Free discussion, decision making by consensus, and constant open debate were ways to insure WILPF's openness and integrity.

The national board's basic complaint about U.S. communists was that they tended to follow a doctrinaire approach to organizing that echoed the Soviet Union's own Stalinist style. WILPF consistently distinguished itself from Communists, contrasting its beliefs with the Communists' alleged support of totalitarianism and rhetoric of "class warfare." What it could not acknowledge was that many of its working-class and African-American members often believed in the solutions to social, economic, and political problems offered by communist ideology, while still embracing the principle of nonviolence. In addition, the leaders could not accept that many "communists" in the United States who might not even be party members believed in open discussion and all the other "democratic" principles to which the WILPF leaders adhered. In a difficult era, the national WILPF leaders' attempts to maintain their organization's integrity resulted in their portraying all communists as violent, dictatorial Stalinists. In doing so, they unintentionally made it all too easy to accept persecution not only of longtime loyal members but also of some of the newer blood they so desperately wanted to attract.

The "Packet on Infiltration and Attack" revealed an inability to distinguish between a person who believed in the concept of communism and an unquestioning supporter of the Soviet Union. The organization seemed to accept without question the government's informal use of the term *communist* to mean any person who was literally controlled by the Communist party, which allegedly got its orders from Moscow—in other words, a person whose primary allegiance was to the Soviet Union. Part 3 of the "Packet," entitled "Dealing with Communist Infiltration," for example, advised branches that there were several "problems" that WILPF members were "obligated to give serious attention to." One of these problems was: "How we may distinguish between the liberal or non-conformist citizen who is loyal to his country and the individual who gives his allegiance to another country by adhering to a party line dictated by that country." Another "problem" stated: "How we may demonstrate to the world that democracy has more to offer than communism *(a)* by upholding at home the things for which democracy stands and *(b)* by helping the underprivileged peoples of the world to achieve the better life which communism promises but cannot deliver." The final "problem" stipulated: "How we may implement our conviction that the one sure defense against communism and related evils is a passionate commitment to the search for truth coupled with eternal vigilance against the enemies of truth and freedom; and how we may express this conviction through positive and constructive programs and activities in which people can engage and by which they may ensure the survival of free institutions" (pp. 4–5).

Next, the committee advised branch leaders on how to identify "Signs of possible infiltration." These included:

> 1. Members who want the branch to select from the WILPF program only those issues in which the Communist Party is interested and to neglect all other parts of the program.
>
> 2. Members who are totally uncritical of the U.S.S.R. and who do not show a balanced judgement in their criticism of U.S. policies.
>
> 3. A group of members fairly new in the WILPF, who seem to be trying to use offices to control program and policy for the Branch (p. 5).

Once these members were identified, they should be guided to recognize on their own that the WILPF principles and program were "genuinely better." Many of these women could become excellent WILPFers. On the other hand, the "Packet" warned that WILPF members who had joined "front" organizations, signed petitions, or had "leftist tendencies" should not be "condemned," as WILPF "welcomed diversity" (p. 5). Where to draw the line and how to define each member's attitudes was left up to the branches. If any branch needed help, it was to report the problem to the Committee on the Special Problems of Branches, which had been set up specifically to meet this crisis. (It is interesting that the "Packet" used the terms *men* and *he,* while most other WILPF documents utilized the term *women.*)

It is amazing that WILPF could be as productive as it was in the 1950s. As the FBI documents released under the Freedom of Information Act indicate, many WILPF branches were placed under surveillance. In addition, in places such as Kentucky, Rhode Island, Florida, and Massachusetts, WILPF members were called before HUAC, even though not overtly as WILPFers. Yet work continued, whether it was in opposition to the Korean conflict or the nuclear arms race or in support of the United Nations or, especially, the civil rights movement. The organization persisted in voicing its opinions through the 1950s and beyond. During this era, however, WILPF did not attract many women who embraced clearly feminist goals. Local tensions such as those in Denver, Chicago, and New York (and there is evidence that these were not the only branches to experience disruption), combined with the national office's rather confusing and often irritating stance on communism, probably kept many prospective members at bay. In addition, although WILPF still emphasized its suffragist roots and relished its female leadership, the organization had ceased emphasizing women's rights issues back in the 1920s. Women who wanted to be more militantly feminist-pacifist and who found no appeal in WILPF turned to two other newly formed organizations in order to work for both world peace and women's rights: the Congress of American Women (CAW) and American Women for Peace (AWP).

Most is known about the Congress of American Women, which grew out of the first World Congress of Women.[49] The meeting, held in Paris on November 26, 1945, was called by the Union des Femmes Françaises, a group of female leaders from the French Resistance movement of World War II. The congress attracted over eight hundred women from forty-one different nations, many from Eastern Europe. Included were representatives from England, China, India, the United States, the

Soviet Union, Spain, Finland, "the liberated European countries," Poland, Greece, Yugoslavia, Hungary, and Czechoslovakia. Unlike WILPF conferences before World War II, which had attracted mostly wealthier women, this congress consisted largely of "housewives, working women, trade unionists, farmers, doctors, lawyers, artists and women in government." The result of the meeting was the founding of the Women's International Democratic Federation (WIDF), whose platform reflected a strong feminist stance: "(1) The eradication of all remnants of Fascism in every country in the world, and the maintenance of world peace; (2) The advance of women into full economic, political and legal status; and (3) The full protection of children in health, in education and the realization of their special talents and abilities."[50]

The founders of the WIDF reiterated the belief held by former suffragists throughout the 1920s that women could not achieve their rights in an unjust society. Political, economic, and social conditions had to change in order to allow for women's equality. In addition, women's advancement depended upon the "liquidation" of illiteracy. Only through open "access to all avenues of education and vocational training" could women become full participants in the "cultural life" of their communities.[51] Like the earlier suffragists, the women of the WIDF noted the importance of national self-determination and the elimination of racism and apartheid as basic elements for the success of their program. Likewise, they embraced the overall concept of world peace and universal disarmament as the ultimate goals of their organization.

During the war, women as well as men had struggled for peace and freedom. Now, the WIDF emphasized, women too should have the right to enjoy the fruits of their labors. Accordingly, the organizers of the Congress of American Women chose International Women's Day, March 8, 1946, to issue a press release on the subject:

> The Congress of Women recounted in many ways the heroic role of women in the struggle against fascism and the place in the life of their countries which they have won and must sustain. The millions of women who plowed fields, sowed the grain and reaped the harvest, the thousands who worked in factories building the planes, the tanks and the ammunition for victory, the women who nursed the wounded, gave themselves to the dangerous work of

> the Resistance, and in an atmosphere of fear and death strove to preserve the remnants of a home for their children—these women in the days of privation and suffering proved that they were superbly capable of sharing responsibility with men for the economic, political, social and cultural regeneration and growth of their countries. These women told of the old and the new status which women hold, of their determination to achieve complete citizenship by reason of the fact that they earned it.[52]

In February 1946, soon after this initial meeting, the U.S. representatives to the conference formed the Congress of American Women, the U.S. branch of the WIDF. In some ways, the women who worked for the CAW resembled those in the local WILPF branches in New York, Chicago, and Denver. There were a number of professionals, such as Dr. Gene Weltfish, an anthropologist at Columbia University; Dr. Beryl Parker, an educator; Jacqueline Cochran, a famous aviator who became the director of Eastern Airlines; Florence Eldridge March, an actress and wife of actor Frederick March; and Cornelia Bryce Pinchot, a former suffragist. There were also several women whose activities concentrated on political or union organizing, including Muriel Draper, chair of the Committee of Women of the Council of American Soviet Friendship; Ann Bradford, a member of the CIO auxiliary; Elizabeth Gurley Flynn, the elderly and respected labor leader and chair of the Women's Commission of the Communist Party of America; and Claudia Jones, another Communist party member. As the CAW intended to build a racially balanced organization from the very beginning, women of color were called on to participate in the initial organizing. These women included Dr. Charlotte Hawkins Brown, Thelma Dale, and Vivian Carter Mason, all active leaders in national African-American and civil rights organizations. The basic difference between national WILPF leadership and the CAW's was that the latter openly involved known Communists in its leadership and did not try to avoid the issue during the McCarthy era. The end result was disastrous.

The CAW got off to an active start. It was the first feminist peace organization to hold celebrations on March 8 for International Women's Day, a holiday celebrated in the communist world at that time but almost ignored here. The festivities pointed up the organization's femi-

21. Congress of American Women protesting President Harry Truman's "containment" policy, March 25, 1947. Courtesy of Swarthmore College Peace Collection.

nist and antifascist roots during one of the most reactionary times in U.S. history. In May the group held its first working conference at New York's Essex House. For the nearly five hundred delegates, the important issues centered around women's postwar unemployment, health care needs, and the equal rights amendment. Soon after this meeting, CAW representatives appeared before a hearing in the nation's capital in favor of the Pepper-Norton Maternal and Child Welfare Act, which would have established a national health program for children and pregnant women. Former suffragists in the 1920s had lobbied for a similar bill, which had passed as the Sheppard-Towner Act, but whose funding ended in June 1927. The CAW, like WILPF, also placed great emphasis on women's rights and on supporting the mission of the United Nations to create "a true peace for the world."[53] In this effort, the CAW women also recognized the importance of building upon their friendship with Soviet women begun in Paris.

A strong multinational, interracial, and cross-class stance of the Congress of American Women reflected its close identity with the WIDF. It ambitiously recruited working-class women and women of color. The organization's pamphlets emphasized the importance of women in U.S. history, using as examples suffragists such as Lucretia Mott, Susan B. Anthony, and Elizabeth Cady Stanton and such African-American leaders as Sojourner Truth and Harriet Tubman. The writings also stressed the importance of the nineteenth-century Lowell mill girls and the women garment workers of the early twentieth century. By 1949, the CAW claimed 250,000 members. There were branches in New York City, Cleveland, Chicago, Pittsburgh, Los Angeles, Detroit, Milwaukee, and Seattle. Affiliates included several labor and social organizations. The CAW's Commission on the Status of Women was chaired by Susan B. Anthony II, the grandniece of the suffrage leader. The commission emphasized the need for equal pay for equal work, job training for women, the elimination of racial discrimination at work, the support of child-care centers, the institution of low-cost carry-home dinners or in-plant feeding for workers, and the benefits of communal kitchens and dining areas in public housing projects. The commission also called for equal educational opportunities for women and the elimination of quotas for admission into medical schools.[54]

In 1948 the full fury of the Red Scare fell upon the CAW. The organization was viewed as particularly suspect because it was a branch of the WIDF, which received substantial support from the Soviet Union. Unlike WILPF, which avoided direct governmental assault, the CAW was placed by the U.S. attorney general on the list of subversive organizations. The California Committee on Un-American Activities referred to the organization as "one of the most potentially dangerous of the many active communist-fronts."[55] Participation in WIDF conferences held in Eastern Europe did not help the CAW's image. The press saw the members as gullible and pro-Soviet and depicted the organization as anti-American. HUAC started an investigation, citing the organization as subversive. In its *Report on the Congress of American Women,* published in 1949, HUAC discredited the CAW's professed connection with the women's rights movement, calling the identification "fraudulent." The report particularly criticized Susan B. Anthony II and Elizabeth Cady Stanton's granddaughter, Nora Stanton Barney, for affiliating with the group.[56] Despite these accusations, the CAW continued to sponsor activities and issue policy statements until January 1950. At that time, the Department of Justice ordered the organization's board to register as "foreign agents." As a means of trying to avoid further harassment, the CAW leaders voted to sever connections with the WIDF. In such a political climate, however, the effort was too little and too late. By later that year, rather than register with the Justice Department, the organization's leaders voted to disband because they could not afford to take on the expense of a legal battle.

About the same time that the Congress of American Women was succumbing to federal pressure, another organization, calling itself American Women for Peace (AWP), emerged. The organization, about which little is known, appears to have existed from August 8, 1950, through at least 1953. Several names from the now defunct CAW appeared on the rolls of the AWP, many of them representing labor unions and organizations of women of color. In the summer of 1951, the organizers of the AWP participated in the Chicago Peace Congress, an event coordinated with the WIDF.

American Women for Peace, reflecting the early suffrage connection between motherhood and peace, in its "Declaration of Principles" stated, "Because the privilege of giving birth is uniquely the labor of women, it becomes a natural responsibility of all women to preserve life, and especially to protect it from the dangers of useless and criminal warfare." The "Declaration" supported the principles of mediation and negotiation as they might be manifested in the workings of the United Nations. It continued: "The lives of our daughters and sons can be secure only in a world at peace—a world which will steadfastly safeguard the health, education and welfare of its future generations." If peace were to be achieved, nuclear weapons had to be banned, confrontations such as the one then taking place in Korea mediated and settled, and the concept of "preventive" warfare rejected. To reach these goals, women of all races, ethnic backgrounds, and classes needed to organize. The AWP was willing to function as an umbrella organization as well as an individual association. Thereby, it could become "a source of strength for all women throughout our great country," so that the voices for peace would "never be hushed" and the fight for peace would be carried on "with greater vigor than ever before."[57]

Within two years American Women for Peace had branches in Chicago, Salt Lake City, Boston, and Los Angeles as well as in five New York City neighborhoods—the East Bronx, Tremont, Harlem, Yorkville, and the Interborough. Addressing issues of peace and justice, the organization considered both domestic and international perspectives. Under the auspices of the group, African-American poet Beulah Richardson (later known as Beah Richards) wrote "A Black Woman Speaks of White Womanhood—of White Supremacy—of Peace," a poem that emphasized the crime of lynching. In addition, the organization worked with local PTAs in the hope of stopping civil defense drills that "terrorized" young children with fears of atomic warfare. Two thousand women marched under its auspices in Los Angeles on Mother's Day, 1951, to protest nuclear weapons; in 1953 the organization sent representatives to the World Congress of Women.[58]

American Women for Peace, like the Congress of American Women, was short-lived. So was another small but intriguing effort to organize women's rights activists for peace during the McCarthy era. This final effort was an attempt by author Dorothy Thompson to "mobilize the women of the world into a single powerful group which can speak out in a unified voice to DEMAND PEACE." Like the AWP, Thompson's World Organization of Mothers of All Nations, known as Woman, Inc., was intended to help individuals or groups "influence public opinion throughout our country and the world."[59] During the existence of Woman, Inc. (from 1946 to early 1952), Thompson tried to organize women, as both mothers and political beings, into letter-writing lobbyists for peace. Thompson argued that "The woman knows that war is the cancer of society, the running amok of its cells, the destroyer of its focussing point, the home, and as such the violator of the purposes of all human activity."[60] Thompson utilized the pages of the *Ladies' Home Journal* to begin her organizing. In February 1946, for example, she wrote an article entitled "A woman says, 'You must come into the room of your mother unarmed.'" In it she attempted, by addressing the "Gentlemen" of the UN Security Council, to convince women that people are naturally peace-loving and peace-seeking.[61] In a follow-up article the next year, she implored women, especially mothers, to create a world movement to achieve peace. She declared: "If women of the world will not fight the destroyers of their children, womanhood itself has failed and with that failure comes the failure of mankind."[62]

While not rooted in the suffrage movement, the Congress of American Women, American Women for Peace and Woman, Inc. all represented new efforts of feminists to work for peace during an unfriendly era. Even though McCarthyism may have tried to obstruct their organizational efforts, the women simply regrouped and persisted. Furthermore, the era Betty Friedan described as spawning "the feminine mystique" may have tried to interfere with feminists' efforts on an individual level, but it did not succeed there either. Whether faced with a hostile government or a restrictive society, these activists all held forth that women had a right and a duty to voice their opinions. The Congress of American Women, American Women for Peace, and Woman, Inc, were but brief moments in a long history of feminist-pacifist activism. Once again, only WILPF survived another difficult era. The longevity of the organization—especially of the leadership, which still claimed women from the suffrage movement—may have aided in its survival. In addition, it had more members, more moneyed supporters, and a more deliberately moderate program, which kept it out of the government's direct eyeshot. Although politically cautious, WILPF members nonetheless stood in the forefront in speaking out for peace, justice, and freedom, taking strong and visible stances against racism, war, and the nuclear arms race.

Although itself untouched by the government, the organization, ironically, was haunted by the nightmare of the McCarthy era well into the 1960s. Hard feelings among members and fear of guilt by association among the average population kept WILPF from attracting a broad range of new participants. Once again, however, the WILPF women remained optimistic and committed to their ideals. This optimism would meet new trials in the 1960s as the Vietnam War became the major national issue leading to the rebirth of feminism within the peace movement.

7

From Civil Rights to the Second Wave of the Feminist Movement, 1960–1975

THE 1950s SET THE STAGE for the political activism of the 1960s. The various movements that took root ever so tentatively during the fifties finally burst forth, attracting many people to their causes—especially students, women, workers, and people of color. At first, racial injustice, the expanding nuclear arms race, and the growing U.S. military involvement in Vietnam were the three most urgent issues behind this new activism. As the decade progressed, however, questions about women's equality also rose to the forefront. The "second wave" of the feminist movement germinated throughout the 1960s. (It was so designated because at the time many historians felt that the "first wave," which began in 1848, had ended once women had gained the vote.)

By 1965 student activists Mary King and Casey Hayden were expressing discontent with the way women and their issues were being treated in such civil rights organizations as SNCC (Student Non-Violent Coordinating Committee) and New Left groups such as SDS (Students for a Democratic Society). From this discontent rose the grassroots women's liberation movement based on community-organized consciousness-raising and self-help groups. Around the same time, in 1966, Betty Friedan and a few other middle-aged professional women organized the National Organization for Women (NOW), a pressure group intent on improving women's lot through legislation and other structural changes within government and business. Emphasizing different populations but often embracing similar issues, the two prongs of the women's movement secured sweeping changes within U.S. society. With the slogan "The personal is political," women moved from their homes into the streets to demand equal wages, equal rights, reproductive freedom, personal opportunity, and respect.[1] For the peace movement as a whole, the women's movement was like a vitamin shot. Spurred on by rage at how they were oppressed by society, women once again pointed an accusing finger at the war machine and the "military-industrial complex." They blamed the men in power for tying the nation's economic prosperity to the production of weapons, thereby militarizing the society. In such a climate, racism, poverty, and sexism had ample opportunity to abound. Even worse, people were made to live their daily lives under the constant threat of a nuclear holocaust.

During the early sixties women fostering this new spurt of interest in feminism focused their efforts largely on the civil rights movement or in trying to understand their discontent with their affluent, but generally boring, suburban lives. Until the escalation of military involvement in Vietnam during the Johnson administration from 1965 on, antiwar work among women still rested primarily with WILPF. That organization, however, was still reeling from the effects of the McCarthy era, even though McCarthy himself had long before fallen into disgrace with the U.S. Senate. In 1960 the U.S. national office of WILPF, in its efforts to attract new members, was still trying to explain its position on communism and the Cold War. In a widely disseminated memo entitled *"W.I.L.P.F. and the Cold War,"* the national leaders once again stressed their position of opposing all wars by nonviolent and "democratic" means: "The WILPF has opposed every war, hot or cold, and has supported negotiation, mediation or arbitration of all international disputes, world disarmament, world organization to insure peace and raise the economic status of vast areas of the world, self determination of peoples, and insurance of basic human rights to every individual man."[2]

In addition, the women felt the need to reiterate their disdain for the "totalitarianism" they perceived in a communist system. Yet they still acknowledged that while they continued to define the Soviet Union as "totalitarian," they also shared goals and phraseology with communists that WILPF would not give up. "If the USSR sings the praises of 'peace' and 'freedom,'" the memo continued, "pleads for disarmament, the meeting of mankind's material needs, or the ending of colonialism, WILPF does not, therefore, feel compelled to demonstrate its anticommunism by dropping 'peace' and 'freedom' from its vocabulary: or declaring itself in favor of the arms race, poverty, or imperialism!"[3]

To avoid harassment from HUAC and to keep its "peace and freedom" position clear, the national WILPF organization took the unofficial position that local branch development should be discouraged in countries that were believed to limit freedom of speech. As a result, neither the international WILPF organization nor the U.S. section would collaborate with the Women's International Democratic Federation, and the WIDF was left without a strong U.S. ally until 1975, when Women for Racial and Economic Equality (WREE) was formed by a group of New York City women. The furthest WILPF would go in its relationship with the WIDF was to allow nonparticipating observers to attend each other's international conferences. WILPF also refused to cosponsor conferences "in which Communist organizations [took] the initiative." This included the widely attended Youth Congresses in Moscow and Vienna.[4]

Despite the national organization's problems during the 1950s and the unstated narrowing of its definition of membership, WILPF members continued to involve themselves in a broad range of issues.[5] From the 1950s on, the major efforts of the national organization were directed against the proliferation of nuclear weapons and against U.S. military intervention wherever and whenever it occurred, and for a strong international community through the United Nations. During the early sixties the organization campaigned for the cessation of nuclear tests, emphasizing the importance of having a test ban treaty that would apply to all nations—but especially the United States and the Soviet Union. Also of great importance was WILPF's work towards an agreement among the military powers not to sell arms to tension-filled underdeveloped areas such as the Middle East, Africa, Latin America, or Central Europe. Understanding the dynamics of the military-industrial complex did not deter the women from this work. Indeed, it spurred them on to create broad international pressure on the big powers to stop both aboveground and underground testing of nuclear weapons.

To develop this pressure, WILPF continued its efforts, begun in 1915, to build international peace links. In 1961 the national WILPF organization sponsored its first seminar intended to establish a network with Soviet women. This meeting at Bryn Mawr College in Pennsylvania opened the door to many other such interchanges held in both the United States and the Soviet Union. Needless to say, these conferences produced a certain amount of criticism from those who saw the Soviets as a threat and any contact with them as treasonous.

Although the national board of WILPF also took a strong stand on the seating of delegates from the People's Republic of China in the UN's Security Council, they did not reach their goal until 1971, just before President Richard Nixon opened the door for détente with that communist nation. WILPF's position on the inclusion of "Red" China in the UN, as stated in 1954, paralleled their previous stands on the Soviet Union. The organizers felt that the 450 million people of China could only "benefit" from their government's exposure to the workings of the international body. As long as the People's Republic was kept isolated from the world community, it was not possible to observe its actions, much less to criticize them. Once a member of the UN, China would be "subject to all its restraints" should it take an aggressive action against another country. In addition, if China were not included, its government, out of a sense of "antagonism rather than cooperation," might come "more completely under the influence of the U.S.S.R."[6] Little did the leaders realize that, even though the Soviet Union and China had the potential to form an enormous united communist front, the two nations would remain on basically unfriendly terms, bickering over borders and taking vastly different stands on international issues—at times worrying that each was conspiring with the U.S. government against the other.

More frustrating to the women than the issue of seating the People's Republic of China on the Security Council was their recognition of the UN's impotence to prevent U.S. military intervention or arms sales in developing countries. Because international WILPF policy continued to allow for the criticism of each nation's government only by the WILPF members of *that* country, the national organizers in the United States had a big job on their hands. U.S. businesses—and hence the government—had emerged from World War II with enormous profits, prestige, and power. As a result, U.S. interests exerted themselves in every part of the globe, and the U.S. section of WILPF found itself addressing worldwide issues. By the mid-1960s, for example, concerns in Asia had shifted from the occupation of Japan and the incursion into Korea to U.S. involvement in Vietnam. As early as 1962, when President John Kennedy was deploying military advisors to South Vietnam, WILPF leader Annalee Stewart acknowledged that the United States was carrying on "an undeclared war" there.[7] In 1965 the women had already announced their support for negotiations that would result in an independent South Vietnam, responsible for determining its own future. By the late sixties, much of the organization's time and effort centered around the Vietnam War, including cosponsorship of and participation in almost every national antiwar demonstration, from Washington, D.C., New York, and San Francisco to hundreds of other cities and towns. Besides protesting the war in Vietnam, the women continued to emphasize that the United States needed to recognize the People's Republic of China and that U.S. military personnel in Asia should cease supporting the counterrevolution of Chiang Kai-shek (Jiang Jieshi).

In the Middle East, where the United States was heavily involved, first in supporting Israel and then also in selling arms to the Arab nations, WILPF took a stand against arms sales and for negotiated settlement in the area. In addition, the women took a strong stand in favor of maintaining the Jewish homeland. The organization consistently spoke out against apartheid in South Africa. The women lobbied the U.S. leaders, who sanctioned extensive trade with the minority-controlled white South African government, to exert pressure on South Africa to abolish apartheid, just as the U.S. was attempting to eliminate racial oppression at home. The women also stressed the importance of allocating U.S. aid to help all the developing African nations. In such an effort, the women preferred that the money be dispersed through such UN organizations as UNICEF, UNESCO, and the World Health Organization. Because the U.S. economy was experiencing such great expansion, WILPFers saw it as the nation's responsibility to share its good fortune with the international community, especially as U.S. companies not only often exploited foreign labor but also obtained raw materials largely from other nations.

In the 1960s, as always, WILPF was greatly concerned about U.S. relations with Latin America. In much of the world, U.S. policy was conditioned by competition with the Soviet Union and China, but Latin America had long been seen as part of the U.S. domain. The terms of the Monroe Doctrine of 1823 stated that foreign nations were unwelcome in the area, and in 1904 the Roosevelt Corollary to the Doctrine provided for U.S. military intervention if those nations south of the border seemed unsettled or in danger of foreign interference. These two policies gave the United States unilateral power to make decisions and take actions that determined the fate of Central and South Americans and all of the peoples of the Caribbean. Exactly as it had done as the Woman's Peace Party in 1915, WILPF spoke out against U.S. military presence in the area and particularly against the U.S. colonization of Puerto Rico. To the women of WILPF, the 1954 invasion of Guatemala, the 1965 invasion of the Dominican Republic, and U.S. troop placement in Puerto Rico, Cuba, and Central America seemed foreboding.

The greatest affront to peace in the Americas during this period was the Bay of Pigs invasion in 1961. The success of the Cuban Revolution in January 1959 had caused great consternation for U.S. government leaders. Fidel Castro, the leader of the new government, established the first communist nation in the Americas. With the Monroe Doctrine as justification, first President Eisenhower and then President Kennedy planned a secret invasion of the island, alleging that Fidel Castro was being controlled by Moscow and thus Cuba was under foreign domination. The two presidents authorized the CIA to train a volunteer force of Cuban exiles to return to Cuba to overthrow the new government. Much to everyone's surprise, when the invaders landed at Playa Giron (the Bay of Pigs), they met with organized resistance and total failure. The entire episode was an embarrassment for the Kennedy administration, which nonetheless continued its trade embargo against Cuba.

Immediately after the Bay of Pigs fiasco, the national board of WILPF issued a statement demanding that Cuban exiles not be encouraged to continue in their vendetta against Castro and that under no circumstances should they be supplied with weapons or trained for the military. In addition, the women favored an end to the economic boycott, stressing that friendly relations with Cuba were desirable and historically natural and that to continue the present policy would only encourage the island's reliance on trade and support from the Soviet Union. A year later they were proved correct when Cuba's request for placement of Soviet-made missiles to deter further U.S. aggression precipitated the Cuban missile crisis. Although people worldwide were frightened by how close the confrontation came to nuclear war, when it was over, the United States continued its economic boycott and political harassment of Cuba. The WILPF members continued to protest. Their position on Cuba, consistent with the organization's stand against U.S. intervention in Latin America, also reflected their point of view that communist nations should be integrated into the "democratic" world so that they might benefit from its openness.

During the sixties WILPF also paid close attention to domestic issues. Of primary concern was continued support of the civil rights movement. WILPFers lobbied tirelessly for the passage of the Civil Rights Act. Members also participated in many demonstrations demanding an end to racial discrimination, including the March for Jobs and Freedom in 1963 and the Selma to Montgomery voting rights march in 1965. WILPFers demanded federal action in the case of the three civil rights workers murdered in Mississippi in 1964. The following year they organized a boycott of products and investments in that southern state; among the companies targeted were Armstrong Tire, International Paper, International Telephone and Telegraph, Kraft Foods, Procter and Gamble, Wurlitzer, Pet Milk, Borden, Swift Dairy Products, and Hunt's Foods. In conjunction with this effort, the organizers once again pressed for U.S. economic sanctions against South Africa until it ended apartheid.

By this time, the Metropolitan New York branch of WILPF was supporting all of the national board's stands on international and domestic issues.[8] They had been able to resolve most of their differences because of UN work, a link resulting in constant communication and greater participation of the local women in the national structure. The local Metropolitan New York branch board was still in the hands of a few dedicated women, often the same ones involved at the UN. The branch, however, continued to attract a more diverse group of members than many other branches. Although recruiting younger women and women of color remained a challenge, Metropolitan New York WILPF members came from both the working and middle classes and represented many ethnic groups, but especially Jews. Indeed, the Metropolitan New York group was still ethnically unique in WILPF. In addition, because New York City was traditionally a home for political dissenters, the branch maintained its attraction for moral pacifists as well as socialists, Communist party members, and labor organizers.

In the early sixties, the Metropolitan New York branch continued

WE MOURN
THE DEATH OF
300 VIETNAMESE EACH DAY

Tonight at $500. a plate dinners, people are listening to Pres. Nixon and enjoying fine food while— in Vietnam, people do not have enough to eat — because our planes have destroyed food crops.

HAVE WE NO SHAME?

Wire Pres. Nixon: Stop all bombing in SE Asia
Withdraw all military forces & equipment now
Not another life wasted / American or Vietnamese!

PAX

Women's International League for Peace and Freedom
Metropolitan New York Branch
201 West 13 Street
New York, New York 10011
___ Plea e send information about your program.
___ I upport your work. Enclosed is a contribution.
Name.......................... Address.......................

22. Flier from WILPF/NY branch demonstration, late 1960s. Courtesy of WILPF Metropolitan New York Branch History Project.

to grow and to pursue its own programming. In 1961, under the presidency of Dr. Rose Mukerji, the branch won the WILPF membership award for having enrolled the largest number of new volunteers. Like the national board, the local women concentrated much effort upon the civil rights movement. Their presence in marches and participation in educational activities reflected a particular concern for their own city as well. Starting in 1964 and continuing for several years thereafter, these women spoke out against the lack of satisfactory results from efforts to integrate the New York City public schools.

At least one of the Metropolitan New York branch's leaders had come to the organization with a history of civil rights activism. Bess Cameron, whose parents had marched in favor of woman suffrage, had become involved in civil rights in the late 1930s when she was a student at the University of Chicago. From her French tutor, an African-American, Cameron learned that they could not eat in the same restaurants; moreover, the tutor could not live in the dorms, and she could join Cameron for a swim only on Friday afternoons (the school's pool was cleaned on Saturday mornings). Cameron, the daughter of a Ku Klux Klan member who had encouraged her to carry a banner in a Klan parade in the 1920s, soon came to know most of the African-American students at the university. Years later, as a faculty member at Indiana University, she became actively involved with the Congress of Racial Equality (CORE) and the National Association for the Advancement of Colored People (NAACP). There she also learned about WILPF and helped a group of women obtain a branch charter. When she moved to New York City a short while later, Cameron joined the local branch. Naturally, she became a great supporter of their civil rights activities.[9]

Both nationally and locally, WILPF had apparently survived the fifties and reemerged in the sixties as a leading force for peace and justice. Yet this was not entirely true. Although the organization did make a comeback, many members were left with a bad taste in their mouths from the incidents of the 1950s. In 1964, Mildred Scott Olmsted, executive director of the U.S. section, remarked in her report at the annual meeting: "It is a mystery to me why an organization with the courage and the standards, the services it provides and the record of accomplishment of the WILPF does not increase in numbers more rapidly than it does."[10] She and most other WILPF leaders had not understood the dynamics of the McCarthy era or their role in it. As a result, there were prospective peace activists who looked for alternatives to WILPF. Some felt the organization was too wishy-washy, while others continued to view it as part of the "Communist front."

Either way, WILPF was losing out. In terms of the reemergence of feminist peace activism as a whole, however, WILPF's fall into disfavor was not an entirely bad thing, for out of the organization's internal convulsions sprang a fresh movement with new ideas, new blood, and, as in the 1920s, a diversity of ideologies.

The initial resurgence of activity, begun in 1961, centered around the nuclear arms race. By the mid-sixties the activities revolved around the Vietnam War. Voice of Women (VOW) became the first alternative to WILPF. Founded in July 1960 in Canada, the organization was adopted by U.S. women on June 25, 1961, in Cleveland, Ohio. In its rhetoric, VOW retained much from the feminist peace movement. Women, as the "givers" of life were "particularly concerned" about their children's survival. Moreover, women worldwide shared not only maternal interests but also an "abhorrence" of nuclear, biological, and chemical warfare. It was thus important, VOW stressed, to utilize "the tremendous creative power" of women in finding a way of easing world tensions and "the turning of men's minds from war."[11] The U.S. branches of VOW existed throughout the 1960s; the Canadian organization is still a large pressure group.

More powerful than VOW was Women Strike for Peace (WSP) (pronounced "wĭsp") organized in the fall of 1961. WSP was not simply an alternative to WILPF; indeed, it was born directly out of the discontent with WILPF's hierarchical structure and anti-Communist stance, as well as from a concern that red-baiting had harmed the organization's credibility and effectiveness. Women Strike for Peace also grew out of the concern over radiation fallout caused by aboveground nuclear bomb tests.[12] (The organization is also known as WISP, from an alternate name, Women's International Strike for Peace, adopted in 1961. It has also been called Women for Peace.) WSP was founded when Dagmar Wilson, a book illustrator based in Washington, D.C., who claimed "wife and mother" as her primary identities, called together a group of women to plan some action around the bomb tests. The women were particularly apprehensive because a three-year Soviet moratorium on nuclear tests had come to an end, and they feared that tensions over the Berlin Wall would set off a nuclear confrontation between the Soviet Union and the United States. Most of the original organizers of WSP—including Wilson, Eleanor Garst, Folly Fodor, Margaret Rus-

HE LIES DEAD IN VIETNAM—WHAT FOR?
For corrupt and power-hungry South Vietnamese "leaders," whose own people do not support them.
HIS PARENTS WEEP.
But the war goes on and the Vietnamese people are no closer to freedom.
HIS WIDOW GRIEVES. WHAT FOR?
For an American policy that sent her man, and continues to send more men, halfway round the world to barge into a civil war between Vietnamese.

The G.I. casualty toll in Vietnam is now over **22,303.**

NOW IS THE TIME TO STOP THE WAR IN VIETNAM.
It is now clear to everyone that American troops do not belong in Vietnam. Whether the Buddhists or the Catholics, the monks or the generals, or the Vietcong National Liberation Front will control South Vietnam must be settled by the people of Vietnam —— themselves.

TELL PRESIDENT JOHNSON WE WANT OUR MEN BROUGHT HOME—ALIVE!
Write, phone or wire the White House, Washington, D.C. today.
Every day's delay costs precious lives.

for further information, write to:
WOMEN STRIKE FOR PEACE • 151 East 50 Street • New York, N. Y. 10022

23. Women Strike for Peace anti-Vietnam War flier, 1960s. Courtesy of Schwimmer/Lloyd Collection, Rare Books and Manuscripts Division, The New York Public Library, Astor, Lenox, and Tilden Foundations.

sell, and Jeanne Bagby—were members of the Washington branch of SANE (National Committee for a Sane Nuclear Policy), but WILPF members also became actively involved in the project.

In September the women began their work by picketing in front of the White House. Within a month they had organized a major demonstration. On November 1, 1961, Women Strike for Peace had its first major success: marches taking place in sixty cities across the nation that involved more than 50,000 women. Taking their babies with them, the marchers headed for their local city halls and federal buildings. The rationale behind the action was that women would call a one-day "strike" in order to illustrate their collective power. On that day women walked off their jobs and out of their kitchens in order to take to the streets. The resounding success of the event inspired Wilson and her friends to establish Women Strike for Peace as a permanent organization.[13] However, as a reaction to the internal red-baiting which had taken place within both SANE and WILPF, they decided not to establish a national hierarchy, not to require or even encourage official membership, not to charge dues, and not even to have any boards of any kind. Rather, WSP would operate as a loosely tied network of women working together to protest the nuclear arms race.

According to historian Amy Swerdlow, who has done a comprehensive study of the organization (she was also an active member), the great appeal of WSP to numbers of women was that it projected an image of "respectable middle-class, middle-aged peace ladies in white gloves and flowered hats."[14] In addition, the organizers exploited the age-old myth of mothers as the protectors of life and the peace movement's portrayal of women as angry citizens. As Swerdlow notes, WSP publicity emphasized that men in power undermined "the ability of American mothers to carry out their assigned role of life-preservation and moral guardianship."[15] Unlike WILPF, the Women's Peace Union, the National Committee on the Cause and Cure of War, and the Woman's Peace Party, whose average member was fifty or older, at first Women Strike for Peace attracted women from their mid-thirties to their late forties. By the late 1960s, WSP was appealing to women in their twenties. The leadership consisted of the usual mixture of pacifists, Quakers, Communists, and socialists, giving the group the variety of liberal to radical participants also characteristic of WILPF. In their public stance, however, the women in WSP generally denied or played down their political backgrounds, relying on their middle-class veneer to produce favorable public reaction.

Unlike WILPF, which managed to avoid a direct hit from HUAC, in December 1962, WSP found a number of its activists, largely from the New York metropolitan area, called before the committee. The subpoenas arrived after the organization had been at work only one full year. Within that time the leaders had sparked the creation of numerous educational programs, demonstrations, and civil disobedience actions. Their immediate goal was to pressure for a treaty that would put an end to atmospheric nuclear testing. Their long-term goal was clearly stated in their motto: "End the Arms Race—Not the Human Race." In June, 1962, a few months before the summons from HUAC, the leading activists had held WSP's first national conference in Ann Arbor, Michigan. The women in attendance adopted a statement to unify their informal membership network:

> We are women of all races, creeds and political persuasions. We are dedicated to the purpose of general and complete disarmament. We demand that nuclear tests be banned forever, that the arms race end and the world abolish all weapons of destruction under United Nations safeguards. We cherish the right and accept the responsibility to act to influence the course of government for peace. . . . We join with women throughout the world to challenge the right of any nation or group of nations to hold the power of life and death over the world.[16]

Women Strike for Peace, which appeared mild in its program, was charged by HUAC with harboring Communists. Because at least two of the specific women subpoenaed were known Communist party members, WSP leaders worried over HUAC's intentions. Accordingly, the main decision-makers took a united stand—much as the WILPF leaders had done—that any woman could join WSP, no matter what her political, religious, or other ideology. All that the organization desired of a prospective member was that she oppose the testing of nuclear weapons by both the United States and the Soviet Union and that she support UN control over a universal disarmament program. In addition, WSP leaders decided to take the initiative in their own defense. In a letter to their membership, they pointed out that HUAC was out to "tarnish" their "image" in order "to intimidate women who might become active" and "to stifle public debate," concluding in the classic suffragist-pacifist style that "more and more it's obvious that it has to be 'the women' who speak for mankind."[17]

Once again in a style echoing earlier years, the leading organizers proclaimed that peace work was "the highest form of patriotism" and proceeded to the hearings.[18] There, HUAC officials attempted to question WSP members about their "united front" activities, especially in its section consisting of Metropolitan New York, New Jersey, and Connecticut.[19] As each woman was called for questioning, the other WSP members broke into applause; Dagmar Wilson was presented with a bouquet of white roses when she took the stand. Furthermore, the women attempted to make the all-male government panel look foolish by hinting that their "masculine minds" could not grasp the concepts supported by WSP.[20] The press had a field day, using such headlines as "Peace Gals Make Red Hunters Look Silly," "Redhunters Decapitated" and "It's Ladies' Day at the Capitol: Hoots, Howls and Charm" to describe the hearings. Certainly, the press no longer took HUAC as seriously as they had during the McCarthy years.

Many of the New York women involved in WSP came from the local branch of WILPF. Minna Kashins, one of the first women to cross over to the Metropolitan New York, New Jersey, and Connecticut section, recalled: "See, we gave birth to Women Strike for Peace. . . . I remember when Bess Cameron, one of our members, came to me one day, and she says, Minna, we're going to start a new organization named Women Strike for Peace."[21] The New York WILPFers, just like several members in Philadelphia and Washington, D.C., were seeking an alternative to their mother organization. In the end, however, they remained active in both. One Metropolitan New York branch member was attracted to WSP because of the anti-Communist stance of the WILPF leadership. She complained that Orlie Pell, president of the local branch, was "violently anti-Communist" and therefore made it close to impossible for New York Communist members to move freely within the group. At one point during the 1950s, Pell had actually recommended that the branch cease having meetings and simply use its efforts to raise money for the national board; that would be one way of limiting the activities of Communist members.[22] Also, in 1961, she voted against WILPF's attending a conference in the Soviet Union and cautioned the organization against cooperating with the Fair Play for Cuba Committee, which she believed was "extremely pro-Castro and anti–United States, if not actually Communist-oriented."[23] WSP was also appealing to some New York WILPF members because its meetings often took place in women's homes rather than in an office or rented hall, thereby giving the participants, as one woman put it, "a communal relationship, whereas with WILPF it's a little impersonal."[24] Nonetheless, there was for many years a core of women, particularly in New York City, who worked for both WILPF and WSP.

The most important "victory" for Women Strike for Peace during the 1960s was its influence on the passage of the 1963 Test-Ban Treaty. This agreement between the Soviet Union and the United States ensured the termination of the aboveground testing of nuclear weapons, a phenomenon which had resulted in over two hundred U.S. and USSR nuclear bomb tests by 1960. The signing of the treaty was partly the result of effective lobbying and protesting on the part of WSP and other peace organizations. As in the HUAC hearings, the organization utilized its unique interpretation of its members' "femaleness." Playing once again on the theme of motherhood, the WSP organizers created their "Mother's Campaign for a Test Ban Treaty." With slogans such as "Let the Children Grow" and "Milk Not Poison," the women emphasized the fact that after each aboveground nuclear explosion, the level of radiation in milk rose dramatically. To bring the point home, WSP leaders encouraged women to have their children's lost baby teeth tested for the radioactive isotope strontium 90, present in nuclear fallout, which is deposited in place of calcium in bone. The teeth, with the lab results, were then forwarded to each woman's senator. In addition, many women organized boycotts of their local dairies and milk delivery services, insisting that their patronage depended upon the installation of equipment capable of removing strontium 90 from the milk.[25]

The signing of the Test-Ban Treaty did not mean the end of WSP protests against the nuclear arms race. Rather, it signaled further commitment and international cooperation. In May 1964, for example, thousands of U.S. and European women joined together at The Hague to voice their anger at NATO for equipping its multilateral naval fleet with nuclear weapons. In addition, WSP members continued WILPF's longtime campaign against the sales, advertising, and production of war toys. Most important to the WSP's program, as for WILPF, was the formation of an international women's network. The woman most influential in this work for WSP was Ruth Gage-Colby, a member of the Metropolitan New York branch of WILPF and, as of 1963, also the coordinator of worldwide activity for WSP.

Gage-Colby came to Women Strike for Peace with much experience in international work.[26] Because of her own opposition to World War I, she was drawn to WILPF as early as 1920, soon after the founding of the international organization. At that time, she was residing with her husband in Vienna, where he was completing his medical studies. During World War II, Gage-Colby joined WILPF's protest against the internment of the Japanese in the U.S., criticizing the policy for its racism. At the end of the war, she took an active interest in the organization's support of the founding of the United Nations and was one of WILPF's representatives at the founding meetings in San Francisco. Soon after, Gage-Colby worked for UNICEF in both Egypt and China. Through her UN efforts she became personally acquainted with Secretary-General U Thant. This friendship, combined with her extensive experience in WILPF and WSP work at the UN, made her an ideal choice for WSP's international coordinator. In addition, from 1966 to 1970 she took on the presidency of the Metropolitan New York branch of WILPF, a striking indication of the spillover from that group to WSP.

The Women's International Strike for Peace appealed to the women of both Eastern and Western Europe, Canada, and Japan, but much of the antinuclear activity centered around Geneva, where the UN often held its disarmament discussions. One of the most successful Geneva protests took place in March 1962, when fifty-one WSP members from the United States, including Dagmar Wilson and Coretta Scott King, flew to Europe to join women from sixteen other nations to lobby for nuclear disarmament. Dagmar Wilson's explanation for their action, as the *New York Times* reported on March 9, was that the nuclear threat had made it impossible for the women to carry on their usual domestic chores. "When women's normal work becomes meaningless in the face of annihilation, international affairs become our direct concern, affecting every hour of our lives."[27]

Soon after the Geneva action, the WSP leaders in the United States voted to send a delegation, headed by Dagmar Wilson, to the Soviet

Union. Because of the HUAC activity, the decision was not an easy one. In 1961, WILPF had met with Soviet women at a conference held at Bryn Mawr College, but now WSP was proposing a visit to the Soviet Union. To gain the approval of the U.S. government and media, the women accepted the argument recommended to them by Arthur Dean, the U.S. delegate to the Geneva disarmament discussions: that the U.S. women's mission was to convince the Russian people that the United States was sincere in its desire for peace. With this rationale, the WSP paid its visit, thereby establishing contact with Soviet women, which Gage-Colby would later develop.[28]

Women Strike for Peace also used a strategy originated by the international WILPF organization. Just as in 1919 when the leaders of WILPF had decided to hold a women's peace conference in Zurich while the major powers were meeting in Versailles, so the WSP leaders decided to hold an alternative conference in May 1964 in the Netherlands at the same time and place as NATO's general meeting at The Hague. Women from all the NATO nations except Turkey attended the conference. U.S. delegate Eleanor Garst was much encouraged. "In two years, we have succeeded in changing the image of the 'ugly American' abroad. . . . we have told the world that there are women on this smug and fat continent who are aware of their existence and determined to fight for their right to exist—but to fight non-violently and non-partisanly, as Gandhi, the American Negro and the peace people . . . have so aptly demonstrated."[29]

The overriding issue for both WILPF and Women Strike for Peace—as for all other peace organizations—from the early 1960s through April 1975, was the U.S. military involvement in Vietnam. Although the United States had become embroiled in the small Southeast Asian country after the French had been defeated in 1954, the use of U.S. troops there did not become a main concern until President Johnson increased the U.S. military presence in 1965. From then until 1972, when the majority of the U.S. soldiers left Vietnam, over 57,000 U.S. military personnel and over two million Vietnamese lost their lives. The Vietnam War ripped the United States apart. Antiwar organizations proliferated to protest the conflict, and super-patriotic groups rose to confront them.

Both WILPF and Women Strike for Peace played key roles in propa-

24. Women Strike for Peace contingent in anti-Vietnam War demonstration, April 22, 1972. Courtesy of Swarthmore College Peace Collection.

gandizing against the war; in working with coalitions like the Fifth Avenue Vietnam Peace Parade Committee to plan massive demonstrations in Washington, D.C., New York, and San Francisco; in supporting draft-counseling centers and other sources of aid to conscientious objectors; and in lobbying Congress and working for the election of peace candidates. The election of Richard Nixon to the presidency in 1968 added fuel to the peace activities. Nixon promised to bring an end to the conflict but, instead, increased the bombing of North Vietnam and Cambodia. As a result, antiwar activity increased. WILPF members worked ceaselessly to bring an end to the war, for the sakes of both the U.S. personnel and for the countless Vietnamese being terrorized, maimed, or killed. One of the most successful coalition efforts the women supported was the Vietnam Moratorium Day, October 15, 1969, which involved millions of U.S. citizens in protest activities throughout the nation. The Moratorium, cited as the largest peace protest up to that day in all U.S. history, involved the expertise of all the local WILPF organizers. At the same time, the national board instituted "Tuesdays in Washington," which included a variety of events to dramatize the war. The nature of these demonstrations pointed the way to the more spectacular theatrics used during the Women's Pentagon Actions in the early 1980s. On one Tuesday, for example, WILPF members formed a procession and carried coffins, each marked with the name of an actual victim of the war, around the Capitol. On another Tuesday, before the White House fence, women acted out what author Catherine Foster described as the "chaining of industry to the U.S. military."[30]

Overall, for many organizations the Vietnam War produced renewed interest in peace work. Young men eligible for the draft sought out help from the War Resisters League, the Fellowship of Reconciliation, and other traditional groups, whose memberships grew each year. In addition, many new organizations, such as SDS, which supported draft resistance, emerged out of the counterculture and student movements of the New Left. Next to these groups, the older women of WILPF seemed staid. Women Strike for peace, however, held some appeal for younger, budding feminists who wanted to protest the war within a female context.

According to economist Nan Wiegersma, who joined WSP around 1967, younger women, especially those with children, found some attraction in the organization's structure and method of decision-making. Like WILPF, WSP relied on reaching a consensus, but unlike WILPF, it was not bogged down in a hierarchy on the local level. Wiegersma contends that even though WSP was commonly viewed as a group for middle-class mothers, in fact, many of the organization's Vietnam-era members were "more of the 60s." They eagerly joined older WSPers in protesting the war as well as the nuclear arms race. In 1969, Wiegersma herself joined a WSP delegation to Cuba. There, she and the other women met with visiting members of the National Liberation Front and became more convinced than ever that the war in Vietnam was wrong.[31]

In the fall of 1969, *Memo,* the national bulletin of Women Strike for Peace, reported on the trip to Cuba. From this one issue, it becomes clear what Wiegersma meant by WSP being "more of the 60s." The issue was dedicated not only to Ho Chi Minh, the leader of the North Vietnamese and a national hero, but also "to all the Vietnamese in that magnificent land who have fought and died, been burned and mutilated" and to those U.S. citizens "who have worked desperately to end our nation's crime: to WSPs and all others who are struggling to change America's direction; students, blacks, third-world, poverty mothers, G.I.'s, deserters, draft resisters, political exiles, burners of draft cards, all those in civil and military prisons."[32] Obviously, WSP of 1968 reflected a New Left approach. The younger women coming into the group, like Nan Wiegersma, were particularly influenced by the student movement and its new interest in Marxism. By 1968, however, some of these women had woken up to the sexism within their student organizations and had sought out separate female groups in order to have a say in decision making and to be part of the power structure. Furthermore, they discovered that men involved in antiwar, draft resistance, civil rights, and student movements were generally not very interested in women's equality. Often crude and condescending in their reactions to the women's assertiveness, the younger men of the New Left unintentionally fostered the formation of the women's liberation movement. By the early 1970s, more and more women were choosing to work within a female environment. The new feminists were walking in the paths of their women's rights foremothers, but, at the time, they were unaware of it.

As the war progressed, WILPF concentrated its efforts more and more in the nation's capital, the seat of the warmakers. In June 1970 the national board called a Women's Emergency Conference on Vietnam. Held in Washington, D.C., the meeting attracted leaders from many organizations. There, the organizers formulated plans on how best to put pressure on Congress to end appropriations for the war. Besides supporting antiwar candidates for local, state, and federal offices and campaigning against those who supported the war, WILPF stressed the importance of maintaining a public presence in Washington. If the public were constantly reminded that large numbers of citizens opposed the war, then they could feel comfortable about adding their own voices to the outcry. Public demonstrations offered an outlet for those who were indignant about the war after watching television news reports showing actual battles and seeing magazine and newspaper photos of never-ending lines of flag-draped coffins returning to the United States.

Many of WILPF's efforts "to bring the war home" were aimed at U.S. women. On International Women's Day, March 8, 1971, for example, WILPF members once again picketed in front of the White House. Demanding that Richard Nixon abide by his promise to withdraw U.S. troops from Vietnam, the women carried multilingual posters with such messages as "Set the Date" and "Out Now." They also delivered to the president 8,000 handwritten postcards from WILPF members demanding an end to the conflict; the cards, which included eight hundred from women then residing in South Vietnam, represented the international community of the organization.[33]

The Metropolitan New York branch, with its office so close to the United Nations, maintained constant antiwar activity. As early as 1964—before Johnson's troop escalation—the women maintained a weekly vigil in Times Square. Every Saturday afternoon from 12:30 to 2:30, while thousands of people scurried to lunch before theater and movie matinees, branch members and sympathizers stood silently in the triangle between Broadway and Seventh Avenue where the Armed Forces recruiting stations were located. That same year, under the leadership of Ruth Gage-Colby, the women held a protest in front of the U.S. Pavilion at the World's Fair, which was then taking place in Queens, a borough where many branch members lived. From 1967 into the 1970s, the Metropolitan New York branch of WILPF also mobilized its members to participate in massive antiwar demonstrations held each spring and fall in their city.

The New York women, like many other antiwar organizers, were pushed into further action by Nixon's escalation of the war in North Vietnam and into Cambodia.[34] After Helen Kusman became president in 1970, the local board instituted a "Never on Tuesdays Shoppers' Stoppage," one small effort in trying to reach the millions of women who shopped in Manhattan stores every day. As residents of a large urban area, the New York women continuously tried to appeal to the consumer side of a very material-oriented but not heartless city. For one such event, the women handed out a leaflet to guests and onlookers outside a reception being given for Nixon. The leaflet, headed with a black bordered box and the hand-written title "We Mourn The

Death of 300 Vietnamese Each Day," contained this message: "Tonight at $500. a plate dinners, people are listening to Pres. Nixon and enjoying fine food while—in Vietnam, people do not have enough to eat—Because our planes have destroyed food crops—*HAVE WE NO SHAME?*"[35] If anger, as exemplified by the "Evict Nixon" campaign, and a sense of simple human compassion, as emphasized in such activities as the 1971 "Rice and Tea for Peace" event intended to raise money for WILPF's support of a Maternal Child Health Center in Hanoi, did not grab people's hearts, then perhaps guilt would.

Women Strike for Peace also utilized several different methods to protest the war. Soon after the Kennedy administration became entangled in the near-nuclear confrontation with the Soviets during the Cuban missile crisis, the organization had also begun addressing the issue of "conventional" wars. The women realized that a small hot spot could lead the nation into a prolonged conventional war, such as the one in Korea. At its June 1963 national meeting in Champaign-Urbana, Illinois, therefore, the WSP leaders attempted to show that the Cuban crisis was not an isolated incident but rather a link in a long chain of U.S. involvement in the affairs of Third World nations. Although the organization took no concrete actions at that time, the discussion set the stage for future work concerning Vietnam.[36]

These talks came to fruition on July 8, 1965, when ten representatives from WSP flew to Indonesia to meet with women delegates of both the National Liberation Front from South Vietnam and the communist government of North Vietnam. At this meeting both groups of women signed a statement expressing their opposition to the U.S. military presence in Vietnam. Throughout the war WSP members consistently opposed the drafting of young men and supported the rights of conscientious objectors. This concern increased as many of the younger, less traditional women joining WSP chapters worked through the National WSP Draft Counseling Service. Traditional WSPers also continued to use their role as mothers and their "feminine" image to attack the "masculine" war machine. In 1967 they employed this tactic in Washington, D.C., when approximately 2,500 of them appeared before the home of the military, the Pentagon, and removed their shoes to bang them on the building's doors.[37]

Younger women contributed greatly to WSP's work. Besides radi-

25. Women Strike for Peace in 1967 march on the Pentagon. Courtesy of Swarthmore College Peace Collection.

calizing the organization in new ways, they also contributed to the group's already contagious sense of humor. One example of this humor invoked a sense of longing for an end to the Vietnam War. In a cartoon appearing in *Peace de Resistance Cookbook #1,* issued by the Los Angeles section of WSP, a mother complete with lacy apron was shown carrying a sign which read, "Bring the Boys Home for Dinner."[38] Also relying on a woman's heart but devoid of all humor was a WSP flier produced by the New York office during Johnson's escalation of troops. On top of the handout in large black block letters were the words "WHAT FOR?" and under them, bordered in black, was the photograph of a soldier's corpse wrapped in a tarpaulin and tied up with rope. The major text, which reflected the Old and New Left elements in WSP, emphasized that the business of running Vietnam belonged to the Vietnamese. The emotional feeling reflected in the text was dramatic:

> HE LIES DEAD IN VIETNAM—WHAT FOR?
>
> For corrupt and power-hungry South Vietnamese "leaders," whose own people do not support them.
>
> HIS PARENTS WEEP.
>
> But the war goes on and the Vietnamese people are no closer to freedom.
>
> HIS WIDOW GRIEVES. WHAT FOR?
>
> For an American policy that sent her man, and continues to send more men, half way round the world to barge into a civil war between Vietnamese.
>
> The G.I. casualty toll in Vietnam is *NOW* over 22,303.[39]

The young age of eighteen of the average U.S. soldier in Vietnam as opposed to the twenty-four or twenty-five year average for World War II was one factor which accounted for the involvement of two generations of women in WSP. The older women feared for their sons. Young men barely out of high school were being drafted into a war very few people understood. The younger women feared for their friends and lovers.

The motherhood theme was also adopted by an organization composed of younger and older women. In March 1967 this group of fifteen "close friends" created Another Mother for Peace.[40] By 1972 this small but effective group of women from the Hollywood film industry had accumulated a mailing list of over a quarter of a million people and had utilized the talents of such stars as Debbie Reynolds, Patty Duke, Mercedes McCambridge, Barbara Rush, Joanne Woodward, and Paul Newman to promote their cause. The founder of Another Mother, Barbara Avedon, an Academy Award–winning screenwriter, became concerned about the war after she had given birth to a son: "Before I know it, he will be old enough to go to war. I wonder which one will be his and where it will be and what it will be about. . . . We are the ones who create life, and we should be the ones to preserve it; yet, here we are, accepting the idea that war is inevitable."[41]

In an attempt to reach out to mothers and to touch their hearts,

26. A small sample of translations of the famous logo designed by Lorraine Schneider for Another Mother for Peace. Courtesy of Swarthmore College Peace Collection.

Avedon and her friends printed one thousand Mother's Day cards to send to congressional representatives. The message on the card read:

> For my Mothers' *[sic]* Day gift this year
> I don't want candy or flowers.
> I want an end to killing.
> We who have given life
> Must be dedicated to preserving it.
> Please, talk peace![42]

Popular response to the card was so enthusiastic that the women kept printing more and more of them. By the end of May, they had sold 200,000 cards. Opening an "Invest in Peace Fund," they used the money to support legislators who would vote against war appropriations. The fact that Donna Reed, the quintessential mother in her television sitcom, was one of the co-chairs of the organization probably reinforced its image.[43]

Another Mother for Peace was not organized by experienced activists. Its bylaws, written in 1967, indicated that there would be no chapters, no endorsements of political candidates, and no political concerns except peace. Intending "to educate women to take an active role in eliminating war as a means of solving disputes between nations, people and ideologies," Another Mother took the position that war was "obsolete—that civilized methods must be creatively sought and implemented to resolve international differences in Vietnam and elsewhere."[44] To promote its educational goals, Another Mother for Peace held its first annual Mother's Day Assembly in Los Angeles in May 1969. At this meeting the organizers introduced their vision of Pax Materna, "a permanent irrevocable condition of amnesty and understanding among mothers of the world" and unveiled their new logo. Created by Lorraine Schneider, the logo consisted of a large flower around which was written in big letters, "War is not healthy for children or other living things."[45] This logo, with its inscription eventually translated into more than twenty languages, retains its popularity today. The assembly was also the beginning of the women's efforts to pass on information about the nuclear arms race, chemical and biological warfare, the environmental effects of the nuclear arms race, and the military budget. Another

Mother for Peace extended its efforts beyond the Vietnam War era. Although it announced its intention to disband after January 1979, it continued producing a newsletter and other peace literature until 1985.

Although the Vietnam War sparked the creation of innumerable antiwar organizations, it also produced a sense of disunity in the older, more established groups. After the election of Nixon in 1968, antiwar organizing became more difficult. Nixon's order to cut back the number of troops in Vietnam anesthetized part of the society into believing the war was ending, while his escalation of the bombing of North Vietnam and the incursions into Cambodia infuriated others. Those whose self-appointed spokesmen styled themselves the "Silent Majority," expressing support for Nixon and such traditional U.S. values as patriotic fervor, came into conflict with the counterculture, represented by hippies, Yippies, and peace activists. As the war moved into the 1970s, the antiwar movement, which had produced a national feeling of disgust for the war, no longer had much momentum, and many younger women opted to move into women's liberation organizations. By January 1973, when the United States and Vietnam signed a cease-fire agreement, the antiwar movement had lost its cohesiveness. Harriet Barron of the Metropolitan New York branch of WILPF had already expressed this feeling very clearly in the summer of 1970. After several years of dedicated activism in protest of the war, Barron still felt a lack of accomplishment. To a fellow WILPFer, Ruth Sillman, who was also feeling disheartened, she wrote, "I know pretty much how you feel because I'm feeling the same way. We've done so many things (not enough I know) and made so little actual headway in ending the war; and the peace movement is splintered."[46]

Nevertheless, WILPF had done a great deal to contribute to the demise of popular support for the war. In fact, membership actually rose during that period. As the effects of McCarthyism became a part of history and the Vietnam War itself became a symbol of the toll of war, the organization once again attracted new members. By the 1980s, it averaged between ten and fifteen thousand members each year. Women Strike for Peace, on the other hand, saw a decline in membership after the war. In 1974 the organization's leaders decided to redirect their attention back to their original concern over nuclear disarmament and to address the issue of amnesty for Vietnam era draft evaders.[47] WILPF, always a multi-issue organization, in the meantime maintained its interest in Vietnam. After the North Vietnamese swept through South Vietnam in April 1975, driving the remaining U.S. military and governmental personnel from the country, WILPF joined many other voices urging the normalization of relations between the two nations, an end to the U.S. economic blockade, and the establishment of U.S. assistance in the rebuilding of a united Vietnam.

The great assortment of people and organizations that participated in the antiwar movement of the Vietnam era bore a surface resemblance to the pro-peace movement of the interwar era. As a popular cause they had indeed affected U.S. government policy in Vietnam and contributed to the termination of the war. For women, however, the significance of the Vietnam-era movement was very different from that of the earlier movement. During the 1920s and 1930s, the former suffragists played a dominant role in the creation of all-female peace organizations. In a feminist voice, they often linked the effects of war with violence against women. By the mid-thirties, this voice had become one of panic, in reaction to the expansion of fascism and the apparently inevitable approach of another world war. The feminist tone was lost, at least in the rhetoric, though not in the women's method of organizing. When World War II began, this voice was drowned out.

The antiwar movement of the mid-1960s had quite the opposite fate. Not only did it influence the end of the war, but it also gave impetus to the rebirth of feminist expression within the peace movement, especially in Women Strike for Peace. This reawakening was part of the emergence of what was then called the "Women's Liberation" movement, an outgrowth of white female discontent within the civil rights, New Left, and antidraft organizations, all of which tended to highlight the importance of male leadership and men's issues. The female exodus from SDS was especially important to the renewal of feminism in the peace movement. In turn, the peace movement was a natural place to cultivate this new feminism. After all, there were already existing organizations of women keeping the issue alive, and, traditionally, feminists had played a central part in peace organizing.

Although younger women were changing the face of Women Strike for Peace and tentatively approaching WILPF, the new feminism officially burst onto the peace movement scene in January 1968, when a

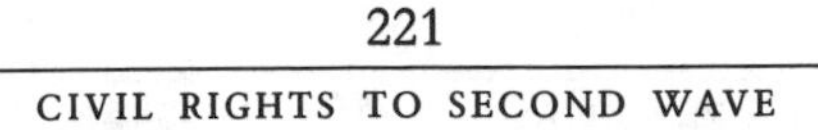

27. Flier about the January 15, 1968, Washington, D.C., demonstration by the Jeannette Rankin Brigade. Courtesy of Swarthmore College Peace Collection.

coalition of women's organizations, including WILPF and WSP, joined together under the name of the Jeannette Rankin Brigade in order "to confront Congress on its opening day, January 15, 1968, with a strong show of female opposition to the Vietnam War."[48] Jeannette Rankin as a member of the House of Representatives had voted against U.S. participation in World War I and had been the only member of Congress to vote against a U.S. declaration of war in 1941. In 1967, Rankin, still committed to a peaceful world, had stated that if 10,000 women would be willing to risk imprisonment to end the war, then the fighting would cease.

Thousands of women responded to Rankin's suggestion, resulting in a WILPF member's proposal that Rankin lead a march on Washington. Between 3,000 and 5,000 women turned out for the occasion. After the women reached the Capitol, Jeannette Rankin and Coretta Scott King entered the building to present the petition to the Speaker of the House and the Senate Majority leader. Beginning "We, the United States women, who are outraged by the ruthless slaughter in Vietnam, and the persistent neglect of human needs at home . . . ," the document demanded the end of the Asian war and the beginning of the healing process at home.[49]

What was most important about the event, however, was not its traditional aspect of presenting a statement to the men in power, but rather its break with tradition. In a ritual organized by a recently formed women's liberation group calling itself New York Radical Women, various members of the Jeannette Rankin Brigade who were disturbed by the nature of the presentation to Congress, marched to Arlington Cemetery carrying the dummy of a rather staid-looking woman to bury as "Traditional Womanhood." Before the event the women distributed the black-bordered invitation, created by Shulamith Firestone, which challenged feminist peace activists to break from their older conservative strategies and to venture into new waters.

> Don't bring flowers . . . Do be prepared to sacrifice your traditional female roles. You have refused to hanky-wave boys off to war with admonitions to save the American Mom and Apple Pie. You have resisted your roles of supportive girl friends and tearful widows, . . . And now you must resist approaching Congress and playing these same roles that are synonymous with powerlessness. We must not come as passive suppliants begging for favors, for power cooperates only with power. We must learn to fight the warmongers on their own terms, though they believe us capable only of rolling bandages. . . . Until we have unified into a force

> to be reckoned with, we will be patronized and ridiculed into total political ineffectiveness.[50]

At Arlington, the New York Radical Women performed a ceremony accompanied by a "Liturgy for the Burial of Traditional Womanhood" written by Peggy Dobbins. The "Liturgy," although intended to break new ground in the way women were to perceive war, actually reflected the sentiments prevalent in feminist peace activism as far back as the early 1800s. Just as in 1836, when William Ladd had admonished women for teaching their children to sing war songs and to play military games and for going themselves to military balls, so the Radical Women blamed their sisters for glorifying the military spirit:

> Oh women
> YOUNG WOMEN (response)
> Civilized women, we have sinned.
> We have sinned to the trill of martial trumpets
> And patriotic hymns
> For the thrill of pride and power
> And to glory in lusty men
> We cheered and waved and goaded
> Our men to murder and maim
> For heroic virility in our eyes.[51]

The ritual also expressed the same sentiments of World War I and interwar activists, who believed that women needed to gain the vote and equal participation in government in order to prevent the scourge of war. During both eras, women actively organized and lobbied, supporting only those political candidates who promised to work for peace legislation, although they were aware that their views on government were more often than not disparaged as being feminine, not masculine ones. The Radical Women promised the same action:

> Women unabashed of feelings
> Loving peace
> And lively bodies
> More than efficiency
> And exigencies
> Of war.

We also *[sic]*
We have sinned
Aquiescing *[sic]* to an order
That indulges peaceful pleas
And writes them off as female logic
Saying peace is womanly.
We sin with brimming hearts conceding
Our arguments are filled with feeling
And feeling must give way to legalese.
We sinned today
If we indulge our hearts
And leave thought and action to men.
We sin tomorrow
If cool computators act out their parts
Blameless, if we cannot find our minds and courage
To force rediscovery of heart.[52]

The Radical Women appeared to assume full blame for the male power structure's lust for blood. Women had made a tradeoff. In exchange for the privileged position of housewife and mother, as exemplified by the suburban dream of the 1950s and the first half of the 1960s, women had allowed the "destruction of our intellect and courage."[53] But times were about to change.

According to Kathie Sarachild (at the time, Kathie Amatniek), one of the spokeswomen for the New York Radical Women, the drafting of large numbers of young men for service in Vietnam indirectly worked against women's desire to gain equality within the antiwar movement and within the larger society.[54] Indeed, the exclusion of women from the draft emphasized all the more that they were second-class citizens. Whereas young men could exert some semblance of power over their own lives by refusing to be drafted, all that the women could do was to support that effort. Women as a group had no concrete way to exert real pressure on governmental leaders.

In "A Call for Women's Liberation," published in the January 1968 issue of *The Resistance,* Sue Munaker observed: "Men are drafted; women can counsel them not to go. Men return their draft cards; women sign complicity statements. That is, men take the stand, women support them."[55] Munaker pointed out that "a new consciousness" was developing among women. "Out of the frustration of trying to find our place in the anti-draft movement, we have come to realize that our total lives have been spent defining ourselves in relation to men."[56] In an address to the Jeannette Rankin Brigade, Kathie Sarachild drew upon the lingering sense of frustration also felt by earlier generations of feminist peace activists as she described a broader vision of equality. Although it was evident that women were "powerless and ineffective over the issues of war and peace," it was also true that women were powerless over their own lives as well. In order to gain power, it was necessary for all women to join together so that men were no longer offered the alternative of the "other woman" when the one they lived with began "acting politically," insisting on such personal equality as shared housework and childcare, "fully and equally, so that we can have independent lives as well." With the insistence that women be allowed their freedom, "as full human beings," Sarachild pointed the way towards a more egalitarian society than even her foremothers had envisioned.[57]

The women of WILPF, in particular, were no strangers to the idea that gender and war were intimately related. Therefore, while some WILPFers may have been taken aback by the new use of women's traditional roles as a form of protest art, others welcomed the revival of feminism into the organization. The Metropolitan New York branch, with its long history of adventurous stands, issued a recruitment flier in 1968 directly acknowledging that autumn's women's liberation demonstration in Atlantic City criticizing the annual Miss America pageant. At this demonstration, women allegedly burned their bras. The flier—headed "All Women are Victims in this Man's War!"—emphasized that until the war in Vietnam was ended, "other important issues," such as the "liberalization of abortion laws, Federal funding for child care, real equality under the law, equal employment opportunities for women and a strong women's political voice" could not be addressed. WILPF, the flier continued, had a "long history in the struggle for peace and women's rights," and, indeed, "women's liberation" had been one of the organization's goals since 1915 when Jane Addams was its president. As the flier pointed out, "She never burned her bra that we know of but she knew how to get things done."[58]

The national WILPF organization also moved towards reaffirming its commitment to feminism. In February 1967, the U.S. section of

WILPF sponsored a conference whose theme was "Women's Response to the Rising Tide of Violence." At this meeting, the organization once again drew connections between the violence of war and violence against women, especially through rape and battering. By 1970 the national board was taking up a theme and its attendant rhetoric from WILPF's earlier days: women were superior to men, and women's liberation proponents should not "Equate equality and similarity—the idealization of masculine attributes."[59] WILPF's national board, however, continued its balancing act as it had on the declarations of the two world wars, on neutrality, on the conscription of women and on Communism. Feminism and equality should be respected, the board emphasized, but so should women's traditional values and roles within the home and family for their moral contribution to society.

With the Vietnam War had come a resurgence of feminism within the peace movement. When the war ended, the women's liberation movement did not evaporate as many antiwar organizations did. That movement continued to thrive, and feminist peace sentiment was one of its beneficiaries. Feminists in the new era would have to continue reaching out to other women. In 1972, on her ninety-first birthday, Jeannette Rankin offered the new generation this advice: "It never did any good for all the suffragettes to come together and talk to each other. There will be no revolution unless we go out into the precincts. You have to be stubborn. Stubborn and ornery." She added, "And when the men make fun of you, that's when you know you're getting on well."[60] As the years after 1975 would show, the younger women took her advice to heart.

{8}

Feminist Peace Activism and the United Nations' Decade for Women, 1975–1985

NINETEEN SEVENTY-FIVE ushered in the United Nations' International Women's Year, which soon evolved into the Decade for Women—ten years of unprecedented global organizing around issues concerning women's social, economic, and political well-being. Peace, of course, was central to the Decade's activities. Not only did established organizations such as WILPF and Women Strike for Peace play instrumental roles in the blossoming of antimilitarist sentiment, but the decade also stimulated the growing commitment of younger women to peace activism.

The Vietnam War of the previous two decades had acted as the catalyst for the renewal of active feminism in the peace movement, and the global nature of the UN Decade for Women added breadth to that new intensity. Feminists committed to peace began to elucidate many sorts of sophisticated connections, linking poverty, sexism, race-hatred, violence against women and children, ecological damage, and a myriad of other social, economic, and political ills with militarism, the nuclear arms race, and Cold War intrusions into the affairs of developing nations. Growing in importance was an emphasis on the practice of nonviolence as epitomized by William Lloyd Garrison, Mohandas Gandhi, and Martin Luther King, Jr. During the Decade for Women, feminist peace activists utilized nonviolent activities and images unique to women in order to dramatize their concerns and demands.

The UN's sponsorship of many events during the Decade ensured that women's issues would not be construed only from a white, western perspective. As a result, the ten years involved as much discussion as it did activities. One woman's definition of peace did not necessarily match with another's. In fact, very often women found themselves at odds over what conditions were necessary to ensure peace. Although most women agreed that a warless world could not be achieved unless everyone on the face of the earth had basic needs fulfilled—food, shelter, health care, education, and employment—they disagreed on political solutions to world tensions. A few of the most dramatic clashes were between Palestinian and Israeli women, between Cuban exiles and Cuban nationals, between white and black South Africans, and between the Taiwanese and the mainland Chinese. Work to define such concepts as *feminism, peace,* and *justice,* begun during the Decade, still galvanizes the women's rights wing of the peace movement.

In spite of the truly global nature of the Decade, until 1980 the traditional U.S. feminist peace organizations continued to reflect a white, middle-class, middle-aged (even elderly) leadership. As in the 1920s and 1930s, younger women were often attracted to mixed-gender groups. From the late 1960s into the mid-1970s, they were also seeking out feminist organizations that combined consciousness raising with political activism. The women's liberation movement, which grew out of these groups, developed radical and socialist feminist strands with varied approaches to peace work. African-American, Native American, and Latina women also continued to shy away from most of the women's rights peace organizations in favor of working more specifically on the issues surrounding race and community. This division of labor did not mean that the peace organizations isolated themselves. Rather, coalition building became more a necessity than a choice, and the national as well as international women's rights networks grew stronger.

Nineteen seventy-five was also the year that the U.S. section of WILPF started to overcome some of its earlier conservative attitudes. In that year, for example, the organization joined its international body and the WIDF in cosponsoring a seminar in New York City entitled "Women of the World United for Peace: Disarmament and Its Social Consequences." Designed as WILPF's first of many meetings during the Decade for Women, the seminar created the opportunity for 250 women from twenty-seven countries to bring together their diverse approaches to achieving world disarmament. As at so many WILPF conferences throughout the twentieth century, the tradition of debating foreign policy issues in order to offer advice to the men in power remained intact.[1]

Throughout the Decade, WILPF organizations at all levels—international, national, and local—concentrated on the global implications of the nuclear arms race. This broad focus allowed the organization to address every conceivable issue. Time and time again, the group illustrated how money being poured into weapons development could be put to better use. One flier issued by the Metropolitan New York branch of WILPF, for example, was headed with the International Women's Year logo and the words "Women Demand Disarmament: 1975 is International Women's Year—Military Spending Threatens the Goals of Equality, Development, Peace." The message was that military spending meant "inflation" and "fewer jobs," especially for women, who were the "last hired, first fired." In a year when the federal government was calling for increased military spending but a $17 billion cut in funds for Medicaid, food stamps, and community health services, the New York branch emphasized that it was up to women to join "women's" community groups "working for peace and equality."[2] This flier reflected that the women of WILPF had begun to acknowledge to themselves that, although they chose to link other issues with peace, large numbers of women preferred to donate their time and money to organizations which addressed more immediate concerns.

The new era, however, did not produce great changes in WILPF's style of activism. The group as a whole continued to rely on the traditional forms of organizing, including small and large meetings, petition campaigns, marches, and participation in many coalition efforts. The two most energetic efforts were the "STAR" campaign, begun on March 8, 1982, and the antinuclear march and rally in New York City on June 12, 1982. "STAR," standing for "Stop the Arms Race," was a massive petition effort. The goal was to collect one million signatures from women who pledged to work for disarmament. The petition also demanded a freeze on U.S. and Soviet nuclear weapons development, a comprehensive test-ban treaty, cutbacks in military budgets, and support for any disarmament proposals put forth by the United Nations. Every woman who signed the petition donated one dollar to WILPF and received a button that proclaimed "One in a Million—Stop the Arms Race." One year later, on March 8, 1983, the entire one million signatures were presented to a NATO meeting in Brussels.

The June march in New York was a massive coalition effort consisting of pre-march conferences, cultural events, lectures, receptions, petition presentations, and civil disobedience actions at embassies of the nuclear powers, especially the United States, the Soviet Union, China, and France. The march itself, numbering somewhere between 750,000 and 1,000,000 people, culminated in a huge rally and concert in Central Park. To date, it is the largest peace demonstration ever held in this nation.

Big demonstrations and petition drives, however, often drove away younger women who wanted to see more evidence of female anger and creativity. Organizing these traditional events was often perceived as old-fashioned and boring. The experience itself did not offer opportunities for further developing one's feminist consciousness nor did it necessarily open the way for dealing more closely with women's more immediate concerns. During the World War I and interwar eras, women's political rights seemed to be the most urgent issue, but in the new era feminist activists were more concerned with concrete social and economic issues. How were women going to achieve wage parity? How were they going to free themselves from abusive relationships? How could women participate in the labor force when they could not secure healthy and affordable child care? How could women of color move forward until racism was confronted directly? How could lesbians participate in a society or movement riddled with homophobia?

WILPF did not always have an easy time adjusting to this new demand on the peace movement to be more active and meaningful to *all* women. Reactions in the Metropolitan New York branch can be seen as a microcosm of those in the larger organization. Its 1968 recruitment flier, which claimed WILPF's historical connection with the issue of women's rights, showed the branch's interest in the new feminism. The branch's actions, however, were not always consistent with its awareness of what a modern feminist would (or should) do. So, although in March 1975 the women advertised a rally for International Women's Day whose speakers and entertainers would represent "all aspects, ages, and conditions of women's struggle," three years later the leadership balked at the suggestion of a younger member, Blanche Wiesen Cook, that a group of feminist academics be included in the branch to give it "a boost" and "to move WILPF along as it desperately needed to move."[3]

The older New York women resisted two changes that threatened their leadership and style: the entrance of feminism into its policy-making and the loss of control over decision making to younger women. In many ways, this situation was a replay of the suffragists' reluctance to hand over the reins of power to younger women who had not been trained through their movement. Their reticence had been one of the factors in the demise of the Women's Peace Society and the Women's Peace Union. Throughout the Decade for Women, there was discussion among younger women over the apparent inability of older women to take a back seat without feeling that they were no longer vital to the organization. The national WILPF leadership also reflected this concern over age. Younger women like Jane Midgley and Libby Frank acted as paid staff, much as Dorothy Detzer had done earlier. The national board and national membership, however, did not begin to reflect the inclusion of younger women, twenty or thirty years old, until the mid-1980s.

Women Strike for Peace also entered the Decade as a matronly organization. The thirty-fiveish mothers of 1960 had become the fifty-ish women of 1975. As in the case of WILPF, younger women who were attracted to the informal, radical nature of the women's movement were put off by the middle-class WSPers. Accordingly, many younger women who had aligned themselves with the organization moved over to more radical women's liberation groups. The mood of the day was not to compromise with the older organizations and leaders but, instead, to challenge them. The WSP leadership was well aware of this situation as early as 1972 when member Rita Handman reported to the national office that the organization's weakness rested in its "inability to consistently replenish [its] ranks with new young women." Handman acknowledged that with U.S. troop withdrawal from Vietnam, WSP could no longer "appeal to women . . . on the basis of their sons, brothers and husbands dying." Rather, the organization needed to appeal to women on the basis of "their own self-interest," namely, domestic and economic problems. Handman pointed out, however, that although the organization often discussed the predicament, the members did not work "seriously" to resolve it.[4]

As a result, after the Vietnam War ended in April 1975, Women Strike for Peace's membership declined rapidly. In addition, some women who had worked for both WILPF and WSP during the 1960s opted to return to their former organization full-time. As one New York City woman explained it, "I felt . . . after the Vietnam War that Women Strike for Peace had sort of out-lived its usefulness, that we did not need two big women's peace movements, that WILPF was much older, was international, had some standing with NGO representation at the U.N. and was able to reach out and to work on a much more fundamentally sound, all-round basis for peace. . . . I felt that at this point, there should have been unification."[5] As a result, WSP needed to rely more on coalition work, placing its own emphasis once again on nuclear disarmament.

WSP generally depended on other organizations to take the lead on many issues it supported, such as reproductive rights, the Equal Rights Amendment, and women's rights. As with WILPF, however, WSP's new approach did embrace the revived feminist spirit especially visible during the UN's Decade for Women. In 1975, as the Decade got underway, WSP issued various fliers utilizing feminist themes. One of these, entitled "Women Strike for Peace and Survival, 1975," posited the age-old question, Why have a specifically *women's* campaign? Much in the spirit of feminist-pacifist foremothers of the interwar era, the leaflet stated:

> When women got the vote, they thought it would mean an end to war. But in fact, wars, weapons and destructive technology have increased. . . . Women must now rebel against those in power who insist that superiority in nuclear weapons can guarantee peace—and who insist that the destruction of small countries and support to corrupt and repressive dictators is necessary to insure national security. . . . WOMEN MUST LIBERATE THEMSELVES FROM MILITARY DOMINATION. . . . WOMEN MUST USE THE POWER OF THEIR PEN, THEIR VOTE AND THEIR ACTIVISM TO INFLUENCE THOSE IN POWER, AND TO PUT INTO POWER PEOPLE WHO WILL PLEDGE THEMSELVES TO THIS DIRECTION.[6]

As part of its work to educate the population about the risks of nuclear war, WSP in 1982 produced a combined flier and mail-in petition entitled "I Refuse to Be One of 20 Million 'Acceptable' Dead!" The appeal was in direct response to the Pentagon's "new strategic master plan" designed to ensure a U.S. military victory in case of a "limited" nuclear war with the Soviet Union. The plan listed a U.S. fatality rate of twenty million as "an acceptable cost" for such a win. The WSP flier included two mail-in coupons. One, addressed to President Ronald Reagan, stated, in part, "I am not a statistic. I and my family refuse to be part of the 20 MILLION ACCEPTABLE DEAD SCENARIO" and demanded a plan for the *"PREVENTION"* of nuclear war. The other coupon asked for donations to cover the cost of more advertising such as this one.[7]

Although both WILPF and Women Strike for Peace identified their chief recruitment problems as an inability to attract younger women and women of color, there is evidence that well into the 1970s the two organizations might still have been feeling the remnants of the anti-Communist spirit of the 1950s. However, so many organizations protested illegal surveillance that in 1975 President Gerald Ford appointed a commission to investigate the CIA's role in all of this. The commission confirmed what women in WSP had already suspected—that the CIA had paid a number of housewives to attend meetings, donate small amounts of money, and take part in activities so that they could be effective informants on the group and its members. As part of its operation, the CIA systematically opened the organization's mail. In 1976, WSP was among 7,200 individuals and 1,000 organizations in a $500 million lawsuit against the CIA and the National Security Agency. Charges of surveillance and infiltration were eventually dropped, but not that of illegally opening the mail. The case was settled out of court, winning the WSP women $5,000. One member recalled, "We used part of the money for our campaign to abolish the CIA."[8]

A few years later, on October 6, 1982, just four months after the monumental New York rally on June 12 and when the U.S. section of WILPF had rebuilt to approximately 15,000 members, the *Washington Post* described both it and WSP as "Soviet Fronts." Three days later the paper retracted its accusations, stating that the two organizations denied any "Soviet funding or control." The same editorial nonetheless reaffirmed that the U.S. State Department had recently "characterized the WILPF as an international front for the Soviet Union, and has designated the group as Communist-affiliated for purposes of granting visas to foreigners," though adding that the State Department's designation was aimed at the international organization, not the U.S. section.[9] Of course, the general public could not grasp the distinction.

As late as 1988, author Guenter Lewy, in his book *Peace and Revolution: The Moral Crisis of American Pacifism,* attacked WILPF, the War Resisters League, and the Fellowship of Reconciliation for being Communist dupes. According to Lewy, all three organizations took a sharp turn to the left during the 1960s, throwing in their lot with world communism by supporting revolutions such as those in Cuba, Nicaragua, and Grenada. In addition, according to Lewy, the leaders were naïve in that they never truly evaluated the politics of the situation. Rather, they blindly slanted their organizational rhetoric and programming away from pacifism and toward Communist agitating. With such accusations still in the wind, it is not surprising that WILPF and WSP had problems attracting new members, young or not.[10]

One seemingly new group which started forming locally in New York City in 1974, Women for Racial and Economic Equality, was actually the rebirth of the Congress of American Women, which had been forced to disband during the McCarthy era. The WREE organizers, although acquainted with some of the original members of the CAW, did not intend their organization to be a revival of the former group, nor were they necessarily even aware that the former group had even existed.[11] However, WREE, in its ultimate shape, resembled the CAW in its program, its interracial make-up, and its affiliation with the Women's International Democratic Federation.

From the beginning, WREE organizers reflected a clear class- and race-consciousness unparalleled in the history of the women's rights peace movement. Norma Spector, one of WREE's original New York founders, explained that the group was a direct reaction to the white, middle-class nature of the second wave of the women's movement. As new organizations multiplied, the women responsible for the birth of WREE reacted to what they perceived as "a vacuum," that is, the lack of a movement addressing concerns of the poor and women of color.[12] Accordingly, a small group of New York City women decided to form a grassroots organization that would confront basic issues, such as racism, sexism, welfare reform, reproductive rights, child care, housing, health care, food, and employment. The theme tying it all together was "peace."

The women who organized the initial WREE in 1974 and 1975 also believed in the power of women as a "sisterhood . . . around the world . . . a powerful force for peace" and felt a special responsibility to the women of such nations as Vietnam, Chile, and South Africa, "where the U.S. government and U.S. corporations play[ed] a vital role against liberation movements."[13] Because, like many organizers throughout the history of the feminist peace movement, several WREE organizers followed an anti-imperialist ideology and favored socialist solutions to economic ills, it was natural for them, like WILPF, to have contact with the WIDF, an organization most popular in communist nations. WREE's relationship with the WIDF, however—unlike WILPF's—was vital to WREE's efforts. The WIDF was, in effect, WREE's international base, just as the international WILPF organization was for the U.S. section. It was through attendance at the World Congress of Women in East Berlin in 1975, sponsored in part by the WIDF and the international organization of WILPF, that news of WREE's existence spread, resulting in a small organizational conference in Chicago the next March for the purpose of expanding WREE into a national organization. The following year, 1977, WREE held its first national meeting, again in Chicago. Women heard about the meeting through word of mouth because no money was available for advertising. The six hundred women who came together at that meeting included a bus of welfare mothers from Pittsburgh. Among the participants was WREE's first president, Josetta Lawus, a domestic worker who had organized the Philadelphia chapter.[14]

By 1977, WREE had chapters in twenty-five U.S. cities from coast to coast. While expanding, WREE continued to focus on peace. "The world peace we seek," stated Sondra Patrinos in her keynote address at WREE's first national convention, "is not an abstraction, but a necessary basis on which to build a movement for equality. As long as our country is controlled by those who profit from arms and war, so long will equality remain out of reach. . . . For us, peace is not simply the absence of a shooting war. It is a way of life that includes constructive normal relations between our country and other countries on the basis of equality among all nations."[15]

Even though WREE did not come from the long line of women's rights peace groups having their roots in the suffrage movement, the organization's spirit and beliefs paralleled those of the more traditional groups. Where WREE differed was in its commitment to including the young, the poor, and women of color in all levels of the organization, even the top leadership positions. No other feminist peace organization had been able to do this. In 1976 Georgia Henning, a leading WREE organizer, emphasized the importance of changing the course of women's organizations: "The acquiescence to racism that became the fundamental weakness of the women's suffrage movement is the part of the heritage we seek to erase. It is an un-natural, grafted-on characteristic which serves none but our enemies—those who wish to grow stronger by our division."[16] In a later speech Henning focused on the necessity for addressing racism within women's groups: "We must pledge ourselves as organizers in the women's movement never to allow ourselves to be a tool to divide race from race, women from women, nationality from nationality. If unity was EVER needed, it is needed now. Women are a powerful tool for that unity."[17]

The basis for WREE's work is the "Women's Bill of Rights," conceived at the original Chicago convention. As Georgia Henning explained, each point in the "Women's Bill of Rights" helped to "link" WREE with a variety of other organizations, such as labor unions, health groups, women's organizations, and the peace movement.[18] The list of demands made WREE's goals clear and indicated the nature of the organization's projects. The original document read:

> The organization is defined and directed by WREE's Women's Bill of Rights. WREE believes that full equality for women cannot be achieved until the following are in force:
>
> 1. Peace and security, an end to the arms race, freedom from racist and sexist violence.
> 2. A safe job at a living wage or a guaranteed annual income.
> 3. Equal pay for equal or comparable work.
> 4. Affirmative action to end discrimination in training, hiring and promotion.
> 5. Organization of the unorganized women to make the trade union movement reflect the interests of all workers.
> 6. A culture free from racist and sexist images of women, a culture that reflects our multi-national history and multi-lingual character.
> 7. Federally funded, nonracist, nonsexist child care for all who want or need it.

8. Federally funded nonracist, nonsexist public education.
9. A federally funded national health care system.
10. Full reproductive freedom, including maternity leave with pay, the right to federally funded abortion, and an end to experimentation and sterilization abuse.
11. Decent affordable housing.
12. An environment free from toxic wastes and industrial pollution.[19]

Later "The Women's Bill of Rights" was revised to stress not only peace through nuclear disarmament but also the cessation of U.S. military intervention in other nations, an end to the militarization of the U.S. economy and society, and the redirecting of the military budget into social programs.

Even though WREE's membership, which included a number of WILPFers, hovered around only 2,000, its outreach and reputation were national. Often WILPF and WREE cosponsored events, but WREE consistently attracted women who were younger, poorer, or members of minority groups. Like WILPF and Women Strike for Peace, WREE relied upon conferences, petitions, newsletters, and lectures for its outreach to the general public. In this respect WREE was still quite traditional.

WILPF, Women Strike for Peace and WREE were the three dominant women's rights peace organizations throughout the Decade for Women. Except for WREE's unique success in incorporating women of color and working and poorer women in both its leadership and its rank and file, they included similar types of women—middle-aged, middle-class, and white. All three organizations relied on the traditional tools for women's peace work: lobbying, petitioning, writing, and demonstrating. All three suffered from the age-old problems of raising enough money and recruiting enough volunteers to keep their work going.

Other smaller groups, also based on traditional organizing techniques, sprang up during the Decade for Women. None of them was a huge success, but a few are worth mentioning, primarily because they serve to illustrate the growing diversity within the women's rights peace movement during this period. During World War I, a woman wishing to join a feminist peace organization had as her only choice the Woman's Peace Party; by the mid-1980s, however, she could give her time, money, and effort to several groups.

One group of the early eighties seemed to be an offshoot of Women Strike for Peace. This was Women, USA, an organization headed by WSP member and former congresswoman Bella Abzug. Because of Abzug's dynamic feminism and popularity, Women, USA often utilized the services of WSP members, and the two organizations also cosponsored events. In general, Women, USA was intended to act as a funnel for concerns to be addressed through lobbying. It ended up being almost a one-woman show, with Abzug and her few staff people doing all the work.

One of the more successful activities of Women, USA was a forum cosponsored with WSP, the Metropolitan New York branch of WILPF, the Riverside Church Disarmament Program, and the Manhattan Women's Political Caucus to address President Jimmy Carter's 1979 recommendation to reinstitute registration for the military draft, which Richard Nixon had suspended. This time, however, registration threatened to include women as well as men. The initial public outcry to Carter's proposal was quite vociferous. For the first time since the early 1970s, there were campus protests and demonstrations in the major cities. Young women carried signs reminiscent of the ones carried by Vietnam-era draft resisters, with statements like "Hell, No, I Won't Go." Added on were sentiments such as "And neither will my boyfriend." On June 10, 1980, soon after the House Armed Services Military Personnel Committee rejected Carter's proposal to register women, Women, USA met at New York University for a "Women Against War Forum." The meeting focused on such questions as "Should Women Be Drafted?" and "Can Feminism and Militarism Live Together?"[20]

The draft issue forced feminists to confront their feelings about militarism. In some ways, it became an issue that divided them. "Peace" had always been a controversial topic among women's rights activists, but the draft issue of the early 1980s—a time when the U.S. was being particularly meddlesome but not involved in a major war—opened up more complicated issues concerning women's equality, especially as the Equal Rights Amendment was then before states for ratification. (It failed in 1982.) Many women, including those in NOW, for example, felt that if women wanted true equality, then they had to accept the bad along with the good, including the military draft. Other women, especially those in the peace movement and including Women, USA, agreed that men and women should be treated equally, but that neither of them should be faced with conscription. Still other women, particularly those concerned with women's work opportunities, felt that drafting women was to be applauded because it would open the way for them to obtain equality in another job area. These women also supported the idea that women should serve in combat along with men and be given every opportunity that male soldiers received for training, travel, and professional advancement. More cynical activists argued back that women might be drafted, but in the end they would be assigned secretarial, nursing, and domestic duties. Anti-ERA proponents like Phyllis Schlafley and her "Stop ERA" campaign used the draft issue to instill fear in uninformed women, suggesting that the very existence of the question proved that the ERA had to be defeated or all women would end up in the army, wearing fatigues, being placed in unfeminine positions, and being denied their rightful place as wives and mothers.

Such was the furor within the government and among the populace that the issue was brought before the Supreme Court. In its ruling, on June 25, 1981, in *Rostker v. Goldberg,* the Court upheld that women did not have to face conscription on the grounds that they were ineligible for combat. The previous March, when the Court had heard the case, Justice William H. Rehnquist claimed that Congress's decision not to register women was "not the accidental by-product of a traditional way of thinking about women." The justice then added that since "Women as a group, unlike men as a group, . . . not being eligible for combat . . . the exemption of women was closely related to the congressional purpose in instituting registration which was to prepare for a draft of combat troops, and, rather than being invidious, realistically reflected the fact that the sexes were not similarly situated."[21] In its final decision in June, the Court held that the ruling concerning women was "not violative of Fifth Amendment equal protection."[22]

Once the decision was announced, most draft debates ceased except for an occasional discussion centered around women and work. Feminist peace activists nonetheless persisted in their commitment that neither gender should have to register or be drafted. Women, USA kept its offices open into the mid-eighties, trying to arouse support for peace lobbying work. In 1984, a similar effort, Women's Peace Initiatives, was organized, primarily to join the Nuclear Freeze movement in lobbying for a U.S. governmental budget freeze on all nuclear arms testing and deployment.

In fact, during the Decade for Women, the few other organizations of the traditional mold that are covered in this study centered all their work around nuclear disarmament. In 1981, the Canadian group, Women's Party for Survival, founded by Dr. Helen Caldicott, changed its name to Women's Action for Nuclear Disarmament (WAND) and began to attract U.S. organizers. The group consisted of chapters—that used the WAND name—and affiliates. Men were as welcome to join as women. The original founding statement, however, emphasized the important traditional connections between peace and women's role as mothers:

> As women, we have traditionally been assigned the responsibility of caring for and raising children. The first priority of women, throughout history and throughout the world, is the survival of our offspring, and this survival is endangered by the present militaristic policies of those in power. . . . As women and mothers of the world, we speak with one voice. We must move into the political arena and assume leadership in order that the perspective of women, more oriented towards common sense, sensitivity, nurturance and survival, becomes predominant in U.S. policy. Women are the best organizers around. Accustomed to managing a home, a family, and a job, they can organize the United States for survival.[23]

As an organization, WAND dedicated itself to supporting continuous lobbying efforts and to informing the public about candidates' positions on nuclear arms development. The organization utilized telephone committees, newsletters, coalition building, membership conferences, and demonstrations. WAND was one more alternative for women interested in peace. But, unlike WILPF and WREE, WAND limited its concern to one aspect of peace: the nuclear arms race. This was a safe issue for women who wanted to work together but who did not want to delve into more politically controversial matters.[24]

Another similar group was Women for a Meaningful Summit,

formed in 1985 as a result of discussions at the final conference of the UN Decade for Women, held in Nairobi, Kenya. This small group, composed largely of women with graduate degrees and professional status, saw as its goal the presence of women's ideas at all of the summit meetings being held between the United States and the Soviet Union. Accordingly, the leaders traveled to each meeting, visiting with diplomats and organizing lobbying efforts, in a mission reminiscent of the many efforts made between 1919 and 1932 for women to be present as a pressure group at major meetings of the League of Nations. As much as feminists had tried to incorporate women equally and fully into the decision-making power structures of the world, Women for a Meaningful Summit clearly showed how futile their efforts had been. The meetings concerning major world issues were still limited to men; women, allotted embassy visits and quick encounters in hotel lobbies, remained on the periphery.

Another response to the frustration of being excluded from the power structure was the formation of Women Against Military Madness (WAMM) in Minneapolis in the fall of 1981. WAMM was an effort to revive the spirit that had spurred women to protest the Vietnam War; indeed, its founders had been friends during that era. Four issues had inspired them to establish yet another organization: (1) the nuclear arms race; (2) the extremely high military budget, resulting in (3) cutbacks in social programs, and (4) U.S. military intervention in Third World countries. WAMM's rationale for forming an all-female group, which echoed all the others of the period, made it poignantly clear that whether because of lack of communication, locale, political views or whatever, the women's rights peace movement was falling into redundancy. In response to their own question, "Why a Women's Group?," the members wrote, "All of society is victimized by rampant militarism. However, women lack access to the policy making levels of the three institutions which run the United States, the government, the Pentagon and the corporations. Thus women are doubly victimized and can only liberate themselves."[25] WAMM also emphasized the connection between the nuclear arms race and the destruction of our planet's ecological balance, a connection that was being explored in some detail throughout the Decade. As a local organization, WAMM achieved some success, with membership lists in 1983 growing to over one thousand. During that same year the group sponsored a Mother's Day march that attracted 7,000 participants, held approximately 140 smaller demonstrations at freeway entrances, and also participated at 55 demonstrations in the centers of Minneapolis and St. Paul.[26]

Throughout the decades of feminist peace activism, anger had been a major driving force. This emotional response to powerlessness was made very visible by the most dramatic, most feminist-defined, most aggressive, and most effective of the women's rights peace activities to date: the international peace encampment movement. Actually, this movement grew out of the continuous attention being paid to women's issues through efforts during the UN Decade, the development of new feminist-pacifist literature, the introduction of feminist-pacifist debate within the women's liberation movement, and the creation of the Women's Pentagon Action. From 1975 to 1985 women's rights activists worldwide received a nod of acceptance (I hesitate to use the word *approval*) from the broader international community. Perhaps, because peace was a major concern for the UN—as well as the chief underlying reason for its existence—it was the UN's sponsorship of the Decade that made it more feasible for feminists to organize around the peace issue.

The first women's peace encampment was established at Greenham Common, England, in August 1981, in response to a NATO announcement that ninety-six U.S. cruise missiles were to be deployed at a U.S. Air Force base there. To make matters worse, the U.S. military, not the British themselves, were to control the weapons. Placement of cruise missiles—not only in England but in several western European nations, including West Germany, Denmark, the Netherlands, and Italy—aroused great consternation, especially in those people already involved in the peace movement. In Wales the anxiety was a catalyst for positive action: a small group of women organized a 125-mile protest march from Cardiff in South Wales to Greenham Common. After the women, some with children in tow, arrived at Greenham on September 5, a number returned home, while others decided to stay and establish an ongoing protest camp on the town "common," a public open space outside the base. Attracted by media attention and word-of-mouth communication, other women joined in the effort, staying anywhere from a day to months or, in the case of a few, years. The women at Greenham Common served as a role model for the development of other peace encampments designed to confront the nuclear arms empire on its own turf but by using nonviolent, uniquely feminist, means of protest.[27]

In the United States the women's peace encampment movement grew out of a new feminist presence in the peace and women's rights movements. The new activists all reflected a resurgence, or the "second wave," of nonviolent resistance within the women's rights peace movement. Many of them were then exploring the connections between ecology and feminism, the new feminist spirituality, and the use of direct nonviolent action. Because the second wave of feminism and the UN Decade for Women had fostered the acceptance of women's intellectual and spiritual sides, women's writings, whether from the past or newly composed, had a steadily growing audience. In this favorable climate came the "discovery" of such pacifist theorists as Jane Addams and Emily Greene Balch, but new voices were constantly being added.

One of these voices was that of Barbara Deming, an outspoken pacifist, civil rights worker, and lesbian.[28] Deming was born in New York City in 1917, a descendant on her mother's side of Elihu Burritt, an early abolitionist and peace advocate. Educated in Quaker schools through high school, Deming in her early adult years delved into theater and editorial work and was from 1942 to 1944 a film analyst for the Library of Congress. In 1959, after a trip to India, she began reading the works of Gandhi. His views, and those of Martin Luther King, Jr., helped to shape her own. Deming's, though, took a decidedly feminist slant, especially after her experiences in both the peace and civil rights movements of the 1960s. This involvement resulted in a twenty-four-day jail sentence in Albany, Georgia, in 1964 and her deportation from Saigon, South Vietnam, in 1966 for peace protest. Throughout the sixties Deming clarified her views of the connections between the power of patriarchy and sexual violence. Such connections had global implications, she wrote in 1976, for "imperialist actions do seem to me, more and more clearly, to be patriarchal acts, acts of rape. . . . I now put my hopes for real social change above all else in the feminist movement and also my hopes for the further invention of nonviolence. I think the root violence in our society is the attempt by men to claim women and children as their property."[29]

Deming did not blame all men for violence. And, like her feminist nonresistant predecessors, she was careful to blame the concepts and the system rather than individuals. "The feminist vision . . . abandons the concept of naming enemies," she wrote, "and adopts a concept familiar to the nonviolent tradition: naming behavior that is oppressive, naming abuse of power that is held unfairly and must be destroyed, but naming no person whom we are willing to destroy. If we can destroy a man's power to tyrannize, there is no need, of course, to destroy the man himself."[30]

Deming, like many nonresisters, had great faith in the future possibility of a nonviolent world. She felt that men had to realize that they were constantly "living a lie," and this pretense was the cause of all their personal violence and anger. If men could stop "living the lie," they would change and so would life. "We ARE one kind—women and men," Deming insisted. "And that world IS possible. When more and more of us find we can believe it, and can hold to that belief, then perhaps we'll be able to release all our anger . . . without fear."[31] The feminist peace movement lost a great voice when Barbara Deming died of cancer in 1984.

During the last half of the Decade for Women, several other powerful feminist voices arose, and numerous books, articles, and pamphlets were published. One of the first anthologies of feminism and peace to emerge in this country was *Reweaving the Web of Life: Feminism and Nonviolence,* edited by Pam McAllister. Published in 1982, this book presented essays, poems, and stories that followed Barbara Deming's approach to feminism and nonviolence. In the introductory essay McAllister explained the need for feminist nonviolence as a tool against patriarchal brutality:

> The peculiar strength of nonviolence comes from the dual nature of its approach—the offering of respect and concern on the one hand and of defiance and stubborn noncooperation with injustice on the other. Put into the feminist perspective, nonviolence is the merging of our uncompromising rage at the patriarchy's brutal destructiveness with a refusal to adopt its ways—a refusal to give in to despair or hate or to let men off the hook by making them the 'other' as they have made those they fear 'others.'[32]

McAllister supported Deming's view that it was harmful ideas and social structures—not the individuals behind them—that were to be condemned.

In an effort to strike out against a clear and identifiable institution, the Women's Pentagon Action (WPA) emerged. This group was pulled together by Ynestra King, then a graduate student, and several other women who were frightened and outraged over the nuclear power plant accident at Three Mile Island, Pennsylvania, in the fall of 1979. By the following March, King had done much of the organizational work needed for a conference on "Women and Life on Earth: Ecofeminism in the Eighties." Over seven hundred women from the Northeast attended the event, from which the Pentagon emerged "as a symbol of all the male violence we opposed." The Pentagon, King further explained, "is the real workplace of the American generals who plan the annihilation of the world as their daily work, far removed from the lives they imperil and the murders they commit. We wanted it to be clear to women around the world that there is feminist awareness of, and opposition to, the imperialist role of the United States military over the globe."[33]

The new women's nonresistance movement, as exemplified by the Women's Pentagon Action and the peace encampments, did not make legislative lobbying and the changing of laws its focus. Instead, the women chose to work largely outside the political mainstream. This trend reflected the changes that had occurred within the women's liberation movement in the early 1970s. At that time, "radical" feminists and "socialist" feminists divided over their differing interpretations of women's situation. In the view of radical feminists, the oppressors of women were men; socialist feminists, on the other hand, saw the oppression in terms of the class struggle. From the two ideologies came different forms of political expression. Radical feminists felt it was necessary to change society culturally and philosophically in order for women to gain equality. Therefore, women needed to develop separately from men—culturally, politically, organizationally, socially, and personally. Socialist feminists, in contrast, believed that a reconstruction of the economic and political components of the society would result in women's rights and that, accordingly, it was necessary to work within political organizations that included men.[34]

By the 1980s the many new organizations and the women's culture—self-sufficient with exciting literature, music, and intellectual debate—filled the women's rights peace movement with renewed energy.

Older feminist pacifists could easily identify with the idea of a separate women's culture. After all, they themselves had chosen that route in their peace work. But the new feminists, besides being younger, also included a good number of lesbians who had nurtured radical feminism. These women added a new element, to which older pacifists were resistant. Throughout the UN Decade for Women, the issue of homophobia within the traditional movement arose time and time again. As a result, separate peace organizations, such as the Women's Pentagon Action, developed. The newer organizations embraced radical feminists, socialist feminists who preferred to work in women-centered groups, lesbian feminists, and the initial ecofeminists. Many women used more than one of these labels to describe themselves.

Ecofeminism evolved out of the peace activism within radical and socialist feminism. It also paralleled the wider ecology movement. Soon after the 1980 "Women and Life on Earth" conference, Ynestra King became a leading spokeswoman and theorist for the idea. In "Healing the Wounds: Feminism, Ecology, and the Nature/Culture Dualism," King explained that radical feminists, who believed that the "subordination of women [was] the root of human oppression," also closely related this oppression to the association of women with nature.[35] If society were rid of patriarchy, then not only women but other parts of society as well would be liberated.

The "woman/nature" connection, however, presented a personal dilemma for radical feminists. For some, accepting the link meant retaining society's traditional belief that women belonged in the realm of nature, which, in turn, reinforced sex-role stereotyping. King referred to this faction as "radical rationalist feminism." For others, the link meant that women needed "a separate feminist philosophy from the vantage point of identification with nature and a celebration of the woman/nature connection." "Radical cultural feminism," as King termed it, "celebrated life" within a "female ghetto," producing a "deeply woman-identified movement" that emphasized women's connection with nature in music, art, literature, poetry, and in communes. Among the offshoots of radical cultural feminism was a spirituality movement, which favored goddess-worship, covens, paganism, or some combination thereof. Its most commonly shared religious belief was that women "should celebrate their connection to the rest of life" and to use protest action to protect the earth.[36]

According to Ynestra King, ecofeminism combined the strengths of socialist feminism and radical cultural feminism. From the socialists came the historical critique of women's place in society, an approach through which it could be possible "to understand, and transform, history." From the radical culturalists, the ecofeminists adopted the concept that the personal was indeed political and that women needed "a beloved community, recognizing our connection with each other—and with nonhuman nature." Combining the two approaches, ecofeminism, as King defined it, used nature as "the central category of analysis . . . of the interrelated dominations of nature—psyche and sexuality, human oppression, and non-human nature—and the historic position of women in relation to those forms of domination."[37]

The ecofeminists quickly identified themselves with struggles in the Third World, with the poor in the United States, with people of color, and with ecological issues. They acknowledged that for most of the world's women, "interest in preservation of the land, water, air, and energy [was] no abstraction but a clear part of the effort to survive."[38] Militarization, the testing of nuclear weapons, toxic waste, and the devastation of the rain forests were all important issues to address. Furthermore, this destruction of "Mother Earth" reflected the age-old patriarchal belief that women's bodies were made for male consumption. Just as men raped the earth, so they raped women. In following this connection, ecofeminists, like their foremothers, continued to insist that world peace was a prerequisite for ending violence against women.

By September 11, 1980, many of the women who had attended the "Women and Life on Earth" conference had come together to form the Women's Pentagon Action, an organization which acted collectively, hoping to discourage the rise of media stars. Racism, U.S. imperialism, military spending, and nuclear weapons development were all singled out for attack in WPA literature. In the "Unity Statement of the Women's Pentagon Action" of 1980, drafted largely by author Grace Paley, an ecofeminist position was made quite clear: "We understand all is connectedness. The earth nourishes us as we with our bodies will eventually feed it. Through us, our mothers connected the human past to the human future. We know the life and work of animals and plants in seeding, reseeding and in fact simply inhabiting this planet. Their exploitation and the organized destruction of never to be seen again species threatens and sorrows us."[39]

Uniquely female creative protests, evolving from radical cultural feminism, became much in vogue during the Decade for Women. These demonstrations attracted media attention because of their theatrical use of traditional female imagery. For example, a small group of Vermont women who had woven the gates of a nuclear power plant closed with colorful yarns joined the Women's Pentagon Action on November 17, 1980, to repeat their action on the doors of the Pentagon. There they were joined by approximately two thousand women and huge, twenty-foot-high mourning puppets. The women planned four stages of action: mourning, rage, empowerment, and defiance. Mourning consisted of a walk through Arlington National Cemetery accompanied by drumbeats and moans. Upon reaching the Pentagon, the women created their own cemetery of unknown women, "victims of the war machine." Rage followed, with women angrily shouting their disdain for the military in chants including such slogans as "No More War" and "Take the Toys Away from the Boys." During empowerment, the two thousand women encircled the Pentagon, either hand-in-hand or using scarves to expand their reaches, and sang peace and women's songs. Finally, during defiance, the women moved up the steps, blocking the entrances to the Pentagon with their bodies in a show of nonviolent civil disobedience. Those arrested received sentences of from ten to thirty days in a federal prison.[40]

The next year, three thousand women repeated the action. Forty-three were imprisoned. While in the Arlington Jail in Virginia, the women issued a statement that reiterated their commitment not only to "direct nonviolent confrontation" but also to their global vision as ecofeminists: "We came to resist the patriarchy because we fear for our lives and for the life of the planet at the hands of these power-hungry men." Drawing an explicit connection between military violence and violence against women, they continued: "We acted because we fear for our own lives, and because we oppose the military mentality; that of rule by the biggest weapons, of penetration and domination. . . . We see this military mentality as intimately tied to the oppression and fears we women live with every day—the fear of rape, the oppression of having our reproductive choices taken from us, the coercion of compulsory heterosexuality." The statement ended with the connection of the personal with broader global issues: "This mentality works hand in glove with racism, using racism to justify imperialist aggression against Third World and native peoples in this country and abroad. These white men have stolen much from us and the theft is still going on."[41] This statement exemplifies the maturation and level of sophistication that the feminist peace movement had reached by the 1980s. Although statements of suffragists and early peace activists reflected these same emotions, it took the feminist education and literature of the second wave of the women's movement to turn latent images into a strong political agenda.

The two demonstrations of the Women's Pentagon Action eventually led to the founding of the Women's Encampment for a Future of Peace and Justice (also known as the Seneca Women's Peace Encampment), one in a series of efforts throughout the United States and various European nations. The Seneca encampment evolved out of the planning for the June 1982 Anti-Nuclear march and protests in New York City and a one-day meeting sponsored by WILPF and the Quaker-based American Friends Service Committee the day before the big march. This "Conference on Global Feminism and Disarmament" attracted several women from the Upstate [New York] Feminist Peace Alliance who were all alumnae of the Women's Pentagon Actions of both 1980 and 1981. After these women spoke of their own local demonstration the month before at the Seneca Army Depot, where the cruise and Pershing missile parts were stored until their deployment to Greenham, England, and other European destinations, the gathering hit upon the idea of establishing a women's peace encampment near the Seneca Depot in Romulus, New York, in solidarity with the British women who were encamped outside the Greenham base. WILPF agreed to raise money to buy an available farm bordering the base so that U.S. women could have a legal, safe space where they would not face eviction, a constant threat for their British sisters.[42]

The Seneca Women's Peace Encampment opened in July 1983. In many ways, the encampment embodied the utopian ideal that had motivated the women's rights peace movement since its inception in Garrisonian abolitionism. One member of the encampment described it as "a bold experiment in a communal life of nonviolence where women cooperate and share decision-making through consensus."[43] The basis of the encampment was to foster a communal atmosphere, a cooperative nature of work, and a nonhierarchical structure. Throughout its

28. Women from Seneca Women's Peace Encampment preparing for a demonstration at Seneca Army Depot, July 1983. Author's personal collection.

existence the Seneca encampment attracted many types of women—from a variety of professions, races, classes, religions, and political views. Loraine Hutchins' article, "Seneca—Summer of Action and Learning," which appeared in the feminist newspaper *Off Our Backs* in October 1983 described the diversity:

> The women who came were students, auto mechanics, book publishers, waitresses, army captains, elected officials, clergy-women, secretaries, artists, economists, teachers, social workers, and farmers. Our politics ranged from those believing women are naturally nurturing and must therefore change society for the better, to those supporting the system and the freeze but not disarmament, to those feeling only emotional outrage at the arms race, to those seeing feminism as an uprooting of all oppressions (capitalism, patriar-

chy, hierarchy), to those believing in mystical, spiritual, and apolitical methods (witches to Buddhist and Catholic nuns). We were lesbian, anarchist, communist, heterosexual, democrat, socialist, republican.[44]

The women relied on a dramatic flair for their demonstrations, utilizing the expression of a uniquely women's culture. The "Washer Woman Action" of 1983 exemplified this technique. During this demonstration, women acted out the daily washing, wringing, and hanging up of clothes. One participant wrote, "The silent ritual became a beautiful dance at times, as a tribute to the work of the washer woman and all women's work. The clothes stretched out on the length of the [Army base] fence symbolized women bringing themselves and their concerns (society's dirty laundry) to the Depot. The clothes were taken from the 'line,' folded and put away. Signs remained stating women's concerns."[45]

Unlike the usual peace action, which required extensive advance planning for a one-day event, the Seneca encampment depended on constant planning for a continuous series of actions, especially during its high point, the summer of 1983. Rhoda Linton, one of the many Women's Pentagon Action participants who became a part of Seneca's summer activities, described "The Governance System" at the encampment.[46] She noted the intricate structure devised, which allowed for constant group discussion and consensus, whether the number of residents equaled three or three thousand (as it did for the major demonstration held on August 1). Issues to which the peace movement had long been sensitive, such as racism and homophobia, were discussed in small, open groups, resulting in the beginnings of broader understanding and commitment to overcoming old prejudices in an effort to improve society. Nurturing the earth was also incorporated in the encampment's list of "respected policies." Campers were to recycle trash, collect only dead wood for fires, use designated paths in order to preserve the soil, and observe water conservation practices. Every woman who came to the encampment was expected to sign up for work, to donate money for food and other supplies, or both. Yet, as in several of their foremothers' organizations, there were to be no leaders or "stars."

The Seneca encampment was an experiment in feminist peace organizing. From the beginning, the women had to deal with external pressure as well as internal issues. The presence of the encampment in the Finger Lakes district served to highlight the polarities between hawks and doves in upstate New York.

On the one hand, the participants could expect support from a variety of sympathetic sources. Syracuse, for example, was the home of the Syracuse Cultural Workers Project, the Syracuse Peace Council, and the Syracuse University Center for Peace and the Resolution of Conflict. Rochester was the base for one of the oldest grassroots Peace Councils in the nation as well as the site of Susan B. Anthony's home. Seneca Falls was the birthplace of the women's rights movement. The Women's Rights National Park, situated in Seneca Falls, had already preserved Elizabeth Cady Stanton's home and was working on other sites important to the first women's rights convention in 1848. Harriet Tubman's home was in Auburn. Not only were there these associations with the present and recent past, but history indicated that in the 1590s, Iroquois women had met in Seneca in order to ask all the local tribes to put an end to warfare.

On the other hand, many local people supported the military presence. Upstate New York, once a bustling industrial region dependent on the intricate canal system, had become somewhat economically depressed. The Seneca Army Depot meant jobs for many people and customers for many businesses. The growth of the peace encampment was apparently threatening to both the townspeople, who felt allegiance to the military personnel as well as to the patriotic ideal, and the military, who did not want outsiders encroaching on the base.

The first confrontation with the townspeople was also a test for the inner workings of the camp itself.[47] The official opening ceremony for the encampment was scheduled for July 4. Just before that holiday, a local resident offered the women a U.S. flag to display, as was the townspeople's custom. The dilemma for the women was a complex but old one. If the camp was meant to reflect international solidarity, would it be appropriate to fly a national symbol? After prolonged discussion, the women made a decision: they would make flags of many nations or design flags of personal statements, none to exceed the size of a pillowcase. These flags could then be used at marches and demonstrations or simply hung along a clothesline on the front lawn, which faced the much-traveled Route 96. Although the long discussions and the reaching of a consensus helped to unite the women, the results served to alienate the town. So did many of the other actions designed to reflect a global ecofeminist perspective, such as the pledge recited at the opening ceremonies on the Fourth of July:

> We pledge allegiance to the earth
> And to the life which she provides
> One planet interconnected
> With beauty and peace for all.[48]

The tensions between the local population and the women reflected all the age-old harassment that women's rights peace activists had faced. Townspeople held placards at every demonstration; local newsmedia portrayed the women as threatening lesbian, Communist traitors out to cripple the nation's manhood or to set the stage for a Soviet, Nicaraguan, or Cuban takeover. The worst expression of this antagonism took place during the encampment's major weekend of demonstrations. The activities began on Saturday, July 30, when a group of about one hundred women left the town of Seneca Falls for a twelve-mile march to the encampment.[49] Some of the marchers carried large cutouts of former women's rights activists, such as Susan B. Anthony, Elizabeth Cady Stanton, and Sojourner Truth. Their intentions were to show the connection between the everyday oppression of women and the violence of war, a connection dating back to their role models' own roots in the abolitionist movement. At first the march promised to be peaceful and uneventful, but when the women reached the town of Waterloo, they were greeted by a large sign spanning the yard between two houses: "NUKE THEM TILL THEY GLOW, THEN SHOOT THEM IN THE DARK."[50]

As the women turned the corner to cross the Waterloo bridge, several hundred local residents, a number of them screaming epithets, met them. Some of the townspeople were carrying flagpoles, and as they became more and more enraged, they combined their insults with jabs. The women, with some justification, felt terrified. They decided to use the nonresistant technique of sitting down so that the violence might dissipate and the two sides might begin conversing. Ironically, the end result was that the women were arrested for disorderly conduct, and the provokers of the violence were sent on their way. In all, fifty-four women, all going under the name "Jane Doe," were arrested and spent five days in a makeshift jail at the Interlaken High School. Although on August 3 all charges against them were dropped, the incident, followed by an August 1 march of almost 3,000 women, raised many questions among the public. A few of the townspeople secretly took part in encampment events; one man and his son even drove up to the reception area and apologized for their neighbors' behavior. A group of Waterloo women appeared at the trial with placards reading "WE SUPPORT YOUR RIGHT TO WALK THROUGH OUR TOWN. THE CONSTITUTION SHELTERS YOU."[51]

The Seneca Peace Encampment served as a model for many other encampments across the United States: Palo Alto, California; Puget Sound, Washington; Tucson, Arizona; Sperry, Minnesota; Ann Arbor, Michigan; and Savannah, Georgia, to name but a few. The international movement begun in Greenham Common spread throughout Great Britain and into Europe—the Netherlands, Germany, Italy, Switzerland, Denmark, and Sweden—as well as to Canada and Australia. In addition, since soon after World War II, the Shibokusa women, who resided near Mount Fuji in Japan, continually disrupted U.S. military maneuvers on farmland formerly owned by local people.

Not only did the encampment capture the spirit of the United Nations Decade for Women, but it also invigorated the worldwide antinuclear movement. When on December 8, 1987, President Ronald Reagan of the United States and President Mikhail Gorbachev of the Soviet Union signed the Intermediate Nuclear Forces Treaty (the first international agreement ever signed to reverse the nuclear arms race), film clips, newspaper and magazine articles, and television documentaries all acknowledged that the international women's peace encampment movement had been instrumental in building public pressure in favor of nuclear arms reduction. Of all the women's rights peace activists' actions up to that time, the peace encampment movement was clearly the most far-reaching, the most clever, and the most successful—at least in the public's eyes. It was not, however, the longest-lasting. By 1985 the Seneca encampment, which had been active during the summer of 1984 and held sporadic demonstrations thereafter, was nearly defunct. The farm was still occupied by a small group of women, but the land became overgrown and unused. Part of the cause was the local government's refusal to grant the farm "camp" status; other causes had to do with disunity and lack of funding within the movement itself. Most of the other encampments became inactive soon after the signing of the 1987 treaty.

Equally notable for women's rights peace activists was the meeting in Nairobi, Kenya, in July 1985 to mark the end of the Decade's activities. The meeting, entitled "World Conference to Review and Appraise the Achievements of the U.N. Decade for Women: Equality, Development, and Peace," actually consisted of two separate meetings. The "official" sessions involved those representatives sent by their governments to discuss women's issues. For many women, especially those involved in grassroots organizing, the real conference was the one that took place at the same time, in the same place, but with different intentions. Known as the NGO Forum, these meetings were designed to parallel the official sessions but to include women from all over the globe who worked for UN-recognized nongovernmental organizations. Approximately 14,000 women flocked to these sessions.

Edith Ballantyne, the international president of WILPF, chaired the committee that planned discussions and activities focusing on the peace issue; under her guidance, the idea emerged for a "peace tent," a place where women could discuss the issues that the official conference planners appointed by their governments considered "too political."[52] These topics included apartheid in South Africa, imperialism by the great powers, and the resulting militarization of Third World countries, and, most important and sensitive, the antagonisms between the Israelis and the Palestinians over the question of a Palestinian homeland. The bright blue- and white-striped tent became a symbol of the NGO sessions. Generally, women would gather and as each spoke, the others would remain silent. There was a no-interruption policy. As one participant described it, "Here Soviet and American women pledged to work together. . . . Here also Palestinian and Israeli women came together in search of ways to end the conflict. Thousands of women passed through the tent. And when there were emotional contributions, every fifth speaker was interrupted by a singer leading the audience in a peace song."[53]

Through the UN activities sponsored during the Decade for Women and also as a result of the growing visibility of the feminist peace movement, peace as a global issue made its greatest advances during these ten years. No doubt the official sanctioning of women's issues by the United Nations had a tremendous impact on the numbers of women attracted to the three official conferences—in Mexico City, Copenhagen, and Nairobi—as well as on the diversity of women attracted to the peace encampments. Of course, the UN's validation of feminist concerns was not the only impetus for the activity. The invention of such Cold War weapons as the neutron bomb, the Pershing and cruise missiles, and the Strategic Defense Initiative (commonly called "Star Wars") frightened many people, while the imperialism implicit in the U.S. or Soviet involvement in Grenada, Nicaragua, Southern Africa, and Afghanistan angered many others. The Reagan era in the United States was characterized by a growth in military pride, yet the memories of Vietnam refused to fade. Edith Ballantyne summed up the sentiment of the Decade quite precisely when she spoke of the importance of peace to all women's lives. "Some governments and even NGO's," she said, "warn against the 'politicization' of the [Nairobi] conference and forum and want to see only 'women's issues' discussed. We should understand that every women's issue is political. One cannot seriously discuss questions of health, education, employment, development, and all others without considering each in its political and economic realities and possibilities. Peace is a political issue above all and it is a women's issue."[54]

WILPF, the foremother of all other women's rights peace organizations, continued to be in the leadership position as far as peace was concerned. In the United States, the national organization began making plans to continue its work beyond the official closing of the UN Decade for Women. In June, just before the Nairobi meeting, the national board held a biennial meeting in Asheville, North Carolina. At that time, the organization's membership adopted a comprehensive two-year program "based on redefining national security from a women's point of view." The program, planned "to challenge the myth that security comes from the barrel of a gun," consisted of five parts: (1) the "Stop Star Wars" campaign, (2) efforts to bring an end to U.S. intervention in Central America, (3) efforts to fight racism at home, (4) a campaign to pressure the U.S. government into withdrawing aid from South Africa until apartheid was abolished, and (5) the composition of a plan in which priorities in the national budget would be reordered so that the basic needs of women and children could be met.[55]

The focal point of this program was *The Women's Budget,* a 1985 study written by Jane Midgley, then executive director of the U.S. section of WILPF. *The Women's Budget* was one of the most important documents emerging from the Decade for Women, for it reflected WILPF's—and, indeed, the entire movement's—growth in understanding differences among economic classes, in directing attention to racism and global interconnectedness, and in committing itself anew to working for a world peace that would reflect not only the end of war but a just world for all people. *The Women's Budget* evolved from a poll of 17,000 women in forty-seven communities and twenty-three states about U.S. military and domestic policy issues. According to the poll, sponsored by the WILPF national board, a vast majority of the respondents favored a decrease in military spending, decreased involvement of the U.S. military in Central America, a nuclear freeze, increased funding for child care, and the passage of the Equal Rights Amendment. From this perspective, the WILPF leadership constructed *The Women's Budget,* illustrating how military dollars could better be spent on societal needs.[56]

The Women's Budget was meant as a response to the imbalance reflected by the official U.S. government budget. In her introduction Midgley pointed out: "Recent budgets have revealed inequities in the allocation of these resources. Building weapons takes precedence over feeding children. Insuring maximum corporate profits through tax giveaways is more essential than constructing decent public housing. Funding CIA attacks on Nicaraguans is more acceptable than assisting victims of domestic violence."[57] *The Women's Budget* was designed to turn the U.S. budget's emphasis away from the military and weapons development so that concentration could be placed on eliminating the high unemployment rate, hunger, homelessness, the rising illiteracy and infant mortality rates, and violent crime. As a result, racism, homophobia, and sexism would decline, and a more equitable distribution of the nation's resources might be possible. In particular, from WILPF's viewpoint, women's economic and political lives would be vastly improved.

Many parts of *The Women's Budget* reflected a continuation of WILPF's program from its origins as the Woman's Peace Party. The approach to each concern, however, showed modification from WILPF's earlier positions. The desire to see the military budget cut had been a WILPF priority since World War I. So had the concerns for women's employment and even the ideas for how the government could better spend its money. New was the idea of "economic conversion," a process by which workers, businesses, and communities would plan ways to transform military industries into other ventures that would actually increase, not decrease, employment in an area if a base, such as the Seneca Army Depot, were to be closed. In this way, people, communities, and the federal government would all benefit economically and socially.

Housing, health care, and education had always been critical issues for WILPFers. *The Women's Budget,* however, added the idea that concerns for these areas could not be separated from concerns for community development and environmental responsibility. In this sense, WILPF had benefited from the beliefs and actions of the ecology movement, but especially from its own exposure to ecofeminism. In its introduction to the issue of environmental protection, *The Women's Budget* stated: "'We have not inherited this earth from our parents, rather it was loaned to us by our children' reads an instructive Kenyan proverb, which should serve as a cornerstone of environmental policies at every level of government. Instead, the environmental legacy that we are leaving our children is dominated by contaminated drinking water, radioactive waste, polluted air, acid rain, and rampant depletion of our natural resources."[58]

WILPF's concern for the environment and its insistence that the U.S. government take concrete and forceful actions to protect it was a new and major addition to its program. The other major concern, which had been a basic part of the organization's structure from the beginning, was a commitment to improving women's situations in areas unique to the gender. WILPF had always recognized, for example, that a war mentality often led to actions of violence against women, whether on or off the battlefield. *The Women's Budget* specifically emphasized the need for the government to find shelters for rape victims and battered women. It also emphasized the need to ensure a legally protected world for elderly women, displaced homemakers, children, and—a new stance for WILPF—for lesbians and gay men. Unfortunately, except for a brief commendation of a family planning clinic that had helped 816,000 women avert "unintended pregnancies," the organization did not take a strong position on the reproductive rights issue; this unfortunate omission was sadly reminiscent of some of WILPF's neglect of important feminist concerns of an earlier period.

Finally, *The Women's Budget* enhanced WILPF's internationalism by recommending that U.S. military assistance and foreign aid be transferred to agencies like the United Nations that enhanced human life rather than destroying it. *The Women's Budget* concluded, "The themes of the U.N. Decade for Women were 'Equality, Development, and Peace.' These themes are the keys to solving the global crises confronting us and can also serve as guidelines for measuring U.S. foreign and military policy."[59]

The UN's Decade for Woman had a profound effect upon the development of global feminism. Unlike earlier periods when international links in the women's rights peace movement really meant links with Europe, this new era pointed the way towards a truly international movement crossing all sorts of class, race, ethnic and sexual barriers. The world, however, was also more complex: the issues of nuclear development, environmental protection, and imperialistic militarism could not be dealt with apart from the recognition that large numbers of the world's women lived in poverty, were illiterate, and had no political or personal power.

{9}

Conclusion

THE REVIVAL OF PATRIOTIC MILITARISM in the United States began in 1981, just six years after the nation's defeat in Vietnam. In that year Ronald Reagan was inaugurated as president. Determined to re-establish an aggressive military stance among the nations of the world and thereby to make U.S. "patriots" glow with pride, he sought pretexts for overseas adventurism. Claiming that the socialist government of the tiny Caribbean island of Grenada was building an airport to land Soviet military jets, in 1983 he ordered an invasion—which could hardly fail to succeed. His stationing of U.S. troops in Lebanon was marred by the needless deaths of 240 young soldiers in a suicide attack by Arab nationalists. Having failed in Lebanon, he was somehow able to find means of extracting funds from Congress to back the "contras" who had begun a civil war against the duly-elected Sandinista government in Nicaragua.

Reagan's militaristic policies continued with the election of his former vice-president, George Bush. After the apparent success of the UN-sanctioned attack on Iraq in January 1991—orchestrated by the Bush administration—many felt that the United States had regained its "manhood."

It was in 1990, even as official national policy was becoming increasingly militaristic, that the U.S. section of WILPF, the longest-lasting U.S. feminist peace organization, celebrated its seventy-fifth anniversary. The group had survived the most difficult of times. During both world wars and the McCarthy era, for example, there were moments when the leadership's actions were more accommodating to the government's policy than at other times, but the feminist-pacifist spirit of

WILPF's founding members never died. The generations of women who have made the organization's history have consistently and optimistically stood for a world without war in which all peoples lead productive lives without fear of any kind of injustice. Moreover, WILPF has persisted as a *women's* organization. Even during the years from 1920 through 1967, when the group promoted peace without necessarily stressing women's rights, the organizational structure remained feminist.

The need to develop a separate women's culture has been part of the feminist peace movement, in fact, since its roots in abolitionism. Everything about this movement was designed to differentiate it from the masculine. First, the method of decision making was intended to expand leadership rather than to narrow it. The Woman's Peace Party, the Women's Peace Union, Women Strike for Peace and WREE all stated openly that they worked by consensus. Second, the relationship among the women in the movement has always been intimate and caring. Women's lives have been intertwined for decades—with such pairings as Mildred Scott Olmsted and Hannah Clothier Hull, Jane Addams and Emily Greene Balch, Elinor Byrns and Caroline Lexow Babcock. Although these teams may have had difficult moments together, they stayed together in a tightly knit working relationship. This warmth has extended beyond the organization's home space to include a humanitarian concern for all people. The feminist peace movement, in other words, has created a value system based on an ethic of caring—caring for each other and for the world as well. Emotionalism is not only allowed; it is encouraged. Third, the movement has developed a rhetoric of its own, employing concepts not traditionally used by men. Whether a group has spoken about motherhood, violence against women, citizenship rights, or oppression, the language has embodied a women's point of view. World peace has been interpreted through women's eyes, in women's images, and with women's needs in mind. This is why the ecofeminist vision is appealing. It roots peace soundly in nature, making femaleness the very essence of life and survival. War belongs to men; peace to women.

Throughout their history, WILPF members have treasured the control that, as women, they could have only in a female-centered environment. In addition, they have valued the camaraderie and nurturance the organization has offered. They have mirrored the same separatist attitudes that radical feminists have fostered since the 1960s. Historian Blanche Wiesen Cook, herself a member of WILPF, has noted that the organization provided "a women's space" before the second wave of feminism popularized the concept.[1] During the three years in which Brenda Parnes, Yvette Tomlinson, and others interviewed members of the Metropolitan New York branch of WILPF for the group's history project, it became apparent time and time again that most of them placed a high value on their relationships with other women in the branch with whom they had worked for years. This emotional gratification is poignantly described in Blanche Wiesen Cook's interview, for it was as a member of WILPF that Cook met the woman she has been with for over twenty years. Cook explained, "So WILPF brought us together and one doesn't think of WILPF as a safe space for serious romance." Yet the two women found a community that accepted them, even though the organization has only just begun to deal with its homophobia. Cook continued, "It was where women met to have fun together, to have a social life together and to do very wonderful important politics." Women who never would have consciously thought of themselves as "feminists" are, in fact, according to Cook, "very women-loving and liked to do their politics with women, *chose* to do their politics with women."[2]

Another New York WILPFer, Evelyn A. Mauss, whose grandmother and mother had both been members of the organization, also values the "personal friendships" and the "feeling of sisterhood" that she has perceived through her own work. "It's very palpable," Mauss declared. "It's a real thing, the sense of working together with other women who feel as you do. You get that also from working with men on an issue you care about, but I do think it's stronger and more enduring [with women], and you get more of a high out of it."[3]

The foremothers of WILPF understood all too well that before the Woman's Peace Party of New York City was formed in November 1914, the U.S. peace organizations were male-controlled. They purposely founded an all-women's organization so that they would no longer be "simply assistants," as Dorothy Detzer expressed it.[4] Emily Greene Balch observe that the predominantly male organizations had to be dominated by men "to hold men."[5] No respectable man could maintain his proper image if his organization was led by women. Detzer also felt that, in any case, women approached matters "differently." She did not personally know whether a woman's approach was better; she simply stressed its difference.[6]

The uniqueness of female perception and behavior was a dominant theme for the World War I activists, just as it has been for women's rights peace activists since the feminist movement reemerged in the 1960s. Certainly the emphasis on the role of women as mothers and life-givers plays an important role in the movement: motherhood is the one continuous theme running through every organization represented in this book and through every historical era covered. Every generation of women's rights peace activists has stressed that women's ability to conceive and reproduce children, whether she chooses to do so or not, gives her an innate aversion to war and violence. This tendency to accept biological determinism for women has led to discussions about whether men are unavoidably violent. Rarely, however, have the activists given thought to the number of their sisters who have supported war and accepted the conscription and death of their loved ones as a valid sacrifice for a particular cause. Nor has this view of women led to a discussion of why some of them join the military. Men, the 1920s and 1930s activists claimed, were violent only because of social conditioning. Women, however, were biologically oriented towards peace but socially trained to accept war. For ecofeminists, the connection goes even deeper: their position is that the earth is our mother, and she is being ravaged by militarism and male-created toxic substances. The ecofeminists have taken the motherhood theme to a radical conclusion, but their message does not appear unacceptable to most feminist peace activists. Instead, it has been embraced to some extent by WILPF and WREE, two of the formal organizations still vital to the movement.

The motherhood theme, though continuous, has not guaranteed the longevity of an organization. One reason WILPF has been able to span the decades may be that it has addressed other issues as well. Some groups, such as the Women's Peace Society, American Women for Peace, and Another Mother for Peace, have not been able to last long. In fact, Women Strike for Peace could not maintain its high level of activism much beyond the Vietnam War. For fifteen years the organization tried to maintain a public presence, but in the summer of 1991, it finally closed its national office. WILPF and WREE, however, address all social injustice—from apartheid to poverty, from health care needs to child care.

Motherhood is only one aspect of a distinct women's perception. Another major consideration has been women's political subordination throughout U.S. history. Certainly, until 1920, women did not even have the vote on a national scale. Even so, the vote never brought with it the political equality that the suffragists had envisioned. Women, quite simply, still do not have power within the governmental structure nor do they wield great decision-making authority within mixed-gender organizations. As a traditionally oppressed group, women may be perceived by those in power as "outsiders." Perhaps that is why they have never truly been initiated into the fraternity of war. Even female military personnel are kept on the margins of combat—in medical units or in offices. If a woman leads a military exercise, as happened in Panama in 1989, she becomes the focal point of a media event, and her role is eventually minimized as an accident or an exception to the rule. In 1920, Emily Greene Balch perceived this tendency to overlook women as beneficial, for in wartime, women had "greater freedom" because they were not forced into the military.[7] Part of the benefit of this "greater freedom," of course, was that women, as outsiders, could organize against war.

However, as citizens not fully integrated into the infrastructure of the society, women have not been seen as a serious threat by the power brokers. The few times that feminist peace activists have appeared to be gaining some degree of public acceptance, the government has stopped their forward momentum by accusing them of being "Communists" or "subversives"—in other words, by displacing their image from their normal place on the periphery into the realm of the unwanted. Yet, by questioning their own part in their lack of success, the women themselves have largely tried to fight against their position of powerlessness and otherness.

Although the various feminist peace organizations have, throughout the years, lambasted the patriarchal system that obstructs their efforts to bring about a peaceful and just world, they also criticize themselves for what they consider self-imposed impediments. As much as the suffragists in all the peace organizations wished to attract large numbers of new voters as members, they never felt they had succeeded. In addition, all the groups have shared WILPF's concern about attracting poorer and younger women, and women of color. Part of the problem with signing up poorer women, of course, has always been money: belonging to an organization entails membership dues, carfare, and lunch fees. Moreover, working-class and poor women have traditionally had little time for volunteer work. Their lives have usually consisted of long working hours, endless domestic and child-care tasks, or both. Women of the working class often prefer to give whatever free time they have to community work, labor organizations, PTAs, or social activities rather than to peace groups. For poor women, world peace is too abstract to contemplate when there is little food to eat, rent to pay, and children to tend. Thus, the dearth of poorer and working-class women in feminist peace organizations can perhaps be attributed more to extrinsic causes, such as the potential members' lack of funds and the poverty of the organizations' treasuries, than to failure by activists in the organizations to attract such new members.

The problem of attracting younger women is more easily traceable to the women themselves. I will never forget the first time I attended a meeting of the Metropolitan New York branch of WILPF. I had just turned forty, but as I walked into the room and sat down, at least three elderly women approached and said how wonderful it was to see a "young person" there. Sure enough, as I looked around, almost all I saw were white-haired, sixtyish-looking women. As Blanche Wiesen Cook has noted, there was great reluctance on the part of the old guard to relinquish control to younger women. The phenomenon I have observed in recent years is, however, far from new: some decades ago, aging suffragists could not quite trust authority to younger women who had not paid their dues in the campaign for attaining the vote. This obstinacy was one of the causes for the demise of the Women's Peace Union, and it certainly did not help WILPF survive the difficult years leading up to World War II. Women Strike for Peace was even less successful in bridging the age gap. As the proper suburban mothers grew matronly and the younger feminists left for the women's movement, few chose to take up the slack. The organization stagnated.

The antinuclear thrust of the 1970s and 1980s has brought younger women into WILPF, particularly in the newer branches forming throughout the United States and among the paid staff in the national Philadel-

29. Members of WILPF protesting U.S. action in the Persian Gulf, 1991. Courtesy of WILPF.

phia office. Nonetheless, the age issue remains a serious one—and one that has been raised generation after generation. As I think of the elderly image associated with WILPF, I wonder how the organization has survived and how it attracts new members. Do new members find their way to WILPF only after gaining the maturity that comes with age or experience? Must a woman have passed the "dating age," or does she simply have to be fed up with working with men? Although I don't have the answers, I do notice a style which prospective members associate with white, middle-class, elderly women—a style that seems moderate, homophobic, and barely feminist, no matter how radical some individual members have been. Such a "style" turns off women who have grown up in the era of the new feminism. Perhaps WILPF needs to find an appropriate new style, one that is influenced by the young—women under the age of thirty-five.

WREE, in contrast, has been relatively successful in attracting younger women. Because these members are encouraged to make decisions and create new projects, they feel vital to the organization's success. They meet with no resistance from older women who fear that they will be pushed aside. Rather, all ages, and all races, commingle and support each other's efforts.

A more complex issue in the movement is one of race. Throughout this book, I have tried to illustrate the efforts and frustrations involved in attracting women of color, especially African-American women, to WILPF. (To date, it has been difficult to document attempts to appeal to Latina, Asian, and Native American women—at least in the geographical areas I have emphasized here.) WILPF branches, especially in New York and Philadelphia, made concerted efforts to recruit African-American women, but neither branch had a high success rate. Women Strike for Peace also met with little success. WREE, although a relatively small organization, has done better. One reason is that WREE was created with an interracial leadership, while WILPF has had very few women of color in positions of responsibility. During the 1920s and 1930s, three African-American women were on WILPF's national board: Mary Church Terrell, Addie Hunton, and Bertha McNeill. Terrell, the founder of the National Association of Colored Women (1897), had been a U.S. representative at the founding meeting of WILPF in Zurich in 1919. At that time, she commented openly on the fact that she was the only African-American woman there. Hunton, a key participant in the Intra-Racial Committee effort, was also active in the New York branch. McNeill, who became most important as chair of the Committee on the Special Problems of Branches during the 1950s, had the difficult task of sorting through the McCarthy-era complexities within WILPF. Even today, the number of women of color on WILPF's national board is small. In the summer of 1990, there were only two women of color out of a board of approximately thirty-five.

Although outright racism has shown itself on some occasions in a few WILPF branches, such cases are rare. Nevertheless, women of color felt at times ill at ease within the organization. One possible explanation might be that WILPF, unlike WREE, did not address race on a personal level until recently. WILPF's many issues were global. Although the organization was always committed to the abolition of racism, its members addressed it as an abstract concept rather than as a concrete problem. For example, the New York branch had an ugly squabble in the 1930s over whether to write a letter in support of anti-lynching legislation. Those in favor won the debate, but the issue of racism left the women at odds with each other. Yet the branch members did not try to analyze why they divided on this issue. By the 1960s, civil rights had become one of the organization's chief concerns; among the members of WILPF was Fanny Lou Hamer, one of the most prominent leaders of the civil rights movement. Once again, however, WILPF did not look at its own membership's race relations.

In 1988, WILPF finally faced racism as an internal organizational issue when its membership voted "Racial Justice" as one of its three priority issues for the period 1988–1990. As part of that work, the organization considered its own structure, questioning why WILPF remained primarily a white women's group even though it worked against racism. The leadership decided to undertake a program "to re-educate" its national board, staff and members "about racism, both individual and institutional racism, in a way we had not done before." WILPF's goals for this phase of their campaign were four:

- Recognize and undo racist patterns within WILPF;
- Prepare WILPF members to take action against racism;
- Protest and publicize incidents of racial violence;

  and
- Build networks between WILPF and other organizations working for racial justice.[8]

Yet the organization is still disproportionately white.

Perhaps it is not accurate to evaluate WILPF's positions on race by counting the number of faces represented by women of color in any given year or at any given meeting. Perhaps it is not even wise to try to determine why the organization still appeals primarily to white women. Perhaps, as they propose, WILPFers themselves should try to evaluate their past actions and attitudes and change those that do not please them; but perhaps, more wisely, they should also understand and accept themselves as an organization that works against racism no matter how its membership is constituted. Blanche Wiesen Cook, in particular, has given serious thought to this issue. She remembers how, in the 1960s, WILPF changed dramatically from an antiracist organization with some racist members to a truly active opponent of racism. Cook feels, however, that since WILPF is basically a white organization that is also antiracist, the organization should emphasize as its work the fighting of racism within the white community.

Jane Addams, founder of the national organization, also felt that WILPF "could never be a popular or mass movement."[9] The organization largely attracts white members, most of them educated professional or working women with strong political views and great energy and dedication. Perhaps the organization should spend some energy on recruiting more such women and in putting their resources into action. In any case, the 1990s promises to be the decade in which WILPF finally faces racism head-on. If so, there will be some big changes. As an experienced WILPFer, Blanche Wiesen Cook feels great optimism for the future of the organization, pointing to the new feminist leadership that has moved into the national headquarters with "a really new vision and a really anti-heterosexist attitude and real embrace for our differences, for gender justice and racial justice and a real embrace for a lesbian membership and reality."[10]

Both WILPF and WREE face new challenges in the years to come. As the 1990s began, both organizations put forward their plans for a new era of growth and commitment based on the elimination of racism. WREE's newsletter announced that the organization was "Setting a Fighting Women's Agenda for the '90s."[11] Fighting both racism and sexism is the core of WREE's program, and workshops scheduled for the organization's fourth national convention in 1990 emphasized the importance of organizing African-American, Latina, Asian, and Native American women to work on domestic issues as well as the need to build international solidarity.

Unlike WILPF's newsletter, the *WREE-View* is always presented in a bilingual English/Spanish format, inviting to women in the Hispanic community. In addition, WREE's rhetoric about race is much more forceful than WILPF's, probably because articles and convention calls are planned by a multiracial membership with a well-formed class-consciousness. WREE's 1990 Convention Call is a good example:

> The past decade under Reagan and the years to come were and will be characterized by the many attempts to divide us by race and sex, by income and social status, by our political views. Drastic setbacks for women of color are a direct result of the deterioration of our economy and rampant union busting; of the Supreme Court reversals of affirmative action and reproductive rights; of the attacks on all civil rights and the alarming increase in racist and anti-Semitic violence across our country.
>
> Racism is institutionalized by an economic system that profits from it at home and abroad. Racism is systematically woven throughout our political, educational, housing, health care and judicial systems. It poisons our social and cultural life.[12]

Racial and cultural diversity have also been concerns for radical cultural feminists and ecofeminists. From the first, radical feminists embraced the concept of a nonracist world. In the development of women's culture, however, women of color were often excluded. One reason, similar to WILPF's, was that white women did not easily accept women of color into their ranks. On the other hand, women of color often opted to support the peace issue by working through civil rights organizations. Since the Decade for Women, this trend has been changing, and radical feminist concepts have elicited a surge of activity from women of color. Ecofeminists have been more successful in reaching out to all kinds of women because of their work in ecology. From the rain forests of Brazil to the forests of India to the toxic waste sites in the United States, women are organizing to save the environment. Such issues affect us all.

It seems in some sense that if WILPF and WREE could merge, perhaps some of the issues could be solved. After all, WREE attracts the membership which WILPF feels it lacks, while WILPF has the national organization and avenues to money that WREE lacks. Both have NGO status in the United Nations. Why, I ask myself, is the division between these two vital women's rights peace organizations so deep? Even though membership in the two groups does not seem to overlap to the same extent as it did between WILPF and Women Strike for Peace, there is some crossover. In addition, the two groups seem to feel comfortable about cosponsoring events. Is the problem one of personalities? Of class? Are WREE's politics more leftist than WILPF's? If so, is WREE nervous about censorship and WILPF skittish about red-baiting? Does WREE find that WILPF has a history of too much compromise, and too often? Does WILPF perceive WREE as too militant? Is it a question of power? Would WREE simply be swallowed up by WILPF's large size and Philadelphia power structure? Are their differing emphases and goals divisive? Does WREE stress domestic issues more than WILPF prefers? Does WILPF emphasize nuclear disarmament to the detriment of other issues? The reason I have posed all these questions is that I really am not sure of the answers myself. I feel much as our foremothers must have felt about having separate organizations working on the same issues. Although there are perhaps some advantages, such as the possibility of diversity in membership and types of activities, there is the great disadvantage of losing collective power. In the case of WILPF and WREE, there is a basic difference between the two organizations that cannot be denied: a subtle personality difference hard to define but clearly felt by women who choose one group or the other.

What, then, is the future for these angry, nonviolent women of peace? Certainly, with the great changes now taking place in Eastern Europe and the former Soviet Union, there will be less emphasis on the effects of U.S. opposition to communism in Europe. The issue of nuclear weapons is still present, although it may be a difficult task to convince the general public that antinuclear work is still necessary. The existence and further development of nuclear weapons in other nations and the use of nuclear power, however, makes the issue of the utmost importance.

With the changes in the former Soviet Union comes the realignment of the world's political polarity along north-south lines, rather than east-west ones. Developing nations have been speaking of this power shift for years. In retrospect, it seems apparent that the United States and the Soviet Union had each accepted the existence of the other's sphere of influence, and thus each had come to tolerate the other's interference in Third World nations. Hence, in 1989, when the U.S. invaded Panama, the Soviets remained silent, and in 1991, when the Soviets had tense moments with a Lithuania desiring its independence, the United States stayed away from the issue. Moreover, if the Cold War had still been in full swing, would the United Nations have approved the military destruction of Iraq?

The issue of interference by big powers raises new questions for feminist peace activists and a more urgent need for organizing women on a truly international scale. WILPF and WREE, with their emphasis on race and gender equality, have provided the groundwork necessary for forming effective alliances with women from Africa, Latin America, the Middle East, and Asia. Furthermore, as the radical feminists and ecofeminists continue to develop their theories and either form new organizations or join these two, the issues of feminism and ecology will no doubt play a major role in feminist peace organizing. The embracing of the concept of interconnectedness by WILPF's and WREE's organizational agendas for the 1990s indicates that these two active groups have been influenced by the ecofeminist presence. Much of the antinuclear literature emphasizes the importance of each life system to every other: to destroy one is to destroy all.

New feminist peace efforts continue to emerge as the world situation changes. The Gulf War, in particular, brought together all kinds of peace coalitions. One which particularly intrigued me as a historian was "The Women's Ship for Peace," which left Algeria in December 1990, with medicine, sugar, and powdered milk for Iraqi children.[13] On board were two hundred women from Europe, the United States, Japan, and several Arab nations. *Ms.* reported: "Two days before reaching Iraq, they were stopped by U.S. and coalition forces. Marines boarded the ship from helicopters, shot over the women's heads, released tear gas, and kicked the women, forcing them into their cabins."[14] After two weeks of the enforced delay, the ship reached Iraq on January 14, the day before the "allied" bombing raids began. Fortunately, the women had just left.

Another effort, called the International Women's Gulf Peace Initiative, consisted of a delegation that traveled to Baghdad to try to avert war. Among these women were some from organizations discussed in previous chapters: Flora Abdrakhmanova of the WIDF, Joan Drake and Kay Camp of WILPF, and Maude Barlow of VOW. Others represented Arab women's groups and MADRE, an organization devoted to the issues of Latin American women. Margarita Papandreou, representative of the newly formed Women for Mutual Security, reported that if women had the power, "we would sit at the negotiating table and we would search—for as long as it takes—for a peaceful solution."[15]

30. Seventh-grade antiwar protester from New York state demonstrating against the Persian Gulf war at the January 26, 1991, march on Washington, D.C. Author's personal collection.

These two new international efforts, plus the statements issued by WILPF, WREE, and the remaining members of WSP against military action in the Gulf, hark back to the experiences of the World War I–era feminist-pacifists who traveled on the *Noordam* to meet with the women of war-torn Europe at The Hague and who then traveled to all the ruling houses to encourage mediation. When I read the reports of these two endeavors, I could almost hear the foremothers cheering. What an incredibly dramatic and optimistic illustration of the courage and self-assuredness of the generations of feminist peace activists!

The nineties require continued commitment to women's solidarity, as WILPF, WREE, and the international networks begun during the UN's Decade for Women all recognize. WILPF took a major step in this direction in 1990 by starting an international campaign to confront the issue of violence against women, on both a domestic and an international level. In 1991 the organization continued this effort by devoting an entire issue of their newsletter, *Peace and Freedom,* to homophobia and gay rights. The most far-reaching of feminist concerns, violence against women, includes personal affronts, economic degradation, and political and legal discrimination as well as ecological questions and international affairs. Violence against women, an issue encompassing every aspect of a woman's life, will take the feminist peace movement full circle to its abolitionist roots.

What WREE, WILPF, and the numerous smaller radical feminist and ecofeminist groups propose for themselves is not an easy task, but it is thoroughly consistent with their feminist roots. The work requires such a strong commitment that not every woman will be able to sustain her level of involvement. Rather, women will come and go and come again—burning out and recovering as feminist peace activists have done since 1914. A ninety-year-old member of the Metropolitan New York branch of WILPF put it well: "I feel that we just have to carry on, and not to get discouraged when we don't succeed, but to keep on trying. As far as I am concerned, so long as I have breath in me, I will fight for what is right, and one of the greatest wrongs in the world is war."[16]

APPENDIX A
APPENDIX B
NOTES
SELECTED BIBLIOGRAPHY
INDEX

APPENDIX A

A Chronological Listing of U.S. Women's Rights Peace Organizations and Committees

AN ASTERISK (*) designates an organization whose roots, organizers, or both can be traced back to the abolitionist/early women's rights/suffrage movement. The organizations are arranged in alphabetical order within each era.

1820–1914

Bowdoin Street Ladies' Peace Society
Essex County Olive Branch Circle
National Council of Women (committee)*
National American Woman Suffrage Association (committee)*
Woman's Christian Temperance Union (committee)

1914–1919

Woman's Peace Party of New York*
Woman's Peace Party (later known as the Women's International League for Peace and Freedom, or WILPF)*

1919–1935

National Committee on the Cause and Cure of War*
Pan American International Women's Committee
Peace and Disarmament Committee of the International Council of Women*
WILPF*
Women's Peace Society*
Women's Peace Union*

1935–1945

National Committee on the Cause and Cure of War*
National Committee to Oppose the Conscription of Women*
WILPF*
Women's Action Committee for Victory and Lasting Peace* (NCCCW)
Women's Peace Union*

1945–1960

American Women for Peace
Congress of American Women
Jane Addams Peace Association*
WILPF*
Woman, Inc.

1960–1975

Another Mother for Peace
Jeannette Rankin Brigade*
Voice of Women
WILPF*
Women Strike for Peace*

1975–1985

The Women's Encampment for a Future of Peace and Justice (also known as Seneca Women's Peace Encampment)*
WILPF*
Women Against Military Madness
Women for a Meaningful Summit
Women for Racial and Economic Equality
Women Strike for Peace*
Women, USA*
Women's Action for Nuclear Disarmament
Women's Pentagon Action*

APPENDIX B

A Partial Chronology of the Metropolitan New York Branch of WILPF

This is a partial chronology highlighting the work of the New York City women of WILPF. The data was part of the work of the WILPF Metropolitan New York Branch History Project.

August 1914	War breaks out in Europe
November 1914	Founding of the Woman's Peace Party of New York City (later changed to Woman's Peace Party of New York); New York City women belong to both local and state WPP branches
January 1915	Founding of national Woman's Peace Party; New York City group becomes a local branch
April 1915	Madeline Doty, of N.Y.-WPP, attends first meeting in The Hague of International Committee of Women for Permanent Peace
January 1916	N.Y.-WPP sponsors mass meeting at Cooper Union to protest military training in public school physical education classes
Spring 1916	N.Y.-WPP sponsors "War Against War" art exhibit that travels from Brooklyn to Manhattan and then to Chicago and Massachusetts
April 1917	U.S. joins war effort in Europe
July 1917	*Four Lights,* newsletter of the N.Y.-WPP, prints its most infamous issue, which criticizes women who knit socks for soldiers for taking jobs away from mill workers.

December 1917	N.Y.-WPP changes its name to Women's International League (WIL)
November 1918	World War I ends
November 1919	U.S. Woman's Peace Party becomes the U.S. Section of the Women's International League for Peace and Freedom; New York WIL becomes N.Y. branch of the U.S. section
1919–1921	N.Y.-WIL splinters into three parts: N.Y.-WILPF, Women's Peace Society, and Women's Peace Union and almost goes out of existence
January 1925	N.Y. branch revives and once again becomes part of official state branch
1925–1930	Katherine Devereux Blake's recruitment efforts rebuild N.Y.C. branch; also institutes programs to recruit women of color
1927	Brooklyn branch of WILPF in full swing; Bronx branch also organizing; results in three branches within city
1930	Helen Curtis, one of first N.Y.-WILPF African-American members, makes citywide speaking tour on branch's behalf
March 1934	N.Y. branch argues over whether to support a national Anti-Lynching Bill; resolution passes
1933–1936	National organization and N.Y.-WILPF branches face conflict over national board's endorsement of the American League Against War and Fascism; foreshadows McCarthy-era "Red Scare"
1936	Brooklyn members support boycott of German goods and services sponsored by American Jewish Congress—against national board policy
1936	All three N.Y. branches oppose the U.S. government's embargo on selling war materials to Spain unless same embargo is placed on *all* belligerents—opposite of national board policy
1937	Brooklyn and Bronx branches lose members because of alleged Communist infiltration by members of American League Against War and Fascism and

	because of national board's neutrality stance regarding Germany, Italy, and Spain
March 1939	Brooklyn, Bronx, and Manhattan branches join to form Greater New York branch of WILPF
December 1941	U.S. enters World War II
1942–1945	In spite of falling membership, N.Y. branches maintain active program throughout war, emphasizing refugee work, self-education, and recruiting women of color
1948	National WILPF office for UN work opens in New York City; New York branches revive and consolidate into the Metropolitan New York branch after shrinking to small numbers during war; Sarah Lifton accepts chair, but is unsuccessful; Far Rockaway branch emerges
1950s	Metropolitan N.Y. branch (hereafter referred to as MNYB) has trouble finding meeting places; finally finds space in the Carnegie Endowment for International Peace building; works against nuclear arms race, Korean War, HUAC
October 1950	Orlie Pell agrees to work as leader in effort to revive MNYB-WILPF
1953–1954	Most members of Chelsea Women's Committee for Peace join MNYB-WILPF, adding numbers and enthusiasm
1954	MNYB plans campaign against H-bomb
June 1955	MNYB-WILPF members arrested in New York City protests against Civil Defense drills
May 1958	By-laws for MNYB of WILPF adopted
1960	MNYB wins WILPF membership award for having largest number of newly enrolled members
1960s	MNYB protests war in Vietnam, nuclear arms race and testing, HUAC; puts much effort in supporting civil rights movement
1961	MNYB establishes Committee on Disarmament

October 1962	MNYB opposes U.S. intervention in Cuba
1964–1975	N.Y. members work actively against U.S. intervention in Vietnam
April 1965	MNYB participates in March on Washington to protest Vietnam War
November 1966	MNYB supports Fifth Avenue Vietnam Peace Parade Committee plans
1970	MNYB initiates Shoppers' Stoppage Campaign, "Never on Tuesdays"
March 1971	MNYB sponsors "Rice and Tea for Peace" Day; raises $300 for Maternal Child Health Center in Hanoi
April 1971	MNYB participates in peace rallies in Central Park and Washington, D.C.
April 1973	MNYB sponsors open membership meeting on the problems facing Native Americans
March 1974	First time that MNYB and Women Strike for Peace cosponsor International Women's Day events
1975	MNYB protests human rights violations in Chile
March 1978	MNYB sponsors march from Union Square to Herald Square to "defend" women's rights
1979	MNYB sponsors poster contest on UN International Year of the Child theme; "The World I'd Like to Make" posters displayed at District 65 headquarters
1980s	MNYB urges ratification of SALT II (Strategic Arms Limitation Talks) treaty; opposes registration for draft; protests U.S. intervention in El Salvador, Grenada, Nicaragua, the Middle East; opposes apartheid in South Africa; works for nuclear weapons freeze
September 1981	"Feed the Cities, Not the Pentagon" march
1982	MNYB participates in WILPF "STAR" campaign (Stop The Arms Race)
July 1983	MNYB members spend two days at Seneca Women's Peace Encampment in Upstate New York

March 1984	MNYB joins WILPF "Listen to Women for a Change" speak-out at Capitol Building on International Women's Day
1984–today	MNYB protests turning New York harbor into homeport for nuclear destroyer, USS *Iowa*
April 1985	MNYB goes to Peace, Jobs and Justice rally in Washington, D.C.
1987	MNYB circulates Comprehensive Nuclear Test Ban Treaty petitions
January 1990	MNYB joins national U.S. section of WILPF in celebrating 75 years of good work
August 1990	MNYB joins nationwide peace effort to prevent war in Middle East
January 1991	MNYB joins nationwide protest over Gulf War and continues to seek ways to bring peace to Middle East and rest of world.

NOTES

1. Coming to Terms

1. For a thorough discussion of the origins of the term "feminism," see Nancy F. Cott, *The Grounding of Modern Feminism* (New Haven: Yale Univ. Press, 1987), 1–50.

2. Developing a Feminist-Pacifist Consciousness, 1820–1914

1. This composite view of the emerging feminist of the nineteenth century was compiled from the following works: Margaret Hope Bacon, *Mothers of Feminism: The Story of Quaker Women in America* (San Francisco: Harper and Row, 1986); Ann Braude, *Radical Spirits: Spiritualism and Women's Rights in Nineteenth-Century America* (Boston: Beacon, 1989); Blanche Glassman Hersh, *The Slavery of Sex: Feminist-Abolitionists in America* (Urbana: Univ. of Illinois Press, 1978); William Leach, *True Love and Perfect Union: The Feminist Reform of Sex and Society* (New York: Basic Books, 1980); and Jean Fagan Yellin, *Women and Sisters: The Antislavery Feminists in American Culture* (New Haven: Yale Univ. Press, 1989).
2. Hersh, *The Slavery of Sex,* 61, 140–146.
3. Barbara Welter, "The Cult of True Womanhood: 1820–1860," *American Quarterly* 18 (1966): 151–174.
4. Elizabeth Margaret Chandler, *The Poetical Works of Elizabeth Margaret Chandler: With a Memoir of Her Life and Character by Benjamin Lundy* (1836; reprint, Miami: Mnemosyne, 1969).
5. "Mental Metempsychosis," ibid., 118.
6. Chandler, 23.
7. "Kneeling Slave," ibid., 59.
8. William Lloyd Garrison, quoted in Peter Brock, *Pacifism in the United States: From the Colonial Era to the First World War* (Princeton: Princeton Univ. Press, 1968), 529.
9. Maria Weston Chapman, quoted in Hersh, 34.

10. Chapman, quoted in Edward T. James, et al., eds., *Notable American Women, A Biographical Dictionary,* s.v. "Chapman, Maria Weston."

11. Garrison, *I will Be Heard, 1822–1835,* vol. 1 of *The Letters of William Lloyd Garrison,* ed. Walter M. Merrill (Cambridge, Mass.: Harvard Univ. Press, Belknap Press, 1971), 209.

12. Lydia Maria Child to E. Carpenter, Mar. 20, 1838, in *Lydia Maria Child: Selected Letters, 1817–1880,* ed. Milton Meltzer and Patricia G. Holland (Amherst: Univ. of Massachusetts Press, 1982), 71–72.

13. Sarah Grimké quoted in *Turning the World Upside Down: The Anti-Slavery Convention of American Women Held in New York City May 9–12, 1837* (New York: The Feminist Press of the City Univ. of New York, 1987), 17.

14. Angelina Grimké, quoted in ibid., 13.

15. Sarah T. Smith, "Address to Anti-Slavery Societies, Second National Anti-Slavery Convention of American Women, Philadelphia, Pennsylvania, 15 May 1838," quoted in Mari Jo Buhl and Paul Buhl, eds., *The Concise History of Woman Suffrage: Selections from the Classic Work of Stanton, Anthony, Gage, and Harper* (Urbana: Univ. of Illinois Press, 1978), 71–72.

16. Lydia Maria Child, quoted in Ronald G. Walters, *American Reformers, 1815–1860* (New York: Hill and Wang, 1978), 105–106.

17. Sarah Grimké, *Letters on the Equality of the Sexes and the Condition of Women and Other Essays,* ed. Elizabeth Ann Bartlett (New Haven: Yale Univ. Press, 1988), 35, 38–39.

18. Angelina E. Grimké, *Letters to Catherine E. Beecher, in Reply to an Essay on Slavery and Abolitionism, Addressed to Angelina Grimké, Revised by the Author* (1838; reprint, Freeport, N.Y.: Books for Libraries, 1971), 116–119.

19. Lydia Maria Child, letter of May 27, 1841, quoted in Brock, 561.

20. Sarah Grimké, quoted in Gerda Lerner, *The Grimké Sisters from South Carolina: Pioneers for Woman's Rights and Abolition* (New York: Schocken, 1967), 176.

21. *Liberator,* Oct. 22, 1835, quoted in Judith Papachristou, *Women Together: A History in Documents of the Women's Movement in the United States* (New York: Knopf, 1976), 6.

22. The description of this incident was adapted from Margaret Hope Bacon, *Mothers of Feminism,* 106.

23. Angelina Grimké to Sarah M. Douglass, Feb. 25, 1838, quoted in Yellin, 42.

24. William Ladd, *On the Duty of Females to Promote the Cause of Peace* (1836; reprint, New York: Garland, 1971), 3.

25. Garrison, quoted in Papachristou, *Women Together,* 17.

26. *Proceedings of the Peace Convention,* quoted in Brock, 544.

27. Chapman, "The Lords of Creation," quoted in Yellin, 66.

28. Elizabeth Cady Stanton, "Speech to the 1860 Anniversary of the American Anti-Slavery Society," quoted in Ellen Carol DuBois, *Feminism and Suffrage: The Emergence of an Independent Women's Movement in America, 1848–1869* (Ithaca: Cornell Univ. Press, 1978), 34.

29. Susan B. Anthony et al., eds., *History of Woman Suffrage* (1881; reprint, New York: Arno and New York Times Press, 1969), vol. 1, 419.

30. "Declaration of Sentiments," ibid., 70–73.

31. "Pauline Wright Davis Presiding Over First National Woman's Rights Convention in Worcester, Massachusetts, 1850," quoted in Judith Papachristou, *Women Together: A History in Documents of the Women's Movement in the United States* (New York: Knopf, 1976), 31.

32. Susan B. Anthony, "Resolutions and Debate, Woman's National Loyal League Meeting, New York City, 14 May 1863," quoted in Mari Jo Buhl and Paul Buhl, eds., *The Concise History of Woman Suffrage: Selections from the Classic Work of Stanton, Anthony, Gage, and Harper* (Urbana: Univ. of Illinois Press, 1978), 200.

33. Lucretia Mott, "Discource on Women: Delivered in Philadelphia, December 17, 1849," quoted in *Lucretia Mott: Her Complete Speeches and Sermons,* ed. Dana Greene (Lewiston, N.Y.: Edward Mellen, 1980), 147.

34. Elizabeth Cady Stanton, "Speech to the 1860 Anniversary of the American Anti-Slavery Society," quoted in Ellen Carol Dubois, *Elizabeth Cady Stanton/ Susan B. Anthony: Correspondence, Writings, Speeches* (New York: Schocken, 1981), 83, 85.

35. Mott to Richard Webb, Jan. 22, 1872, quoted in Margaret Hope Bacon, *Valiant Friend: The Life of Lucretia Mott* (New York: Walker, 1980), 212.

36. Mott, "'A Warlike Spirit,' Remarks Delivered at the Woman's Peace Festival, 2 June 1876," quoted in Mott, *Speeches and Sermons,* 379.

37. Mott, "'Place Woman in Equal Power,' Delivered at the Thirtieth Anniversary of the Seneca Falls Convention, July, 1878," quoted in Mott, *Speeches and Sermons,* 393.

38. Stanton, "Address Delivered at Seneca Falls, July 19, 1848," quoted in Stanton and Anthony, *Correspondence, Writings, Speeches,* 27–35.

39. Stanton, quoted in Jean Bethke Elshtain, *Women and War* (New York: Basic Books, 1987), 6.

40. Stanton, "Proposal to Form a New Party," May 1872, quoted in Stanton and Anthony, *Correspondence, Writings, Speeches,* 169.

41. Stanton, "Address of Welcome to the International Council of Women," March 25, 1888, quoted in ibid., 212.

42. The American Woman Suffrage Association and the National Woman Suffrage Association were founded as a result of a schism in the suffrage movement over the issue of enfranchising black men but not women. The AWSA supported the idea, while the NWSA would not relinquish its claim to votes for all women.

43. Julia Ward Howe, *Woman's Journal,* November 5, 1870, and July 6, 1872, as quoted in Hersh, 166.

44. "Proceedings of a Peace Meeting Held at Union League Hall, New York, December 23, 1870, for the Purpose of Free Consultation on the Subject of a Woman's Peace Congress for the World, as Proposed by Mrs. Julia Ward Howe of Boston," Woman's Peace Congress Papers, SCPC.

45. Julia Ward Howe, "Bits of Remembrances Written Summer of 1907," Julia Ward Howe Papers, Schles.

46. Hersh, 48.

47. Amelia Bloomer, quoted in ibid., 48; and in Elizabeth Pleck, *Domestic Tyranny: The Making of American Social Policy Against Family Violence From Colonial Times to the Present* (New York: Oxford Univ. Press, 1987), 58 n. 17.

48. Stanton to Anthony, July 20, 1857, quoted in Hersh, 199, 20.

49. Anthony, untitled speech, quoted in ibid, 109.

50. "The W.C.T.U. in Relation to Peace and Arbitration," n.d., box 1, folder 8, HB: SCPC.

51. Hannah Bailey, "Woman's Place in the Peace Reform," n.d., HB: SCPC.

52. Elizabeth P. Gordon, "Catechism on the World's W.C.T.U." n.d., HB: SCPC. Gordon was Superintendent of the Department of Schools of Methods in the World's W.C.T.U.

53. *Woman's Journal,* Jan. 18, 1896, quoted in Papachristou, "American Women and Foreign Policy, 1898–1905," *Diplomatic History* 14, no. 4 (Fall 1990): 493–509.

54. "To the President of the United States:," n.d., HB: SCPC.

55. National Council of Women, *Fourth Triennial Report, 1902,* quoted in Papachristou, "American Women and Foreign Policy," 502–503.

56. *Woman's Tribune,* June 3, 1899, quoted in ibid., 502.

57. Ibid. For a more detailed account of this period, see Papachristou, "American Women and Foreign Policy," 493–509.

58. Stanton, "Address of Welcome to the International Council of Women," March 25, 1888, quoted in Stanton and Anthony, *Correspondence, Writings, Speeches,* 214–215.

59. *International Woman's Suffrage News* 8, no. 9 (May 1, 1914), quoted in Edith F. Hurwitz, "The International Sisterhood," in *Becoming Visible: Women in European History* ed. Renate Bridenthal and Claudia Koonz (Boston: Houghton Mifflin, 1977), 335.

3. Suffragist-Pacifists versus the Great War, 1914–1919

1. Fanny Garrison Villard, "A Real Society," WPS: SCPC; Background information on foreign policy throughout this book was adapted from Thomas G. Paterson et al., *American Foreign Policy: A History/Since 1900* (Lexington, Mass.: Heath, 1983).

2. Parade Committee, quoted in C. Roland Marchand, *The American Peace Movement and Social Reform, 1898–1918* (Princeton: Princeton Univ. Press, 1972), 184.

3. Jane Addams, speech given in Chicago on April 30, 1899, quoted in Allen F. Davis, *American Heroine: The Life and Legend of Jane Addams* (New York: Oxford Univ. Press, 1973), 142.

4. Jane Addams, *Democracy and Social Ethics,* ed. Anne Firor Scott (1907; reprint, Cambridge, Mass.: Harvard Univ. Press, Belknap Press, 1964), 275.

5. Jane Addams, *The Newer Ideals of Peace* (New York: Macmillan, 1907), 24–26.

6. Charlotte Perkins Gilman, *Women and Economics* (1898; reprint, New York: Harper and Row, 1966), 41.

7. Gilman, *Our Man-Made World,* quoted in Marchand, 203.

8. Carrie Chapman Catt in Letter to the *New York Times,* Feb. 6, 1915, box 1, folder 1, CCC: NYPL.

9. Addams, quoted in Linda Kay Schott, "Women Against War: Pacifism, Feminism, and Social Justice in the United States, 1915–1941" (Ph.D. diss., Stanford Univ., 1985), 52.

10. Catt to Jane Addams, Dec. 16, 1914, WPP: SCPC.

11. Addams to Catt, Dec. 21, 1914, WPP: SCPC.

12. Addams to Lucia Ames Mead, Dec. 28, 1914, quoted in John M. Craig, "Lucia True Ames Mead: American Publicist for Peace and Internationalism" (Ph.D. diss., College of William and Mary, 1986), 148–149.

13. Catt to Addams, Dec. 16, 1914, WPP: SCPC.

14. Catt to Addams, Dec. 29, 1914, WPP: SCPC.

15. "Speeches from Mass Meeting at Woman's Peace Party Organizing Conference, January 10, 1915," p. 26, WPP: SCPC.

16. Anna Garlin Spencer to the Reverend Marion Murdock, Jan. 18, 1915, reel 1, B 1, folder 2, AGS: SCPC.

17. Spencer to Addams, Jan. 18, 1915, reel 1, box 1, folder 2, AGS: SCPC.

18. "Woman's Peace Party Preamble and Platform Adopted at Washington, January 10, 1915," Subject Files 463, S/L: NYPL.

19. For more information on the formative years of the Woman's Peace Party, see Marie Louise Degen, *The History of the Woman's Peace Party* (1939; reprint, New York: Garland, 1972) and Barbara Jean Steinson, "Female Activism in World War I: The American Woman's Peace, Suffrage, Preparedness and Relief Movements, 1914–1919" (Ph.D. diss., Univ. of Michigan, 1977).

20. Steinson, 123.

21. Crystal Eastman to Addams, June 28, 1917, reel 12.6, box 9, WPP: SCPC.

22. "Report of the International Congress of Women, The Hague," quoted in Steinson, 50.

23. Jane Addams, Emily G. Balch, and Alice Hamilton, *Women at The Hague: The International Congress of Women and Its Results* (New York: Macmillan, 1915), 147.

24. "Program from the International Women's Congress, April 28, 29, 30, 1915," series A, box 3, folder 2, WPP: SCPC.

25. Addams et. al., *Women at The Hague,* 11–15.

26. Rosika Schwimmer, quoted in Steinson, 62.

27. Jane Addams, "The Revolt Against War," reprinted from the *Survey,* July 17, 1915, Subject File 464, S/L: NYPL.

28. Jane Addams et al., *Women at The Hague:* 59, 127–128.

29. "Mass Meeting at Cooper Union" announcement, Jan. 31, 1916, WPP: SCPC.

30. Press release, May 15, 1916, WPP: SCPC.

31. Press release, April 17, 1916, WPP: SCPC.

32. Cable to Mexico from Margaret Lane, June 1916, WPP: SCPC.

33. Eleanor Karsten to Addams, June 24, 1916, WPP: SCPC.

34. Blance Wiesen Cook, "Woodrow Wilson and the Anti-militarists, 1914–1917" (Ph.D. diss., Johns Hopkins Univ., 1970), 185.

35. "Dear Member" letter from Executive Board, June 12, 1917, WPP: SCPC.

36. Spencer to Catt, Feb. 17, 1917, reel 1, box 1, folder 2, AGS: SCPC.

37. Spencer to Catt. Mar. 1, 1917, reel 1, box 1, folder 2, AGS: SCPC.

38. Spencer to Catt, Mar. 12, 1917, reel 1, box 1, folder 2, AGS: SCPC.

39. Catt to Spencer, Mar. 19, 1917, reel 1, box 1, folder 1, AGS: SCPC.

40. Catt to Spencer, Mar. 21, 1917, reel 1, box 1, folder 2, AGS: SCPC.

41. Spencer to Addams, Mar. 4, 1917, reel 1, box 1, folder 2, AGS: SCPC.

42. New York City Woman's Peace Party to President Woodrow Wilson, n.d., WPP: SCPC.

43. For a discussion of Jane Addams's food relief work, see Jane Addams, *The Second Twenty Years at Hull-House—September 1909 to September 1929* (New York: Macmillan, 1930), 144–146.

44. "Statement of the Executive Board of the National Woman's Peace Party," Oct. 25, 1917, WPP: SCPC.

45. "A Program During War Time," publication of the Woman's Peace Party, quoted in Degen, 193–195.

46. Addams, *Peace and Bread,* 127–128.

47. Anne Herendeen to Marge, Dec. 1, 1917, Reel 12.14, WPP: SCPC.

48. "Dear Member" letter from Executive Board, June 12, 1917, WPP: SCPC.

49. Unsigned letter to Lou Rogers, Apr. 9, 1917, WPP: SCPC.

50. Katherine Anthony, "The 'Sister Susie' Peril," *Four Lights,* July 14, 1917, WPP: SCPC.

51. Press release, Aug. 13, 1917, WPP: SCPC.

52. Degen, 224–238.

53. *Toward Peace and Freedom,* Aug. 1919, Subject File 465, S/L: NYPL.

54. "Report of the International Congress of Women, Zurich, May 12–17, 1919," quoted in Degen, 232.

55. "Lists Americans as Pacifists," *New York Times,* Jan. 25, 1919, 1:4, 4:4.

56. See Mercedes Randall, *Improper Bostonian: Emily Greene Balch* (New York: Twayne, 1964), 236–257; and *Report of the Joint Legislative Committee Investigating Seditious Activities, Filed 24 January in the Senate of New York: Revolutionary Radicalism,* Pt. 1: Vol. 1, Clayton R. Lusk, chm. (Albany: J. B. Lyon Company, Printers, 1920), 967–1111.

57. "Statement Recommended by the Board of Officers of the Woman's Peace Party to the Annual Meeting, November 3d and 4th, 1919," reel 2, box 3, folder 1, AGS: SCPC.

4. Former Suffragists for Peace during the Interwar Years, 1919–1935

1. The death tolls for World War I were: U.S.—112,432 (over 52,000 from the worldwide influenza epidemic of 1918); U.K.—947,000; France—1.38 million; Russia—1.7 million; Italy—460,000; Germany—1.8 million; Austria-Hungary—1.2 million; Turkey—325,000. These figures do not include deaths of civilians. In addition, over 20 million soldiers were wounded. Statistics were taken from Paterson et al., 293–294.

2. Carrie Chapman Catt, "A Call to Action," Apr. 13, 1921, CCC: NYPL.

3. Grace Hankett to Caroline Lexow Babcock, Nov. 2, 1921, WPU: SCPC.

4. Statement, New York Branch, 1919, WPP: SCPC.

5. Jessie Wallace Hughan, "Women Pacifists in 1920," *The Call Magazine,* 8, JWH: SCPC.

6. Madeline Doty to Hannah Clothier Hull, Dec. 30, 1924, reel 75.1, HCH: SCPC.

7. Dorothy Detzer to Hull, Jan. 9, 1925, reel 75.1, HCH: SCPC.

8. Undated, untitled, reel 2, box B3, folder 1, AGS: SCPC.

9. Anna Garlin Spencer to Owen Lovejoy, Feb. 5, 1920, reel 41, WILPF/US: SCPC.

10. "Objects as Stated in the Constitution Adopted at Annual Meeting in Chicago" flier, 1920, reel 2, box 3, folder 1, AGS: SCPC.

11. From this point on, I will be concentrating on the New York City women of WILPF, who, as the reader will see, did not always constitute one unified branch. It may be helpful to understand the structure of WILPF as it has emerged since World War I. The international WILPF, whose office is headquartered in Geneva, represents all national WILPF sections. Every three years, an international congress composed of delegates from each national section meets to determine international WILPF policy. Since 1919, U.S. women have been able to join the U.S. section of WILPF, either as members-at-large or as part of a local branch. Local branches can also form larger units (for example, state branches) while still maintaining their local autonomy. In the 1920s and 1930s, for instance, the various New York City branches were also part of the New York State branch. All units, however, are called branches.

Initially, the national board consisted of members elected by the entire U.S. membership. In 1972, the U.S. WILPF set up geographical regions. Since the late 1980s, the national board has reflected this regional emphasis since the number of board members depends on the number of members in any one region. Most of WILPF's activities are organized on the local level. However, the national board, through congresses, newsletters, and the national office in Philadelphia, determines national policy and acts as a central networking point for all U.S. WILPF members and branches. The WILPF national congresses are open to all members, as are the international congresses, although only official delegates can vote.

12. Statement, 1918, New York City WPP, WPP: SCPC.

13. "Conference Call," Feb. 15, 1919, WPP: SCPC.

14. "Goals of the Women's International League, 1919," WPP: SCPC.

15. Unsigned to Mrs. Gavrilowitch, Mar. 7, 1919, reel 12.14; Unsigned to Margaret, May 12, 1919, reel 12.15, WPP: SCPC.

16. Anna Garlin Spencer to Lucia Ames Mead, Aug. 3, 1919, reel 1, box 1, folder 2, AGS: SCPC.

17. For more information on the major players and history of the Women's Peace Society and the Women's Peace Union, see Harriet Hyman Alonso, *The Women's Peace Union and the Outlawry of War, 1921–1942* (Knoxville: The Univ. of Tennessee Press, 1989).

18. Elinor Byrns, "The Women's Peace Society: A NonResistant Organization—Founded October, 1919—Its Aim, Program and Arguments," 1921, WPU: SCPC.

19. Elinor Byrns to Fanny Garrison Villard [1921], WPS: SCPC.

20. [Elinor Byrns] to Mary Abbott, Apr. 11, 1921, WPS: SCPC.

21. "Senate Joint Resolution 100—69th Congress, 1st Session," Apr. 19, 1926, WPU: SCPC.

22. "The Boy Scout Movement: A Blessing or a Menace?" n.d., WPU: SCPC.

23. Spencer to Amy Woods, Sept. 21, 1923, series C, box 3, New York, WILPF/US: SCPC.

24. Christine Miller to New York Branch, Dec. 8, 1923, reel 40, WILPF/US: SCPC.

25. Mabel Hyde Kittredge to Woods, Dec. 9, 1923, reel 40, WILPF/US: SCPC.

26. For a more detailed discussion of the U.S. Section of WILPF, including its personalities and politics, during the interwar years, see Carrie Foster-Hayes, "The Women and the Warriors: Dorothy Detzer and the WILPF" (Ph.D. diss., Univ. of Denver, 1984; forthcoming from Syracuse Univ. Press) and Anne Marie Pois, "The Politics and Process of Organizing for Peace: The United States Section of the Women's International League for Peace and Freedom, 1919–1939," (Ph.D. diss., Univ. of Colorado, 1988).

27. Detzer to Spencer, Apr. 9, 1925, reel 53, WILPF/US: SCPC.

28. Katherine Devereux Blake, "The Star Spangled Banner," box 5, WPU: NYPL; "The Star-Spangled Banner" was not officially adopted as the national anthem until 1931. Blake's biographical sketch is based on "Miss Blake Bids Young People Enter Politics," *New York Herald Tribune,* June 9, 1946.

29. Rosalyn Terborg-Penn, "Discontented Black Feminists: Prelude and Postscript to the Passage of the Nineteenth Amendment," in *Decades of Discontent: The Women's Movement, 1920–1940,* ed. Lois Scharf and Joan Jensen, (Boston: Northeastern Univ. Press, 1987), 270–271.

30. Mary Church Terrell, *A Colored Woman in a White World,* quoted in Carrie Foster, *The Women and the Warriors: The U.S. Section of the WILPF, 1915–1946* (Syracuse: Syracuse Univ. Press, forthcoming).

31. Ibid.

32. "Report of the New York State Branch of WIL for Year 1928–1929, Given at Annual Meeting in Detroit, April 26, 1929," series b2, box 1, WILPF/US: SCPC.

33. "Report of the New York State Branch, 1930," series b2, box 1, WILPF/US: SCPC.

34. Sadie A. Cohen to Detzer, Mar. 15, 1934, reel 60, WILPF/US: SCPC.

35. Biographical information about Addie Hunton was drawn from Cynthia Neverdon-Morton, *Afro-American Women of the South and the Advancement of the Race, 1895–1925* (Knoxville: Univ. of Tennessee Press, 1989), 196, 199, 200, 226.

36. Hunton to Detzer, Sept. 1934, reel 59, WILPF/US: SCPC.

37. Hunton to Detzer, Jan. 8, 1935, reel 59, WILPF/US: SCPC.

38. Dorothy Detzer Denny to Barbara Miller Solomon, Jan. 27, 1979, quoted in Barbara Miller Solomon, "Dilemmas of Pacifist Women, Quakers and Others, in World Wars I and II," in *Witnesses for Change: Quaker Women Over Three Centuries,* ed. Elisabeth Potts Brown and Susan Mosher Stuard (New Brunswick: Rutgers Univ. Press, 1989), 131.

39. Emily Greene Balch to Fanny Garrison Villard, Mar. 15, 1920, quoted in Foster-Hayes, 102. See no. 30 for the forthcoming book from this dissertation.

40. Catt to Florence Allen, Dec. 28, 1923, CCC: NYPL.

41. "General Information," 1935, NCCW: SCPC.

42. "Historical Introduction," n.d., NCCW: SCPC.

43. "The New Work of the New Woman," n.d., reel 84.3, box 3, folder 4, AGS: SCPC.

44. Statement to the National Council of Women, n.d., reel 53, WILPF/US: SCPC.

45. "Slacker Oaths Should Forfeit Citizenship," *The Woman Patriot,* 7, no. 13 (July 1, 1923), 3.

46. Anita Phipps to Assistant Chief of Staff, June 25, 1924, MI: NA.

47. Press release to *Evening Graphic,* Apr. 16, 1925, WPU: SCPC.

48. R. M. Whitney, "Peace at Any Old Price" (New York: Beckwith Press, 1923), reel 75.5, HCH: SCPC.

49. File #35, Report #19—Women's International League for Peace and Freedom, May 31, 1924, MI: UPA.

50. For additional information on the "Pax-Special," see Foster-Hayes, 148–149.

51. "The Socialist-Pacifist Movement in America Is an Absolutely Fundamental and Integral Part of International Socialism," chart compiled by Lucia R. Maxwell, 1922–23, MI: N.A.

52. Emily Greene Balch, "Statement of Facts Concerning the Women's International League in Regard to Certain Misrepresentations," *PAX,* n.d., reel 33, WILPF/US: SCPC.

53. H. A. Jung to Major Sidney L. Smith, July 13, 1926, MI: UPA.

54. J. V. McConville, Captain, Cavalry to Major Cowles, May 13, 1922, MI: UPA.

55. Carrie Chapman Catt to Aletta Jacobs, May 27, 1924, CCC: NYPL.

56. Catt to Daughters of the American Revolution, 1927, CCC: NYPL.

57. Ibid.

58. Catt, "Monroe Doctrine," 1924, CCC: NYPL.

59. Catt to Emma Swiggett, Oct. 30, 1924, PanAm Women's Auxiliary: LC.

60. For additional information on Latin American efforts of the Women's Peace Union, see Alonso, *The Women's Peace Union and the Outlawry of War, 1921–1942,* 129–130.

61. Pois, 301, n. 22.

62. Sara Weeks Roberts to Swiggett, May 9, 1921, PanAm Women's Auxiliary: LC.

63. Minutes of Women's Auxiliary Committee Meeting, May 8, 1917, PanAm Women's Auxiliary: LC.

64. "Proceedings and Report of the Columbus Day Conferences Held in Twelve American Countries on October 12, 1923," 1926, PanAm Women's Auxiliary: LC.

65. Caroline Lexow Babcock to Isabel Ashby, May 27, 1926, WPU: SCPC.

66. Carrie Chapman Catt, "The Problem Stated," 1924, CCC: NYPL.

67. Ibid.

68. "Women's Memorial to the London Naval Reduction Conference," Jan. 29, 1930, CCC: NYPL.

69. "Petition," 1931, P & D: SCPC.

70. WILPF Press Release, Mar. 16, 1931, WILPF/US: SCPC.

71. "Abolition of Aggressive(?) Armaments," n.d. [c. 1932], P & D: SCPC.

72. For a detailed account of Woolley's appointment, see Dorothy Detzer, *Appointment on the Hill* (New York: Holt, 1948), 112–115.

73. Ibid., 112.

74. Mary E. Woolley, "Woman as World Citizen: A New Role," *New York Times Magazine,* July 10, 1932.

75. For a more detailed account of the "Peace Caravan," see Foster-Hayes, 371–375, and Pois, 352–358.

76. Gertrude Bussey and Margaret Tims, *Pioneers for Peace: Women's International League for Peace and Freedom, 1915–1965* (1965; reprint, Oxford: Alden, 1980), 96.

77. Frieda Langer Lazarus, "Why Women Failed at Geneva," *Eagle Magazine for Women,* Apr. 3, 1932, [Section M of the *Brooklyn Eagle*], 1–2.

78. For additional information on the Nye Committee, see Pois, 412–416.

5. Dilemmas, Quandaries, and Tensions during War, 1935–1945

1. "Dorothy Detzer—'Useful American,'" in *Equal Rights,* 1, no. 4 (Jan. 26, 1935), series 1, box 1, DD: SCPC.

2. Pois, 273.

3. Emily Greene Balch, quoted in Pois, 48. Pois has a detailed discussion on the use of consensus within WILPF.

4. Mildred Scott Olmsted, "Editorial Comments—Women for Peace," Feb. 1965, series 3, box 8F, "Articles 1938–79," MSO: SCPC.

5. Dorothy Detzer, *Daily Worker,* Oct. 13, 1933. Within the context of this book, "communist" refers to those who follow the general Marxist-Leninist ideology,

and "Communist" refers to those who were members of the Communist Party, USA; "anti-communist" and "anti-Communist" follow the same pattern.

6. Detzer to Mrs. A. Rosenberg, Mar. 30, 1934, reel 60, WILPF/US: SCPC.

7. Detzer to a Mrs. Seelman, Oct. 9, 1934, reel 60, WILPF/US: SCPC.

8. "Memorandum prepared by Miss Caroline Singer at the request of the Board of Directors of the Manhattan Division of the Women's International League," n.d. [c. 1935], series b2, box 4, WILPF/US: SCPC.

9. Eleanor D. Brannan to Detzer, Feb. 14, 1936, reel 60, WILPF/US: SCPC.

10. Eleanor A. Eaton, Executive Secretary, "Report of the State President and State Executive Secretary to the State Board, at the Quarterly Meeting, December 1, 1939," box 2, series 1, WILPF/US: SCPC.

11. Eaton to Detzer, Jan. 31, 1940, series B,2, box 4, WILPF/US: SCPC.

12. Resolutions Passed at the Annual Meeting of the New York State Branch of the Women's International League for Peace and Freedom, February 21, 1940, series B2, box 1, WILPF/US: SCPC.

13. "People's Mandate" flier, 1935, subj. file I 10, S/L: NYPL.

14. "The Conference Report" [Weekly of the National Affairs Conference Board] 1, no. 11, (Sept. 16, 1939), 20, "A Red Pilgrimage," HCH: SCPC.

15. Detzer, "The Pro-Neutrality Pattern," appended to Branch Letter 70, Feb. 28, 1939, quoted in Solomon, 137.

16. "First Interview Between Mildred Scott Olmsted and Mercedes Randall in New York City," Feb. 1972, series 4, box 9, MSO: SCPC.

17. Ibid.

18. Balch, "A Foreign Policy for the W.I.L.," appended to Branch Letter 70, Feb. 28, 1939 quoted in Solomon, 137.

19. Balch to Alice Hamilton, Feb. 20, 1941, quoted in ibid., 153.

20. Minutes of Quarterly Meeting, State Board of Directors—New York Branch, Feb. 14, 1937, WILPF/US: SCPC.

21. Sadie Cohen, Eva Antin and Rachel Sellinger of the Bronx Branch to Hannah Clothier Hull, Nov. 21, 1938, reel 66, WILPF/US: SCPC.

22. "First Interview Between Mildred Scott Olmsted and Mercedes Randall in New York City," Feb. 1972, series 4, box 9, MSO: SCPC.

23. Tracy Mygatt to Elinor Byrns, Jan. 19, 1940, WPU: NYPL.

24. Catt to Clark M. Eichelberger, Sept. 6, 1939, CCC: NYPL.

25. "Program for 1940, the 15th Conference on the Cause and Cure of War," Box 3, NCCCW: SCPC.

26. Women's Peace Union leaflet, "For Twice a Year," n.d. [c. 1936–37], WPU: NYPL.

27. "Secretary's Report, 1938–39," WPU: SCPC.

28. Press release by Tracy Mygatt, Apr. 6, 1939, WPU: NYPL.

29. Detzer, "America and the Next Peace," radio address, Mar. 27, 1940 quoted in Foster-Hayes, 543.

30. Foster-Hayes, 561–569.

31. Detzer to a Mrs. Cohen, Mar. 17, 1934, reel 60, WILPF/US: SCPC.

32. W. Katharine Bennett to Mrs. Morgan, May 27, 1936, NCCCW: SCPC.

33. Catt to Mrs. Thomas Nicholson, Aug. 2, 1933, CCC: NYPL.

34. Catt to Dr. Ernest M. Patterson, Sept. 11, 1933, CCC: NYPL.

35. Ibid.

36. Catt to Elizabeth S. Medvene, Oct. 6, 1933, box 1, folder 10, CCC: NYPL.

37. Catt to Samuel Untermyer, Sept. 12, 1933, box 1, folder 10, CCC: NYPL.

38. Catt to Clark M. Eichelberger, Sept. 6, 1939, CCC: NYPL.

39. "Statement Adopted at an Emergency Meeting of the National Board of the Women's International League for Peace and Freedom Held in Washington, D.C. on December 10, 1941," reel 1, WILPF/US: SCPC.

40. "Statement of WIL Policy prepared by Emily Greene Balch and Amy Woods," *Stepping Stones,* Jan. 1942, series B2, box 8, WILPF/US: SCPC.

41. "Statement Adopted at an Emergency Meeting of the National Board of the Women's International League for Peace and Freedom Held in Washington, D.C. on December 10, 1941," reel 1, WILPF/US: SCPC.

42. Anna Graves to Balch, Apr. 5, 1942, quoted in Solomon, 140.

43. Mildred Scott Olmsted, "Report to National Board—Westport, Connecticut," Jan. 23–24, 1942, reel 11, WILPF/US: SCPC.

44. "Report by Caroline Singer, Intra-American Chairman, New York State Boards, W.I.L.," Feb. 25, 1938, WILPF/US: SCPC.

45. "The Conscription of Women?", leaflet, May 1943, series A, box 1, folder 3, WCOC: SCPC.

46. "Statement of Purpose," 1943, series A, box 1, folder 2; General Statement, n.d., series A, box 1, folder 2, WCOC: SCPC.

47. Olmsted, "The Drafting of Women for the Armed Forces," presented on the Town Meeting of the Air, Feb. 3, 1944, WCOC: SCPC.

48. Ibid.

49. Ibid.

50. Ibid.

51. "News Flash," from the New York Branch, June 1942, series B2, box 3, WILPF/US: SCPC.

52. "Twenty Questions on the International Police Force," leaflet, June 1943, NCCCW: SCPC.

53. National Committee on the Cause and Cure of War Minutes of National Committee, Apr. 8, 1943, CCC: NYPL.

54. Catt to Margery Corbett-Ashby, Aug. 1, 1945, Box 3, folder 11, CCC: NYPL.

55. Detzer, "An Effective Organized National Office," n.d. [c. 1945], reel 2, WILPF/US: SCPC.

56. Detzer to Olmsted n.d. [c. 1930], quoted in Margaret Hope Bacon, *One Woman's Passion for Peace and Freedom: The Life of Mildred Scott Olmsted* (Syracuse: Syracuse Univ. Press, 1993), 171.

57. Roberta C. Kramer, Chair, "Report of the Special Committee on Youth and the W.I.L.," 1944, reel 12, WILPF/US: SCPC.

58. Ibid.

6. The Effects of McCarthyism on Feminist-Pacifists, 1945–1960

1. For a detailed description of the Manhattan Project and the scientists' feelings about the bomb, see Richard Rhodes, *The Making of the Atomic Bomb* (New York: Simon and Schuster, 1988); and Alice Kimball Smith, *A Peril and a Hope: The Scientists' Movement in America, 1945–47* (Chicago: The Univ. of Chicago Press, 1965).

2. Dorothy Detzer, "The Future of the W.I.L.," report of the national secretary, Jan. 1946, reel 12, WILPF/US: SCPC.

3. "The Women's International League and the United Nations," Series no. 1; "How the WIL Works With and For the U.N.," one pamphlet, n.d., reel 37, WILPF/US: SCPC.

4. "WILPF, US Section—Principles," n.d. [c. 1948], reel 1, WILPF/US: SCPC.

5. Ibid.

6. Ibid.

7. "The Atomic Bomb and Its Message to You," 1945, box 30, WILPF/ US: SCPC.

8. Emily Greene Balch et al. to the editor of the *New York Times,* Oct. 6, 1949, reel 37, WILPF/US: SCPC.

9. Radio Spot #1, n.d. [1950s], reel 37, WILPF/US: SCPC.

10. Radio Spot #2, n.d. [1950s], reel 37, WILPF/US: SCPC.

11. Sarah Lifton to Mildred Scott Olmsted, June 1, 1948, reel 78, WILPF/US: SCPC.

12. Olmsted to Louise Lesson, Oct. 25, 1950, reel 82, WILPF/US: SCPC.

13. The Exeuctive Committee of the Metropolitan New York Branch of the Women's International League for Peace and Freedom to Members, June 23, 1955, reel 90, WILPF/US: SCPC.

14. Brenda Parnes, interview with Bess Cameron, Dec. 30, 1987, NYHP.

15. Senator Hubert Humphrey to Annalee Stewart, Mar. 27, 1952, reel 30, WILPF/US: SCPC; Thomas W. Beale, Sr., to Mary Ford Hann, Mar. 25, 1955, courtesy of JAPA.

16. "Freedom of Thought and Speech," statement at 1949 annual meeting, reel 1, WILPF/US: SCPC.

17. Balch, 1926 and 1950, quoted in "Materials for Discussion: Not for distribution," n.d. [c. 1952], WILPF/US: SCPC.

18. "Information From the Files of the Committee on Un-American Activities: U.S. House of Representatives," June 30, 1953, courtesy of JAPA.

19. "Materials For Discussion, Not For Distribution," n.d. [c. 1952], WILPF/US: SCPC.

20. Olmsted to national board meeting, Jan. 29–31, 1953, reel 4, WILPF/US: SCPC.

21. "Principles and Policies, 1954–1955," reel 1, WILPF/US: SCPC.

22. "Our Patriotic Duty to Dissent," WILPF pamphlet, May 1957, reel 37, WILPF/US: SCPC.

23. "Principles and Policies, 1954–1955," reel 1, WILPF/US: SCPC.

24. "Report of Administrative Secretary to Board of Directors Meeting," Feb. 8–10, 1951, reel 4, WILPF/US: SCPC.

25. Mildred Scott Olmsted, "Report of Administrative Secretary to Board of Directors Meeting," Feb. 8–10, 1951, reel 4, WILPF/US: SCPC.

26. "The Women's International League for Peace and Freedom Human Rights Series No. 2—International Security," n.d. [c. 1952], reel 37, WILPF/US: SCPC.

27. Olmsted to national board meeting, Jan. 29–31, 1953, reel 4, WILPF/US: SCPC.

28. Anonymous comment to member of WILPF Metropolitan New York Branch History Project.

29. Citations for notes 29, 32, 33, 34, 36, 37, 38, 39, 40, 41, 42, 43, 45, 46, and 47 have been eliminated because I have not been able to reach the people involved for permission to use their names. I have contacted the national WILPF office and the Denver branch, but my search has been unsuccessful. Because the material in this section is sensitive, neither I nor Syracuse University Press wishes to infringe on anyone's privacy. The names of Denver branch members are used because these people were cited from newspaper articles within the public domain. These include notes 30, 31, and 35.

30. *Denver Post,* Jan. 15, 1954.

31. "Battle Seen on League Red Charge," *Denver Post,* Feb. 21, 1954, sec. 3A.

32. The citations are in the possession of the author of this book.

33. Ibid.

34. Ibid.

35. "Battle Seen on League Red Charge," *Denver Post,* Feb. 21, 1954, sec. 3A.

36. The citations are in the possession of the author of this book.

37. Ibid.

38. Ibid.

39. Ibid.

40. Ibid.

41. Ibid.

42. Ibid.

43. Ibid.

44. "First Interview between Mildred Scott Olmsted and Mercedes Randall," Feb. 1972, series 4, box 9, MSO: SCPC.

45. The citations are in the possession of the author of this book.

46. Ibid.

47. Ibid.

48. "Packet on Infiltration and Attack Issued by the National Board of the WIL," received May 17, 1954, WILPF/US: SCPC. Hereinafter cited in the text by page number.

49. The following account of the Congress of American Women is derived from primary documents, as indicated in nn. 50–53, or from Amy Swerdlow, "The Politics of Motherhood: The Case of Women Strike for Peace and the Test Ban Treaty," (Ph.D. diss., Rutgers Univ., 1984), 59–70.

50. "What Is the Congress of American Women?" leaflet, n.d. [c. 1946], S/L: NYPL.

51. "Constitution and Programme of the WIDF, 1963 addendum," courtesy of WREE National Office.

52. Press release, Congress of American Women, Mar. 8, 1946, subj. file I4, S/L: NYPL.

53. "Report of Commission on Action for Peace and Democracy," submitted by Muriel Draper, May 25, 1946, I7, S/L: NYPL.

54. "Report on the Commission on the Status of Women," submitted by Susan B. Anthony, May 25, 1946, as quoted in Swerdlow, 63.

55. California Committee on Un-American Activities Report, 1948, quoted in Swerdlow, 104, n. 42.

56. *Report on the Congress of American Women,* quoted in Swerdlow, 65.

57. "Declaration of Principles" as appeared in *The Peacemaker,* 1, no. 2 (Nov. 1950), folder 1, AWP: SCPC.

58. Clementina Jaolone, "Report on Women's Activities at the Chicago Peace Congress, June 29–July 1, 1951," folder 1, AWP: SCPC.

59. "How to Establish a Local Chapter of Woman, Inc." leaflet, n.d. [c. 1947], CDGA, Woman, Inc. Papers: SCPC. For a detailed description of Woman, Inc., see Susan F. Dion, "Challenge to Cold War Orthodoxy: Women and Peace, 1945–1963," (Ph.D. diss., Marquette University, 1991).

60. Dorothy Thompson, "A Woman's Manifesto," n.d., [c. 1946–47], CDGA, Woman, Inc. Papers: SCPC.

61. Dorothy Thompson, "A woman says, 'You must come into the room of your mother unarmed,'" *Ladies' Home Journal* 63 (Feb. 1946), 24.

62. Dorothy Thompson, "If No One Else—We, the Mothers," *Ladies' Home Journal* 64 (July 1947), 11–12.

7. From Civil Rights to the Second Wave of the Feminist Movement, 1960–1975

1. For a good summary of the development of the women's movement of the 1960s, see Sara Evans, *Personal Politics: The Roots of Women's Liberation in the Civil Rights Movement and the New Left* (New York: Vintage, 1979); Myra Marx Ferree and Beth B. Hess, *Controversy and Coalition: The New Feminist Movement* (Boston: Twayne, 1985).

2. *"W.I.L.P.F. AND THE COLD WAR,"* statement, Aug. 23, 1960, courtesy of JAPA.

3. Ibid.

4. Ibid.

5. The summary of WILPF's activities was derived from Eleanor Fowler, "The WILPF Story . . . Then and Now," booklet, 1986, WILPF/US: SCPC and a scanning of the Reports of National Board Meetings from 1960–1975, WILPF/US: SCPC.

6. Ibid.

7. Annalee Stewart to Beatrice Pearson, Dec. 13, 1962, OP: RU.

8. The summary of the activities of the Metropolitan New York Branch of WILPF reflects a scanning of the branch's reports to the national board, 1960–1975, WILPF/US: SCPC.

9. Bess Cameron, interview by Brenda Parnes, Dec. 30, 1987, NYHP.

10. Olmsted, quoted in Margaret Hope Bacon, *One Woman's Passion for Peace and Freedom,* 306.

11. Voice of Women, USA leaflet, n.d., CDGA, VOW: SCPC.

12. Details about Women Strike for Peace were derived from both primary sources as indicated in the following notes and from the work of historian Amy Swerdlow, "The Politics of Motherhood."

13. Swerdlow, 1–3, 14.

14. Swerdlow, 2–3.

15. Ibid., 3.

16. "Historical Background," box 1, series 1, DG115, WSP: SCPC.

17. "Dear WISPs," Dec. 16, 1962, quoted in Swerdlow, 308.

18. "Women Strike for Peace Statement on 'House Un-American Activities Subpoenas' to WSP Participants in New York," quoted in Swerdlow, 309.

19. Swerdlow, 329–330.

20. U.S. Congress, House Committee on Un-American Activities, *Communist Activities in the Peace Movement,* quoted in Swerdlow, 346.

21. Minna Kashins, interview by Brenda Parnes, Oct. 7, 1986, NYHP.

22. Bess Cameron, interview by Brenda Parnes, Dec. 30, 1987, NYHP.

23. Orlie Pell to Savina Weisman, Apr. 3, 1961, OP: RU.

24. S.B., interview by Harriet Alonso, Nov. 20, 1987, NYHP. (The interviewee requested that initials be used in place of her full name.)

25. Swerdlow, 379–420.

26. Biographical information about Gage-Colby is drawn from Swerdlow, 245–251.

27. Swerdlow, 256.

28. Swerdlow, 274.

29. Eleanor Garst, "NICH Issues for Discussion, #4," Oct. 11, 1963, quoted in Swerdlow, 294.

30. Catherine Foster, *Women for All Seasons: The Story of the Women's International League for Peace and Freedom* (Athens: Univ. of Georgia Press, 1989), 51–52.

31. Nan Wiegersma, interview with author, Fitchburg, Mass., May 1, 1991.

32. *Memo* (Fall 1969), 2, personal collection of Nan Wiegersma.

33. Catherine Foster, *Women for All Seasons,* 66–70.

34. Metropolitan New York branch activities derived from branch minutes, 1960–1975, WILPF/US: SCPC.

35. "We Mourn the Death" flier, n.d. [c. 1970], NYHP.

36. Swerdlow, 211–214.

37. "Historical Background," DG115, series 1, box 1, WSP:SCPC.

38. Kathie Sarachild, "Taking in the Images: A Record in Graphics of the Vietnam Era Soil for Feminism," *Vietnam Generation* 1, nos. 3–4 (Summer–Fall, 1989): 235.

39. "What For?" flier, n.d. [c. 1968] subj. file I6, S/L: NYPL.

40. "Historical Background," AMP: SCPC.

41. Martin Hall, "Another Mother for Peace," *New Perspectives: Journal of the World Peace Council* 2, no. 5 (Sept.-Dec. 1972): 79–82.

42. Ibid.

43. "Historical Background," AMP: SCPC.

44. "By-Laws," 1967, series 1, box 1, folder 2, AMP: SCPC.

45. "Historical Background," AMP: SCPC.

46. Harriet Barron to Ruth Sillman, Aug. 19, 1970, series B,6 box 27, WILPF/US: SCPC.

47. "Historical Background," WSP: SCPC.

48. Shulamith Firestone, quoted in Jenny Brown, "Women for Peace or Women's Liberation? Signposts from the Feminist Archives" *Vietnam Generation* 1, nos. 3–4 (Summer-Fall 1989): 248. For a good analysis of this event, see Ruth Rosen, "The Day They Buried 'Traditional Womanhood': Women and the Politics of Peace Protest," *Vietnam Generation* 1 nos. 3–4 (Summer–Fall, 1989): 208–234.

49. *Congressional Record,* 90th Cong., 2d sess., vol. 114, no. 4, Thursday, Jan. 18, 1968.

50. "Invitation to 'Burial of Traditional Womanhood,'" Jan. 15, 1968, quoted in Brown, 248.

51. Peggy Dobbins, "Liturgy for the Burial of Traditional Womanhood," Jan. 15, 1968, quoted in Sarachild, 239.

52. Ibid.

53. Ibid.

54. Ibid., 241.

55. Sue Munaker, quoted in Brown, 251.

56. Ibid.

57. Sarachild, 249.

58. "All Women are Victims in This Man's War!" flier, n.d. [c. 1968], NYHP.

59. Kay Camp, "Up With Women," *Peace and Freedom,* March 1970, quoted in Catherine Foster, 56.

60. Elizabeth Frappollo, "At 91, Jeannette Rankin is the Feminists' New Heroine," *Life,* Mar. 3, 1972, 65.

8. Feminist Peace Activism and the United Nations' Decade for Women, 1975–1985

1. The summary of WILPF events is derived from Eleanor Fowler, "The WILPF Story . . . Then and Now" booklet, 1986, WILPF/US: SCPC; and a scanning of the "Reports of the National Board Meetings" from 1975–85, WILPF/US: SCPC.

2. "Women Demand Disarmament . . . 1975 is International Women's Year" flier, 1975, NYHP.

3. "Women's International League for Peace and Freedom, Metropolitan New York Branch-Occasional Newsletter #14," Mar. 1975, NYHP; Blanche Wiesen Cook, interview by Brenda Parnes, Harriet Alonso, and Yvette Tomlinson, May 24, 1990, NYHP.

4. Rita Handman, untitled report n.d. [c. 1972], WSP: SCPC.

5. S.B., interview by Harriet Alonso, Nov. 20, 1987, NYHP.

6. "Women Strike for Peace and Survival, 1975" leaflet, 1975, WSP: SCPC.

7. "I Refuse to Be One of 20 Million 'Acceptable' Dead!" flier, n.d. [c. 1982], WSP: author's personal collection.

8. Ethel Barol Taylor, summarized and quoted in Judith Porter Adams, *Peacework: Oral Histories of Women Peace Activists* (Boston: Twayne, 1990), 11–18.

9. "The Peace Groups," *Washington Post,* Oct. 9, 1982.

10. See Guenter Lewy, *Peace and Revolution: The Moral Crisis of American Pacifism* (Grand Rapids, Mich.: Eerdmans, 1988).

11. I discovered that WREE members were unfamiliar with their CAW roots while interviewing Norma Spector, one of the original founders and leading organizers of WREE. Norma Spector, interview with author, Brooklyn, New York, Nov. 22, 1988.

12. Ibid.

13. "Keynote Address to WREE's First National Convention" by Sondra Patrinos, n.d. [c. 1977], WREE National Office, New York City.

14. Ibid.

15. Ibid.

16. Georgia Henning, "Conference Keynote," *The Wree-View,* Pilot Issue, May 1976, WREE National Office, New York City.

17. Georgia Henning, "Presentation Made at Fannie Lou Hamer Awards Luncheon, 1987," WREE National Office, New York City.

18. Ibid.

19. "Women for Racial and Economic Equality: Statement of Purpose and By-Laws" as decided in Convention in Chicago, Sept. 1977, WREE National Office, New York City.

20. "Founding Call," n.d. [c. 1980], Women, USA: SCPC.

21. *Facts on File,* 1981, 439–440.

22. *Rostker v. Goldberg, Decisions of the United States Supreme Court: 1980–81 Term,* 386–387.

23. "Organizational Packet for Women's Party for Survival," n.d. [c. 1981–82], WAND: SCPC.

24. Ibid., and "The Women's Party for Survival" leaflet, July 1981, WAND: SCPC.

25. "Origin and History" leaflet, 1984, WAMM: SCPC.

26. Ibid.

27. For more information on Greenham Common, see Alice Cook and Gwyn Kirk, *Greenham Women Everywhere: Dreams, Ideas, and Actions from the Women's Peace Movement* (Boston: South End Press, 1983); and Jill Liddington, *The Long Road to Greenham: Feminism and Anti-Militarism in Britain Since 1820* (London: Virago, 1989).

28. For more information on Barbara Deming, see "Introduction" by Jane Meyerding in Barbara Deming, *We Are All Part of One Another: A Barbara Deming Reader,* ed. Jane Meyerding (Philadelphia: New Society, 1984), 1–17; and Robert Cooney and Helen Michalowski, eds., *The Power of the People: Active Nonviolence in the United States* (Philadelphia: New Society, 1987), 204.

29. Barbara Deming, quoted in *The Power of the People: Active Nonviolence in the United States,* ed. Robert Cooney and Helen Michalowski (Philadelphia: New Society Publishers, 1987), 204.

30. Ibid., 218–219.

31. Deming, quoted from Mab Segrest, "Feminism and Disobedience: Conversations with Barbara Deming," in Pam McAllister, *Reweaving the Web of Life: Feminism and Nonviolence* (Philadelphia: New Society Publishers, 1982), 55, 59.

32. McAllister, iii.

33. Ynestra King, "All is Connectedness: Scenes from the Women's Pentagon Action, USA," in *Keeping the Peace: A Woman's Peace Handbook* 1, ed. Lynne Jones, (London: Women's Press, 1983), 44.

34. A good analysis of the differences between radical and socialist feminists can be found in Barbara Epstein, *Political Protest and Cultural Revolution: Nonviolent Direct Action in the 1970s and 1980s* (Berkeley: Univ. of Calif. Press, 1991), 167–183.

35. King, "Healing the Wounds: Feminism, Ecology, and the Nature/Culture Dualism," in *Reweaving the World: The Emergence of Ecofeminism,* ed. Irene Diamond and Gloria Feman Orenstein (San Francisco: Sierra Club Books, 1990), 109.

36. Ibid., 110.

37. Ibid., 117.

38. Ibid., 118.

39. "Unity Statement" quoted in King, "All is Connectedness," 42–43. The following description of Women's Pentagon Action is based on this essay, pp. 40–63.

40. King, "All is Connectedness," 45–51.

41. "Why We're Here" statement from Arlington Jail, Nov. 19, 1981, quoted in *Keeping the Peace,* ed. Lynne Jones, 58–59.

42. "Women's Encampment for a Future of Peace and Justice: Resource Handbook," Summer 1983, author's private collection.

43. Mima Cataldo et al., eds. *The Women's Encampment for a Future of Peace and Justice: Images and Writings* (Philadelphia: Temple Univ. Press, 1987), 3.

44. Loraine Hutchins, quoted in Cataldo et al., 30.

45. Kathryn Kirk, quoted in Cataldo et al., 49.

46. Rhoda Linton, "Seneca Women's Peace Camp: Shapes of Things to Come" in *Rocking the Ship of State: Toward a Feminist Peace Politics,* ed. Adrienne Harris and Ynestra King (San Francisco: Westview, 1989), 239–259.

47. Ruth Putter, as cited in Cataldo et al., 59.

48. Ibid., 21.

49. The description of the march is based on Grace Paley, "The Seneca Stories: Tales from the Women's Peace Encampment" *Ms.,* Dec. 1983, 54–62, 108.

50. Ibid., 56.

51. Ibid., 62.

52. Catherine Foster, *Women for All Seasons,* 95.

53. Elizabeth Mattick, quoted in ibid., 95–96.

54. Edith Ballantyne, quoted in ibid., 96.

55. WILPF mailing, 1988, author's personal collection.

56. Jane Midgley, *The Women's Budget* (New York: Jane Addams Peace Association, 1985).

57. Ibid., 1.

58. Ibid., 25.

59. Ibid., 36.

9. Conclusion

1. Blanche Wiesen Cook, interview by Brenda Parnes, Harriet Alonso and Yvette Tomlinson, May 24, 1990, NYHP.

2. Ibid.

3. Evelyn A. Mauss, interview by Clay Dalferes, Sept. 21, 1987, NYHP.

4. Oral History of Dorothy Detzer by Rosemary Rainbolt, June 28, 1974, SCPC.

5. Emily Greene Balch to Anna Garlin Spencer, Apr. 1, 1920, quoted in Foster-Hayes, 40–41.

6. Oral history of Dorothy Detzer by Rosemary Rainbolt, June 28, 1974, SCPC.

7. Balch, quoted in Foster-Hayes, 41.

8. Ursula Bowring, "WILPF's Racial Justice Campaign: An Evaluation, 1988–90," *Peace and Freedom* 50, no. 4 (July–Aug. 1990): 8.

9. First Interview between Mildred Scott Olmsted and Mercedes Randall, Feb. 1972, MSO: SCPC.

10. Blanche Wiesen Cook, interview May 24, 1990, NYHP.

11. "Pre-Convention Bulletin—Spring, 1990" of Women for Racial and Economic Equality, author's personal collection.

12. Ibid., insert.

13. The information on women's international actions in the Gulf War was drawn from the "International News" section of *Ms.*, 1, no. 5, (Mar.–Apr. 1991): 11–13.

14. "Troubled Waters: The Women's Ship for Peace," ibid., 11.

15. Margarita Papandreou, "When I Become One of Them," ibid., 13.

16. S.B., interview by Harriet Alonso, Nov. 20, 1987, NYHP.

SELECTED BIBLIOGRAPHY

Manuscript Collections

Jane Addams Peace Association. New York, New York
  Women's International League for Peace and Freedom Files.
Library of Congress. Washington, D.C.
  Women's Auxiliary of the Pan American Scientific Congresses Papers
National Archives. Washington, D.C.
  War Department General Staff Military Intelligence Division, 1917–1941 Papers.
New York Public Library, Rare Books and Manuscripts Division, Astor, Lenox, and Tilden Foundations. New York, New York
    Carrie Chapman Catt Papers
    Cathrine Curtis Papers
    Frieda Langer Lazarus Papers
    Rosika Schwimmer/Lola Maverick Lloyd Collection
    Women's Peace Union Papers
Rutgers University Libraries. Special Collections and Archives. New Brunswick, New Jersey
    Orlie Pell Papers
Arthur and Elizabeth Schlesinger Library on the History of Women in America. Radcliffe College, Cambridge, Massachusetts.
    Julia Ward Howe Papers
Swarthmore College Peace Collection. Swarthmore, Pennsylvania
  American School Peace League Papers
  American Women for Peace Papers
  Fannie Fern Andrews Papers
  Another Mother for Peace Papers
  Hannah Bailey Papers

Katherine Devereux Blake Papers
Elise Boulding Papers
Dorothy Detzer Papers
Jessie Wallace Hughan Papers
Hannah Clothier Hull Papers
Lucia Ames Mead Papers
Tracy Mygatt and Frances Witherspooon Papers
National Committee on the Cause and Cure of War Papers
Mildred Scott Olmsted Papers
Alice Park Papers
Peace and Disarmament Committee of the Women's International Organizations Papers
People's Mandate to Governments to End War Papers
Mercedes Randall Papers
Jeannette Rankin Papers
Anna Garlin Spencer Papers
Voice of Women Papers
Woman, Inc. Papers
Woman's Peace Congress Papers
Woman's Peace Festival Papers
Woman's Peace Party Papers
Women Against Military Madness Papers
Women for Peace Papers
Women Strike for Peace Papers
Women, USA Papers
Women's Action for Nuclear Disarmament Papers
Women's Committee for World Disarmament Papers
Women's Committee to Oppose Conscription Papers
Women's International League for Peace and Freedom, U.S. Section Papers
Women's International League for Peace and Freedom, U.S. Section, 1919–1959, Scholarly Resources Microfilm Edition
Women's Peace Society Papers
Women's Peace Union Papers

University Publications of America, Inc.
U.S. Military Intelligence Reports: Surveillance of Radicals in the United States, 1917–1941

Women for Racial and Economic Equality Materials. WREE National Office, New York, New York.

Oral Histories and Interviews

James Lerner, interview with author, Brooklyn, New York, May 24, 1991.

Norma Spector, interview with author, Brooklyn, New York, Nov. 22, 1988.

Nan Wiegersma, interview with author, Fitchburg, Massachusetts, May 1, 1991.

Oral History of Dorothy Detzer by Rosemary Rainbolt, June 28, 1974. Swarthmore College Peace Collection.

WILPF Metropolitan New York Branch History Project.

S.B., November 20, 1987.

Bess Cameron, December 30, 1987.

Blanche Wiesen Cook, May 24, 1990.

Minna Kashins, October 7, 1986.

Evelyn A. Mauss, September 21, 1987.

Books and Articles

Adams, Judith Porter. *Peacework: Oral Histories of Women Peace Activists.* Boston: Twayne, 1990.

Addams, Jane. *Democracy and Social Ethics.* Edited by Anne Firor Scott. 1907. Reprint. Cambridge, Mass.: Harvard Univ. Press, Belknap Press, 1964.

———. *Jane Addams: A Centennial Reader.* Edited by Emily Cooper Johnson. New York: Macmillan, 1960.

———. *The Newer Ideals of Peace.* New York: Macmillan, 1907.

———. *Peace and Bread in Time of War.* 1922. Reprint. Silver Springs, Md.: National Association of Social Workers, 1983.

———. *The Second Twenty Years at Hull-House—September 1909 to September 1929.* New York: Macmillan, 1930.

Addams, Jane, Emily G. Balch, and Alice Hamilton. *Women at The Hague: The International Congress of Women and Its Results.* New York: Macmillan, 1915.

Alonso, Harriet Hyman. *The Women's Peace Union and the Outlawry of War, 1921–1942.* Knoxville: Univ. of Tennessee Press, 1989.

Anthony, Susan B., Matilda Joslyn Gage, and Elizabeth Cady Stanton, eds. *History of Woman Suffrage,* Vol. 1. 1881. Reprint. New York: Arno and New York Times Press, 1969.

Bacon, Margaret Hope. *Mothers of Feminism: The Story of Quaker Women in America.* San Francisco: Harper and Row, 1986.

———. *One Woman's Passion for Peace and Freedom: The Life of Mildred Scott Olmsted.* Syracuse: Syracuse Univ. Press, 1992.

———. *The Quiet Rebels: The Story of the Quakers in America.* New York: Basic Books, 1969.

———. *Valiant Friend: The Life of Lucretia Mott.* New York: Walker, 1980.

Banner, Lois W. *Elizabeth Cady Stanton: A Radical for Woman's Rights.* Boston: Little, Brown, 1980.

Barry, Kathleen. *Susan B. Anthony: A Biography.* New York: New York Univ. Press, 1988.

Biehl, Janet. *Rethinking Ecofeminist Politics.* Boston: South End Press, 1991.

Bosch, Mineka, with Annemarie Kloosterman. *Politics and Friendship: Letters from the International Woman Suffrage Alliance, 1902–1942.* Columbus: Ohio State Univ. Press, 1990.

Boulding, Elise. *Women in the Twentieth Century World.* New York: Wiley, 1977.

Braude, Ann. *Radical Spirits: Spiritualism and Women's Rights in Nineteenth-Century America.* Boston: Beacon, 1989.

Brock, Peter. *Pacifism in the United States: From the Colonial Era to the First World War.* Princeton: Princeton Univ. Press, 1968.

Brown, Jenny. "Women for Peace or Women's Liberation? Signposts from the Feminist Archives." *Vietnam Generation* 1, nos. 3–4 (Summer–Fall 1989): 253–260.

Buhl, Mari Jo, and Paul Buhl, eds. *The Concise History of Woman Suffrage: Selections from the Classic Work of Stanton, Anthony, Gage, and Harper.* Urbana: Univ. of Illinois Press, 1978.

Bussey, Gertrude, and Margaret Tims. *Pioneers for Peace: Women's International League for Peace and Freedom, 1915–1965.* 1965. Reprint. Oxford: Alden Press, 1980.

Carroll, Berenice A. "The Outsiders: Comments on Fukuda Kideke, Catherine Marshall and Dorothy Detzer." *Peace and Change: A Journal of Peace Research* 4, no. 3 (Fall 1977): 23–26.

Cataldo, Mima, et al., eds. *The Women's Encampment for a Future of Peace and Justice: Images and Writings.* Philadelphia: Temple Univ. Press, 1987.

Chambers, John Whiteclay, II, ed. *The Eagle and the Dove: The American Peace Movement and United States Foreign Policy, 1902–1922.* New York: Garland, 1976.

Chandler, Elizabeth Margaret. *The Poetical Works of Elizabeth Margaret Chandler: With a Memoir of Her Life and Character by Benjamin Lundy.* 1836. Reprint. Miami: Mnemosyne, 1969.

Chatfield, Charles. *For Peace and Justice: Pacifism in America, 1914–1941.* Knoxville: Univ. of Tennessee Press, 1971.

———, ed. *Peace Movements in America.* New York: Schocken, 1973.

Child, Lydia Maria. *Lydia Maria Child: Selected Letters, 1817–1880.* Edited by Milton Metzer and Patricia G. Holland. Amherst: Univ. of Massachusetts Press, 1982.

Cook, Alice, and Gwyn Kirk. *Greenham Women Everywhere: Dreams, Ideas, and Actions from the Women's Peace Movement.* Boston: South End Press, 1983.

Cook, Blanche Wiesen. "The Woman's Peace Party: Collaboration and Non-Cooperation." *Peace and Change: A Journal of Peace Research* 1, no. 1 (Fall 1972): 36–42.

———. "Woodrow Wilson and the Antimilitarists, 1914–1917." Ph.D. diss., Johns Hopkins Univ., 1970.

Cooney, Robert, and Helen Michalowski, eds. *The Power of the People: Active Nonviolence in the United States.* Philadelphia: New Society, 1987.

Cott, Nancy F. *The Grounding of Modern Feminism.* New Haven: Yale Univ. Press, 1987.

Craig, John M. "Lucia True Ames Mead: American Publicist for Peace and Internationalism." Ph.D. diss., College of William and Mary, 1986.

Curti, Merle. *Peace or War: The American Struggle: 1636–1936.* New York: Norton, 1936.

Davis, Allen F. *American Heroine: The Life and Legend of Jane Addams.* New York: Oxford Univ. Press, 1973.

DeBenedetti, Charles. *An American Ordeal: The Antiwar Movement of the Vietnam Era.* Assisted by Charles Chatfield. Syracuse: Syracuse Univ. Press, 1990.

———. *Origins of the Modern American Peace Movement, 1915–1929.* Millwood, N.Y.: KTO Press, 1978.

———. *The Peace Reform in American History.* Bloomington: Indiana Univ. Press, 1980.

Degen, Marie Louise. *The History of the Woman's Peace Party.* 1939. Reprint. New York: Garland, 1972.

Deming, Barbara. *Prison Notes.* Boston: Beacon, 1966.

———. *Revolution and Equilibrium.* New York: Grossman, 1971.

———. *We Are All Part of One Another: A Barbara Deming Reader.* Edited by Jane Meyerding. Philadelphia: New Society, 1984.

Detzer, Dorothy. *Appointment on the Hill.* New York: Holt, 1948.

Dion, Susan F. "Challenge to Cold War Orthodoxy: Women and Peace, 1945–1963." Ph.D. diss., Marquette Univ., 1991.

DuBois, Ellen Carol. *Feminism and Suffrage: The Emergence of an Independent Women's Movement in America, 1848–1869.* Ithaca: Cornell Univ. Press, 1978.

Dunn, Mary Maples. "Latest Light on Women of Light." In *Witnesses for Change: Quaker Women Over Three Centuries,* edited by Elisabeth Potts Brown and Susan Mosher Stuard, 71–85. New Brunswick: Rutgers Univ. Press, 1989.

Du Pre Lumpkin, Katharine. *The Emancipation of Angelina Grimké.* Chapel Hill: Univ. of North Carolina Press, 1974.

Eagan, Eileen. *Class, Culture, and the Classroom: The Student Peace Movement of the 1930's.* Philadelphia: Temple Univ. Press, 1981.

Early, Frances. "Feminism, Peace, and Civil Liberties: Women's Role in the Origins of the World War I Civil Liberties Movement." *Women's Studies* 18 (1990): 95–115.

———. "An Interview with Mildred Scott Olmsted: Foremother of the Women's International League for Peace and Freedom." *Atlantis* 12, no. 1 (Fall 1986): 142–150.

Eastman, Crystal. *Crystal Eastman on Women and Revolution.* Edited by Blanche Wiesen Cook. New York: Oxford Univ. Press, 1978.

Echols, Alice. "'Women Power' and Women's Liberation: Exploring the Relationship Between the Antiwar Movement and the Women's Liberation Movement." In *Give Peace a Chance,* edited by William D. Hoover and Melvin Small, 171–181. Syracuse: Syracuse Univ. Press, 1992.

Elshtain, Jean Bethke. *Women and War.* New York: Basic Books, 1987.

Epstein, Barbara. *Political Protest and Cultural Revolution: Nonviolent Direct Action in the 1970s and 1980s.* Berkeley and Los Angeles: Univ. of California Press, 1991.

Erickson, Nels. *The Gentleman from North Dakota: Lynn J. Frazier.* Bismarck: State Historical Society of North Dakota, 1986.

Evans, Sara. *Personal Politics: The Roots of Women's Liberation in the Civil Rights Movement and the New Left.* New York: Vintage, 1979.

Ferree, Myra Marx, and Beth B. Hess. *Controversy and Coalition: The New Feminist Movement.* Boston: Twayne, 1985.

Ferrell, Robert H. "The Peace Movement." In *Isolation and Security,* edited by Alexander DeConde, 82–106. Durham, N.C.: Duke Univ. Press, 1957.

Filene, Peter. "The World Peace Foundation and Progressivism, 1910–1918." *New England Quarterly* 36 (1963): 478–501.

Fite, Gilbert C., and H. C. Peterson. *Opponents of War: 1917–1918.* Madison: Univ. of Wisconsin Press, 1957.

Flexner, Eleanor. *Century of Struggle: The Woman's Rights Movement in the United*

States. Rev. ed. Cambridge, Mass.: Harvard Univ. Press, Belknap Press, 1975.

Foster, Carrie. *The Women and the Warriors: The U.S. Section of the WILPF, 1915–1946.* Syracuse: Syracuse Univ. Press, forthcoming.

Foster, Catherine. *Women for All Seasons: The Story of the Women's International League for Peace and Freedom.* Athens: Univ. of Georgia Press, 1989.

Foster-Hayes, Carrie A. "The Women and the Warriors: Dorothy Detzer and the WILPF." Ph.D. diss., Univ. of Denver, 1984.

Fowler, Robert Booth. *Carrie Catt: Feminist Politician.* Boston: Northeastern Univ. Press, 1986.

Friedman, Andrea. "Feminist Pacifism During World War I: A Study of Ideology and Organization in the United States and Great Britain." M.A. thesis, Ohio State Univ., 1985.

Garrison, William Lloyd. *I Will Be Heard, 1822–1835.* Vol. 1 of *The Letters of William Lloyd Garrison.* Edited by Walter M. Merrill. Cambridge, Mass.: Harvard Univ. Press, Belknap Press, 1971.

———. *No Union With Slave Holders.* Vol. 3 of *The Letters of William Lloyd Garrison.* Edited by Walter M. Merrill. Cambridge, Mass.: Harvard Univ. Press, Belknap Press, 1971.

Giles, Kevin. *Flight of the Dove: The Story of Jeannette Rankin.* Beaverton, Oreg.: Touchstone, 1980.

Gilman, Charlotte Perkins. *Women and Economics.* 1898. Reprint. New York: Harper and Row, 1966.

Gioseffi, Daniela, ed. *Women on War: Essential Voices for the Nuclear Age.* New York: Simon and Schuster, 1988.

Gluck, Sherna. *From Parlor to Prison: Five American Suffragists Talk about Their Lives.* New York: Vintage, 1976.

Griffin, Walter R. "Louis Ludlow and the War Referendum Crusade, 1935–1941." *Indiana Magazine of History* 64, no. 4 (Dec. 1968): 267–288.

Griffith, Elisabeth. *In Her Own Right: The Life of Elizabeth Cady Stanton.* New York: Oxford Univ. Press, 1984.

Grimké, Angelina E. *Letters to Catherine E. Beecher, in Reply to an Essay on Slavery and Abolitionism, Addressed to Angelina Grimké, Revised by the Author.* 1838. Reprint. Freeport, N.Y.: Books for Libraries 1971.

Grimké, Archibald H. *William Lloyd Garrison: The Abolitionist.* 1891. Reprint. New York: Negro Universities Press, 1969.

Grimké, Sarah. *Letters on the Equality of the Sexes and the Condition of Women and Other Essays.* Edited by Elizabeth Ann Bartlett. New Haven: Yale Univ. Press, 1988.

Gustafson, Melanie Susan. "Lola Maverick Lloyd: 'Truly a live wire and a brick and everything else that goes to make up a militant pacifist.'" M.A. thesis, Sarah Lawrence College, 1983.

Halstead, Fred. *Out Now!: A Participant's Account of the American Movement Against the Vietnam War.* New York: Monad, 1978.

Hare, Lloyd C. *The Greatest American Woman: Lucretia Mott.* 1937. Reprint. New York: Negro Universities Press, 1970.

Harris, Adrienne, and Ynestra King, eds. *Rocking the Ship of State: Toward a Feminist Peace Politics.* San Francisco: Westview, 1989.

Hersh, Blanche Glassman. *The Slavery of Sex: Feminist-Abolitionists in America.* Urbana: Univ. of Illinois Press, 1978.

Higonnet, Margaret Randolph, et al. *Behind the Lines: Gender and the Two World Wars.* New Haven: Yale Univ. Press, 1987.

Howlett, Charles F., and Glen Zeitzer. *The American Peace Movement: History and Historiography.* Washington, D.C.: American Historical Association, 1985.

Hurwitz, Edith F. "The International Sisterhood." In *Becoming Visible: Women in European History,* edited by Renate Bridenthal and Claudia Koonz, 325–345. Boston: Houghton Mifflin, 1977.

James, Edward T., et al., eds. *Notable American Women: A Biographical Dictionary.* Cambridge, Mass.: Harvard Univ. Press, Belknap Press, 1971. S.v. "Maria Weston Chapman," by Alma Lutz.

Jensen, Joan M. "All Pink Sisters: The War Department and the Feminist Movement in the 1920s." In *Decades of Discontent: The Women's Movement, 1920–1940,* edited by Lois Scharf and Joan M. Jensen, 199–222. Boston: Northeastern Univ. Press, 1987.

———. "When Women Worked: Helen Marston and the California Peace Movement, 1915–1945." *California History* (June 1988): 118–131.

Johnson, Dorothy E. "Organized Women as Lobbyists in the 1920's." *Capitol Studies* 1, no. 1 (Spring 1972): 41–58.

Johnson, Oliver. *W. L. Garrison and His Times.* 1881. Reprint. Miami: Mnemosyne, 1969.

Josephson, Hannah. *Jeannette Rankin: First Lady in Congress: A Biography.* New York: Bobbs-Merrill, 1974.

Josephson, Harold, ed. *Biographical Dictionary of Peace Leaders.* Westport, Conn.: Greenwood, 1985.

King, Ynestra. "All is Connectedness: Scenes from the Women's Pentagon Action, USA." In *Keeping the Peace: A Woman's Peace Handbook* 1, edited by Lynne Jones, 40–63. London: Women's Press, 1983.

———. "Healing the Wounds: Feminism, Ecology, and the Nature/Culture Dualism." In *Reweaving the World: The Emergence of Ecofeminism,* edited by Irene Diamond and Gloria Feman Orenstein, 106–121. San Francisco: Sierra Club Books, 1990.

Kirk, Gwyn. "Blood, Bones, Connective Tissues: Issues for Feminist Peace Politics," Paper prepared for seminar at Douglass College, spring 1989. Typed draft.

Kraditor, Aileen. *The Ideas of the Woman Suffrage Movement, 1890–1920.* New York: Columbia Univ. Press, 1965.

Ladd, William (a.k.a. Philanthropos). *On the Duty of Females to Promote the Cause of Peace.* 1836. Reprint. New York: Garland, 1971.

Lasch, Christopher, ed. *The Social Thought of Jane Addams.* New York: Bobbs-Merrill, 1965.

Leach, William. *True Love and Perfect Union: The Feminist Reform of Sex and Society.* New York: Basic Books, 1980.

Lemons, J. Stanley. *The Woman Citizen: Social Feminism in the 1920's.* Urbana: Univ. of Illinois Press, 1973.

Lerner, Gerda. *The Grimké Sisters from South Carolina: Pioneers for Woman's Rights and Abolition.* New York: Schocken, 1967.

Lewy, Guenter. *Peace and Revolution: The Moral Crisis of American Pacifism.* Grand Rapids, Mich.: Eerdmans, 1988.

Liddington, Jill. *The Long Road to Greenham: Feminism and Anti-Militarism in Britain Since 1820.* London: Virago, 1989.

Lindquist, Adah Donnan. "A Study of Jeannette Rankin and Her Role in the Peace Movement." Honors paper, Swarthmore College, 1971.

Link, Arthur S. "What Happened to the Progressive Movement in the 1920s." *The American Historical Review* 64, no. 4 (July 1959): 833–851.

Linton, Rhoda. "Seneca Women's Peace Camp: Shapes of Things to Come." In *Rocking the Ship of State: Toward a Feminist Peace Politics,* edited by Adrienne Harris and Ynestra King, 239–262. San Francisco: Westview, 1989.

Lutzker, Michael. "Jane Addams: Peacetime Heroine, Wartime Heretic." In *Peace Heroes in Twentieth-Century America,* edited by Charles DeBenedetti, 28–55. Bloomington: Indiana Univ. Press, 1986.

McAllister, Pam, ed. *Reweaving the Web of Life: Feminism and Nonviolence.* Philadelphia: New Society, 1982.

———. *This River of Courage: Generations of Women's Resistance and Action.* Philadelphia: New Society, 1991.

———. *You Can't Kill the Spirit.* Philadelphia: New Society, 1988.

Marchand, C. Roland. *The American Peace Movement and Social Reform, 1898–1918.* Princeton: Princeton Univ. Press, 1972.

Merrill, Walter M. *Against Wind and Tide: A Biography of Wm. Lloyd Garrison.* Cambridge, Mass.: Harvard Univ. Press, 1963.

Midgley, Jane. *The Women's Budget.* New York: Jane Addams Peace Association, 1985.

Mott, Lucretia. *Lucretia Mott: Her Complete Speeches and Sermons.* Edited by Dana Greene. Lewiston, N.Y.: Edwin Mellen, 1980.

Murray, Robert K. *Red Scare: A Study of National Hysteria, 1919–1920.* New York: McGraw-Hill, 1955.

Nelson, John K. *The Peace Prophets: American Pacifist Thought, 1919–1941.* Chapel Hill: Univ. of North Carolina Press, 1967.

Neverdon-Morton, Cynthia. *Afro-American Women of the South and the Advancement of the Race, 1895–1925.* Knoxville: Univ. of Tennessee Press, 1989.

Newberry, Jo Vellacott. "Anti-War Suffragists." *History* 62 (Oct. 1977): 411–425.

O'Neill, William L. *Everyone Was Brave: A History of Feminism in America.* New York: Quadrangle/The New York Times Books, 1969, 1971.

Paley, Grace. "The Seneca Stories: Tales from the Women's Peace Encampment." *Ms.* Dec. 1983, 54–62; 108.

Papachristou, Judith. "American Women and Foreign Policy, 1898–1905." *Diplomatic History* 14, no. 4 (Fall 1990): 493–509.

———. "An Exercise in Anti-Imperialism: The Thirties." *American Studies* 15, no. 1 (Spring 1974): 61–75.

———. *Women Together: A History in Documents of the Women's Movement in the United States.* New York: Knopf, 1976.

Paterson, Thomas G., et al. *American Foreign Policy: A History/Since 1900.* Lexington, Mass.: Heath, 1983.

Peace, Roger C., III. *A Just and Lasting Peace: The U.S. Peace Movement from the Cold War to Desert Storm.* Chicago: Noble, 1991.

Peck, Mary Gray. *Carrie Chapman Catt: A Biography.* New York: H. W. Wilson, 1944.

Pierson, Ruth Roach, ed. *Women and Peace: Theoretical, Historical and Practical Perspectives.* London: Croom Helm, 1987.

Pleck, Elizabeth. *Domestic Tyranny: The Making of American Social Policy Against Family Violence From Colonial Times to the Present.* New York: Oxford Univ. Press, 1987.

Pois, Anne Marie. "The Politics and Process of Organizing for Peace: The United States Section of the Women's International League for Peace and Freedom, 1919–1939." Ph.D. diss., Univ. of Colorado, 1988.

Rainbolt, Rosemary. "Women and War in the United States: The Case of Dorothy Detzer, National Secretary W.I.L.P.F." *Peace and Change: A Journal of Peace and Research* 4, no. 3 (Fall 1977): 18–22.

Randall, Mercedes. *Improper Bostonian: Emily Greene Balch.* New York: Twayne, 1964.

Reardon, Betty A. *Sexism and the War System.* New York: Teachers College Press, 1985.

Report of the Joint Legislative Committee Investigating Seditious Activities, Filed April 24, 1920, in the Senate of the State of New York: Revolutionary Radicalism. Pt. 1, Vol. 1. Clayton R. Lusk, chairman. Albany: J.B. Lyon Company, Printers, 1920.

Rhodes, Richard. *The Making of the Atomic Bomb.* New York: Simon and Schuster, 1988.

Rosen, Ruth. "The Day They Buried 'Traditional Womanhood': Women and the Politics of Peace Protest." *Vietnam Generation* 1, nos. 3–4 (Summer–Fall 1989): 208–234.

Ruddick, Sara. *Maternal Thinking: Toward a Politics of Peace.* Boston: Beacon, 1989.

Rupp, Leila J., and Verta Taylor. *Survival in the Doldrums: The American Women's Rights Movement, 1945 to the 1960s.* New York: Oxford Univ. Press, 1987.

Russell, Diana E. H., ed. *Exposing Nuclear Phallacies.* New York: Pergamon, 1989.

Sarachild, Kathie. "Taking in the Images: A Record in Graphics of the Vietnam Era Soil for Feminism." *Vietnam Generation* 1, nos. 3–4 (Summer–Fall 1989): 235–245.

Savell, Isabelle K. *Ladies' Lib: How Rockland Women Got the Vote.* New City, N.Y.: Historical Society of Rockland County, 1979.

Schaffer, Ronald. "Jeannette Rankin, Progressive-Isolationist." Ph.D. diss., Princeton Univ., 1959.

Schott, Linda Kay. "The Woman's Peace Party and the Moral Basis for Women's Pacifism." *Frontiers: A Journal of Women's Studies* 8, no. 2 (1985): 18–24.

———. "Women Against War: Pacifism, Feminism, and Social Justice in the United States, 1915–1941." Ph.D. diss., Stanford Univ., 1985.

Schwarz, Judith. *Radical Feminists of Heterodoxy: Greenwich Village—1912–1940.* Lebanon, N.H.: New Victoria, 1982.

Segrest, Mab. "Feminism and Disobedience: Conversations with Barbara Deming." In *Reweaving the Web of Life: Feminism and Nonviolence,* edited by Pam McAllister, 45–62. Philadelphia: New Society, 1982.

Sewall, May Wright. *Women, World War and Permanent Peace.* 1915. Reprint. Westport, Conn.: Hyperion, 1976.

Showalter, Elaine, ed. *These Modern Women: Autobiographical Essays from the Twenties.* Old Westbury, N.Y.: Feminist Press, 1978.

Smith, Alice Kimball. *A Peril and a Hope: The Scientists' Movement in America, 1945–47.* Chicago: Univ. of Chicago Press, 1965.

Sochen, June. *The New Woman: Feminism in Greenwich Village, 1910–1920.* New York: Quadrangle/The New York Times Books, 1972.

Solomon, Barbara Miller. "Dilemmas of Pacifist Women, Quakers and Others, in World Wars I and II." In *Witnesses for Change: Quaker Women Over Three Centuries,* edited by Elisabeth Potts Brown and Susan Mosher Stuard, 123–148. New Brunswick: Rutgers Univ. Press, 1989.

Stanton, Elizabeth Cady, and Susan B. Anthony. *Elizabeth Cady Stanton/Susan B. Anthony: Correspondence, Writings, Speeches.* Edited by Ellen Carol DuBois. New York: Schocken, 1981.

Steinson, Barbara Jean. "Female Activism in World War I: The American Women's Peace, Suffrage, Preparedness and Relief Movements, 1914–1919." Ph.D. diss., Univ. of Michigan, 1977.

Stoner, John Edgar. "Salmon O. Levinson and the Peace Pact: How the Outlawry of War was Engineered to Acceptance." Ph.D. diss., Univ. of Chicago, 1937.

Swerdlow, Amy. "Ladies' Day at the Capitol: Women Strike for Peace Versus HUAC." *Feminist Studies* 8, no. 3 (Fall 1982): 493–520.

———. "The Politics of Motherhood: The Case of Women Strike for Peace and the Test Ban Treaty." Ph.D. diss., Rutgers Univ., 1984.

Terborg-Penn, Rosalyn. "Discontented Black Feminists: Prelude and Postscript to the Passage of the Nineteenth Amendment." In *Decades of Discontent: The Women's Movement, 1920–1940,* edited by Lois Scharf and Joan M. Jensen, 261–278. Boston: Northeastern Univ. Press, 1987.

Turning the World Upside Down: The Anti-Slavery Convention of American Women Held in New York City May 9–12, 1837. With an Introduction by Dorothy Sterling. New York: The Feminist Press at the City Univ. of New York, 1987.

Tuttle, Florence Guertin. *Alternatives to War.* New York: Harper, 1931.

Van Voris, Jacqueline. *Carrie Chapman Catt: A Public Life.* New York: The Feminist Press at the City University of New York, 1987.

Walters, Ronald G. *American Reformers, 1815–1860.* New York: Hill and Wang, 1978.

Welter, Barbara. "The Cult of True Womanhood: 1820–1860." *American Quarterly* 18 (1966): 151–174.

Wilson, Joan Hoff. "'Peace is a woman's job . . .' Jeannette Rankin and American Foreign Policy: The Origins of Her Pacifism." *Montana: The Magazine of Western History* 30, no. 1 (Jan. 1980): 28–41.

———. "'Peace is a woman's job . . .' Jeannette Rankin and American Foreign Policy: Her Lifework as a Pacifist." *Montana: The Magazine of Western History* 30, no. 2 (Apr. 1980): 38–53.

Wiltsher, Anne. *Most Dangerous Women: Feminist Peace Campaigners of the Great War.* Boston: Pandora Press, Routledge and Kegan Paul, 1985.

Wittner, Lawrence S. *Rebels Against War: The American Peace Movement, 1933–1983.* Philadelphia: Temple Univ. Press, 1984.

Yellin, Jean Fagan. *Women and Sisters: The Antislavery Feminists in American Culture.* New Haven: Yale Univ. Press, 1989.

Zaroulis, Nancy, and Gerald Sullivan. *Who Spoke Up? American Protest Against the War in Vietnam, 1963–1975.* New York: Holt, Rinehart and Winston, 1984.

Zeiger, Susan. "Finding a Cure for War: Women's Politics and the Peace Movement in the 1920s." *Journal of Social History* 24 (Fall 1990): 69–86.

INDEX

Abdrakhmanova, Flora, 272
Abolitionism, 16, 22, 24–25, 26–39
Abyssinia, 136–37
Abzug, Bella, 238
Acorn (periodical), 49
Addams, Jane: African-American women and, 102; American Union Against Militarism and, 71; Anti-Imperialist League and, 52; Balch and, 105, 261; Catt and, 16, 61–62; childlessness of, 11; Congressional testimony of, 70; *Democracy and Social Ethics,* 59; Eastman and, 93; The Hague Conference (1915) and, 66; Hoover and, 121; International Committee of Women for Permanent Peace and, 69; *The Newer Ideals of Peace,* 60; Nobel Peace Prize for, 112–13; "Red Scare" and, 111, 112, 180; Spencer and, 76; UN Decade for Women and, 243; wartime relief work and, 77; Woman's Peace Party and, 63, 65, 72, 73, 78; Women's International League for Peace and Freedom and, 82, 83, 90, 91, 126, 269. *See also* Jane Addams Peace Association (JAPA)
Africa, 197
African-American men, 148–49
African-Americans, 29, 31, 183, 209
African-American women: abolitionism and, 8, 31; Congress of American Women and, 187, 189; Ethiopia and, 139; recruitment of, 101–3, 148; Women's International League for Peace and Freedom and, 102–5, 142, 267
African troops, 102
Alcohol abuse, 22, 24–25, 47–49
Alien Registration Act, 158, 170
Allen, Florence, 121
"All Women Are Victims in This Man's War!" (WILPF), 225
Amatniek, Kathie, 224, 225
American Anti-Slavery Society, 43
American Committee for Protection of the Foreign Born, 158
American Committee for the Outlawry of War, 88, 96
American Friends Service Committee, 99, 249
American Hebrew Award, 142
American Jewish Congress, 142
American League Against War and Fascism, 129–34; Detzer and, 169; House Special Committee on Un-American Activities and, 158; WILPF New York branches and, 147, 166, 172, 173
American League for Peace and Democracy, 134

American Legion, 111
American Peace Society, 36–37; on Civil War, 41; founded, 35; Mead and, 62; Villard and, 57; women members of, 47
American School Peace League, 47
American Union Against Militarism, 71, 77
American Woman Suffrage Association, 45
American Women for Peace (AWP), 160, 185, 190–91, 192, 263
Andrews, Fannie Fern, 47
Another Mother for Peace, 216–19, 263
Anthony, Katherine, 65, 80
Anthony, Susan B., 42; Katherine Anthony and, 80; on Civil War, 41; Congress of American Women and, 189; home of, 252; Seneca Encampment and, 153; Stanton and, 48
Anthony, Susan B., II, 189, 190
Anti-Imperialist League, 52, 59
Anti-lynching legislation, 103, 104, 142, 268
Anti-Semitism. *See* Jewish issue
Anti-Slavery Convention of American Women (1838), 34
Apartheid, 197, 199
"Appeal to the Christian Women of the South, An" (A. Grimké), 31
Arab nations, 197
Arms limitations treaties, 117; peace encampment movement and, 254; Women for a Meaningful Summit and, 241; Women's International League for Peace and Freedom and, 195; Women Strike for Peace and, 205, 207
Army, U.S., 109, 110
Arnett, Kitty, 178–79, 181
Ashby, Isabel, 122
"Atomic Bomb and Its Message to You, The" (WILPF), 164
Atomic bombs, 155–56, 157–58, 164. *See also* Nuclear arms race
Atomic Energy Commission, 164
Atwood, Charlotte, 10[illegible]
Austin-Wadsworth National War Service Act, 149, 151
Avedon, Barbara, 216, 218

Babcock, Caroline Lexow, 93, 96, 126, 261
Bacon, Margaret Hope, 34
Baer, Gertrud, 146
Bagby, Jeanne, 203
Bailey, Hannah, 49
Balch, Emily Greene: Addams and, 261; on atomic weapons, 164; childlessness of, 11; on Communism, 168; economic sanctions and, 138; as international delegate, 69; on male domination, 262; on military service, 264; National Committee to Oppose the Conscription of Women and, 149; neutrality and, 137–38; New York City organizations and, 106; Nobel Peace Prize for, 154, 159, 160, 161; *Occupied Haiti,* 114; "Red Scare" and, 111–12; UN Decade for Women and, 243; W. Wilson and, 69; Women's International League for Peace and Freedom and, 83, 91, 99, 105, 126–27; on World War II, 144–46
Baldwin, Roger, 71
Ballantyne, Edith, 255, 256
Barker, Christine Ross, 95
Barlow, Maude, 272
Barney, Nora Stanton, 190
Barron, Harriet, 219
"Battle Hymn of the Republic, The" (Howe), 45
Bay of Pigs invasion, 198
Beard, Mary, 57

Berger, Meta, 119
Big business, 85–86, 113, 196, 199. *See also* Munitions industry
"Black Woman Speaks of White Womanhood—of White Supremacy—of Peace, A" (Richardson), 191
Blake, Katherine Devereux: African-American women and, 103; L. D. Blake and, 51; at League of Nations Disarmament Conference, 119; National Committee to Oppose the Conscription of Women and, 149; outlawry of war and, 117; Women's International League for Peace and Freedom and, 99, 100, 101, 105, 128, 147; Women's Peace Society and, 93
Blake, Lillie Devereux, 51, 100
Blatch, Harriot Stanton, 57, 59
Bloomer, Amelia, 48
Boissevain, Inez Milholland, 79
Bombings: Hiroshima and Nagasaki, 155, 156; Pearl Harbor, 144
Borah, William, 88, 100
Boston Female Anti-Slavery Society, 29, 34
Bowdoin Street Ladies' Peace Society, 36
Boycotts. *See* Economic sanctions
Boy Scouts, 9, 97
Bra burning, 225
Bradford, Ann, 187
Brannan, Eleanor D., 133
Briand, Aristide, 88
British Guiana, 51
British women, 67, 242–43
Brown, Charlotte Howkins, 187
Bryan, William Jennings, 58
Bryn Mawr College conference (1961), 209
Budget, U.S., 257
Bureau of Legal Advice, 76
Burns, Josephine, 124
Burritt, Elihu, 243
Bush, George, 260
Business interests. *See* Big business
Bussey, Gertrude, 146
Butler, Nicholas Murray, 113
Byrns, Elinor: Babcock and, 261; Villard and, 93, 95; Women's International League for Peace and Freedom and, 92; Women's Peace Union and, 96, 126, 139–40

Caldicott, Helen, 240
California Committee on Un-American Activities, 189
"Call for Women's Liberation, A" (Munaker), 224–25
Calvinism, 24
Cameron, Bess, 168, 201, 206
Camp, Kay, 272
Carnegie Endowment for International Peace, 167
Carrazil incident, 72, 73
Carter, Jimmy, 238
Catt, Carrie Chapman: Addams and, 16, 61–62; childlessness of, 11; Congressional Union and, 62–63; on disarmament conferences, 118; Jewish issue and, 142–43; Latin American work of, 113; on male violence, 86; National Committee on the Cause and Cure of War and, 74–76, 106–9; neutrality and, 140; on outlawry of war, 117, 118; PanAm Women's Auxiliary and, 115; Peace Parade Committee and, 57, 58; "Red Scare" and, 112; Terrell and, 102; Woman's Peace Party and, 59, 60, 74, 75–76; Women's Action Committee for Victory and Lasting Peace and, 152–54
Central Intelligence Agency, 233
Central Park rally (1983), 230

Challenge (newspaper), 173
Chandler, Elizabeth, 26–28, 29
Chapman, Maria Weston, 29, 37–38
Chelsea Women's Committee for Peace, 173
Chiang Kai-shek, 197
Chicago Peace Congress (1951), 190
Child, Lydia Maria, 31, 32, 33, 34
Children, 23, 24, 48
Chile, 51
China, People's Republic of, 196, 197
Chinese refugees, 149
Christian anarchy. *See* Nonresistance
Christian values, 49
Churchill, Winston, 147
Civil defense drills, 167–68, 191
Civil Rights Act, 199
Civil rights movement, 194, 199, 200–201, 268, 270
Civil War, U.S., 40–42, 51
Class warfare, 132, 158, 168, 245
Clubs, women's, 106–8
Cochran, Jacqueline, 187
Coffin family, 29
Cohen, Sadie A., 103
Cold War, 157, 172, 194, 271
Color, women of: Women for Racial and Economic Equality and, 234, 236, 269; women's culture and, 270; Women's International League for Peace and Freedom and, 265, 267. *See also* African-American women
Communism: Addams and, 112; Alien Registration Act and, 158; American League Against War and Fascism and, 130, 132; Balch on, 168; Congress of American Women and, 187; decline of, 271; Detzer on, 132; Pell and, 206–7; Women's International League for Peace and Freedom and, 169, 170, 182–84, 194–95, 233–34; Women Strike for Peace and, 212. *See also* McCarthy era; "Red Scare"
Communist Control Act, 170
Concentration camps, 136, 148. *See also* Internment camps
Conference on Global Feminism and Disarmament (1982), 249
Conference on Reduction and Limitation of Arms (1932). *See* League of Nations Conference on Reduction and Limitation of Arms (1932)
Congressional Union, 5, 62–63, 64, 65, 66
Congress of American Women (CAW), 185–90; American Women for Peace and, 160–61, 191; Women for Racial and Economic Equality and, 234; Women's International League for Peace and Freedom and, 18; mentioned, 7, 192
Congress of Mothers, 52
Congress of Racial Equality (CORE), 201
Conscientious objectors, 42, 76–77, 214
Conscription. *See* Military draft
Consejo Nacional de Mujeres Mexicanas, 114
Constitution, U.S.: Fifth Amendment, 239; Nineteenth Amendment, 84; proposed amendments to, 41, 96–97, 117–18, 126, 140. *See also* Equal Rights Amendment
"Continuous Mediation without Armistice" (Wales), 68
Cook, Blanche Wiesen, 230, 262, 265, 269
Cook, Elizabeth Ellsworth, 96
Corbett-Ashby, Margery, 143, 152
Cott, Nancy, 5
Council of Congregational Ministers of Massachusetts, 31
Council of Jewish Women, 53
Counterculture, 219

Courtney, Kathleen, 67, 120
Cruise missiles. *See* Missiles, cruise
Cuba, 51, 198–99, 211–12
Curtis, Helen, 103

Daily Worker, The (newspaper), 171
Dale, Thelma, 187
Daughters of the American Revolution, 111, 112
Davis, Pauline Wright, 40
Dean, Arthur, 209
Decade for Women, 18–19, 227–59
Decision making, 128, 211, 261, 264
Declaration of Independence, U.S., 40
"Declaration of Principles" (AWP), 190
"Declaration of Sentiments" (Garrison), 37
"Declaration of Sentiments" (Seneca Falls Women's Rights Convention), 40
Defense, Department of, 170–71. *See also* War, Department of
Defensive war, 117–18
Deming, Barbara, 243–44
Democracy, 184
Democracy and Social Ethics (Addams), 59
Dennett, Mary Ware, 93
Depression economics, 124, 126
Detzer, Dorothy: American League Against War and Fascism and, 129–30; on atomic age, 161–62; Cohen and, 103; Eaton and, 134; House Special Committee on Un-American Activities and, 169; Hunton and, 104–5; on male domination, 87, 262, 263; National Committee to Oppose the Conscription of Women and, 149; neutrality and, 137, 138, 141–42; Nye and, 123; outlawry of war and, 117; WILPF and, 99–100, 126, 164, 231; WILPF branches and, 132, 133, 142, 147; on Women's Action Committee, 154; on Woolley, 121
Developing countries, 195, 196, 271
Dingman, Mary A., 120, 152
Disarmament, 117, 118, 120; Women's International League for Peace and Freedom and, 169, 229; Women's Peace Society and, 94; Women's Peace Union and, 96; Women's Peace Union of the Western Hemisphere and, 95; Women Strike for Peace and, 205, 208, 219
"Disarm the Nursery" (WILPF), 110
Divorce, 48
Dobbins, Peggy, 223
Dock, Lavinia, 57
Dodge, David Low, 35
Dolan, Eunice, 173–80
Dolan, Graham "Cozey," 173, 177
Dominican Republic, 114
Doty, Madeline Zabrisky: on male domination, 87; Pethick-Lawrence and, 58; "Red Scare" and, 111; Woman's Peace Party and, 65, 66; Women's International League for Peace and Freedom and, 99, 105, 128
Douglass, Grace and Sarah, 31
Draft. *See* Military draft
Drake, Joan, 272
Draper, Muriel, 187
Drier, Mary, 57

Eastman, Crystal: American Union Against Militarism and, 71; Balch and, 99; Pethick-Lawrence and, 58; in Washington Square demonstration, 79; Woman's Peace Party and, 65, 66; Women's International League for Peace and Freedom and, 92–93

Eaton, Eleanor, 134
Ecofeminism, 10, 246–47, 272; appeal of, 261, 270; motherhood and, 263; Women's International League for Peace and Freedom and, 258; Women's Pentagon Action and, 248
"Economic conversion" proposal, 258
Economic issues, 86, 230, 231, 234
Economic sanctions: against Cuba, 198; on German imports, 142; against Jewish businesses, 135; in Mississippi, 199; on slave-produced items, 26, 29–30; on war materials, 138
Edelman, Rose K., 101
Egalitarianism, 29, 225
Embargoes. *See* Economic sanctions
Emergency Committee of Atomic Scientists, 165
Enabling Law (Germany), 135
Encampments, 242–43, 249–55
England. *See* Great Britain
Equal Rights Amendment, 105, 238, 239, 257
Espionage Bill, 76, 80
Ethiopia, 136–37, 139

Fair Play for Cuba Committee, 207
Fascism, 116, 124, 125, 129, 135–36, 137
Federal Bureau of Investigation (FBI), 176–77, 185
Fellowship of Reconciliation (FOR), 152, 211, 234
Feminism: radical, 245, 246–47, 248, 270, 272; socialist, 245, 246, 247
Feminist movement, 18; early, 21–25; New Left and, 212; UN Decade for Women and, 243; Vietnam War and, 220; on violence, 10; Women's International League for Peace and Freedom and, 225–26
Feminists, European, 143–44
Fifth Amendment. *See* Constitution, U.S.
Fifth Avenue Vietnam Peace Parade Committee, 210
Film industry, 216
Firestone, Shulamith, 222–23
Fiske, Bradley Allen, 109
Flags, 252–53
Flynn, Elizabeth Gurley, 187
Fodor, Folly, 202
Fogarty, William B., 174, 175–78, 179
Food Administration, Department of, 77
Ford, Gerald, 233
Foreign policy, U.S., 51, 113, 129, 171, 228
Forten family, 31
Foster, Catherine, 211
Four Lights (newsletter), 74, 80–81, 103, 148
Fourteen Points (W. Wilson), 78
Fourth of July, 252–53
France, 137
Franco, Francisco, 137
Frank, Libby, 231
Frazier, Lynn Joseph, 96, 114, 123, 126
Freedom of Information Act, 185
Freeman, Ruth, 162
Free Produce Movement, 29
Free speech, 169, 170, 171, 195
French colonial African troops, 102
Friedan, Betty, 192, 193
Friendships, 261, 262
Fries, Amos A., 111
Fuchs, Klaus, 158
Fuller, Margaret, 80
Fuller, Walter, 71

Gaffney, Fannie, 52
Gage-Colby, Ruth, 208, 209, 213
Gandhi, Mohandas: Deming and, 243;

Garrison and, 6, 89, 93; Garst on, 209; UN Decade for Women and, 227; Women's Peace Union and, 140
Garment workers, 189
Garrison, William Lloyd: on Civil War, 40–41; "Declaration of Sentiments," 37; Gandhi and, 6, 89, 93; Motts and, 30; New England Anti-Slavery Society and, 36; nonresistance and, 6, 26, 28, 227; seizure of, 34; Seneca Falls Women's Rights Convention and, 39–40; Stanton and, 38; women's equality and, 29; on women slaves, 31; Women's Peace Society and, 93, 94
Garst, Eleanor, 202, 209
Gay rights, 258, 274. *See also* Homophobia
General Federation of Women's Clubs, 52–53
Geneva demonstration (1962), 208
Geneva Disarmament Conference (1932). *See* League of Nations Conference on Reduction and Limitation of Arms (1932)
Genius of Universal Emancipation (newspaper), 26, 28, 30
Genoni, Rosa, 69
German imports, 142
Germany: in World War I, 73–74; in interwar period, 135–36, 137, 139, 142–43; in World War II, 144, 171
Gestapo, 144
Gilman, Charlotte Perkins, 57, 60–61
Gorbachev, Mikhail, 254
Government employees, U.S., 159
Grassroots organizing, 14–15
Graves, Anna, 114, 146
Great Britain, 51, 137
Greenham Common (England), 242–43, 249, 254
Grenada, 260
Grimké, Angelina, 31, 33–34, 35
Grimké, Sarah, 32–33, 34
Guam, 51

The Hague conferences: 1899: 52–53; 1915: 66–69, 273; 1964: 207, 209
Haiti, 72, 114
Hamer, Fanny Lou, 268
Hamilton, Alice, 138
Handman, Rita, 231
Harding, Warren, 88, 117
Hayden, Casey, 193
"Healing the Wounds" (Y. King), 246–47
Henning, Georgia, 236
Herendeen, Anne, 65, 79
Hersh, Blanche, 24
Heterodoxy (organization), 65, 93
Hiroshima bombing. *See* Bombings
Hiss, Alger, 124
History of Woman Suffrage (Stanton), 38
Hitler, Adolf, 116, 125, 135–36, 141
Ho Chi Minh, 212
Hollywood. *See* Film industry
Homophobia, 10, 230, 246, 262, 274
Hoover, Herbert, 77, 114, 121, 122
Howe, Julia Ward, 45–47, 54
Howe, Marie Jenny, 57
Hughan, Jessie Wallace, 86
Hughes, Antoinette Carter, 115
Hughes, Charles Evans, 73, 115
Hull, Hannah Clothier: Detzer and, 137, 138; at League of Nations Disarmament Conference, 119; National Committee to Oppose the Conscription of Women and, 149; Olmsted and, 261; Women's International League for Peace and Freedom and, 99, 127, 139; mentioned, 101
Hull House, 59, 91, 99, 112
Hunton, Addie: Addams and, 102; Anti-Lynching Bill and, 103; in

Hunton, Addie (*continued*)
Haiti, 114; Women's International League for Peace and Freedom and, 104–5, 148, 267
Hutchins, Loraine, 250–51

Immigration laws, 149
Imperialism: Japanese, 116, 124, 125, 136; superpower, 256; U.S., 51–52. *See also* Military intervention
Infant damnation, 24
"Inner light" (Quakerism), 22, 24
Integration, racial, 201
Intermediate Nuclear Forces Treaty, 254
Internal Security Act, 159
International Alliance of Women for Suffrage and Equal Citizenship, 54, 120, 143, 152
International Committee of Women for Permanent Peace, 69, 78, 90
International Congress of U.S.-WILPF (1924), 110
International Congress of Women, 66–69, 81–83, 273. *See also* World Congress of Women
International Council of Women (ICW), 54–55, 56, 118–20, 122, 123
International Council of Women of the Darker Races, 104
International Labor Organization, 116
International organizations, women's, 119–20
International Police Force, 152
International Summer School (Chicago), 110
International Union of Mine, Mill and Smelter Workers, 173
International Woman Suffrage Alliance, 54, 56, 58, 59
International Woman Suffrage Congress (1913), 58
International Women's Day, 186, 187, 213, 230
International Women's Gulf Peace Initiative, 272
International Women's Year, 227
Internment camps, 146, 208. *See also* Concentration camps
Interwar period, 85–144
Invest in Peace Fund, 218
Iraq, 260, 271
"I Refuse to Be One of 20 Million 'Acceptable' Dead!" (WSP), 232–33
Israel, 197
Italy, 136–37, 144

Jacobs, Aletta, 66, 69
Jane Addams Peace Association (JAPA), 162
Japan, 144, 145
Japanese Americans, 146, 208
Japanese imperialism. *See* Imperialism
Jeannette Rankin Brigade, 221–23, 225
Jencks, Virginia, 174, 179
Jesus Christ, 24
Jewish businesses, 135
Jewish issue, 141, 142–43, 148
Jewish women, 17, 101, 199; antilynching legislation and, 103, 142; German boycott and, 142; neutrality and, 139
Jiang Jieshi. *See* Chiang Kai-shek
Johnson administration, 194, 209
Jones, Claudia, 187
Justice, Department of, 78, 81, 190

Kaplan, Louis, 167
Karsten, Eleanor, 73, 91
Kashins, Minna, 206
Keep America Out of War Committee (KAOW), 133
Kellogg, Frank, 88

Kellogg-Briand Peace Pact, 88, 109, 117–18; Detzer and, 100; Women's Peace Union and, 97, 120
Kennedy, John, 197
King, Coretta Scott, 208, 222
King, Martin Luther, Jr., 227, 243
King, Mary, 193
King, Ynestra, 245, 246–47
Kirchwey, Freda, 65, 99
Kittredge, Mabel Hyde, 91, 98
"Kneeling Slave" (Chandler), 28
Kramer, Roberta, 155
Kusman, Helen, 213

Ladd, William, 35–36, 88, 223
Lane, Margaret, 65
Lansing, Eleanor, 115
Latin America, 113–16, 197–98, 199
Lawus, Josetta, 235
Lazarus, Frieda Langer, 122–23
Leach, Agnes, 99
League for Permanent Peace, 78
League of Nations, 88, 116–17; charter, 120; International Congress of Women on, 81–82; Japan and, 136; UN and, 154, 163; Women for a Meaningful Summit and, 241; Women's International League for Peace and Freedom and, 83, 90; Women's Peace Union and, 97
League of Nations Conference on Reduction and Limitation of Arms (1932), 13, 118, 119, 123, 135
Lebanon, 260
Lesbians, 230, 246, 258
Letters on the Equality of the Sexes and the Condition of Women (S. Grimké), 32–33
Letters to Catherine E. Beecher (A. Grimké), 33–34
Levinson, Salmon O., 88, 96
Lewis, Lucy Biddle, 91
Lewy, Guenter, 234
Libby, Frederick, 149
Liberation movement, women's. *See* Feminist movement
Liberator (periodical), 26, 27, 29, 31
Lifton, Sarah, 166
Lily (newspaper), 48
Lincoln, Abraham, 41
Linton, Rhoda, 251
Lithuania, 271
"Liturgy for the Burial of Traditional Womanhood" (Dobbins), 223
Local organizing, 14–15
Lockwood, Belva Ann, 47
London Naval Reduction Conference (1930), 118
London War Resisters' International, 13
"Lords of Creation, The" (Chapman), 37–38
Love, Albert, 43, 45
Lowell mill girls, 189
Loyalty oaths, 170
Luisi, Paulina, 113
Lundy, Benjamin, 26
Lusitania, 69
Lusk Commission, 83, 111

McAllister, Pam, 244
McCarran Act, 159, 170
McCarthy era, 17–18, 130, 157–92, 194, 201, 219. *See also* "Red Scare"
McConville, J. V., 112
Macmillan, Chrystal, 66, 67, 69
McNeill, Bertha, 175, 178, 179, 267
MADRE (organization), 272
Mail surveillance, 176, 233
Male domination: of American Peace Society, 36; L. D. Blake on, 51; Chandler on, 27–28; Deming on, 244; McAllister on, 244; of national peace organizations, 61–62, 262; of

Male domination (*continued*)
New England Anti-Slavery Society, 29, 30–31; of New Left, 212; radical/socialist feminists and, 245; S. Grimké on, 32–33; Stanton on, 44; Woman's Peace Party and, 87; Women's International League for Peace and Freedom and, 92; Women's Peace Union and, 13
Male violence, 86, 263
"Mammy Statue," 104
Manhattan Project, 157
Manus, Rosa, 120, 144
March, Florence Eldridge, 187
March for Jobs and Freedom (1963), 199
Married Women's Property Acts (N.Y. State), 20
Mason, Vivian Carter, 187
Massachusetts Peace Society, 35
Maternal and Child Welfare Act, 188
Maternal Child Health Center (Hanoi), 214
Mauss, Evelyn A., 262
Maxwell, Lucia R., 111
Mead, Lucia Ames, 47, 91; Addams and, 62, 65; Anti-Imperialist League and, 52; Eastman and, 93
Mediation: American Women for Peace on, 190; Doty and, 58; The Hague Conference (1915) and, 68; neutrality and, 74; F. Roosevelt and, 138; W. Wilson and, 69–70; Women's Peace Union and, 139, 140
Membership pledges, 109
Memo (periodical), 174
Men. *See* African-American men; Male domination; Young men
"Mental Metempsychosis" (Chandler), 26
Mexico, 72, 73, 114
Middle East, 197
Midgley, Jane, 231, 257
Militant Liberty, 170–71
Militarism, 163, 171, 194, 256, 260; alcohol abuse and, 49; Y. King on, 245; violence against women and, 8–10, 16, 97, 258; Women for Racial and Economic Equality on, 237; *The Women's Budget* on, 259; Women's Peace Union on, 97; Women Strike for Peace and, 232–33
Military draft, 238–39; National Committee to Oppose the Conscription of Women and, 149–52; Sarachild on, 224; Women Strike for Peace and, 214, 216, 219
Military-industrial complex, 124
Military intervention: in Asia, 197; in Haiti, 114; in Japan, 254; in Latin America, 198; Women for Racial and Economic Equality on, 237; Women's International League for Peace and Freedom and, 195, 196. *See also* Imperialism
Military spending, 229, 257
Military training, 9, 95; for boys, 55, 70–71
Milk, 207
Miller, Christina, 98
Miss America pageant, 225
Missiles, cruise, 242
Mississippi boycott (1965), 199
Monroe Doctrine, 88, 113, 197–98
Morgan, Laura Puffer, 152
Motherhood, 10–12, 16, 86, 263–64; Another Mother for Peace and, 216; Woman's Christian Temperance Union on, 49; Women's Action for Nuclear Disarmament and, 240; Women Strike for Peace and, 204, 207
Mother's Day Assembly (1969), 218
Mother's Day cards, 218
Mother's Day for Peace, 47
Mother's Day marches, 242; in Los Angeles, 191

Mott, James, 29, 30, 43
Mott, Lucretia, 29–31, 43–44; Civil War and, 41–42; Congress of American Women and, 189; nonresistance and, 35; Philadelphia Female Anti-Slavery Society and, 34; Stanton and, 38; on women reformers, 42–43
Mukerji, Rose, 200
Munaker, Sue, 224–25
Munitions industry, 123–24
Mussolini, Benito, 116, 125, 136
Muste, A. J., 149
Mygatt, Tracy, 126, 139, 140, 141, 147

Nagasaki bombing. *See* Bombings
National Affairs Conference Board, 135
National American Woman Suffrage Association (NAWSA): on British Guiana, 51; Catt and, 59; Congressional Union and, 62, 63, 65, 66; Mead and, 47; National League of Women Voters and, 152; on Philippines, 52; war service and, 74–75
National Association for the Advancement of Colored People (NAACP), 201
National Association of Colored Women, 102, 104
National Committee for a Sane Nuclear Policy (SANE), 203, 204
National Committee on the Cause and Cure of War (NCCCW), 106–9; demise of, 152–54, 155; International Council of Women and, 120; Jewish issue and, 142–43; Latin American efforts of, 113; League of Nations and, 116, 118, 121; neutrality and, 136, 137, 140; outlawry of war and, 117; Women's Action Committee for Victory and Lasting Peace and, 125; Women Strike for Peace and, 204; World War II and, 17, 144; mentioned, 6, 90
National Committee to Oppose the Conscription of Women, 135, 149, 151–52, 154
National Council of Mexican Women, 114
National Council of Women, 47, 51, 52, 109
National Equal Rights Party, 47
National Goodwill Day, 121
National League of Women Voters, 113, 152
National Liberation Front: in Cuba, 211; of South Vietnam, 214
National Organization for Women (NOW), 193, 238–39
National Security Agency, 233
National Woman's Party, 5, 121
National Woman's Relief Society, 52
National Women's Committee to Oppose Conscription. *See* National Committee to Oppose the Conscription of Women
National WSP Draft Counseling Service, 214
Native Americans, 23
NATO, 207, 209, 229, 242
Nazism, 135–36, 137, 140–41; Catt and, 142–43; Olmsted on, 171; Soviet Union and, 129
Neutrality, 136–37, 138, 139, 140–41, 147
Neutrality Acts, 125, 136, 137–38
"Never on Tuesdays Shoppers' Stoppage," 213
New England Anti-Slavery Society, 26, 29, 30–31, 36
New England Non-Resistant Society, 37
New England Women's Club, 45
Newer Ideals of Peace, The (Addams), 60
New Left, 212

New York activists. *See* Woman's Peace Party (WPP), New York City branch; Women's International League for Peace and Freedom (WILPF), New York branches
New York City: abolitionist convention in, 31–32; antiwar marches in, 56–58, 229–30, 249; Board of Education, 100; feminist peace network in, 106; public schools of, 201
New York Peace Society, 35, 47
New York Radical Women (organization), 222–24
New York State: Defense Emergency Act, 167; Employer's Liability Commission, 65; legislation, 20, 70; Lusk Commission, 83, 111; suffrage, 81; Woman's Temperance Society, 48; Woman Suffrage Association, 74
NGO Forum (1985), 255
Niagara conference (1921), 95
Nicaragua, 114, 260
Niera de Calvo, Ester, 113
Nine-Partners Boarding School, 29
Nineteenth Amendment. *See* Constitution, U.S.
Nixon, Richard, 210, 213–14, 219, 238
Nobel Peace Prize, 112–13, 154, 159, 160, 161
No More War parades (1922, 1923), 117
Nongovernmental organizations, 163, 255, 256
Nonresistance, 6; abolitionism and, 34–35; Communism and, 183; Deming on, 244; Gandhi on, 89, 140; Garrison and, 6, 26, 28, 227; McAllister on, 244; Mott and, 41, 43; in Quakerism, 23; UN Decade for Women and, 227, 243, 245; Women's Peace Society and, 93; Women's Pentagon Action and, 248
Nuclear arms race: Detzer on, 162; early, 157–58; in 1960s, 202; in 1990s, 271; peace encampment movement and, 254; UN Decade for Women and, 240; Women's International League for Peace and Freedom and, 164, 195, 229; Women Strike for Peace and, 205, 207, 208, 219, 232–33
Nuclear Freeze movement, 240
Nuclear power plants, 245, 248
Nye, Gerald, 123–24, 129

Occupied Haiti (Balch), 114
Olive Branch Circles, 36
Olmsted, Mildred Scott: on Communism, 170; drafting of women and, 149, 150–51; economic sanctions and, 138; in Germany, 141; Hull and, 261; on militarism, 171; neutrality and, 137, 139; WILPF and, 104, 127, 162, 173, 201; WILPF branches and, 166, 175, 176, 179, 180; on World War II, 146–47; mentioned, 101, 105
On the Duty of Females to Promote the Cause of Peace (Ladd), 35–36
O'Reilly, Leonora, 57
Organizational methodology, 6
Organizations, women's international, 119–20
Our Man-Made World (Gilman), 61
Outlawry of war movement, 88, 96–97, 117–22, 122, 139
Overman Senate Subcommittee, 83

Pacific Banner (periodical), 49
"Packet on Infiltration and Attack," 182–85
Paley, Grace, 247
Panama, 271

Pan American Association for the Advancement of Women, 113
Pan American Congress (1922), 113
Pan American International Women's Committee, 115
Pan American Scientific Congresses, 115, 116
PanAm Women's Auxiliary, 115–16
Papandreou, Margarita, 272
Parker, Beryl, 187
Parnes, Brenda, 262
Passports, 171
Patrinos, Sondra, 235
Patriotism, 52, 260
Paul, Alice, 5
PAX (periodical), 111
"Pax Special" (train), 110
Peace and Revolution (Lewy), 234
"Peace at Any Old Price" (Whitney), 110
Peace Caravan (1931–32), 121–22, 135
Peace de Resistance Cookbook #1 (WSP), 215
Peace encampments, 242–43, 249–55
Peace Parade Committee, 57–58
Peace principle. *See* Nonresistance
"Peace Without Victory" (W. Wilson), 73
Pearl Harbor bombing. *See* Bombings
Pell, Orlie, 162, 166–68, 206–7
Pennsylvania Hall, 34–35
Pennsylvania Peace Society, 43, 47
Pentagon demonstrations, 214, 215, 248
People's Mandate Committee, 135
Pepper-Norton Maternal and Child Welfare Act, 188
Persian Gulf War, 260, 266, 272–73
Personal relationships, 261, 262
Pethick-Lawrence, Emmeline, 58, 59, 60, 65, 67
Philadelphia Female Anti-Slavery Society, 29, 31, 34
Philanthropos. *See* Ladd, William
Philippines, 51, 52
Physical education, 9, 70–71, 95
Picon, Elsie, 162
Pinchot, Cornelia Bryce, 187
Political power, 20, 87, 264
Political responsibility, 12–13
"Polyglot Petition for Disarmament" (ICW), 118
Post, Alice, 66
Post Office Department, U.S., 80
"Program During Wartime, A" (WPP), 77
Protestant churches, 21–22
Public schools, 201. *See also* Physical education
Puerto Rico, 51, 114, 198
Pugh, Sarah, 35
Purvis, Harriet Forten, 31

Quakerism, 22–24; in Pennsylvania, 23

Racism: Henning on, 236; McCarthyism and, 171; suffragist, 101–2; Women's International League for Peace and Freedom and, 104–5, 148–49, 267–69; Women's Pentagon Action on, 248–49
Radical feminism. *See* Feminism
Radio broadcasts, 164–65
Ramondt-Hirsch, Cor, 69
Randall, Mercedes, 148
Rankin, Jeannette, 76, 80, 221–22, 226. *See also* Jeannette Rankin Brigade
Raushenbush, Steve, 123–24
Reagan, Ronald, 233, 254, 256, 260
"Red Scare," 109–13; National Committee on the Cause and Cure of War and, 108; Women's International League for Peace and Free-

"Red Scare" (*continued*)
dom and, 83–84, 99, 110–11, 130. *See also* McCarthy era
Reed, Donna, 218
Reformers, 21–25
Rehnquist, William H., 239
Relief work, 77, 78, 80
Religion, 21–24, 25, 49, 89, 246
Report on the Congress of American Women (HUAC), 189–90
Reproductive rights, 258–59
Responsible citizenship, 12–13
Revivalism, 25
"Revolutionary Radicalism" (Lusk Commission), 83, 111
Reweaving the Web of Life (McAllister), 244
"Rice and Tea for Peace" event, 214
Richards, Beah, 191
Richardson, Beulah, 191
Riff-Raff (film), 133
Riseman, Meta, 162
Robinson, Dorothy, 146
Rochester, N.Y., 252
Rogers, Lou, 80
Roosevelt, Franklin Delano: as mediator, 138; National Committee on the Cause and Cure of War and, 140; Neutrality Acts and, 136; UN and, 147; USSR and, 129; Women's Action Committee and, 153
Roosevelt Corollary to the Monroe Doctrine, 197–98
Rosenberg, Mrs. A., 130, 132
Rosenberg, Ethel and Julius, 158, 169
Rostker v. Goldberg, 239
Russell, Margaret, 202–3

Sandinistas, 260
SANE. *See* National Committee for a Sane Nuclear Policy (SANE)
Sarachild, Kathie, 224, 225
Schlafley, Phyllis, 239
Schneider, Lorraine, 217, 218
Schneiderman, Rose, 57
Schwimmer, Rosika, 58, 59, 60, 68, 69
Selective Service Bill, 76
Self-criticism, 7
Selma/Montgomery voting rights march (1965), 199
Seneca Falls Women's Rights Convention (1848), 24, 38, 39–40
"Seneca—Summer of Action and Learning" (Hutchins), 250–51
Seneca Women's Peace Encampment, 249–55
Separatism, 58, 246
Sex roles: traditional, 149–50, 224, 226, 246, 248. *See also* Motherhood
Sewall, May Wright, 52, 54
Shaw, Anna Howard, 55, 63
Sheppard-Towner Act, 188
"Silent Majority," 219
Sillman, Ruth, 219
Singer, Caroline, 132–33, 147
Sisterly Voices (newsletter), 36
"'Sister Susie' Peril, The" (K. Anthony), 80
"Slacker's Oath," 109
Slater Bill, 70
Slavery. *See* Abolitionism
Smith, Sarah, 32
Smith Act, 158, 170
Sobel, Morton, 158
Social issues, 230, 231, 234
Socialist feminism. *See* Feminism
Socialist party, 93
South Africa, 197, 199
Soviet Union. *See* USSR
Spanish-American War, 51–52, 56, 59, 72
Spanish Civil War, 125, 134, 137, 138
Spector, Norma, 234
Spencer, Anna Garlin: Anti-Imperialist League and, 52; Catt and, 74–75;

Detzer and, 100; Eastman and, 93; on feminist power, 87; on National Committee on the Cause and Cure of War, 108; New York City organizations and, 106; New York Peace Society and, 47; Woman's Peace Party and, 64, 76, 77; Women's International League for Peace and Freedom and, 83, 84, 90, 91, 98, 99
"Spider Web Chart," 111
Stalin, Joseph, 147, 168
Stanton, Elizabeth Cady: Anthony and, 48; Congress of American Women and, 189; home of, 252; International Council of Women and, 54; Mott and, 38–39, 42, 43; on peace, 44–45; Seneca Encampment and, 253; Woman's National Loyal League and, 41; mentioned, 57, 190
"STAR" campaign, 229
"Star-Spangled Banner, The," 100
State, Department of, 159, 233
Steinson, Barbara, 65–66
Stepping Stones (newsletter), 148
Stevenson, Archibald, 83
Stewart, Annalee, 162, 197
"Stop ERA" campaign, 239
"Stop the Arms Race" campaign, 229
Strontium 90, 207
Student Non-Violent Coordinating Committee (SNCC), 193
Students for a Democratic Society (SDS), 193, 211, 220
Submarine warfare, 73
Subversive Activities Control Board, 159
Suffrage: New York State, 81; U.S., 41, 76, 84; Wyoming, 20
Suffrage Alliance, 143
Suffragism: The Hague Conference (1915) and, 68; Mott and, 44; Woman's Christian Temperance Union and, 49; Woman's Peace Party and, 16, 60, 62, 63, 64
Summit meetings, 241
Supreme Court, U.S., 239
Surrez de Coronado, Narrva, 113
Swarthmore College, 127
Swerdlow, Amy, 204
Syracuse, N.Y., 252

Talbert, Mary B., 102
Tatum, Arlo, 176
Teachers, 101
Temperance, 22, 24–25, 47–49
Terrell, Mary Church, 102, 104, 267
Test-Ban Treaty (1963), 207
Thant, U, 208
Thomas, Margaret Loring, 103
Thompson, Dorothy, 191–92
Threats Against the President Act, 73
Three Mile Island disaster, 245
Times Square vigil (1964), 213
Tomlinson, Yvette, 262
Tone, Gertrude Franchot, 96
Torres, Elena, 113
Toys, 207–8
Tripartite Agreement, 144
True womanhood, cult of. *See* Womanhood, true
Truman, Harry, 159, 171, 188
Truth, Sojourner, 189, 253
Tubman, Harriet, 189, 252
"Tuesdays in Washington," 211

Union des Femmes Françaises, 185
Unitarianism, 24
United Nations: Africa and, 197; American Women for Peace and, 190; China and, 196; Congress of American Women and, 188–89; Gage-Colby and, 208; Iraq and, 271; League of Nations and, 88,

United Nations (*continued*) 154, 163; National Committee on the Cause and Cure of War and, 152; Olmsted and, 147, 162; Thompson and, 191; *The Women's Budget* on, 259; Women's International League for Peace and Freedom and, 154, 162–64, 195, 199, 232; Women Strike for Peace and, 205
United Nations' Decade for Women, 18–19, 227–59
United Nations' International Women's Year, 227
United Order of True Sisters, 101
"Unity Statement of the Women's Pentagon Action," 247
Universal Declaration of Human Rights, 163
Universalism, 24
Universal Peace Union, 43, 45, 47, 57
Upstate Feminist Peace Alliance, 249
U.S. Congress, 136
U.S. Congress, House, Armed Services Military Personnel Committee, 238
U.S. Congress, House, Special Committee on Un-American Activities, 159; Congress of American Women and, 189–90; Women's International League for Peace and Freedom and, 158, 168–69, 185, 195; Women Strike for Peace and, 205, 206, 207, 209
U.S. Congress, Senate, 73, 88, 194; Overman Subcommittee, 83; Special Committee Investigating the Munition Industry's Work, 124, 129; Sub-Judiciary Committee, 97
USSR: atomic bomb and, 157–58, 164; China and, 196; conferences in, 206, 208–9; Cuba and, 198; in 1990s, 271; "Packet on Infiltration and Attack" on, 183–84; Test-Ban Treaty (1963) and, 207; U.S. relations with, 129, 171, 195, 202; women of, 189, 195–96, 209; Women's International League for Peace and Freedom and, 169, 194–95, 233; in World War II, 137
Utah, 53

Varela, Capurro de, 113
Venezuela, 51
Vernon, Mabel, 111, 120–21, 135
Versailles Treaty: criticism of, 85; German repudiation of, 136; International Congress of Women on, 81–82; Mygatt on, 141; U.S. Senate and, 88; Women's International League for Peace and Freedom and, 83, 90
Vietnam: North, 220; South, 197, 220
Vietnam Moratorium Day, 211
Vietnam War, 194, 202; Jeannette Rankin Brigade and, 221; UN Decade for Women and, 227; Women's International League for Peace and Freedom and, 197, 209–11, 212–14, 219–20
Villa, Pancho, 72
Villard, Fanny Garrison: death of, 117, 125; New York City organizations and, 106; Peace Parade Committee and, 57, 58; Women's International League for Peace and Freedom and, 92; Women's Peace Society and, 6, 93–94, 95, 96
Violence, 86, 263. *See also* Militarism
Violence against women: feminist peace movement and, 274; militarism and, 8–10, 97, 258; slavery and, 32–34; temperance and, 47–48
Virgin Islands, 72
Voice of Women, 202

Wald, Lillian, 57, 71, 93
Wales, Julia Grace, 68
War, Department of, 83, 109, 111
"War Against War" (art exhibit), 71, 72
War of Independence, U.S., 23
Waring, Mary F., 102
War Resisters League, 126, 167, 176, 211, 234
Washer Woman Action (1983), 251
Washington Naval Conference (1921), 117
Washington Post (newspaper), 233
Wellesley College, 83, 111
Welter, Barbara, 25
Weltfish, Gene, 187
White, Grace Hoffman, 103
Whitehouse, Vera, 74, 75, 76, 152
Whitman, Charles Seymour, 74, 79
Whitney, R. M., 110
Wiegersma, Nan, 211, 212
Willard, Frances, 49
"W.I.L.P.F. and the Cold War," 194
Wilson, Dagmar, 202, 206, 208
Wilson, Woodrow: Addams and, 69; Catt and, 76; Congressional Union and, 62–63; declares war, 76; Fourteen Points and, 78; mediation and, 69–70; Peace Parade Committee and, 57; Schwimmer and, 58; Threats Against the President Act and, 73; U.S. Senate and, 88; Woman's Peace Party and, 72
Winsor sisters, 99
Witherspoon, Frances, 147
Wolforth, Robert, 124
Woman, Inc., 191–92
Woman Patriot (newspaper), 109, 112
Woman's Association for the Aid of the Freedmen, 42
Woman's Christian Temperance Union (WCTU), 48–51, 52, 53
Woman's Freedom Conference (1919), 92
Woman's National Loyal League, 41
Woman's Peace Congress for the World (proposed), 45
Woman's Peace Party (WPP), 16, 56, 59, 63–66; African-American women and, 102, 103; Catt and, 76; feminist power and, 87; internal operation of, 72–73, 261; International Committee of Women for Permanent Peace and, 69; interwar trends and, 89; Massachusetts branch, 78; military training classes and, 70–71; motherhood and, 86; *New York City branch:* 15, 65–66, 78–81, 98, Catt and, 74, 75, Cooper Union protest of, 70, divisions in, 84, "War Against War" exhibit and, 71, Women's Peace Society and, 93–94, Women's Peace Union and, 96; in wartime, 76–81; W. Wilson and, 70, 73–74; Women's International League for Peace and Freedom and, 83, 90, 144, 198, 257; Women's Peace Union and, 97, 139; mentioned, 16, 204, 237–38, 262
Women: French, 67; German, 102; Hispanic, 269; Iroquois, 252; Japanese, 254; married, 20, 22, 23, 28, 48; military, 264; poor, 234, 236, 265; Quaker, 26; Shibokusa, 254; Southern, 101–2; Soviet, 189, 195–96, 209. *See also* African-American women; Jewish women; Young women
Women Against Military Madness (WAMM), 241–42
Women Against War Forum (1980), 238
Women and Economics (Gilman), 60
Women and Life on Earth (1980), 245, 246, 247

Women for a Meaningful Summit, 240–41
Women for Mutual Security, 272
Women for Peace. *See* Women Strike for Peace (WSP)
Women for Racial and Economic Equality (WREE), 7, 195, 234–37; decision making in, 261; on racism, 270; women of color and, 267; Women's International League for Peace and Freedom and, 263–64, 269–74; young women in, 267
Women of the World United for Peace (1975), 228
Women's Action Committee for Victory and Lasting Peace, 125, 152–54, 166
Women's Action for Nuclear Disarmament, (WAND), 240
"Women's Bill of Rights, The" (WREE), 236–37
Women's Budget, The (WILPF), 257–59
"Women's Charter" (proposed), 82
Women's Emergency Conference on Vietnam (1970), 212
Women's Encampment for a Future of Peace and Justice, 249–55
Women's International Democratic Federation (WIDF), 186–87; Congress of American Women and, 189, 190; Women for Racial and Economic Equality and, 234, 235; Women's International League for Peace and Freedom and, 195, 228
Women's International League for Peace and Freedom (WILPF), 7–8, 14; Addams and, 82, 83, 90, 91, 126, 269; African-American women and, 102–5, 142, 267; American Friends Service Committee and, 249; British section, 144; Catt on, 112; Chicago branch, 128, 130, 180–82; Cold War and, 194; Committee on the Special Problems of Branches, 178, 185; Communist countries and, 195–96; Congress of American Women and, 187, 188; Denver branch, 128, 130, 173–80; disarmament and, 117; founded, 60, 78, 83–84; House Special Committee on Un-American Activities and, 158; International Congress sponsored by, 110; International Council of Women and, 120; in interwar period, 90–91, 97, 98–106, 125, 126–39, 141–42; "Intra-American" committees of, 148; Intra-Racial Committee, 104; Jeannette Rankin Brigade and, 221; Latin American work of, 113, 114; League of Nations and, 116, 118, 120–22, 123; McCarthyism and, 17–18, 130, 158–85, 192, 194, 201, 219; National Committee on the Cause and Cure of War and, 108; National Council of Women and, 109; national security program of, 256–59; *New York branches (including Bronx and Brooklyn):* 138–39, 140, 172, African-American women and, 103, 268, American League Against War and Fascism and, 130–32, 134, consolidation of, 139, disarmament and, 229, Fogarty and, 176, friendships in, 262, Gage-Colby and, 208, in interwar period, 91–93, 100–101, 128, 142, Jewish membership of, 101, 142, McCarthyism and, 165–68, 172–73, on male violence, 86, neutrality and, 142, in 1960s, 199–201, predecessors of, 15, *Riff-Raff* and, 133, UN Decade for Women and, 230–31, Vietnam War and, 213–14, Women's Liberation and, 225, Women Strike for Peace and, 206–7, in World War II, 147–48, mentioned, 17; in 1940s,

144–52, 154–56; in 1960s, 194–202; in 1990s, 260–74; nonresistance and, 6; Nye Committee and, 124; "Red Scare" and, 110–12; Soviet women and, 209; UN Decade for Women and, 18–19, 227, 228–30; Vietnam War and, 209–11, 212–14, 219–20; Women for Racial and Economic Equality and, 237, 263–64, 269–74; Women's International Democratic Federation and, 195, 235; Women's Liberation and, 225–26; Women Strike for Peace and, 203, 204, 207–8, 209, 232, 233
Women's International Strike for Peace (WISP). *See* Women Strike for Peace (WSP)
Women's Liberation. *See* Feminist movement
Women's Party for Survival. *See* Women's Action for Nuclear Disarmament (WAND)
Women's Peace Festivals, 46–47
Women's Peace Initiatives, 240
Women's Peace Society (WPS), 93–96; demise of, 125, 126, 231, 263; disarmament and, 117; League of Nations and, 116; membership pledge of, 109; National Committee on the Cause and Cure of War and, 109; nonresistance and, 6; outlawry of war and, 117; suffragists in, 101; mentioned, 17, 90, 97, 98, 105, 106, 134
Women's Peace Union (WPU), 96–97; decision making in, 261; demise of, 125, 126, 139–40, 155, 231, 265; disarmament and, 117; International Council of Women and, 120; Latin American efforts of, 113–14; League of Nations and, 116–17, 121, 122–23; London War Resisters' International and, 13; membership pledge of, 109; National Committee on the Cause and Cure of War and, 109; Nazism and, 140–41; neutrality and, 136, 137; nonresistance and, 6; Nye Committee and, 124; origins of, 134–35; outlawry of war and, 117–18; suffragists in, 101; Women Strike for Peace and, 204; mentioned, 17, 90, 105, 106
Women's Peace Union of the Western Hemisphere, 95
Women's Pentagon Action (WPA): founded, 245; peace encampments and, 242; philosophy of, 247, 248–49; Women's International League for Peace and Freedom and, 211; Women's Liberation and, 246
Women's Political Union, 59
Women's Response to the Rising Tide of Violence (conference), 226
Women's Rights Convention (1848), 24, 38, 39–40
Women's Rights National Park, 252
Women's Ship for Peace, 272
Women Strike for Peace (WSP), 202–10; decision making in, 261; decline of, 18–19, 219, 263, 265; Jeannette Rankin Brigade and, 221; New Left and, 212; Persian Gulf War and, 273; UN Decade for Women and, 227, 231–33; Vietnam War and, 211, 214–16; Women for Racial and Economic Equality and, 237; women of color and, 267; Women's International League for Peace and Freedom and, 270; Women's Liberation and, 220; Women, USA and, 238
"Women Strike for Peace and Survival, 1975," 232
Women, USA, 238, 239–40
Woods, Amy, 98, 144–46
Woolley, Mary, 121
Worcester, Noah, 35

Workers' compensation law, 65
"World Charter for Women" (Catt), 152
World Conference to Review and Appraise the Achievements of the UN Decade for Women (1985), 255, 256
World Congress of Women, 185, 191, 235. *See also* International Congress of Women
World Court, 88, 97, 118
World Disarmament Day, 122
World Organization of Mothers of All Nations, 191–92
World's Anti-Slavery Convention (London), 38
World's Fair (1964), 213
World's Woman's Christian Temperance Union, 49–51
World War I, 16, 56–84, 123–24, 141, 222
World War II, 17, 144–56, 222
WREE-View (newsletter), 269–70
Wyoming Territory, 20

Young men, 216
Young women: in Women for Racial and Economic Equality, 236, 267; in Women's International League for Peace and Freedom, 154, 231, 265–66; in Women Strike for Peace, 204, 211, 212, 214–15, 231
Youth Congresses, 195

Zurich conference (1919), 81, 209

PEACE AS A WOMEN'S ISSUE
was composed in 12 on 13 Bembo on Digital Compugraphic equipment
by Metricomp;
printed by sheet-fed offset on 50-pound, acid-free Natural Smooth,
Smyth-sewn and bound over binder's boards in Holliston Roxite B
and notch bound with paper covers,
with dust jackets and paper covers printed in 2 colors,
by Braun-Brumfield, Inc.;
and published by
Syracuse University Press
Syracuse, New York 13244-5160